Malcolm
Cooper

Your College Experience

Nov. 10 - tues - tawes Ctr 12:30 pm
Rothskeller

Nov 12 - Thurs 1992 - Library 12:30 pm
Mr. Robinson

▼▼▼▼▼▼▼▼▼▼▼▼▼▼▼▼▼

Your College Experience
Strategies for Success

Edited by

John N. Gardner

Director, University 101
Associate Vice Provost, Regional Campuses and
Continuing Education
Professor, Library and Information Science
University of South Carolina, Columbia

A. Jerome Jewler

Professor, Journalism and Mass Communications
University of South Carolina, Columbia

Wadsworth Publishing Company
Belmont, California
A Division of Wadsworth, Inc.

The Freshman Year Experience_SM Series
Editor: Angela Gantner

Development Editor: Alan Venable

Editorial Assistant: Tricia Schumacher

Production Editor: Vicki Friedberg

Designer: Carolyn Deacy

Print Buyer: Randy Hurst

Copy Editor: Tom Briggs

Art Editor: Edie Williams,
Vargas/Williams/Design

Permissions Editor: Jeanne Bosschart

Photo Researcher: Judy Mason

Cover Illustrator: John Nelson

Signing Representative: Henry Staat

Compositor: Thompson Type, San Diego, CA

Printer: Courier Companies, Inc.,
Kendallville, IN

▼▼

The Freshman Year Experience is a servicemark of the University of South Carolina. A license may be granted upon written request to use the term *The Freshman Year Experience* in association with educational programmatic approaches to enhance the freshman year. This license is not transferable and does not apply to the use of the servicemark in any other programs or on any other literature without the written approval of the University of South Carolina.

3 4 5 6 7 8 9 10 — 96 95 94 93 92

Gardner, John N.
    Your college experience : strategies for success /
John N. Gardner, A. Jerome Jewler.
        p.   cm. — (The Freshman year experience_SM series)
    Includes bibliographical references (p.) and index.
    ISBN 0-534-16140-5
    1. College student orientation — United States.
    2. Study, Method of.   3. Success — United States.
    I. Jewler, A. Jerome.   II. Title.   III. Series.
LB2343.32.G37 1992
378.1'98 — dc20   91-28601

Illustration and Photo Credits

John Nelson: Exercise, Journal, Commuter box icons; chapter numerals; and the illustrations on the following pages: 22, 45, 72, 82, 84, 89, 98, 145, 168, 280, 302, 341, 365, 378, A4, A11.

Mary Ross: Freshman Survey box icon and the illustrations on the following pages: 27, 60, 81, 132, 169, 185, 193, 269, 282, 296, 317, 340.

Robert Ariail: Illustrations on the following pages: 2, 14, 26, 48, 66, 80, 96, 111, 126, 140, 160, 178, 198, 210, 232, 244, 264, 278, 294, 306, 322, 334, 359, 376, 390.

Richard Tauber: Photos on the following pages: 39, 50 (left), 69 (left), 70, 101, 147, 150, 163, 183, 212, 246, 314, 324, 326, 328, 330, 347.

Other Photo Credits: p. 4, Spencer Grant/Monkmeyer Press; p. 5, North Wind Picture Archives; p. 8 (left), Druskis/Photo Researchers Inc.; p. 8 (right), Spencer Grant/Photo Researchers Inc.; p. 11, Beringer/Dratch/The Image Works; p. 17, Lane/Photo Researchers Inc.; p. 43, Anestis Diakopoulos/Stock, Boston; p. 50 (right), Michael Kagan/Monkmeyer Press Photo; p. 67, Zimbel/Monkmeyer Press Photo; p. 69 (right), Courtesy of Stanford University; p. 76, Hugh Rogers/Monkmeyer Press Photo; p. 85, The Bettmann Archive; p. 120, Reuters/Bettmann Newsphotos; p. 131, Steven Goldblatt/Swarthmore College; p. 133, Addison Geary/Stock, Boston; p. 135, Robert John Mihovil; p. 142, Joseph Schuyler/Stock, Boston; p. 174, James Woodcock Photography; p. 180, The Bettmann Archive; p. 194, Bettmann Newsphotos; p. 200, UPI/Bettmann Newsphotos; p. 224, Ken Andreyo/Carnegie Mellon; p. 239, Tony Cardoza/Impact Visuals; p. 250, Reagan Bradshaw; p. 273, Michael Kagan/Monkmeyer Press Photo; p. 267, Hugh Rogers/Monkmeyer Press Photo; p. 299, Irene Bayer/Monkmeyer Press Photo; p. 308, Rick Reinhard; p. 329, Joe Wrinn/Harvard University; p. 363, Judy Gelles/Stock, Boston; p. 367, Tom Grill/COMSTOCK; p. 381, Courtesy of Stanford University; p. 383, Akos Szilvasi/Stock, Boston.

▼ ▼

We thank our wonderful families for their patience over the past several years as we watched this book take shape. We thank our students for proving to us that the basic assumptions in this book really do work. We thank faculty, staff, and administrators at colleges and universities for believing in those same basic assumptions. Most important of all, we welcome all new first-year students to their "college experience" and urge them, in the words of Tennyson, to be "strong in will to strive, to seek, to find, and not to yield."

▼ ▼

Brief Contents

**I am a part of all that I have met;
Yet all experience is an arch wherethro'
Gleams that untravelled world. . . .**

From "Ulysses" by Alfred, Lord Tennyson

Contents

▼▼▼▼▼▼▼▼▼
Chapter 2   Time Management: The Foundation of Academic Success 25

▼▼▼▼▼▼▼▼▼
Chapter 3   Learning Styles 47

Minorities: The Coming Majority 244

You're Never Too Old to Go to Class 264

▼▼▼▼▼▼▼▼▼▼▼▼▼▼▼▼▼▼▼▼▼▼▼▼▼▼▼▼▼▼▼

Preface to the Instructor

The lines from Alfred, Lord Tennyson's famous poem "Ulysses" quoted on page viii capture the spirit and purpose of *Your College Experience*. College definitely is an experience in itself — the arch, if you will — that prepares us for the "untravelled world" of our future lives. College is a journey of numerous explorations, embarked upon with interest, excitement, and some trepidation. *Your College Experience* is the guide for this journey, the roadmap to success, the stone supporting the triumphal arch.

As founders and dedicated supporters of The Freshman Year Experience_SM movement over the past twenty years, we have found ourselves in a uniquely privileged position: Not only have we taught many freshman seminars on our own campus, we also have had the deeply rewarding experience of working with colleagues in every kind of institution of higher learning to help them develop their own versions of freshman seminar courses.

Your College Experience is based on that rich experience in two ways. First, it derives from our own knowledge of first-year students and the teachers striving to prepare them for college or university life. Second, the book itself has many authors — many voices — whose ideas we have structured into a complete and unified tool. Your students will hear from a wide range of faculty and student affairs professionals who have themselves helped to develop some aspects of the course. Your students will also hear from other students — men and women of diverse ages and backgrounds — who have faced similar challenges in the first year of college. Whether an individual student's needs seem at the outset mainly academic or mainly social in nature, we believe that *Your College Experience* reflects a deeper, broader understanding of the problems of the first-year student than that found in any other book.

PREMISES OF THE 101 COURSE

College teachers and administrators around the country now agree that, at its best, any course on the freshman year experience is a dynamic, holistic, and challenging class. They also concur with regard to several major themes, which we have embodied in the principal tenets of this book:

- Although in the final analysis a student must succeed by his or her own efforts, each student deserves a reasonable amount of support in college. The course is not a "survival" course but a tool for true success.
- Most first-year students profit from learning or reviewing basic study skills and habits, but college faculty also want them to go beyond study fundamentals to become active, critical, and creative thinkers.
- The course should help students begin to master the indispensable art of writing.
- First-year students need more than advice about what to do or not to do in order to succeed in college. They need concrete information on a number of topics, objective feedback about themselves, and candid information about their teachers and classmates. And they also need someone who will lend a sympathetic, yet unbiased, ear.
- One of the best ways to ensure a student's college success is to help him or her form friendships and other supportive relationships with peers and teachers.
- The success of the class depends in large part on the teacher's ability to generate lively, meaningful classroom discussions.

As a textbook, this is how *Your College Experience* will support you and your students in relation to each of those concerns:

Success for Every Student

Every student who has been admitted to your school and who earnestly desires to succeed should feel a full sense of partnership with the institution. Chapter 1, "Setting Goals for College," summarizes the key factors for success and explains how and where the book addresses each one. Furthermore, the book focuses on the needs of students of both sexes and of every age, color, and background, as well as addressing specific problems of commuting and returning students. Throughout, and particularly in its multipart Chapter 12, "The New Diversity," the book also provides you, the instructor, with the means to initiate and direct discussion and exercises related to problems of gender and diversity, in whatever form these concerns arise on your own campus.

Study Skills and Beyond

This book teaches sound, state-of-the-art study techniques, beginning with a goal-setting strategy in Chapter 1 and continuing with separate chapters on time management (Chapter 2), learning styles (Chapter 3), note-taking (Chapter 4), reading (Chapter 5), and test-taking (Chapter 6). In addition, the book discusses the importance of a college education (the second section of Chapter 1), introduces the key elements of critical thinking (Chapter 10), and provides a chapter-long exercise designed to give each student a solid, "hands-on" appreciation of your college library (Chapter 8).

Writing in the Class

This book provides writing opportunities in every chapter, including exercises built on writing and end-of-chapter or end-of-section journal assignments that challenge students to think critically and creatively about academic and personal growth. And Chapter 9, "Writing for Success," tackles the anxieties of reluctant writers and explains writing as a tool for learning.

Filling the Need for Information

Students need and want concrete information on many vital topics. This book provides it in a variety of ways:

- ► *Self-assessments* in many areas, especially learning styles, time management, majors and career choices, wellness, alcohol consumption, and stress management
- ► *The Freshman Survey* series of features based on yearly surveys conducted among first-year students across the country showing the changing attitudes of students on a wide variety of issues, from choice of major to political outlook
- ► *Scientific and medical information* on numerous topics, including diet, AIDS and other sexually transmitted diseases, nutrition, and alcohol
- ► *References and Suggestions for Further Reading* for every chapter, providing a valuable bibliography of relevant contemporary material

Personal Connections

Students who persist and succeed in college are greatly helped by the supportive relationships they form with peers and teachers. For this reason, this book takes every opportunity to help the student form such associations, relying wherever possible on group activities rather than on exercises aimed at the individual. Chapter 7, "Professor and Student," is devoted to helping every first-year student have at least one friendly, significant, one-on-one, face-to-face meeting with a member of the faculty. The book also discusses the benefits of study groups and provides an exercise in forming one. Finally, Chapter 14, "Person to Person," addresses issues of assertiveness, personal relationships, and campus involvement to further support students' efforts to form lasting, constructive relationships with classmates and teachers.

Enriching Classroom Participation

If you have already taught the freshman seminar, you probably share our conviction that the most important measure of course success is lively, meaningful classroom discussion. This book respects the knowledge and experience that students bring to college and encourages them to explore, express, and enhance their own viewpoints. In addition to carefully constructed classroom exercises, each chapter includes numerous features to make it easier for you to generate open, constructive discussion:

- ► Frank, humorous, sometimes misinterpreted and controversial section-opening remarks "from the back of the classroom," which are conceived as "typical" first-year-student comments and which acknowledge common feelings and anxieties (see p. 2, for example)
- ► Lively, humorous, and sometimes provocative cartoons, well worth collective interpretation
- ► Carefully chosen brief personal statements and other readings to generate discussion on topics that first-year students and their teachers often find hard to address, such as discrimination and alcoholism

In these parts of the book you may find things you or your students frankly *disagree* with. We hope you'll take advantage of that to make your classes provocative and lively!

THE FLEXIBILITY OF THIS BOOK

If our years in The Freshman Year Experience$_{SM}$ movement have taught us anything, it's that while there is growing consensus about the aims and the means of the freshman seminar, there is also great diversity in how the course is structured and in what topics are emphasized. Each campus and student body has its own particular needs, resources, and constraints that greatly affect the first-year-student course. Individual instructors also have their own valid reasons for shaping the course one way or another. With that need for adaptability in mind, we have provided what we hope are more than sufficient materials in each chapter, leaving you with the relatively simple and pleasant task of selecting those units and exercises that best suit your needs.

We believe this book offers great flexibility in choosing topics and teaching them in the order you find works best for your students. We've structured the table of contents so that you can teach the topics in a variety of orders, in harmony with the needs of your students and the time constraints of your campus schedule. We have also divided the book into fifteen chapters and further divided some chapters into sections, from which you can customize your course. For instance, you may want to use the section in Chapter 11 on academic advising together with Appendix A, "How to Read Your College Catalog." Depending on the backgrounds of your students, you may choose to focus on one of the sections in Chapter 12 on women, minorities, or older students, respectively. The comprehensive instructor's manual that goes with this book provides many suggestions for coordinating various chapters.

If your course meets twice a week for twelve weeks or more, you should be able to cover at least one chapter or one section from a chapter each week. If your course meets somewhat less often, you should not have difficulty building your class meeting around selected chapters or chapter sections and assigning others for individual reference. Suggestions for topic coverage for courses meeting twice a week for eight, twelve, and fourteen weeks, respectively, can be found in the instructor's manual.

WHAT WE WANT FROM YOU

We want you to do more than just use *Your College Experience* in your course. We want you to help us write the next edition. We feel good about asking this of you, because we know from experience that the more we have shared our insights and problems with others, the more we have benefited in return. Here are several ways you can help not only us but yourself and other teachers:

1. Communicate with us about your experience teaching from this book, ℅ Wadsworth Publishing Company, 10 Davis Drive, Belmont, CA 94002.

2. Encourage your students to communicate with us, using the tearsheet at the back of this book to summarize their comments. We're eager to know how they respond to individual chapters — and eager to make improvements!

3. Ask to be added to the mailing list of The Freshman Year Experience$_{SM}$ at the University of South Carolina. You will receive information, announcements, and calls for proposals for an invaluable series of conferences, resource seminars, workshops, and publications designed to show higher educators how to help their first-year college students achieve success.

4. Attend a meeting of The Freshman Year Experience$_{SM}$. Between 1982 and 1991, thirty-eight conferences in this series, held across the United States and in Canada and the United Kingdom, have drawn more than 13,000 college faculty, administrators, and student affairs professionals, including freshman seminar instructors like yourself. Let us know you'd like more information by writing to The Freshman Year Experience$_{SM}$, University of South Carolina, 1728 College Street, Columbia, SC 29208.

ACKNOWLEDGMENTS

We're extremely grateful for the help of literally hundreds of faculty, academic administrators, and student affairs professionals who have shaped this book, either as direct contributors or as colleagues, advisors, and friends. We are equally grateful for the insights of students, as well as for their sometimes deeply personal and moving written contributions.

First of all, we wish to thank our many advisors, reviewers, survey respondents, and focus group participants: **Alabama:** Martha Ann Cox, Samford University; Fran Johnson, Alabama A&M University. **Arizona:** Josephine S. Ong, Grand Canyon University. **Arkansas:** Lee DeMarais, John Brown University; Sally Kirst, University of Arkansas at Monticello. **California:** Steve Alley, Pacific Christian College; Gale Auletta, California State University, Hayward; Jim Carter, Woodbury University; Robert F. Giomi, Holy Names College; Carey Harbin, Chabot College; Irene Hunandy, Fullerton College; Diane Jennings, St. Joseph's College; Terry Jones, California State University, Hayward; William H. Jones, Monterey Peninsula College; Pat Ladousier, Merced Community College; Dean Mancina, Golden West College; Robert Morrow, University of the Pacific; William Ott, West Valley College; Bruce Peterson, Sonoma State University; Carol Rossi, Santa Clara University; Terry Spearman, El Camino College; Robert Spier, Hartnell College; Walter Stangl, Biola University; Dwayne D. Van Rheenen, Pepperdine University; Marci Winans, Fresno Pacific College. **Connecticut:** Donna L. Wagner, University of Bridgeport. **District of Columbia:** Steve Weiner, Gallaudet University. **Florida:** J. Cebulski, University of South Florida; David K. Hosman, Valencia Community College; Alfonsa James, Chipola Junior College; Eileen McDonough, Barry University; Audrey Roth, Miami-Dade Community College; Rita J. Sordelline, Barry University; Wayne White, University of West Florida. **Georgia:** Lew S. Akin, Abraham Baldwin College; Susan H. Chin, DeVry Institute of Technology; Patricia W. Hughes, West Georgia College; Dean Tucker, Oglethorpe University; Sharon Vance, Crandall Junior College. **Hawaii:** Laurence R. Test, University of Hawaii at Hilo. **Illinois:** Gary Ayres, Lewis and Clark Community College; Thomas G. Eynon, Southern Illinois University; Cynthia Hill, Rock Valley College; Eva Mae Moats, Springfield College; Christopher P. Moderson, Rockford College; Daniel Nadler, Southern Illinois University; Vivian Snyder, Southern Illinois University. **Indiana:** Drew Appleby, Marian College; Jerry E. Davis, Huntington College; Linda Duttlinger, Purdue University; Pete Gustavson, Rose-Hulman Institute of Technology; Robert P. Mathisen, Grace College; M. Elise Kress, Saint Francis College. **Iowa:** Roseanne Cook, St. Ambrose University; Tucki Folkers, North Iowa Area Community College; James Hard, Teikyo Westmar University; David B. Straley, University of Dubuque. **Kansas:** Jerry Headrick, Seward County Community College; Judith Lynch, Kansas State University; Dixie Schierlman, Independence Community College; Barb Thoman, Garden City Community College; Karlene Tyler, McPherson College; Faye Vowell, Emporia State University. **Kentucky:** Carmen Garland, Murray State

University; Jerry W. Warner, Northern Kentucky University. **Louisiana:** Joseph L. Capers, Grambling State University; V. M. Johnson, Tulane University. **Maine:** Marvin Druker, University of Southern Maine. **Maryland:** Christine Doerfler, Washington Bible College; Jane Forni, College of Notre Dame of Maryland; James C. Lackie, Salisbury State University; Mannine Smith, Garrett Community College. **Massachusetts:** Charlene Doyon, University of Lowell; Jack Meade, Massachusetts Bay Community College; Carl Petersen, Wentworth Institute of Technology; Mary M. Sullivan, Curry College. **Michigan:** Elizabeth M. Church, Mercy College of Detroit; Rita Grant, Grand Valley State University; A. Sherlyn Kah, Detroit College of Business; Shirley McClellan, Suomi College; Curtis Shivar, Wayne Community College; Susan Vantil, Ferris State University; Suzanne Waring, Great Falls Vocational-Technical Center. **Minnesota:** Kristin Anderson, Augsberg College; Joan Costello, Saint Mary's College of Minnesota; Joe Rine, Minneapolis Community College; Myron Umerski, Saint Cloud State University. **Mississippi:** Lisa J. Allen, Belhaven College. **Missouri:** Jane Ellen Ashley, Stephens College; Robert P. Dowis, Tarkio College; Elsie Gaber, Northeast Missouri State University; Elaine Grev, Columbia College; Frederick T. Janzow, Southeast Missouri State University; John Jasinski, Northeast Missouri State University; Lori LeBahn, Missouri Southern State College. **Nebraska:** Jennifer Nelson, Peru State College. **New Hampshire:** Debra Nitschke, New England College; Neal Steiger, New Hampshire Technical College. **New Jersey:** David Cohen, Union County College; G. Jan Colijn, Stockon State College; Marshall S. Harth, Ramapo College; Jane Sullivan, Glassboro State College. **New York:** William R. Barnett, Le Moyne College; Kathleen Best, Dominican College; Jean Carlson, Iona College; Tami Conway-Grieg, Concordia College; Martha H. Dietz, Colgate University; Deborah Durnam, Ithaca College; Jean Trevarton Ehman, Saint Bonaventure University; Adina Elfant, Mount Saint Mary College; Jason Finkelstein, City College of New York; Katherine R. Lammon, St. Francis College; Patricia A. Morris, Molloy College; Margot C. Papworth, Cazenovia College; Carol Parmentier, Polytechnic University; L. Schaffer, State University of New York at Plattsburgh; Harriet E. Spitzer, New York Institute of Technology; L. Susan Stark, Tobe-Coburn School of Fashion Careers; Carl M. Wahlstrom, Genesee Community College. **North Carolina:** Gladys Haunton, Methodist College; Linda King, Lees-McRae College; Linda S. Kraft, Mount Olive College; Raymond Ledford, Western Carolina University; James Pearson, Appalachian State University; Edward S. Perzel, University of North Carolina at Charlotte; Lela Faye Rich, Elon College; Mike Riley, Lenoir-Rhyne College; Sam Sink, Wilkes Community College; Norma J. Thompson, Pembroke State University; Dean W. Turner, Concord College. **North Dakota:** Sally Olsen, University of Mary. **Ohio:** Arthur Acton, Ohio Northern University; Laura Cross Chapman, Ohio University; Constance Dubick, Kent State University; William Hartel, Marietta College; Mimi Lewellen, The College of Wooster; Dorothy J. Ling, Walsh College; Arnold Mokma, Ohio State University; Stephen Schwartz, Marietta College; David Skeen, Muskingum College; Randie L. Timpe, Mount Vernon Nazarene College. **Oklahoma:** Carole Lewandowski, Oral Roberts University; Marita Morgan, Oral Roberts University; Tracy Wood, Seminole Junior College. **Oregon:** Becky J. Leithold, Western Baptist College; Bonnie M. Meyer, Linfield College; Leon Young, Umpqua Community College. **Pennsylvania:** Jerry Bowman, Pennsylvania State University at Schuylkill; Kathy Hacker, Pennsylvania State University, Beaver Campus; Mary Lou Kennedy, Community College of Allegheny County; A. F. Kreisler, Susquehanna University; Lois Sculco, Seton Hill College; Robert Willey, Jr.,

Lancaster Bible College; Mary B. Wolf, Lycoming College. **Puerto Rico:** Nelida Rivera, Universidad Central del Caribe. **Rhode Island:** David E. Melchar, Roger Williams College; John Rok, Salve Regina College; Wilder M. Snodgrass, Providence College. **South Carolina:** Arthur Hartzog, Coker College; E. Marcia Hougen, Columbia Junior College; Katy Murphy, University of South Carolina at Spartanburg; Carole Obermeyer, Newberry College; Beth Triplett, College of Charleston; James Von Frank, Francis Marion College. **Tennessee:** Harley F. Acton, Middle Tennessee State University; Bonnie Buckland, Lincoln Memorial University; Janet Byrne, Roane State Community College; Lynn M. Gipson, Memphis College of Art; James C. Perry, Tennessee Technical University; Mary Ruth Stone, Lee College; Thomas R. Van Dervort, Middle Tennessee State University; Marianne Woodside, University of Tennessee at Knoxville; Connie L. Wright, Cumberland University. **Texas:** L. A. Barnes, Tyler Junior College; Kim Brookshire, Paris Junior College; Leigh A. Crane, McMurry University; Vicki Davis, East Texas State University; J. Emily Evans, Palo Alto College; Rusty Jergins, Tarleton State University; Jud Mather, Our Lady of the Lake University; Tom McNeely, Midwestern State University; James N. Twohig, Angelina College; Steve Wilkinson, Wharton County Community College. **Utah:** Marlene Cousens, Weber State University. **Vermont:** Bruce Berryman, Lyndon State College; A. C. Hessler, St. Michael's College; C. R. Landgrien, Middlebury College. **Virginia:** Mary Kaye Benton, Longwood College; Pauline M. Donaldson, Liberty University; Emily Harbold, Sweet Briar College; Julie L. Jones, Lord Fairfax Community College; Nancy Lukic, Virginia Wesleyan University. **Washington:** Kathy Calvert, Yakima Valley Community College; Mary Conley Law, Saint Martin's College; Patricia Palmer, Griffin College. **Wisconsin:** Maureen Josten, Moraine Park Technical College; Dorothy Poulsen, Carroll College. **Wyoming:** Andrea Reeve, University of Wyoming.

We are especially appreciative of the efforts of our contributing writers: Steven Blume, Marietta College; H. Thorne Compton, University of South Carolina; Charles C. Curran, University of South Carolina; Ray Edwards, East Carolina University; Dorothy S. Fidler, University of South Carolina; Ruthann Fox-Hines, University of South Carolina; Robert A. Friday; Mary Stuart Hunter, University of South Carolina; N. Peter Johnson, University of South Carolina; Preston Johnson, undergraduate at Emory University; Kevin W. King, University of South Carolina; Kenneth F. Long, University of Windsor; Carolyn Matalene, University of South Carolina; Lisa Ann Mohn, University of South Carolina; Richard L. Morrill, University of Richmond; Hilda F. Owens, Spartanburg Methodist College; Marie-Louise A. Ramsdale, Harvard University School of Law; Laura I. Rendón, Arizona State University; Debora A. Ritter, University of South Carolina; Sue V. Rosser, University of South Carolina; Linda B. Salane, Columbia College; and Foster E. Tait, University of South Carolina.

We would also like to thank Robert Rice, Oregon State University, for his contributions on commuting students, and Kenneth C. Green, University of Southern California, for generously sharing results of The Freshman Survey, which appear throughout the book. We offer special thanks to Debora Ritter for coordinating all the exercises in the book and for writing many of them herself. For their efforts we also are grateful to Peter Elias Sotiriou, Los Angeles City College; Richard Wertz, University of South Carolina; Ray Murphy, University of South Carolina; and Dennis Pruitt, University of South Carolina. To Robert Ariail, editorial cartoonist for *The State* newspaper in Columbia, South Carolina, we offer our appreciation for his series of distinctive cartoons and congratulate him on his growing collection of national and regional awards. For the comprehensive instructor's manual, we are indebted to William Hartel, Marietta College; Stephen Schwartz, Marietta College; and Arthur Acton, Ohio Northern University. We also thank the Higher Education Research Institute, UCLA, for permission to use the data in the Freshman Survey features. Finally, we offer special thanks to Vicky Howell of the University 101 staff at the University of South Carolina, who helped us keep this manuscript in shape during its many months of revisions.

In conclusion, we thank you for choosing this book, which represents the efforts of an incredible number of educators who work with first-year students throughout the United States and Canada, and congratulate you for being an important part of the work we are all doing to help more entering students become successful and productive citizens.

John N. Gardner

A. Jerome Jewler

▼▼▼▼▼▼▼▼▼▼▼▼▼▼▼▼▼▼▼▼▼▼▼▼▼▼▼▼▼▼▼▼▼▼

Preface to the Student

In his classic poem "Ulysses," published in 1842, Alfred, Lord Tennyson recounts the story of the legendary Greek who, even at the end of a lifetime of wild adventure and perilous travel, never ceases to yearn for new and ever greater challenge. We open this book with Ulysses' words because, as they so eloquently remind us, we are each a part of all we have met — the people and the events, the joys and the sorrows. And as we move through the archways of our own experiences, where "gleams that untravelled world," we continue to change, to grow, and to become more of what we are.

Welcome to *Your College Experience*, quite possibly the most dynamic experience of your life. Each of us who has contributed to this book has been there. We were once new college students, and we vividly recall this time of challenge and excitement, of uncertainty and concern. In this respect we believe that college as we first knew it was much the same as it is today. In other respects it has changed dramatically.

For one thing, female students today outnumber their male counterparts on most American campuses, a major reversal of earlier trends. And not only are more women in college than ever before, but colleges are also serving more students of color, more returning students who may be 25 or older, and more students from other countries.

Another great change is the heightened sense of responsibility colleges feel about welcoming and developing *all* entering students. As a result, freshman seminar or freshman orientation courses, perhaps similar to one you are taking now, have cropped up on a majority of American campuses over the past 20 years. If you're presently enrolled in such a course, congratulations! Studies indicate it's going to help you make it through the first year.

You should know that the greatest percentage of college students who leave college without graduating do so during their first year — and that students who actively participate in freshman seminar or orientation courses tend to complete their first year successfully at a higher rate than those who don't take such a course. Once you've completed your first year, the odds that you will graduate are definitely in your favor.

Determined to provide the best introduction to college, we've created this book to directly support those factors that keep students in college, as indicated by national surveys: good study habits, good relationships with professors and fellow students, critical thinking skills, strong writing skills, involvement in activities outside class, and many others.

Bearing in mind that college is more than an intellectual experience, we have also included sections on aspects of personal development that affect most entering college students.

We begin in Chapter 1 with a roadmap for what's to follow and some ideas for setting goals. The next few chapters get right to the task of helping you sharpen key study skills — managing time, understanding different learning styles, taking lecture notes, reading textbooks, and studying for exams.

Chapter 7 moves on to getting the most out of the valuable relationship between professor and student. And from there? To another key relationship, between you and the library! Chapter 8 walks you through an information search that will get you ready to write your first college term paper. And speaking of writing, you'll learn how to overcome "blank paper anxiety" in Chapter 9.

Chapter 10 begins to explore the value of the liberal arts and some basics of critical thinking. In Chapter 11, you'll learn how to work with your academic advisor in planning courses for each term, and you'll complete a number of exercises to help you decide on a career path.

Chapter 12, "The New Diversity," will make you more aware of what it means to say that women, minorities, and returning students have each become an important and respected presence in American higher education.

While the opening chapters deal with academic skills, the final chapters deal with personal growth: values in Chapter 13; assertiveness, relationships, and campus involvement in Chapter 14; and health and wellness issues in Chapter 15.

Finally come two valuable appendixes, "How to Read Your College Catalog" and "How to Manage Your Money and Obtain Financial Aid," followed by a glossary of terms that are highlighted in **boldface** type throughout the text.

That's the general idea. From this feast of topics, your instructor will undoubtedly choose those that he or she feels are most immediately relevant to you and your classmates. Of course, we hope you will find time to read other sections in your spare time or after the term is over.

To keep things interesting, there's a cartoon to kick off each section by South Carolina award-winning editorial cartoonist Robert Ariail. We believe you'll find it intriguing to discuss what they say and to what extent you agree with them. Our colleague Debora Ritter has organized and written a number of classroom and individual exercises to help you become involved in learning about college. And our friends Robert Rice and Kenneth C. Green offer perspectives on commuting to college and on what today's freshmen are like, respectively.

This book is full of exercises that will help you size up your progress this term and get to know the people around you. There's also a journal assignment for you at the end of each section or chapter, a way to record your thoughts as you complete each part of this book so that you can reflect on them later.

We sincerely wish you the best as you begin *Your College Experience* and urge you, in the words of Tennyson, to be "strong in will to strive, to seek, to find, and not to yield."

John N. Gardner

A. Jerome Jewler

C H A P T E R

Keys to Success

Setting Goals for College
John N. Gardner
A. Jerome Jewler

The Value of College
Hilda F. Owens

Setting Goals
for College

Orientation made it sound like college was going to be fun. Well, it's no fun today. First day of the term, and I've just spent over a hundred dollars on books, I have three exams scheduled the same week in October, and I'm broke. But all is not lost, thank goodness. At least my roommate's a human being. Pretty easy-going. Would you believe I have to read two chapters of history before Wednesday?! Don't they realize I need to relax?

JOHN N. GARDNER *has been the director of University 101, the freshman seminar program at the University of South Carolina, since 1974 and has hosted national and international conferences on The Freshman Year Experience$_{SM}$. He is also an administrator and faculty member at the university. As a freshman in 1961 at Marietta College in Ohio, he found himself close to flunking out.*

"There were lots of reasons for my bad grades during my first term in college," he says. "I didn't know how to take notes; I lacked proper study habits; I didn't seek out professors for help, and I didn't understand them or know how to relate to them."

Ultimately he was saved by some of the same "persistence factors" that he and his co-author describe in this section.

A. JEROME JEWLER, *a professor in the College of Journalism and Mass Communications at the University of South Carolina, directed the University 101 course and faculty development workshops from 1983 to 1989 and has taught University 101 since the mid-1970s. A former advertising copywriter who now teaches courses in advertising copy and design, he emphasizes that mastering the writing process is one of the critical elements for success in college and in life. Like Gardner, he also threatened to quit college in the middle of his freshman year and was saved when he joined the staff of the college newspaper at the University of Maryland.*

"I think many of us who enjoy being a mentor to students went through a trying period as college freshmen," he notes. "Maybe that's why we're able to identify with so many of the everyday concerns of students today."

ROBERT L. RICE, *an assistant professor of college student services administration at Oregon State University, contributed the text in this section related to the special problems of commuting, as well as features and exercises throughout this book addressing the needs of commuting students.*

"Commuter students represent one of the largest student groups in colleges and universities," he notes. "Yet they are often treated as invisible members of the campus and are seldom afforded special academic or student services. My years of teaching, advising, and counseling freshman commuters have led me to pay special attention to this neglected population."

Rice is very interested in finding the national record-holding freshman commuter—the student who commutes the greatest distance to college. If you think you qualify as the national long-distance-commuter champion, please send your name, address, college, distance you travel, and means of transportation to:

Robert Rice
313 Snell Hall
Oregon State University
Corvallis, Ore., 97331

You've just taken another major step in life: You've decided to invest in a college education. It doesn't matter whether you're male or female; 18, 28, or older; "majority" or "minority." You've started college. Welcome. Your life will never be the same.

You probably already know that college is very different from high school: more freedom, more work, also more responsibility. The work is more difficult, the grading tougher. You may not make the grades you made in high

school, at least not in your first year of college. If some of your ideas about college come from people who attended some time back, you're going to find it different from how they described it: perhaps more complex, more diverse, also more necessary.

In the first half of this century, going to college was an intellectual privilege largely reserved for white males from the upper reaches of society. Then, following World War II, thousands of veterans took advantage of the GI Bill to get their college degrees. More than ever before, colleges were admitting students who saw a college education as a path not only to intellectual growth but also to a better career.

Now as we approach the twenty-first century, college is becoming less of an option. New technology, the information explosion of the 1980s, and especially the computer have changed the workplace so drastically that few people will be able to adequately support themselves and their families without at least some education beyond high school. That may not have been true for your parents' generation, but it's true for yours.

It's a great achievement that this country sends a higher percentage of high school students to college than any other country in the world (about 60 percent). At the same time, it's distressing that 40 percent of those who start college never earn their degrees. In fact only 40 percent complete their **bachelor's degree*** in four years, while another 20 percent take up to ten years to finish — and this at a time when, more than ever before, the vast majority of colleges want every student to succeed. It's generally not academic unreadiness that causes college students to stop short of their degree. Most (about three-fourths) leave college in good academic standing, not because they have flunked out. So why do so many more fall by the wayside?

There are certainly many reasons, but one of the simplest is confusion: A generation back, students typically went to college, chose a major, followed an established curriculum, and earned their degrees four predictable years

*Terms set in boldface type are defined and/or discussed in the Glossary.

"Knock, Knock."
"Who's There?"

With the founding of Harvard College in 1636, American colleges began a 200-year-long aristocratic mission of preparing well-to-do white males for the professions and for government. The Morrill Act of 1862 helped to change that by establishing the land grant colleges that brought **higher education** to a broader range of society. For the next hundred years, new kinds of schools emerged for a broader range of Americans, gradually including more women, more minorities, and more scholarship students.

In the mid-1960s the junior college movement went into high gear, as colleges became less exclusively focused on traditional academic areas and more oriented toward education for personal and job-related knowledge. By the late 1980s more than a third of all American colleges were two-year schools. Today, over 55 percent of college freshmen are starting in two-year colleges. At the same time, four-year schools have admitted increasing numbers of students — white and nonwhite, rich and poor — through special admissions programs that offset deficiencies in background and preparation. Colleges now also accept many older, largely part-time learners, many of whom have family responsibilities that have interrupted or delayed their higher education.

Student "digs" at Harvard — back when most American colleges were more like men's clubs.

In 1900 fewer than 2 percent of people of traditional college age attended college. Today 50 percent attend, with over 3,400 colleges serving more than 13 million students. According to a recent Gallup Poll almost two-thirds of Americans today believe that a college education is "very important" — nearly double the number that felt that way in 1978.

later. Today's students often have a staggering number of courses to choose from, and programs offer so many options that most students need a trained advisor to help them choose and coordinate courses. Your own college is probably anxious to provide an advisor to help you plan your courses and connect with other campus services like career planning, personal counseling, writing labs, and academic skills centers. Make getting to know your advisor a top priority.

This book won't take the place of a living, breathing advisor. What it will do, however, is help you not only obtain your degree but also get the most out of your college experience. At the very least it will help you avoid some common pitfalls that many freshmen encounter.

TWENTY-ONE WAYS TO SUCCEED IN COLLEGE

Researchers have identified certain things students can do to ensure success in college. Ironically students are often unaware of what these "persistence factors" — or keys to success — are and how much they really matter. Here are twenty-one basic things you can do to thrive in college. This book is built on these suggestions and will, we hope, show you how to implement them. If you regularly practice the following suggestions, you can and most likely will succeed.

1. **Find and get to know one individual on campus who knows you are there and who cares about your survival.** One person, that's all it takes. It might be the leader of your freshman seminar or some other professor (see Chapter 11), an academic advisor (see Chapter 7), or someone at the career or counseling center (see Chapter 11). Like the freshman seminar on most campuses, this book is designed to help you get out on campus and meet that person.

2. **Learn what helping resources your campus offers and where they are located.** Follow the suggestions throughout this book for how to get in touch with the people who are there to serve you. Most campuses have career planning offices, personal counseling centers, and academic skills centers, as well as many other resources.

3. **Understand why you are in college.** Your college experience will be much more productive if you can identify specific goals you wish to accomplish. The second section of this chapter should help you clarify your reasons for being in college. Chapters 12 and 13 also address this issue.

4. **Set up a daily schedule and stick to it.** Now that no one is around to tell you when to study or when to sleep, you need to do this for yourself. If you can't do it alone, find someone on campus who can help — perhaps someone in your academic skills or personal counseling center. Chapter 2 will get you started at assigning sufficient time for study, work, sleep, and recreation.

5. **If you're attending classes full-time (12–15 hours per semester), don't work more than 20 hours a week.** Most people begin a downhill slide in the quality of learning beyond 20 hours. Don't be one of them. If you need more money, borrow it from a reliable source or talk to a financial aid officer. Try to work on campus. Students who work on campus tend to do better in classes and are more likely to stay enrolled than those working off campus. Appendix B discusses what to do if you have serious money problems.

6. **Assess and improve your study habits.** An integral part of your success in college involves assessing your own learning style, taking better notes in class, reading more efficiently, and doing better on tests. If your campus has an academic skills center, by all means visit it. Chapters 3–6 focus on these important issues.

7. **Choose professors who involve you in the learning process.** Attend classes in which you can actively participate. You'll probably learn more, more easily and more enjoyably. Chapter 7 will tell you how to get to know more about professors — and how to get closer to some good ones.

Commuter Power

About how many of America's 13.9 million college students would you guess are **commuters**? (The answer appears at the bottom of the next page.)

a. 2.78 million (20 percent)

b. 5.56 million (40 percent)

c. 8.34 million (60 percent)

d. 11.12 million (80 percent)

The fact that you commute may work to your advantage in some ways. In others you will need to work harder than the campus resident. Look over the twenty-one "persistence factors." Do you think any of these will be harder for you to achieve because you commute? Compensate with special effort. Interact fully with your campus. Use the goal-setting process at the end of this section to ensure that you do *get involved* in a campus activity, do *explore* campus resources, and do *find* someone on campus who knows and cares about you.

8. **Know how to use your campus library**. The library isn't as formidable as it might seem, and it offers a wealth of information and resources. Chapter 8 will get you launched.

9. **Improve your writing**. Your writing skills will serve you well throughout life if you take some pains now to improve and secure them. Write something every day — the more you write, the better you write. Remember, writing is for life, not just for English 101. Chapter 9 focuses on writing for success. In addition each section in this book concludes with journal suggestions to give you more practice.

10. **Develop critical thinking skills**. Challenge. Ask why. Look for unusual solutions to ordinary problems and ordinary solutions to unusual problems. There are few absolutely right and wrong answers in life, but some answers come closer to being "truthful" than others. Chapter 10 introduces you to college-level critical thinking and will help you develop what is called "tolerance for ambiguity."

11. **Find a great academic advisor and fight to keep him or her**. The right advisor can be an invaluable source of support, guidance, and insight throughout your college years. Chapter 11 tells how to find that person.

12. **Visit the career center**. Even if you think you have chosen your academic major, the career center may offer valuable information about careers and about yourself. Chapter 11 provides additional help in choosing a major and a career.

13. **Make one or two close friends among your peers**. College represents a chance to form new and lasting ties. It also offers great diversity in terms of the people on your campus. Choose your friends for their own self-worth, not for what they can do for you. Remember that

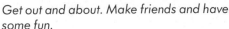

Get out and about. Make friends and have some fun.

Of course it's confusing; there's so much to choose from!

in college, as in life, you become like those with whom you associate. Chapters 12–14 discuss how you might go about forming close ties with other students.

14. **If you're not assertive enough, take assertiveness training**. It's never too late to learn how to stand up for your rights in a way that respects the rights of others. Chapter 14 introduces some techniques to help you do just that.

15. **Get involved in campus activities**. Work for the campus newspaper or radio station. Join a club. Play intramural sports. Yes, most campus organizations do welcome freshmen — you're their lifeblood. Chapter 14 tells you how to become involved in campus life.

16. **Take your health seriously**. How much sleep you get, what you eat, whether you exercise, and the kinds of decisions you make about drugs, alcohol, and sex all contribute to how well or unwell you feel. Get into the habit of being good to yourself and you'll be both a happier person and a more successful student. Chapter 15 addresses health-related issues.

17. **If you can't avoid stress, learn how to live with it**. While stress is an inevitable part of modern life, there are ways of dealing with it. Your counseling center can introduce you to techniques that will help you worry less and study more. Chapter 15 also suggests ways to manage stress and learn how to relax.

18. **Show up at class**. Professors tend to test on what they discuss in class, as well as grade in part on the basis of class attendance (and participation). Don't abuse your new freedom. Being there is your responsibility. Simply being in class every day (unless you are sick) will go a long way toward helping you graduate. Remember the adage: 95

ANSWER (to question in box on p. 7): d — commuters account for 11.12 million of America's 13.9 million college students. That number is more than the combined populations of Norway and Israel. There are more commuter students than there are people in the greater Boston and Philadelphia areas combined. If all commuter students parked in the same parking lot, the lot would have to be larger than the city of Boston. No wonder parking is often cited by commuters as one of their major problems!

percent of success is simply showing up! Chapter 4 tells you what to do once you get there.

19. **Remember that you are not alone**. Thousands of other first-year students are facing the same uncertainties you now face. This book was written to help you talk with other freshmen. Find out how much you have in common. There's strength in numbers. Again, Chapter 14 can help you form mutually supportive relationships with your fellow freshmen.

20. **Learn to appreciate yourself more**. Hey, you got this far! Chapter 13 discusses how you go about forming a set of personal values.

21. **Try to have realistic expectations**. At first you may not make the grades you made in high school. Or, even if you were a star athlete in high school, you might not be anything special in college. This book, and especially this section, can help you develop more realistic goals.

Do most of these suggestions sound simple? We guarantee that if you follow them, they will make a difference in your life, as they already have for thousands of graduates.

ELIMINATING THE NEGATIVES

A *self-fulfilling prophecy* is something you predict is going to happen, and by thinking that's how things will turn out, you greatly increase the chances that they will. For instance, if you decide that today just isn't going to be your day, chances are it won't be. You'll look for ways that things can go wrong — and you'll find them. Students entering college bring with them a good many negative self-fulfilling prophecies and other mental baggage. Widespread fears and problems include the following:

► Fear of freedom, of not being able to manage your time without the family around
► Depression
► Fear that college will be too difficult
► Homesickness
► Lack of good study habits
► Difficulty in understanding professors
► Fear of competition from brighter, younger, or older students
► Fear of disappointing your parents
► Roommate problems
► Worry over choosing the wrong major
► Shyness
► The expectation that you may have to cheat to survive
► Fear of being perceived as a klutz or some other type of undesirable by other students

If some of these concerns sound familiar, take comfort: Most other entering students share the exact same fears. Your concerns are normal transition pains. Remember also that each of the worries is attached to a negative self-fulfilling prophecy that you can exchange for a positive one. That's basically what setting goals is all about: creating and implementing positive self-fulfilling prophecies.

EXERCISE 1.1   Dreams and Nightmares

Briefly write down as many good dreams (ambitions, hopes, wishes) as you can think of in the next few minutes related to entering or completing college. Assume you'll accomplish or gain everything you set out for in life from this point on. Be optimistic.

1. _Become rich_
2. _Find a wife_
3. _help out my community_
4. _have children some day_
5. _____
6. _____
7. _____
8. _____

Now take an equal amount of time to record your worst nightmares and expectations. Be brutally pessimistic — assume the worst will happen.

1. _Becoming Anothing society a_
2. _Bum_
3. _everyone dieing_
4. _____
5. _____
6. _____
7. _____
8. _____

Compare the two lists. How much will you need to do to tip the scales in favor of the positive?

We'll come back to these lists a little later.

NOTE: Many of the exercises in the book are accompanied by the following icons: ✍ This icon indicates a writing exercise. 👤 This icon indicates an exercise involving class or small-group discussion.

SETTING GOALS

Setting conscious goals and working to achieve them helps you avoid the nightmares and capitalize on the rewards of college and beyond. College is an ideal time to begin setting conscious goals. First, you will need to differentiate between short- and long-term goals. During your first semester begin to test some of the short-term goals. It's okay if you don't yet know what you want to do with the rest of your life or what you should be majoring in. Be

Finding a Mentor

Daniel J. Levinson, a psychiatrist at Yale University, discovered in his study of the aging process in men that individuals who tended to be successful in life had developed a dream during their adolescence that was an idealized conception of what they wished to become. He also found that they went on to find a **mentor** — an older successful individual — who personified that dream. Finally, he discovered that these people also developed friendships with a few other people who encouraged, nurtured, and supported them in pursuit of that dream.*

Perhaps the simplest way to define a mentor is to say that he or she is someone who, in some respect, is now what you hope to be in the future. What mentors can you identify in your life up to now? What specific qualities did you seek to emulate? Do you have any mentors right now? If you do, what might you do to make more use of them? What are you looking for in a college mentor?

What can a mentor give you? Encouragement. Friendship. Inspiration.

*D. J. Levinson et al. *The Seasons of a Man's Life* (New York: Ballantine Books, 1978).

patient. Practice setting and fulfilling some short-term goals by means of the following process.*

1. **Select a goal**. State it in measurable terms. Be specific about what you want to achieve and when (not "improve my study skills" but "master the double-entry system of note-taking by the end of October").

2. **Ask whether the goal is achievable**. Do you have enough time to pursue it, and more important, do you have the necessary skills, strengths, and resources? Modify the goal to make it achievable.

3. **Be certain you genuinely want to achieve this goal**. Don't set out to work toward something only because you feel you should. Be sure that your goal will not have a negative impact on yourself or others and that it is consistent with your most important basic values.

4. **Identify why this goal is worthwhile**. Be sure that it has the potential to give you a sense of accomplishment.

5. **Anticipate and identify difficulties you might encounter**. Plan ways to overcome these problems.

6. **Devise strategies and steps for achieving the goal**. What will you need to do to begin? What comes next? What may you need to avoid? Set a timeline for the steps.

*Adapted from Human Potential Seminars by James D. McHolland and Roy W. Trueblood, Evanston, Illinois, 1972. Used by permission of the authors.

EXERCISE 1.2   Setting a Short-Term Goal

Look over your responses in Exercise 1.1. Pick one dream or problem area that you can begin to work on with a short-term goal. Or identify one "persistence factor" that you can address in a short-term goal (ask your instructor whether this will overlap with work he or she may be assigning later in the course). In discussion and writing complete the six steps for achieving this goal. Establish a date (perhaps a week or month from now) when you will determine whether the goal has been achieved. At that time set at least one new goal.

EXERCISE 1.3   Commuters or Residents: Who Has the Advantage?

Check either residential or commuter students as having an advantage in participating in the following persistence and success factor activities.

Residential	Commuter	
_____	_____	1. Developing close and personally satisfying relationships with other students
_____	_____	2. Having opportunities to meet and make friends with other students
_____	_____	3. Having opportunities to chat with a faculty member about things not related to class
_____	_____	4. Working and studying with other students
_____	_____	5. Using the institution's academic support services — tutors, learning centers, media materials, and so on
_____	_____	6. Participating in co-curricular activities
_____	_____	7. Collecting information about the college
_____	_____	8. Receiving help from a faculty member about a class-related problem
_____	_____	9. Meeting with academic advisors on more than one occasion during the term
_____	_____	10. Studying in the college library
_____	_____	11. Talking with students about course-related material

What pattern emerges? Many commuters will insist they have no desire to become more integrated with their campus or will claim they simply don't have time. But such involvement is clearly related to academic success. Develop short-term goals to compensate in several areas where you feel at a disadvantage.

A First-Year Journal

At the end of each section or chapter in this book, you will find a journal assignment such as the one below. It's important to get into the habit of asking questions as you read and keeping track of your thoughts in writing. Periodically throughout this book you should be asking yourself questions like these:

1. What do I think of what I just read?

2. What did I learn?

3. How do I react to what I've learned?

4. What is there here that I can apply to my own life in the first year of college?

Each journal assignment poses questions to help you focus your thoughts. These are simply suggestions for writing. Use them if they stimulate your thinking. If other, related questions concern you more, write about those instead.

You will get the most out of your freshman year and this course if you actually do keep a regular journal. As your college experience grows, so will your appreciation of the value of expressing yourself, personally and professionally, in clear written form.

Use the journal entries to record how you are adapting to college life and to gain perspective on what is happening. Your instructor may ask you to write these entries strictly for your own private reading and reflection or as a hand-in assignment. Instructors who ask to read your journal entries generally do so because they know this to be an excellent means of individual, private, supportive communication between you and them. You may find this a rare and rewarding opportunity.

Depending on your instructor's preferences, you may record your journal entries on separate looseleaf sheets, on typed pages, or in a journal notebook. Whatever the format, be sure to collect and keep these writings so that you can periodically review them, especially at the end of the semester and later in your college career. Among other benefits they will give you a graphic measure of the progress you are making.

JOURNAL

Which of the "persistence factors" listed in this section have you already begun to incorporate into your college life? Which others can you start working on soon? How might you start? Do any of the discoveries of Daniel Levinson match with your own experience so far? What suggestions do they offer about things you might want to do in the next few months?

SUGGESTIONS FOR FURTHER READING

Hettich, Paul I. *Learning Skills for College and Career.* Pacific Grove, Calif.: Brooks/Cole, 1992.

Kleinke, Chris L. *Coping with Life's Challenges.* Pacific Grove, Calif.: Brooks/Cole, 1991.

The Value of College

Panic. One of my professors says to write about why we're in college. What can I write? That my parents told me I'd better make something of myself? That all my friends were going? Or because I know it's the only way to finally get that BMW?! Great time at the football game Saturday (I actually met someone I'd like to go out with!!!!!). Also had pizza delivered right to my door. Okay, so those aren't really the "important" reasons. So what are?

HILDA F. OWENS *is executive assistant to the president for planning and research at Spartanburg Methodist College in Spartanburg, South Carolina.*

"I can vividly recall my feelings of excitement, anticipation, uncertainty, and fear of the unknown during those first few weeks of my freshman year [at East Carolina University]," she says. Before very long, however, she found "challenge, reward, and satisfaction in my years as a student. Each experience added something to the whole of who and what I am."

Owens taught junior high math and science for five years, earned her doctorate from Florida State University, and is a published author and active community citizen. Along with her other duties she continues to teach freshman and sophomore classes.

EXERCISE 1.4   Before You Read On

Jot down some notes in response to the following questions:

1. Why did you choose to go to college?
2. Why did you choose this particular school?
3. If you've already chosen a major, why did you choose this major?
4. What person(s) or information influenced you in each of these decisions?
5. How do you expect to change between now and graduation?

Few decisions, if any, will have as great an impact on the quality and direction of your life as your decision to go to college. In addition to increasing your knowledge and self-understanding, college can expand your horizons by offering new career opportunities and by helping you make the right decisions. It will also affect your views on family matters, social issues, community service, politics, health care, recreation, and consumer priorities.

This section looks at how college can change your life greatly for the better, in terms of not only career and money-earning prospects but also personal growth, development, and competence.

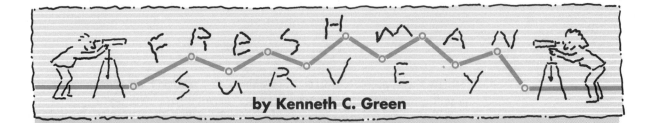

by Kenneth C. Green

1969 – The Year That Was

Woodstock . . . the Apollo mission to the moon . . . the October moratorium in which millions of Americans protested against the Vietnam War . . . campus upheavals over war and racial equality . . . the beginnings of a new movement for women's rights . . .

What matters now about 1969 is that your psychology, math, or lit professor was probably an undergraduate in 1969. He or she may well have been a campus activist — protesting against the war, helping to organize some of the first environmental awareness projects, or working with other students to promote the civil rights or women's movement. Many of the faculty and administrators on campus today were deeply influenced by the events of that era.

Some faculty romanticize their own experiences as college students during the 1960s when they compare themselves to students today. Do you know what some of them say about your generation of college students? Many faculty complain that today's undergraduates may be described as:

► *Greedy and materialistic* — preoccupied with making money

► *Overly career oriented* — interested in college mainly as a way to land a good, well-paying job

► *Intellectually docile* — interested primarily in grades and demonstrating little real interest in learning about issues and ideas

► *Ambivalent or apathetic* — not concerned about social issues or the welfare of others

► *Politically and socially conservative* — ill-informed about the political and social

changes this country experienced in the 1960s and 1970s

Are they right? Since 1966 the Cooperative Institutional Research Program, now based at the University of California, Los Angeles (UCLA), has surveyed hundreds of thousands of college students in annual surveys of entering freshmen at campuses across the country. This data, reported in the UCLA Freshman Survey, allows us to compare the attitudes, aspirations, and behaviors of succeeding generations of freshmen. Your campus may be one of some 600 two- and four-year colleges and universities across the country that participate in this project each year. You may have completed a special survey during freshman orientation or registration that was from the UCLA Freshman Survey project.

There have been some interesting and very important changes in the attitudes, values, and aspirations of college freshmen over the past twenty-six years. Look for data from and comments about the UCLA Freshman Survey in this and following chapters.

NOTE: Kenneth C. Green, formerly associate director of UCLA's Higher Education Research Institute and the annual UCLA Freshman Survey project, wrote the Freshman Survey reports that appear throughout this book. Dr. Green, currently senior research associate at the Center for Scholarly Technology of the University of Southern California, is the co-author (with Daniel T. Seymour) of *Who's Going to Run General Motors: What College Students Need to Learn Today to Become Business Leaders Tomorrow* (Princeton, N.J.: Peterson's Guides, 1991).

Architecture may not be the highest-paying profession, but how many of us literally shape our world?

EDUCATION, CAREERS, AND INCOME

The relationship between education and income is well established. To illustrate, consider the following list from *The Wall Street Journal* on average monthly income for individuals in 1986 in terms of degrees earned:

Education Level	Monthly Income
High school diploma	$ 415
Vocational degree	990
Associate degree	1,188
Bachelor's degree	1,540
Master's degree	1,956
Doctoral degree	2,747
Professional degree	3,439

Furthermore, according to a report by the Carnegie Commission on Higher Education, as a college graduate you will have a more continuous, less erratic job history, will be promoted more often, and are much less likely to become unemployed than your non-college-graduate counterpart. You are also likely to be happier with your work than those who didn't attend college.

Critics of higher education occasionally point out that some people with college degrees are unemployed or underemployed, but you have only to look at the employment figures of high school graduates and high school dropouts to see that the better educated you are, the better your employment and money-earning opportunities. Thus, while you might question whether investing your time, effort, and money in a college education is worth it, the evidence suggests that it most certainly is. As one person put it, "If you think education is expensive, try ignorance."

THE BROADER VALUE OF COLLEGE

Of course college will affect you in many ways besides financially. How will you change in ways that differ from those of people who decided to go directly to work, join the military, or do something else rather than go to

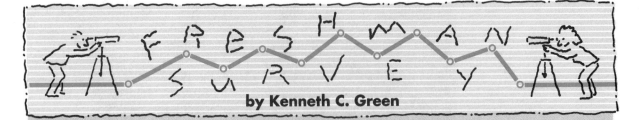

College, Money, and Career

Reasons for Attending College, 1976–1990 (percentage of freshmen indicating "very important")

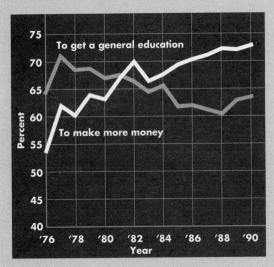

SOURCE: Higher Education Research Institute, UCLA

In the 1980s entering students increasingly thought of college as a link to jobs and money. As the accompanying figure shows, in Fall 1990 a record 73.2 percent of college freshmen indicated that "making more money" was a very important factor in their decision to attend college.

More than ever before, students seem preoccupied with college as a means to financial security and career development rather than as a chance for intellectual growth and personal development.

Why do some college faculty react negatively to this trend? Many of them came of age during the 1960s, a time of great social change. However, the 1960s were also a period of economic growth and prosperity for almost all Americans: The economy was booming, and young people were generally optimistic about future jobs.

But the 1990s are not the 1960s. You have probably experienced first-hand the economic upheaval that has shaken this nation for over a decade: high inflation in the late 1970s, severe recession in the early 1980s, and a dramatic economic restructuring now under way. These events have greatly affected how you and your classmates look at and plan for the future.

Today's traditional-aged college students are what demographers refer to as the "baby bust" generation. Because there are fewer people of this age who will enter the job market in the 1990s, you might feel somewhat confident about your future. Unfortunately the 1990s will also be a time of dramatic change in the U.S. economy. Although demography is on your side, other factors suggest that the 1990s will be a period of significant change for American workers. Corporations across the country are hiring fewer new workers and reducing overall employment; at least that's been the trend between 1988 and 1991. There is little on the horizon to suggest that things will improve dramatically. Increased competition both at home and from abroad means that American businesses — both large corporations and small firms — will make every effort to work faster, wiser, and smarter, *and with fewer people.*

How are students of the 1990s reacting to the prospect of an economically troubled future? One common response among undergraduates is to build a portfolio of skills, contacts, experiences, and credentials to present to potential employers. A growing number of students are making choices about college and majors based in part on what they think will protect them in the job market of the 1990s and the twenty-first century. (Remember, if you are an 18- or 19-year-old college freshman, you will not yet be "thirtysomething" in the year 2000; you'll probably be working until the year 2035 or 2040!) This preoccupation with preparing for what many students regard as an economically insecure future leads a growing number of freshmen to view college primarily as a link to future employment — and to be very concerned about money, jobs, and career.

college? Certainly everyone continues to change somewhat simply because of maturation and increased life experience. But because you chose college, you can expect some significant additional changes.

At the same time, going to college will be stressful and frustrating. For one thing, college is a lot of work! For another, your own natural resistance to new ideas and experiences may at times make you uncomfortable. The "creative tension" caused by the need to learn how to deal with unfamiliar situations can be a powerful stimulus to learning and change. Facing up to crises, or major decision points in your life, is essential for you to continue learning and developing. Intellectual and emotional growth do have their own growing pains.

If you believe that going to college is going to be all fun and games, you should rethink the matter. Doing well in college is at least as demanding as a full-time job. Like all constructive change, learning is hard work.

MAJOR AREAS OF CHANGE IN STUDENTS

A number of studies have greatly expanded our knowledge of how students change during college. In one of the most important, Katz and associates (1968) identified the following as major areas of development for college students:

- ► Authoritarianism declines.
- ► Autonomy grows.
- ► Self-esteem grows.
- ► Capacity for relatedness grows.
- ► Political sophistication grows.
- ► Esthetic capacity grows.
- ► Grasp of theoretical issues grows.

Katz also noted an increase in political and social liberalism and a decrease in formal religious identification and religious activities. These trends basically still hold true, though there has been a recent trend toward more conservative positions with regard to some political and social issues and religious identification.

Increased Knowledge and Cognitive Development

Virtually all the evidence to date suggests that college has a strong positive impact on cognitive learning (content and thought process) whether we compare freshmen with seniors, college students with peers not attending college, or alumni with comparable noncollege people. As a college student you can expect your substantive knowledge, intellectual sensibilities, intellectual tolerance, and interest in lifelong learning all to increase significantly. Colleges seem to do a good job at what they claim to do best — increase the knowledge and spur the development of their students.

Increased Personal Self-Discovery and Emotional Changes

Colleges claim to educate the *whole person*. They claim to improve a person's capacity for personal self-discovery (who one is, what one knows and can do, what one believes and values, and where one fits in the scheme of things) and for internalizing many attitudes and values acquired from others along the way.

Colleges further contend that the collegiate experience gives students the opportunity to clarify and improve their sense of possibility and self-worth, to realize a sense of personal identity, and to improve certain skills, competencies, and behaviors. Evidence strongly suggests that colleges do generally help students in these areas.

When you graduate from college, chances are you will be not only more competent but also more confident than when you arrived. You will also tend to know better who you are, where you fit in the scheme of things, and how you might make a difference in the world. On the other hand, you might also experience some decline in traditional religious values and some increase in behaviors such as drinking and gambling. The former change may be due to the breaking away, at least temporarily, from certain family-held values, while the latter change may be a result of feeling mature enough to handle such behaviors responsibly.

EXERCISE 1.5 Creative Tensions

Is the "fit" between you and your institution comfortable enough that you feel reasonably at home? Is it also challenging enough to stimulate you to develop intellectually, physically, and socially? What "creative tensions" do you feel? Write a brief statement describing the fit between you and your school, including what is comfortable for you and what is not. You may want to consider the size and location of the school, the diversity of the student body, the academic programs offered, social and leisure opportunities, and so on.

EXERCISE 1.6 The Give-and-Take

Begin to get a better focus on what you want to contribute to life as well as what you want to get out of it. List three things you want to get out of life:

1. _____happiness_____
2. _____Financial indepdence_____
3. _____

Now list three contributions you would like to make as your gift to the world or to other people:

1. _____help rebuild homes for the black community_____
2. _____help fights diseases_____
3. _____

Was it more difficult to list what you would like to contribute or what you would like to get? Are there ways in which you expect college to help you accomplish items on both lists? How?

Increased Practical Competence

Colleges frequently espouse the goal of preparing people to handle the practical affairs of life. From a practical and economic standpoint, as a college graduate you will tend to have needed knowledge and skills, and your employment rate will go up accordingly. College further helps you develop the flexibility, mobility, and knowledge needed to adapt to the changing demands of work, life, and relationships. You will also contribute to increased productivity, enjoy greater job satisfaction, and receive a reasonable financial return on the time, energy, and money invested in your college education.

According to research, as a college graduate you will also tend to be more adaptable and more future-oriented, to adopt more liberal views and more ideological thinking, and to develop greater interest in political and public affairs. You will be more likely to vote and to be active in community affairs, and somewhat less prone to criminal activity.

College also has an important influence on family life. The stereotypical division of roles between men and women in the family seems to diminish with education. As more women work (about 60 percent of women in America currently work outside the home) and as women earn more of the family income, child-care and household responsibilities are more likely to be shared or shifted. As a college graduate you will tend to delay getting married and having children, to have fewer children, and to plan your children's births. You will also tend to allocate more thought, time, energy, and money to child rearing. You and your peers will have a slightly lower divorce rate than non-college-educated people, and your children generally will have greater abilities and achieve more than children of non-college-educated parents.

As a college-educated person, in addition to making more money, you will be a more efficient consumer than non-college-educated persons. Chances are you will save more money, take sounder investment risks, and spend more money on home, intellectual, and cultural interests and on your children. As a consumer and citizen you will also be more able to deal with bureaucracies, the legal system, tax laws and requirements, and advertising claims.

In terms of leisure time activities you will spend less time and money on television and movies and more time on intellectual and cultural pursuits, including continuing education, hobbies, community and civic affairs, and vacations.

Finally, you are likely to be concerned with wellness and preventive health care rather than just treatment of physical and mental illness. Through diet, exercise, stress management, a positive attitude, and other factors, you will live longer and suffer fewer disabilities. Your attention to preventive health maintenance will probably reflect a greater feeling of self-worth.

Too many people think of college primarily in terms of its relationship to employment and its effect on income. For example, Bird (1975) argued that a college education is not a good investment. Other critics point to the supply and demand issues related to a college education and argue that the value of college is declining.

Certainly having a fulfilling career and earning enough money are important goals, and a college education should enhance your ability to achieve them. On the other hand, these aren't the only or the best reasons for going to college or the greatest benefits of the college experience. College can and

Who Are You?

Are you beginning to clarify your own identity and philosophy of life? Once you've finished reading this section, compose a letter about who you are and what your personal philosophy is as you now understand it. Write to me, if you would care to do so, at the address below. I assure you, I will not only read your letter with great interest but respond!

Hilda F. Owens
Spartanburg Methodist College
Spartanburg, S.C., 29301

should be much more than a place for you to be "processed" into a higher wage bracket. College should help add meaning and purpose to your life.

Frankel (1969) noted that individuals find meaning and purpose in their lives in three ways: (1) by what they give to the world in terms of their creations, (2) by what they take from the world through encounters and experiences, and (3) by the stand they take with regard to their human predicaments. Research suggests that you will gain skills, knowledge, attitudes, and behaviors during college that help you face — and get the most out of — life.

Kingman Brewster, a former president of Yale University, identified the primary goals of a college education as the development of three senses: (1) a sense of place, (2) a sense of self, and (3) a sense of judgment. Brewster argued eloquently for the broader and more liberating view of education when he concluded:

> The most fundamental value of education is that it makes life more interesting. This is true whether you are fetched up on a desert island or adrift in the impersonal loneliness of the urban hurly-burly. It allows you to see things which the uneducated do not see. It allows you to understand things which do not occur to the less learned. In short, it makes it less likely that you will be bored with life. It also makes it less likely that you will be a crashing bore to those whose company you keep. By analogy, it makes the difference between the traveler who understands the local language and the traveler to whom the local language is a jumble of nonsense words. (Cited in Davis, 1977, p. xv)

The value of college is calculable and incalculable, tangible and intangible. As Eddy (1977) notes, your real task as an educated person is to be able to articulate to yourself and others what you are willing to bet your life on.

EXERCISE 1.7   Interviewing Another Student

Interview another student on campus who is somewhat different from you — maybe from a different cultural background, geographic region, age group, or family background. Compare your respective goals and reasons for attending college. Write a short statement about the interview.

EXERCISE 1.8   On Further Thought

Now that you've read this section, answer the questions in Exercise 1.4 on page 15 again. Write a brief statement comparing your answers. How has this section affected your views on the value of college?

JOURNAL

Think about two people who are or have been significant in your life, one who is a college graduate and one who is not. How were they different and to what extent do you think this is attributable to the college experience? How would you like the college experience to change you and your circumstances? This is another way of asking you why you have come to college.

REFERENCES AND SUGGESTIONS FOR FURTHER READING

Astin, A. W. *Four Critical Years: Effects of College on Beliefs, Attitudes, and Knowledge.* San Francisco: Jossey-Bass, 1977.

Astin, A. W., Kenneth C. Green, and William S. Kern. *The American Freshman: Twenty Year Trends (1966–1985).* Los Angeles: Higher Education Research Institute of the University of California, 1987.

Bird, Caroline. *The Case Against College.* New York: McKay, 1975.

Bowen, H. R. *Investment in Learning: The Individual and Social Value of American Higher Education.* San Francisco: Jossey-Bass, 1977.

Boyer, E. L. *College: The Undergraduate Experience in America.* New York: Harper & Row, 1987.

Chickering, A. W. *Education and Identity.* San Francisco: Jossey-Bass, 1972.

Davis, J. R. *Going to College: The Study of Students and the Student Experience.* Boulder, Colo.: Westview Press, 1977.

Eddy, E. D. "What Happened to Student Values?" *Educational Record* 58, no. 1 (1977): 7–17.

Frankel, V. *The Will to Meaning.* New York: Plume, 1969.

Katz, J., ed. *No Time for Youth: Growth and Constraint in College Students.* San Francisco: Jossey-Bass, 1968.

Levine, A. W. *When Dreams and Heroes Died: A Portrait of Today's College Students.* San Francisco: Jossey-Bass, 1980.

Owens, H. F., C. H. Witten, and W. R. Bailey, eds. *College Student Personnel Administration: An Anthology.* Springfield, Ill.: Thomas, 1982, pp. 121–69.

Parker, C. A., ed. *Encouraging Development in College Students.* Minneapolis: University of Minnesota Press, 1978.

Parks, Sharon. *The Critical Years: Young Adults and the Search for Meaning, Faith, and Commitment.* New York: HarperCollins, 1991.

Pascarella, E. T., and P. Terenzini. *How Colleges Affect Students.* San Francisco: Jossey-Bass, 1991.

Sanford, N. *Self and Society: Social Change and Individual Development.* New York: Atherton Press, 1966.

C H A P T E R ▼▼▼▼▼▼▼▼▼▼▼▼▼▼▼▼▼▼

Time Management: The Foundation of Academic Success

Kenneth F. Long

Time Management

Let's see . . . it's Wednesday. Wednesday!! That big committee meeting's at four and I promised to be in for work. I can't work tonight, I've got a history quiz at nine tomorrow and I need to read two chapters for it. Got to get to English class. Hope she won't mind that my paper's still rough. Better write this all down in my calendar. Now where's that calendar??

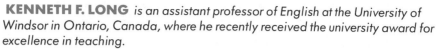

KENNETH F. LONG *is an assistant professor of English at the University of Windsor in Ontario, Canada, where he recently received the university award for excellence in teaching.*

"I was most honored," he says, "that students — both current and recent graduates — played a major role in choosing me. Each semester I look forward to meeting my new students, and it seems that in no time at all I see them at convocation. Their graduation is always a proud moment for me, too, because academic achievement is a shared responsibility between teacher and student. Both need to play their roles well to ensure success. Of all the factors that can contribute to that success, perhaps study skills are the most critical. The strategies I share in these chapters work. Thousands of students are proof of that."

Most experts agree: Time management is one of the most important keys to success in college. Yet many students entering college are weak in this area. Perhaps it's because they did well in high school without consciously practicing time management or because in most high schools students had little control over their own time. That won't work in college. So the central aim of this chapter is to show you how to develop and stick to a time management program.

Time management is a highly sophisticated skill, yet one you practice every day. For instance, whenever you show up at an appointed place at an agreed-upon time, or whenever you say to someone, "Give me five minutes to finish this and I'll go out with you," you are practicing time management. As casual as it may sound, this strategy is the basis for high performance in almost every endeavor.

Whether the task is simple or complex, time management involves planning, judgment, anticipation, and commitment. First, you must know what your goals are and where you will need to be at some future time. Second, you must decide where your priorities lie and how to satisfy competing interests. Third, you must make plans that anticipate future needs as well as possible changes. Finally, you must commit yourself to placing yourself in control of your time and carrying out your plans.

In certain high school courses students are not expected to take much responsibility for controlling their own use of time. College is different. Once courses are selected, you are personally responsible for allocating time to attend classes, to complete assignments, to study for tests, and so on. Generally it's even your decision whether to show up for class — on time or at all! College offers a great deal of freedom. In turn, it requires you to take personal responsibility for planning and managing your time.

SETTING PRIORITIES

To manage your time in college, you must first set priorities. Certain activities should take priority over all others and determine the way you live. The decision to attend college is a commitment to being a professional student for an extended period of time. Any professional — businessperson, athlete,

doctor, or student — attends to his or her professional responsibilities above most other things in life. Usually work comes *before* pleasure. As a student you must identify your priorities and develop a system for living each day accordingly.

What are your current priorities? Managing your time begins with an honest appraisal of what you want to do with it.

EXERCISE 2.1   ## Identifying Your Priorities

A. Rank order the following pursuits in terms of their importance to you. In the left-hand column write 1 beside the most important, 2 beside the second most important, and so on. Next, under "Estimated Hours," record the amount of time per week you believe you spend at this pursuit. Be honest, now!

Rank		Estimated Hours	Actual Hours
1	Class attendance	4 hours	
	Relaxation		
	Volunteer service		
6	Time with family	5 min	
4	Exercise	30 min	
7	Clubs/organizations	1 hour	
	Required reading		
9	Hobbies or entertainment	2 hours	
3	Time with girlfriend/boyfriend or spouse	4 hours	
8	Studying	3 hours	
	Working at a job		
	Time with girlfield/boyfriend or spouse		
5	Religious activities	5 minutes	
	Shopping		
	Nonrequired reading		
	Sleeping		
	Other: _____		

B. Monitor the actual amount of time you spend at each pursuit over the course of one week, and record the total figures under "Actual Hours." Compare your estimates with the actual figures. Are there any important differences? If so, how do you explain them?

C. Discuss your rankings and your use of time with your peers and your instructor. How are your choices and habits similar to or different from theirs? How are your current practices likely to affect your college success? What changes seem to be in order?

How to Beat Procrastination

Procrastination may be your single greatest enemy. Getting started when it's time to start takes self-discipline and self-control. Here are some ways to beat procrastination:

1. Say to yourself, "A mature person is capable and responsible and is a self-starter. I'm that kind of person if I start now." Then start!

2. On a 3 × 5 notecard write out a list of everything you need to do. Check off things as you get them done. Use the list to focus on the things that aren't getting done. Move them to the top of your next day's list and make up your mind to do them. Working from a list will give you a feeling of accomplishment and lead you to do more.

3. Break big jobs down into smaller steps. Tackle short, easy-to-accomplish tasks first.

4. Apply the goal-setting technique described in Chapter 1 to whatever you are putting off.

5. Promise yourself a suitable reward (an apple, a phone call, a walk) whenever you finish something that was hard to undertake.

6. Take control of your study environment. Eliminate distractions — including the ones you love! Say no to friends who want your attention at *their* convenience. Agree to meet them at a specific time later. Let them be your reward for doing what you must do now. Don't make phone calls during planned study sessions. Close your door.

Let's consider a student who has some problems setting priorities. Joe is a bright, well-intentioned, promising student who happens to be in danger of failing his first semester. He complains about having too much work and not enough time. Unfortunately, like many students, Joe wastes many hours every day. How does this happen?

First, Joe socializes at the drop of a hat. Naturally he wants to be popular, so he is available when anyone calls. He also likes to enjoy himself and, consequently, often stays out fairly late, even during the week. Then, to catch up on his sleep, he sometimes skips his 8:00 class, figuring he can make it up later. Other times Joe makes it to class even when he is still tired and manages to take notes, usually from the back of the room. In general Joe's penchant for socializing has made it increasingly difficult for him to keep up with his studies.

Joe is a person of good character, a quality reflected in some other activities. He is a frequent volunteer at a children's center and never disappoints his little friends. He has also undertaken to write an occasional column for the student newspaper and faithfully meets his deadlines, usually at the expense of his studies. This is when Joe complains especially about never having enough time.

Of course Joe has exactly the same number of hours in each day as you or I. But rather than controlling the various attractions of college life, Joe lets these things control him. Rather than deciding what his basic responsibilities are and committing himself to college, he proceeds on a vague agenda of miscellaneous personal preferences.

Look around and you will see that Joe isn't the only one on campus with this kind of problem. One way or another, many students fail to see that with good time management and an extra drop of discipline, they can make studying their number one priority and still have time for other things. Yet, in essence, all time management means is becoming fully conscious of the right priorities and planning accordingly.

EXERCISE 2.2   Analyzing Joe as a Student

Review the description of Joe carefully, and select five characteristics of his behavior that will likely prevent him from being the best student he can be. When you finish, share your choices and the reasons for your choices with your peers and instructor.

1. _Girls_
2. _Friends_
3. _Fun_
4. _Clubs_
5. _hanging out_

TAKING CONTROL IN THE FIRST WEEK: THE TIMETABLE AND MASTER PLAN

Now let's see how a more fully aware and committed student handles priorities. Carmen's first step each semester is to create a personal timetable and master plan (see Figure 2.1). The timetable is determined mostly by her course selections and other fixed responsibilities (shaded in the figure). Note that Carmen's timetable includes five courses, the typical full-time load for students on the semester system. (If you work long hours or have significant family responsibilities, you should take on a proportionately smaller course load.) Of course your master plan will not be the same as Carmen's, but it should be as well thought out.

The classroom time for Carmen's five courses (History, University 101, Geology, Psychology, and Expository Writing) totals only 16 hours per week. That leaves Carmen with lots of free time, right? Well, no. To that figure Carmen adds 2 hours outside of class for *every hour* in class. Thus, based on her 16 hours in class, Carmen anticipates 32 more hours of schoolwork outside of class, for a total of 48 hours. A 48-hour work week?! Who says college students have it easy? Obviously Carmen has to schedule her time wisely and efficiently.

Carmen begins by scheduling 17 hours of study time into her normal weekday hours (see Figure 2.1). Her trick is to make good use of the many hours tucked into the day between her widely scheduled classes. For instance, on Tuesdays and Thursdays she gets an early (but not too early) start,

Figure 2.1 Carmen's Timetable and Master Plan

	Sunday	Monday	Tuesday	Wednesday	Thursday	Friday	Saturday
6:00							
7:00							
8:00		History		History		History	
9:00		Univ. 101	Read/ Study Psych.	Univ. 101	Read/ Study Psych.	Univ. 101	
10:00		Review Hist. & Univ. 101	↓	Review Hist. & Univ. 101	↓		
11:00		Geology	Psych.	Geology	Psych.		
12:00		LUNCH	↓	LUNCH	↓	LUNCH	
1:00		Study Geology	LUNCH	Study Geology, etc.	LUNCH	Read/ Study History,	
2:00		Geology Lab	Work on Writing	↓		Univ. 101, etc.	
3:00		↓	↓			↓	
4:00			↓	Work on Writing			
5:00				↓			
6:00			Expository Writing				
7:00			Workshop				
8:00			↓				
9:00							
10:00							

Total class hours: 16
Total study hours needed: 16 x 2 = 32

Total study hours allotted: 17
Additional study hours needed: 15

completing 4 of the 6 recommended hours of study for Psychology. Now look at Monday, Wednesday, and Friday mornings, which are more complex. Carmen knows that it is best to review right after class, so on Mondays and Wednesdays she uses the hour between University 101 and Geology to review her notes from the two classes she has already attended on those mornings. Nor does she waste the time after lunch on Monday before her Geology lab at 2:00. Noting that Tuesday evening includes her 3-hour writing workshop, Carmen schedules time for writing right before the workshop and again the following afternoon. Although short bursts of study are sometimes ideal for review, writing requires longer, uninterrupted periods.

Now that she has accounted for 17 of the 32 study hours, Carmen should be able to find time for the additional 15 hours. When will she add these hours or, on certain weeks, put in the even longer hours that her courses will sometimes require? The master plan makes it clear that Carmen will most likely be using many Thursday afternoons as well as evenings and weekends to meet her basic commitment. Oh, no, the weekends?! Sad but true. Carmen must plan to work a good portion of many weekends, and so should you. But take heart—it's worth it. Once you have met your academic (and other) commitments, the free time left over will be all yours! It will relax you totally, letting you enjoy yourself and return refreshed to your studies.

Let's review the steps Carmen followed to gain control from the first day of college:

- ► *Step 1.* She obtained a blank timetable form or purchased a calendar organized by day and hour, which often provides blank timetable forms as well.
- ► *Step 2.* As soon as she was registered in her five courses, she filled in the days and times for each course. She also made a list of buildings and room numbers, consulted a campus map, and took a tour before the first day of class. Colleges frequently organize these tours for new students.
- ► *Step 3.* She began to organize her class hours according to effective strategies for study, also including some time for nonacademic pursuits.

Although Carmen is the ideal time manager, and it would be difficult to follow all the tips she provides, you need to consider how she organizes her study time to see which tips fit into your lifestyle as a student. Using just a few of her time management strategies can markedly improve your chances of success as a college student.

EXERCISE 2.3   Your Timetable and Master Plan

Photocopy Figure 2.2 and use the chart to construct your own timetable and master plan. First, fill in your scheduled commitments: classes, job, child care, and other activities. Then block out study hours according to the suggestions discussed previously. Share and discuss these with your peers and instructors. Check particularly to see if your work schedule or family responsibilities are too demanding and prevent you from putting in the necessary study hours.

Figure 2.2 Timetable and Master Plan

(1) List all class meeting times. (2) Try to reserve about one hour of daytime study for each class hour. (3) Reserve time for meals, exercise, free time. (4) Try to plan a minimum of one hour additional study in evenings or on weekends for each class.

	Sunday	Monday	Tuesday	Wednesday	Thursday	Friday	Saturday
6:00							
7:00							
8:00							
9:00							
10:00							
11:00							
12:00							
1:00							
2:00							
3:00							
4:00							
5:00							
6:00							
7:00							
8:00							
9:00							
10:00							
11:00							
12:00							

ORGANIZING THE SEMESTER: THE WEEKLY ASSIGNMENT PLAN

Weekly assignment plans are the next important tool for staying in control. These incorporate into the timetable all the assignments and tests for which you are responsible. In the first week of classes you may receive course outlines, or **syllabi**, that delineate the nature and purpose of each course and establish the criteria and due dates of all assignments. Use these syllabi to structure your weekly study plans. If the instructor does not provide a syllabus, ask him or her for the specific study requirements for that week and mark them on your timetable. If the course syllabus doesn't specify due dates, don't be bashful. Ask the professor, and write the dates on your copy of the syllabus.

EXERCISE 2.4   Semester Assignment Previews

To see the "big picture" of your workload this quarter or semester, fill in the following assignment preview sheet, listing all tests, reports, and other deadline-related activities.

Week	Course	What's Due
1	_____	_____
	_____	_____
	_____	_____
2	_____	_____
	_____	_____
	_____	_____
3	_____	_____
	_____	_____
	_____	_____
4	_____	_____
	_____	_____
	_____	_____
5	_____	_____
	_____	_____
	_____	_____
6	_____	_____
	_____	_____
	_____	_____

7   _____   _____

      _____   _____

      _____   _____

8   _____   _____

      _____   _____

      _____   _____

9   _____   _____

      _____   _____

      _____   _____

10   _____   _____

      _____   _____

      _____   _____

11   _____   _____

      _____   _____

      _____   _____

12   _____   _____

      _____   _____

      _____   _____

13   _____   _____

      _____   _____

      _____   _____

14   _____   _____

      _____   _____

      _____   _____

15   _____   _____

      _____   _____

      _____   _____

16   _____   _____

      _____   _____

      _____   _____

Use photocopies of your timetable as weekly assignment plans, one sheet for each week. Carefully study all of the course outlines, and write in the due dates of all tests, papers, and special assignments. Complete this early in the term. Typically the first two or three weeks will be free of due dates, but the midterm (fifth through seventh weeks) will be full. This lets you see in advance what planning is necessary to handle these demanding weeks.

Let's look at one such week for Carmen, in which she will face the challenge of doing well on three tests while also turning in two essays (see Figure 2.3). Carmen keeps her timetable where she can consult it often, but she knows that good time management is flexible. She will generally stick to her routine, but occasionally, when things are going well, she will slack off a bit. She also knows that certain days and weeks will be unusually demanding.

In order for Carmen to manage this week successfully, she will need to have done some planning and a lot of studying in advance. For example, note her early wakeup on Monday for a "final" study session. In other words Carmen has studied all the important material thoroughly prior to Monday morning. (In subsequent chapters you'll be learning about long-term study techniques for exams.) The same will be true for the lab test on Monday afternoon. Now look at 1:30 on Tuesday. All Carmen can do here is proofread and make minor revisions. This means that the essay itself was researched, written, and revised some days earlier — certainly not the day before, in the midst of preparing for and taking tests on Monday and Tuesday morning!

The rest of the week is not nearly so difficult, but note that for the history essay, only the final draft and proofing stages are planned for. Once again success depends on Carmen's completing the bulk of the work for this essay well in advance of this week. Only by crafting a detailed weekly plan for each week of the semester can Carmen — and you — see in advance how to get everything done well and on time. You don't want to find yourself scrambling to write an essay when you need to be studying for a test!

In the very first weeks of class every college student is called upon to take control of and be responsible for a number of complex situations. Few can keep track of all this complexity without the help of a master plan and weekly assignment plans. Yours should be completed no later than Monday morning of the second week of classes so that you can continue to plan, anticipate, judge, and use your time effectively. You should also purchase some type of pocket calendar (your bookstore has these "week at a glance"–type calendars), use it, and carry it with you everywhere.

Finally, note how versatile the weekly assignment plan is: It reminds you, on a week-to-week basis, of your major assignments during the semester. The master plan serves a more global purpose: It tells you when you must be in class and encourages you to structure the hours outside of class. You should have access to both plans at all times for reference.

ORGANIZING THE DAY: THE DAILY PLAN

With master and weekly plans in place, it will be easy for you to look at each day as an important 24-hour package and plan accordingly. Let's look for a moment at one of Carmen's daily plans, to which we add some comments. This daily plan is nothing more than a note that she has written to herself the prior evening (see Figure 2.4).

Although college study is often demanding and requires a great deal of time, being a good student does not necessarily mean grinding away at studies and doing little else. By planning her time carefully, Carmen is able to balance her academic commitment with a modest number of recreational activities. By working two-thirds of her class and study hours into the normal working day, she has reduced the additional studying she will need to do to

Figure 2.3 Carmen's Timetable and Master Plan — Week 6

	Sunday	Monday	Tuesday	Wednesday	Thursday	Friday	Saturday
6:00							
7:00		Final Study Univ. 101					
8:00		History		History		History ESSAY DUE	
9:00		Univ. 101 TEST	Read/ Study Psych.	Univ. 101	Read/ Study Psych.	Univ. 101	
10:00		Review Hist. & Univ. 101	for Test ↓	Review Hist. & Univ. 101	↓		
11:00		geology	Psych. TEST	Geology	Psych.		
12:00		LUNCH	↓	LUNCH	↓	LUNCH	
1:00		Study Geology Final Review	LUNCH Work	Study Geology, etc.	LUNCH	Read/ Study History,	
2:00		Geology Lab	on Writing Review	↓		Univ. 101, etc.	
3:00		TEST ↓	and Proofread Essay			↓	
4:00			↓	Work on Writing			
5:00				↓			
6:00		Study for	Expository Writing		Review and		
7:00		Psych. Test	Workshop ESSAY DUE	History Essay	Proofread History Essay		
8:00		↓	↓	Final Draft			
9:00				↓			
10:00							
11:00							
12:00							

Figure 2.4 Carmen's Daily Plan

Thursday

7:00 — Up

Scheduling early classes and rising early will give you a jump on the day.

8:00 – 9:00 — Review science and hist. notes with Rob over breakfast

Rob is also a well-organized student — a good study partner.

9:00 – 10:00 — Read/study psych. in library, review notes from last lecture

Reading and reviewing notes will help prepare you for class.

11:00 – 12:30 — Psych. lecture

12:30 – 12:45 — Review/Recall/Recite

As you will discover, to prevent forgetting it's very important to review as soon after class as possible.

12:45 – 1:45 — Lunch

1:45 – 2:30 — Bookstore for supplies, textbook

Right after lunch is a good time for miscellaneous activity. It's hard to study on a full stomach.

2:30 – 4:00 — Read/study history

Always take a short break in the middle of a study session to maintain alertness.

4:00 – 5:30 — 25 min. jog with Alice; shower, sauna

Regular exercise is important. It actually aids studying by promoting alertness.

5:30 – 6:30 — Dinner

6:30 – 7:15 — Free time

Schedule free time. It keeps you balanced emotionally.

7:15 – 10:00 — Study for hist. quiz, prepare for Univ. 101, write schedule for Friday

In extended study sessions schedule a variety of activities, each with a specific objective.

Time management is a lifetime skill. The better the job you have after college, the more likely you'll be managing your own and other people's time.

about 15 hours. Thus a few hours spent studying each evening should account for most of the required study time. Her weekends can remain somewhat free, as can selected regular times during the week, for other commitments and interests.

Note that Carmen honors the age-old principle, "Sound mind, sound body." Thus her timetable includes two commitments to exercise, and she'll work out once more on the weekend. Your schedule should also include regular exercise time of at least an hour (including shower) three times a week. Research consistently shows that regular exercise gives you more, not less, energy.

What are the implications of all this for Joe, our currently unorganized student? There's good news and bad news. The bad news is that Joe does need to examine his current patterns and commit himself to change. Like Carmen, he must begin to manage his time around the basic responsibilities that the freedom of college entails. He needs to see what his academic needs are and to set priorities accordingly. He may have to start saying no sometimes to friends who want him to socialize, and he'll want to take a long, hard look at other ways in which he tends to procrastinate. Most likely he will also have to reduce the hours he spends on interests outside school. Admittedly students like Joe may not be able to adopt all of Carmen's study habits immediately. But such students can gradually begin to get their priorities, time demands, and study habits under better control as the first term progresses.

The good news is that he can also start a time management system like Carmen's. Once he starts changing some of his study habits, Joe will find himself doing a better job of pursuing his interests both inside and outside class. Joe needs to devise and regularly consult his master plan, his weekly plan, and his daily plan, as did Carmen.

Use the following guidelines in your scheduling:

1. Examine your toughest weeks. Can you finish some of these assignments early in order to free up some time to study for tests?

2. Break large assignments like term papers down into smaller steps (choosing a topic, doing research, writing an outline, writing a first draft, and so on). Add deadlines in your schedule for each of these smaller portions of the project.

3. Start working on assignments days before they are due. Good student time managers frequently have assignments finished one or more days before actual due dates to allow for emergencies.

EXERCISE 2.5 Starting Your Time Management System

Review your "Assignment Preview" sheet from Exercise 2.4 on pages 34–35. Then begin to structure a schedule allowing you time to finish all your assignments. Be sure to try to find time during your hours on campus to study. Try to follow this schedule for a week. Then share your experiences with your peers and your instructor. See if you can use some of the time management strategies that your peers introduce in this discussion. If this system gives you problems, talk to your instructor about what you think is not working.

TIME MANAGEMENT FOR COMMUTERS

If you are a commuter you probably have less time to devote to college than students who live on campus. Not only do you spend more time traveling, but you are also more likely to have commitments to family and work that seriously compete with your class and study time. Your greatest problems probably occur during exam time or when papers and projects are due. In addition to the time management strategies already presented in this chapter, you can do several things to help manage your time efficiently.

1. Be Realistic in Your Time Management Plans

To keep your problems to a minimum, the first thing you must do is be realistic. As you fill out your daily and weekly plans, be sure to allow time for travel, family, work, or other responsibilities. If there is really not enough time to meet your commitments and carry the hoped-for number of courses, reduce your course load. Take care to record the critical exam dates and assignment due dates on your family calendar so that you can avoid potential conflicts. Let your family know ahead of time the days or weeks that you will need more time of your own.

EXERCISE 2.6   Do Commuters Have Time for Success?

The following shows how typical *residential* freshmen allocate their time on a weekday.*

Activity	Hours per Day
Class time	3
Studying	3
Employment	1/4
Idle leisure	3
Social	2 1/4
Travel (between classes)	1
Eating	1 1/2
Grooming	1
Resting	6 1/2
Recreation	1 1/2
Other	1

Notice that freshmen who live on campus devote almost 7 hours each day to socializing, recreation, and leisure pursuits. How might a commuter use those 7 hours? The following chart lists some activities that commuters may have to carry out on a typical weekday. If you are a commuter, estimate the time you take for each. Write your response in the "hours per day" column.

Activity	Hours per Day
Class time	4
Studying	4
Employment	_____
Travel	
Home to college	30
Between classes	1-2 hours
College to work	_____
Work to home	_____
Other	_____
Total travel	_____
Home responsibilities	
Shopping	_____
Meals	_____

*Data adapted from David W. Desmond and David S. Glenwick, "Time-Budgeting Practices of College Students: A Developmental Analysis of Activity Patterns," *Journal of College Student Personnel* 28, no. 4 (1987): 318–23.

Activity	Hours per Day
Home responsibilities (cont.)	
Housecleaning	_____
Laundry	_____
Other	_____
Total home	_____
Family responsibilities	
General time	_____
Child care	_____
Care for elderly or disabled	_____
Other	_____
Total family	_____
Civic responsibilities	
Volunteer work	_____
Other	_____
Total civic	_____
Personal	
Grooming/dressing	_____
Newspaper	_____
Rest	_____
Other	_____
Total personal	_____
Other	_____
Total time for all responsibilities	_____

Do you need to make some adjustments? What are they? Use the goal-setting process in Chapter 1 to help you make them.

2. Don't Be a "Blockhead"

As a commuter you may tend to use block scheduling, running all your classes together without any breaks or attending school only one or two days a week. You may be doing this to cut down travel costs and have more free time on other days.

However, you may be unaware of problems associated with block scheduling. Fatigue can kill your enthusiasm for and productivity in classes held later in the day. You will probably tend to forget lecture material because

you don't have enough time between classes to digest information. You may also sometimes feel compelled to miss one class in order to prepare for another. In addition, if you are on a two-day schedule (for example, all your classes on Tuesday and Thursday), you will find it difficult to finish assignments between one class meeting and the next. And if you are on a one-day schedule and fall ill on that day, the consequences of missing all your classes that week can be devastating. You will also feel stress when all your midterm or final exams fall on the same day. With back-to-back block scheduling, you will not have a free period between several exams, which can have a serious impact on how well you do.

Try these suggestions for a more effective schedule:

1. *Arrange a "double-up" schedule.* Try to schedule classes in which instructors teach the same course at different times or on different days. This will give you an extra chance to catch up if you miss a class. Ask your instructors if you can attend an alternate class.

2. *Split your schedule.* Try to alternate classes with free periods. This will give you time to prepare for the next class, visit the library, talk and study with other students, meet with a professor, or just recoup.

3. *Seek a flexible schedule.* Look for teachers who will allow you flexibility in completing assignments. Find out about independent study, project, correspondence, and televised courses.

3. Follow a Routine

Humans have a built-in biological clock that helps them establish a rhythm and routine. However, some psychologists believe this natural rhythm is thrown out of sync when events conflict with our biological expectations.

Perhaps the best-known example of this problem is jet lag. Similarly, many shift workers such as nurses and police officers are less productive and more lethargic and irritable as they adapt to new time schedules. Commuting students likewise may be susceptible to time lag problems when they adjust their schedules to satisfy competing obligations or when block-scheduling patterns require them to vary their schedules. For instance, if you study 2 hours every night Monday through Thursday, then engage in leisure activities during these times Friday through Sunday, you are likely to have trouble getting back into studying on Monday evening. Like the victim of jet lag, you confuse your body about whether it should study, play, or vegetate during this time of day. Likewise, students who sleep in on weekends often find it hard to make Monday morning classes.

As a commuter you face more schedule challenges than the residential student. Keep your biological clock running smoothly by establishing as much routine as possible.

EXERCISE 2.7 Commuter's Telephone Directory

According to the 1985 *Guinness Book of World Records*, the Houston, Texas, telephone directory was the largest in the world with 939,640 entries and 2889 pages. The smallest directory came from Farley, Missouri — it had 221 entries listed on two pages.

Your commuter's telephone directory might be even shorter than the one for Farley, but you should have one and should keep it handy. To get your directory started, record phone numbers for at least the following:

1. All professors
2. Campus security/local police
3. Campus lost and found
4. Campus health service
5. Dean of students
6. Campus counseling center
7. Campus legal services
8. Child-care centers
9. Emergency road service
10. Landlord (home and work)
11. Employer (home and work)
12. Campus tutorial center or learning center
13. Campus commuter student service center (if available)
14. Neighbor
15. Local taxi service
16. Public library
17. Friends and study mates (for each class)
18. College FAX number (to FAX a paper long distance if you get stuck)

Also place your class schedule and the number for campus security in a convenient place at home so that people can reach you in an emergency.

4. Reduce Distractions

Female ticks will remain dormant on a branch or leaf for weeks waiting for an unsuspecting mammal to pass directly beneath. Only the odor of butyric acid, which is emitted from the mammal's skin, will trigger the tick to fall on the animal host. The odor is a "sign stimulus" triggering the tick's behavior.

Are there any such sign stimuli in your life? For instance, just when you are preparing to study, does a host of would-be distractors suddenly descend upon you like so many ticks? When this happens, ask yourself whether you are unwittingly giving them a signal to approach.

"Do Not Disturb"

Read how one single-parent commuter handles distractions:

I made it a point to select one area of the house for serious study. I selected a specific block of time to study. When I entered the room, I would place a red sign outside my door to signal the kids that I was not to be disturbed.

My kids didn't buy into this right away, but they soon learned that I was not going to alter this strategy. I was amazed at how soon they adjusted. Later they were a big help in keeping me on schedule.

I feel much better about working at home because I am no longer under pressure to get things done in a piecemeal fashion. My children feel better too. They feel that they have a part to play in helping me with my studies.

One sign stimulus may be study location. If you study in the living room, in front of the television, or in other places associated with leisure, you may be giving the message that your study isn't serious. Study time is another signal: Studying at times associated with eating or family interaction can signal others that you want to be approached. Method of study also carries a message. Studying while lying on your bed, while walking around the house, or while listening to the radio can signal to others that you really aren't studying.

Use sign stimuli to *reduce* distractions. Set aside specific study times at locations not associated with socialization. Behave in a way that is consistent with academic work and that signals others not to disturb you.

EXERCISE 2.8   ## Study Time Without Distractions

Using the goal-setting process in Chapter 1 and small-group discussion, record your plans for studying with fewer distractions and for sending signals to distractors that you are not to be disturbed.

AT SCHOOL

Time: _____ to _____   Location: _____

Potential distractors (human and physical):

_____

_____

Actions against physical distractions:

_____

_____

Signals to human distractors:

_____

_____

AT HOME

Time: _____ to _____   Location: _____

Potential distractors (human and physical):

_____

_____

Actions against physical distractions:

_____

_____

Signals to human distractors:

_____

_____

JOURNAL

How are things going in your own struggle to manage your time? What are some of your "distractions/distractors"? Compare or contrast yourself with the two students discussed in this chapter — Joe and Carmen.

SUGGESTIONS FOR FURTHER READING

Fanning, Tony, and Robbie Fanning. *Get It All Done and Still Be Human: A Personal Time Management Workshop.* Menlo Park, Calif.: Open Chain, 1990.

Hunt, Diane, and Pam Hait. *The Tao of Time.* New York: Henry Holt, 1989.

MacKenzie, Alec. *The Time Trap: The New Version of the 20-Year Classic on Time Management.* New York: AMACOM (Div. of American Management Association), 1990.

Sotiriou, Peter Elias. *Integrating College Study Skills: Reasoning in Reading, Listening, and Writing,* 2nd ed. Belmont, Calif.: Wadsworth, 1989. See Chapter 2, "Managing Your Time and Your Study Area."

CHAPTER 3

Learning Styles

Steven Blume

Learning Styles

To each his own, they always say. I could sit and listen to old man Moroney lecture on Grant and Lee all day, but there's Janet sitting next to me, so bored she's almost snoring. In Government 101 she's totally wired because no one lectures and they get to argue all the time. That scene freaks me out. She says, "Look, there's more than one way to learn." I say, "Fine, you learn how to stay awake in a lecture and I'll learn how to shoot the bull!"

STEVEN BLUME *is professor of English at Marietta College. He's been in-volved with freshman seminar courses since 1977 and has been the coordinator of a critical thinking project at the college since 1985.*

"I always wanted to be a teacher," he says, "partly out of a desire to commu-nicate my own enthusiasm for literature and my love of poetry. As a younger teacher I discovered there were always some students who found poetry terribly difficult no matter how carefully I tried to explain and reiterate how we arrived at the meaning of a poem. At that time I had never even heard of learning styles. Gradually I realized that not everyone learned in the same way I did and that my failure to pay attention to the divergent ways that students learned adversely af-fected those students whose learning styles differed from my own. Since then I've become more aware of learning styles and more able to present materials in a way that empowers more students and increases their enthusiasm for literature."

Throughout high school certain subjects probably appealed to you more than others, and most likely those subjects you liked best were those that came easiest to you. Perhaps you found history easier than mathematics, or biology easier than English. Part of the explanation for that has to do with what is called your learning style — that is, the way you acquire knowledge.

Learning style affects not only how you process material as you study, read your textbook, and take notes but how you absorb the material. Some students learn more effectively through visual means, others through listen-ing to lectures, and still others through class discussion, hands-on experi-ence, memorization, or various combinations of these.

Your particular learning style may make you much more comfortable and successful in some academic areas than in others. Consider Mark, a stu-dent whose favorite subject is history. Mark generally receives B's on his history exams, and he is satisfied with his performance. One of the things he likes best about history is the study of historical movements — the develop-ment of ideas as they inform historical events. When he studies for his ex-ams, he analyzes those events, trying to determine what is responsible for the various social, political, and historical changes he has been reading about. While he recognizes the importance of names and dates, they are less significant and interesting to him than the analysis of why certain events occurred and what effects have resulted from such occurrences. For exam-ple, he studies to understand *why* the pilgrims came to America and *how* they created the Plymouth Plantation rather than to discover who the leaders of the emigration were, who the first settlers were, when they arrived in America, what crops they grew, and what treaties they signed with the Indi-ans. What he is interested in and how he studies are integral parts of his learning style.

Mark is also taking Introductory Biology, and as is natural for him, he studied for his biology exam in the same way he studied for his history test. Unfortunately he was able to use very little of the knowledge gained from his studying and thus received an F on his biology exam. Instead of studying

Mark's analytical style thrives on the complexities of history. Anne's love for science stems from her satisfaction at mastering facts and understanding how they are related.

facts, committing important terminology to memory, and learning definitions, Mark had stressed concepts when he studied, and this *analytical learning style* turned out to be inappropriate for this course, or at least for the way his instructor taught the course.

The reverse can also be true. Another student, Anne, has a *factual learning style* that makes her comfortable with memorizing facts. Anne would do very well on that same biology test and yet find the history exam that stressed concepts and analysis of material very difficult. Just as we all have different skills, so we have different learning styles. While no one learning style is inherently better than another, it is important to be able to work comfortably no matter what style is required in a given course. An awareness of your learning style can be helpful in emphasizing your strengths and helping you compensate for your weaknesses.

In this chapter we'll examine learning styles of students both in and out of the classroom, as well as discuss the teaching styles of professors.

AN INFORMAL MEASURE OF LEARNING STYLE

To begin to define your own learning style and to understand how it affects your responses in class, complete the following exercise.

EXERCISE 3.1   Your Learning Style: A Quick Indication

List three or four of your favorite courses from high school or college:

1. _____History_____

2. _____Enviromental Science_____

3. _____Business_____

4. _____Lunch_____

What did these courses have in common? Did they tend to be hands-on courses? Lecture courses? Discussion courses? What were the exams like? Do you see a pattern from one course to the next? For example, did your favorite courses tend to use information-oriented tests such as multiple-choice or true-false? Or did they often include broader essay exams? Did the tests cover small units of material or facts, or did they draw on larger chunks of material?

Now list three or four of your least favorite courses from high school or college:

1. _____Math—Geometry_____

2. _____Spanish_____

3. _____Sat Prep_____

4. _____

What did these courses and their exams have in common? How did they tend to differ from the courses you liked?

What conclusions can you draw about your preferences for learning based on these common elements in course presentation or exams? Do you prefer to make lists and memorize facts or to analyze the material, searching for concepts and considering broader implications? If you prefer the former, your learning style is more factual, like Anne's; if you prefer the latter, your learning style is more analytical, like Mark's. Can you understand why Anne prefers biology and Mark prefers history?

If you prefer listening to lectures, taking notes, and reading your notes aloud to yourself, you have a more *auditory learning style*. You might even read your notes into a tape recorder and play them back when you study for an exam. If you prefer instructors who outline their lectures on the blackboard or who make liberal use of the board by illustrating the important points they are trying to make, you have a more *visual learning style*. You probably find that copying and recopying your notes helps you learn the material better.

Being more aware of your learning style preferences can help you exploit your strengths in preparing for classes and also help you better understand why you may be having difficulty with some of your courses and what you might do to improve.

FORMAL MEASURES OF LEARNING STYLE

A number of instruments can help you determine more effectively just what your preferred learning style is and better understand other learning styles as well.

Classroom Behavior

One approach is based on the ways in which students behave in the classroom. For instance, psychologists Tony Grasha and Sheryl Riechmann have put together the *Grasha-Riechmann* instrument. This tool assesses six learning styles based on classroom behavior: (1) *competitive*, (2) *collaborative*, (3) *participant*, (4) *avoidant*, (5) *dependent*, and (6) *independent*.

To understand which classroom learning style you are most comfortable with, you need to answer certain questions. For example, do you find the study questions or review questions passed out by your instructor helpful? Do you enjoy and find helpful studying with and learning from other students in your class? Do you like it when the instructor engages the class in discussion? If so, then you probably have a more collaborative, participant, and dependent learning style and will work best with an instructor who has a correspondent teaching style. On the other hand, you may prefer an instructor who lectures in class with minimal class participation. You may feel that straightforward study of your lecture notes and textbook is the most effective means of study. If so, your learning style is more competitive, independent, and avoidant.

Personality Preferences

Another approach explores basic personality preferences that make people interested in different things and draw them to different fields and lifestyles. The *Myers-Briggs Type Indicator* is based on Carl Jung's theory of psychological types and on four scales:

- ► *EI (Extroversion/Introversion).* This scale describes two opposite preferences depending on whether you like to focus your attention on the outer or the inner world.
- ► *SN (Sensing/Intuition).* This scale describes opposite ways you acquire information — that is, whether you find out about things through facts or through intuition.
- ► *TF (Thought/Feeling).* This scale describes how you make decisions, whether by analysis and weighing of evidence or through your feelings.
- ► *JP (Judging/Perception).* This scale describes the way you relate to the outer world, whether in a planned, orderly way or in a flexible, spontaneous way.

You will often feel most comfortable around people who share your preferences, and you will probably be most comfortable in a classroom where the instructor's preferences for perceiving and processing information are most like yours. But the Myers-Briggs instrument also emphasizes our ability to cultivate in ourselves all processes on the scale.

Exam Preparation and Learning/Teaching Style

Understanding learning styles can help you to perceive more clearly the expectations of an instructor whose teaching style is incompatible with your learning style and thus allow you to prepare more effectively for his or her exam. You saw earlier, for example, how Mark's learning style, essentially an intuitive (N) style, was suited to his history course but not to his biology exam. By contrast Anne's more sensing (S) style was suited to the biology course but not the history course. In order to perform better on that biology exam Mark would need to modify his way of studying.

Let me illustrate further with an experience of my own. When I was learning about the Myers-Briggs Type Indicator, I attended a workshop for college instructors. One of its purposes was to help them understand how different learning styles can cause them to construct exams that will be much easier for students who share the instructor's learning style preference than for students who do not.

According to the Myers-Briggs approach sensing (S) people acquire information by remembering and working with great numbers of facts while intuitive (N) people are more interested in meanings, relationships, and essential patterns, that is, in grasping the "big picture." Those of us attending the workshop were divided into two groups, sensing and intuitive. Each group was given a five-page essay about the effects of divorce on young children and asked to construct a short exam based on the reading. The sensing group was then asked to take the exam constructed by the intuitive group while the intuitive group was asked to take the exam constructed by the sensing group.

In dealing with the questions we could not believe that both groups had read and processed the same essay. Those of us in the intuitive group had been asked to construct lists of details and respond to much factual data that we had regarded as less essential than the more analytical and conceptual themes of the essay. And those in the sensing group were quite taken aback by the very broad thematic questions my group had asked about the implications of divorce on the children and the larger questions about the children's future. (Keep in mind that all of the people at the workshop — sensing and intuitive — were successful professionals.)

Our very different ways of acquiring and processing information (part of our learning styles) had led us to emphasize very different information and to require very different responses to that information. It would have been much easier for those who favored sensing to respond to an exam constructed by other sensing people, and vice versa. That same situation has probably been true for you in classes and will continue to be true — you will be most comfortable in a course taught by an instructor with a teaching style similar to your learning style.

EXERCISE 3.2   Assessing Your Learning Style

PERSONAL STYLE INVENTORY

Just as every person has differently shaped feet and toes from every other person, so we all have differently "shaped" personalities. Just as no person's foot shape is "right" or "wrong," so no person's personality shape is right or wrong. The purpose of this inventory is to give you a picture of the shape of your preferences, but that shape, while different from the shapes of other persons' personalities, has nothing to do with mental health or mental problems.

The following items are arranged in pairs (a and b), and each member of the pair represents a preference you may or may not hold. Rate your preference for each item by giving it a score of 0 to 5 (0 meaning you *really* feel negative about

NOTE: This exercise is an abridgement of the Personal Style Inventory by Dr. R. Craig Hogan and Dr. David W. Champagne, adapted and reproduced with permission from Organization Design and Development, Inc., 2002 Renaissance Blvd., Suite 100, King of Prussia, Pa., 19406. For information on using the complete instrument, please write to the above address.

it or strongly about the other member of the pair, 5 meaning you *strongly* prefer it or do not prefer the other member of the pair). The scores for *a* and *b* must add up to 5 (0 and 5, 1 and 4, or 2 and 3). Do not use fractions such as 2½.

I prefer:

___3___ 1a. making decisions after finding out what others think

___2___ 1b. making decisions without consulting others

___1___ 2a. being called imaginative or intuitive

___4___ 2b. being called factual and accurate

___1___ 3a. making decisions about people in organizations based on available data and systematic analysis of situations

___4___ 3b. making decisions about people in organizations based on empathy, feelings, and understanding of their needs and values

___5___ 4a. allowing commitments to occur if others want to make them

___0___ 4b. pushing for definite commitments to ensure that they are made

___5___ 5a. quiet, thoughtful time alone

___0___ 5b. active, energetic time with people

___4___ 6a. using methods I know well that are effective to get the job done

___1___ 6b. trying to think of new methods of doing tasks when confronted with them

___1___ 7a. drawing conclusions based on unemotional logic and careful step-by-step analysis

___4___ 7b. drawing conclusions based on what I feel and believe about life and people from past experiences

___0___ 8a. avoiding making deadlines

___5___ 8b. setting a schedule and sticking to it

___3___ 9a. inner thoughts and feelings others cannot see

___2___ 9b. activities and occurrences in which others join

___0___ 10a. the abstract or theoretical

___5___ 10b. the concrete or real

___1___ 11a. helping others explore their feelings

___4___ 11b. helping others make logical decisions

___4___ 12a. communicating little of my inner thinking and feelings

___1___ 12b. communicating freely my inner thinking and feelings

___4___ 13a. planning ahead based on projections

___1___ 13b. planning as necessities arise, just before carrying out the plans

_____2_ 14a. meeting new people

_____3_ 14b. being alone or with one person I know well

_____2_ 15a. ideas

_____3_ 15b. facts

_____1_ 16a. convictions

_____4_ 16b. verifiable conclusions

_____4_ 17a. keeping appointments and notes about commitments in note-
books or in appointment books as much as possible

_____1_ 17b. using appointment books and notebooks as minimally as possi-
ble (although I may use them)

_____4_ 18a. carrying out carefully laid, detailed plans with precision

_____1_ 18b. designing plans and structures without necessarily carrying them
out

_____1_ 19a. being free to do things on the spur of the moment

_____4_ 19b. knowing well in advance what I am expected to do

_____1_ 20a. experiencing emotional situations, discussions, movies

_____4_ 20b. using my ability to analyze situations

PERSONAL STYLE INVENTORY SCORING

Instructions: Transfer your scores for each item of each pair to the appropriate
blanks. Be careful to check the *a* and *b* letters to be sure you are recording
scores in the right blank spaces. Then total the scores for each dimension.

Dimension				Dimension			
I		**E**		**N**		**S**	
1b.	2	1a.	3	2a.	1	2b.	4
5a.	5	5b.	0	6b.	1	6a.	4
9a.	3	9b.	2	10a.	0	10b.	5
12a.	4	12b.	1	15a.	2	15b.	3
14b.	3	14a.	2	18b.	1	18a.	4
TOTALS: I	17	E	8	N	5	S	20

Dimension				Dimension			
T		**F**		**P**		**J**	
3a.	1	3b.	4	4a.	5	4b.	0
7a.	1	7b.	4	8a.	0	8b.	5
11b.	4	11a.	1	13b.	1	13a.	4
16b.	4	16a.	1	17b.	1	17a.	4
20b.	4	20a.	1	19a.	1	19b.	4
TOTALS: T	14	F	11	P	8	J	17

PERSONAL STYLE INVENTORY INTERPRETATION

Letters on the score sheet stand for:

I	— introversion	**E**	— extroversion
N	— intuition	**S**	— sensing
T	— thinking	**F**	— feeling
P	— perceiving	**J**	— judging

If your score is: *The likely interpretation is:*

12–13	balance in the strengths of the dimensions
14–15	some strength in the dimension; some weakness in the other member of the pair
16–19	definite strength in the dimension; definite weakness in the other member of the pair
20–25	considerable strength in the dimension; considerable weakness in the other member of the pair

Your typology is those four dimensions for which you had scores of 14 or more, although the relative strengths of all the dimensions actually constitute your typology. Scores of 12 or 13 show relative balance in a pair so that either member could be part of the typology.

DIMENSIONS OF THE TYPOLOGY

The following four pairs of dimensions are present to some degree in all people. It is the extremes that are described here. The strength of a dimension is indicated by the score for that dimension and will determine how closely the strengths and weaknesses described fit the participant's personality.

Introversion–Extroversion

Persons more introverted than extroverted tend to make decisions somewhat independently of constraints and prodding from the situation, culture, people, or things around them. They are quiet, diligent at working alone, and socially reserved. They may dislike being interrupted while working and may tend to forget names and faces.

Extroverted persons are attuned to the culture, people, and things around them, endeavoring to make decisions congruent with demands and expectations. The extrovert is outgoing, socially free, interested in variety and in working with people. The extrovert may become impatient with long, slow tasks and does not mind being interrupted by people.

Intuition–Sensing

The intuitive person prefers possibilities, theories, gestalts, the overall, invention, and the new and becomes bored with nitty-gritty details, the concrete and actual, and facts unrelated to concepts. The intuitive person thinks and discusses in spontaneous leaps of intuition that may leave out or neglect details. Problem solving comes easily for this individual, although there may be a tendency to make errors of fact.

The sensing type prefers the concrete, real, factual, structured, tangible here-and-now, becoming impatient with theory and the abstract, mistrusting intuition. The sensing type thinks in careful, detail-by-detail accuracy, remembering real facts, making few errors of fact, but possibly missing a conception of the overall.

Thinking–Feeling

The feeler makes judgments about life, people, occurrences, and things based on empathy, warmth, and personal values. As a consequence, feelers are more interested in people and feelings than in impersonal logic, analysis, and things, and in conciliation and harmony more than in being on top or achieving impersonal goals. The feeler gets along well with people in general.

The thinker makes judgments about life, people, occurrences, and things based on logic, analysis, and evidence, avoiding the irrationality of making decisions based on feelings and values. As a result, the thinker is more interested in logic, analysis, and verifiable conclusions than in empathy, values, and personal warmth. The thinker may step on others' feelings and needs without realizing it, neglecting to take into consideration the values of others.

Perceiving—Judging

The perceiver is a gatherer, always wanting to know more before deciding, holding off decisions and judgments. As a consequence, the perceiver is open, flexible, adaptive, nonjudgmental, able to see and appreciate all sides of issues, always welcoming new perspectives and new information about issues. However, perceivers are also difficult to pin down and may be indecisive and noncommittal, becoming involved in so many tasks that do not reach closure that they may become frustrated at times. Even when they finish tasks, perceivers will tend to look back at them and wonder whether they are satisfactory or could have been done another way. The perceiver wishes to roll with life rather than change it.

The judger is decisive, firm, and sure, setting goals and sticking to them. The judger wants to close books, make decisions, and get on to the next project. When a project does not yet have closure, judgers will leave it behind and go on to new tasks and not look back.

STRENGTHS AND WEAKNESSES OF THE TYPES

Each person has strengths and weaknesses as a result of these dimensions. Committees and organizations with a preponderance of one type will have the same strengths and weaknesses.

	Possible Strengths	Possible Weaknesses
Introvert	is independent	misunderstands the external
	works alone	avoids others
	is diligent	is secretive
	reflects	loses opportunities to act
	works with ideas	is misunderstood by others
	is careful and avoids generalizations	needs quiet to work
	is careful before acting	dislikes being interrupted
Extrovert	understands the external	has less independence
	interacts with others	does not work without people
	is open	needs change, variety
	acts, does	is impulsive
	is well understood	is impatient with routine
Intuitor	sees possibilities	is inattentive to detail, precision
	sees gestalts	is inattentive to the actual and practical
	imagines, intuits	is impatient with the tedious
	works out new ideas	leaves things out in leaps of logic
	works with the complicated	loses sight of the here-and-now
	solves novel problems	jumps to conclusions

	Possible Strengths	**Possible Weaknesses**
Senser	attends to detail	does not see possibilities
	is practical	loses the overall in details
	has memory for detail, fact	mistrusts intuition
	works with tedious detail	does not work out the new
	is patient	is frustrated with the complicated
	is careful, systematic	prefers not to imagine future
Feeler	considers others' feelings	is not guided by logic
	understands needs, values	is not objective
	is interested in conciliation	is less organized
	demonstrates feelings	is uncritical, overly accepting
	persuades, arouses	bases judgments on feelings
Thinker	is logical, analytical	does not notice people's feelings
	is objective	misunderstands others' values
	is organized	is uninterested in conciliation
	has critical ability	does not show feelings
	is just	shows less mercy
	stands firm	is uninterested in persuading
Perceiver	compromises	is indecisive
	sees all sides of issues	does not plan
	is flexible, adaptable	has no order
	remains open for changes	does not control circumstances
	decides based on all data	is easily distracted from tasks
	is not judgmental	does not finish projects
Judger	decides	is unyielding, stubborn
	plans	is inflexible, unadaptable
	orders	decides with insufficient data
	makes quick decisions	is controlled by task or plans
	remains with a task	wishes not to interrupt work

As you reflect on your performance on the previous exercise, keep in mind that your score merely suggests your preferences; it does not stereotype or pigeonhole you. Remember, too, that no one learning style is inherently preferable to another and that everyone knows and uses a range of styles. The fact that many of us exhibit behaviors that seem to contradict our preferences shows that we each embrace a wide range of possibilities.

Using Knowledge of Your Learning Style

Discovering your own strengths empowers you to recognize what you already do well and provides you with some insights into the kinds of learning experiences in which you are likely to do your best. Discovering your weaknesses is also useful, because it is to your advantage to cultivate your less dominant learning styles. While certain disciplines and certain instructors may take approaches that favor certain styles, no course is going to be entirely sensing or entirely intuitive, entirely thinking or entirely feeling, just as you are not entirely one thing or another.

Knowing your own learning style preferences can also help you to work more effectively with other students on projects or in study groups. Seek out students with opposite preferences, and supplement each other's weakness. When two people take different approaches to a problem, each sees components not visible to the other. But be sure you have some preferences in common as well as in opposition. The best teamwork comes from people who differ on one or two preferences. Their differences help them learn from each other while their common preferences help them communicate.

For example, if you are an intuitive type, you may find it helpful to discuss assignments, go over class notes, or study for a quiz with a sensing type. Sensing types will bring up pertinent facts while intuitive types will bring up new possibilities. Sensing types will apply experience to problems while intuitive types will supply ingenuity. Sensing types will keep track of essential details while intuitive types will supply new essentials. This kind of collaboration works not only in the classroom but also in troubleshooting situations such as car repairs.

EXERCISE 3.3   Working with Other Learning Styles

A. Form a group with one or two other students whose learning style preferences are the opposite of your own in one or two ways and like yours in others. Together, review the chart in Exercise 3.2 on strengths and weaknesses. Discuss what help feelers can give thinkers, introverts can give extroverts, intuitors can give sensers, and perceivers can give judgers, and vice versa. Come up with some ideas about what sort of person would be a good collaborator for you. Try to identify someone in the class with whom to collaborate on future assignments.

B. Try working on an assignment for this or some other class with someone who has a preference that is the opposite of yours on either the sensing–intuitive or thinking–feeling scale. Be prepared to share and discuss this experience. Do you feel you got more out of the assignment? Did you consider more issues or facts than you might have? Did you gain any new techniques for studying? For processing the assignment? Is your final product different than it might have been? Did you each offer an approach that enhanced the other's learning style? What have you discovered about another learning style?

DEALING WITH YOUR TEACHERS' LEARNING/ TEACHING STYLES

Just as your learning style affects how you study, perform, and react to various courses and disciplines, so your instructor's teaching style affects what and how he or she teaches. As you have probably already guessed,

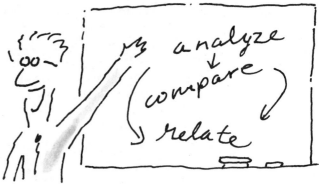

some awareness of your instructor's teaching style might help you study and prepare for exams. The syllabus for the course, the lecture, and the discussion questions as well as handouts, assignments, and exams can provide some helpful hints not only about your instructor's teaching style but also about ways you can utilize the strengths of your own learning style or compensate enough to perform effectively in the class.

The best clue to your instructor's teaching style is the language he or she uses. If your learning style is more visual, you can sense those clues more easily from printed material such as the syllabus or course handouts. If your learning style is more auditory, pay attention to the language your instructor uses when lecturing, asking discussion questions, or phrasing oral test questions.

For example, earlier we discussed two ways of receiving and processing information: (1) sensing, that is, factual and informational, and (2) intuitive, that is, analytical and conceptual. An instructor who uses words like *define, diagram, label, list, outline,* and *summarize* will tend to have a more sensing teaching style. He or she will want you to be extremely specific and provide primarily factual information. Words such as these really ask for very restricted answers. (See Chapter 6, pages 103–105, for more on the meaning of each of these terms.) Whereas Anne will be very comfortable with this instructor, Mark will be less so. Recognizing his instructor's teaching style, however, would be to Mark's benefit since he would have a better idea of what to expect. He could then adjust his approach to the material in order to perform satisfactorily in class and on exams.

On the other hand, an instructor whose syllabus or lecture is sprinkled with words such as *concept, theme, idea, theory,* and *interpretation* will tend to have a much more intuitive and analytical learning style and expect similar kinds of responses from students. On exams or on assignments he or she may use terms such as *describe, compare, contrast, criticize, discuss, evaluate, explain, interpret, justify,* or *relate.* (Again see Chapter 6 for definitions.) You may notice that instead of asking you to provide factual data or information, these words ask you to act on that information, that is, to use it in relation to other pieces of information, to evaluate it, or to examine it in terms of your own experience. An instructor who uses these words has a much more intuitive teaching style and will expect more analytical, imaginative, and conceptual responses. He or she will expect you to see that information in a new context rather than simply restate the facts as they have been given to you or as they appear in the textbook.

How to Develop Other Learning Styles

The key ingredient in developing your less dominant style is awareness. Try to develop one process at a time.

Raising Your Factual (S) Learning Style

1. Whenever you walk, try to notice and jot down specific details of the scenery — shapes of leaves; size, color, and types of rocks; and so on.

2. Three or four times a day pay careful attention to and then describe to a friend, what someone else is wearing.

3. Do a jigsaw puzzle.

4. Break down a physical activity into its component parts.

5. Describe in detail something you just saw, such as a picture, a room, or the like.

Raising Your Intuitive (N) Learning Style

1. Imagine a given situation or circumstance in a new light by considering, "What if . . . ?" For example, what if the pilgrims had landed in California — how would their lifestyle have changed? What if you had gone to a bigger (smaller) school? What if X was your roommate instead of Y?

2. Pretend you saw an article ten years from now about your hometown, your lifestyle, American values, or the like. What would it say?

3. Read a novel and imagine yourself as one of the characters. What would happen to you following the novel's conclusion?

Raising Your Feeling (F) Learning Style

1. Write down a feeling statement about your class, your day, your job, or your emotions, and make sure you use a simile. For example, "I feel like a puppy that's just been scolded." Note that if you use *think* in a statement, it's not a feeling statement. Write down five feeling statements every day.

2. Write down what matters most in your relationship with someone or something else.

Raising Your Thinking (T) Learning Style

1. Have someone write down a problem that's bothering them or a problem related to the college or your environment. Then answer questions that explain who, what, where, when, and why, and provide the details that back up each response. Doing this every day for 15 or 20 minutes will teach you how to be objective.

Mark will, of course, feel far more comfortable with this instructor. Anne will have to recognize when she studies in this course that learning the facts is not enough. She will be expected to see them in other contexts, to think about their relationships to one another. While this may not be easy for her, she can certainly adapt to it if the instructor's teaching style and expectations demand it.

EXERCISE 3.4   Assessing Your Courses and Instructors

Take some time over the next few days to think about the courses you are taking now. How well does your preferred learning style fit the style reflected in the syllabus, handouts, lectures, and study questions in each of your courses?

Do any of the key sensing words mentioned previously (*define, diagram,* and so on) or some close approximation of them appear? If so, list them and place a check mark next to each of them each time the word appears. Do any of the key intuition words (*describe, compare,* and so on) or similar words appear? List them also and note their frequency. Listen carefully in class. What key words do you hear? Write these down also. Which type of word do you hear most frequently? That will begin to give you some idea of each instructor's learning/teaching style.

INSTRUCTOR/COURSE 1: _McFadden_

Sensing Words	Intuition Words
_____	_____
_____	_____
_____	_____
_____	_____
_____	_____
_____	_____

Instructor's preferred style: Sensing _____   Intuition _____

Other teaching style observations:

_____

_____

_____

_____

INSTRUCTOR/COURSE 2: _Wiesse_

Sensing Words	Intuition Words
_____	_____
_____	_____
_____	_____
_____	_____
_____	_____
_____	_____

Instructor's preferred style: Sensing _____   Intuition _____

Other teaching style observations:

_____

_____

_____

_____

INSTRUCTOR/COURSE 3: _____ Mrs Kane _____

Sensing Words   **Intuition Words**

_____   _____

_____   _____

_____   _____

_____   _____

_____   _____

_____   _____

Instructor's preferred style: Sensing _____   Intuition _____

Other teaching style observations:

_____

_____

_____

_____

INSTRUCTOR/COURSE 4: _____ Dr Mathura _____

Sensing Words   **Intuition Words**

_____   _____

_____   _____

_____   _____

_____   _____

_____   _____

_____   _____

Instructor's preferred style: Sensing _____   Intuition _____

Other teaching style observations:

_____

_____

_____

_____

How does your learning style as measured in Exercise 3.2 fit with the learning/teaching style of each instructor? Which courses will require some adjustment on your part? Discuss these problems with other students in your first-year seminar. Keep these problems in mind as you complete the next three chapters, which focus on your study skills.

Are there things your instructors could be doing to help you take advantage of your strengths and learn more efficiently? In your first-year seminar discuss what these ideas are and how you might convey them to the appropriate instructor.

If your instructor's teaching style is compatible with your learning style, then you should be able to perform well simply by keeping up with your work. If your instructor's style is incompatible with yours, you might consider either mastering more factual material or interpreting or analyzing that material in order to be better prepared for exams or papers. In any case a greater awareness of both your learning style *and* your instructor's teaching style can be of real benefit.

A variety of additional tests can help you learn more about your learning style. These are generally available through your college guidance office. A guidance counselor will both administer the test and help you interpret the results. Ask about the following:

- ► The Myers-Briggs Type Indicator
- ► The complete Hogan/Champagne Personal Style Indicator
- ► The Kolb Learning Style Inventory

JOURNAL

What's your learning style? How are you trying to adapt your style to the teaching styles of some of your professors? Outside class, do you tend to associate with people who have learning styles similar to your own or with people whose learning styles are different? Thinking about this may help you uncover some clues about compatibility between you and some of the significant people in your life, in both short-term and long-term relationships. Remember that opposite styles may complement yours, while similar styles may provide comfort and a sense of affinity.

SUGGESTIONS FOR FURTHER READING

Lawrence, Gordon. *People Types and Tiger Stripes.* Gainesville, Fla.: Center for the Application of Psychological Types, 1982.

Malone, John C., Jr. *Theories of Learning: A Historical Approach.* Belmont, Calif.: Wadsworth, 1991.

Pauk, W. *How to Study in College*, 4th ed. Boston: Houghton Mifflin, 1989.

Perry, William. *Forms of Intellectual and Ethical Development in the College Years: A Scheme.* New York: Holt, Rinehart & Winston, 1970.

CHAPTER

4

▼▼▼▼▼▼▼▼▼▼▼▼▼▼▼▼▼▼

Listening and Learning in the Classroom

Kenneth F. Long

▼ ▼ ▼ ▼ ▼ ▼ ▼ ▼ ▼ ▼ ▼ ▼ ▼ ▼ ▼ ▼ ▼

Listening and Learning in the Classroom

I'm looking over my notes from psych. "Personalities affecting behaviors . . . something . . . something . . . abnormal." Wonder what the heck that means. Can't read the next sentence. I write too fast. Guess I missed something in the middle. . . . What's this say? "Ask Jean to go out Friday." That's not psych. Uh oh, today is Friday. Wonder if it's too late. Gee, these notes are useless. I'd better get them from somebody else.

Lecturing is only one mode of teaching, and for a variety of reasons including the relatively short attention span of many people, it is often not the best. Nevertheless it remains an important mode of college teaching. Therefore, to succeed in college, you should know what lecturing entails and how to deal with it. The lecture method is teacher-dominated (they talk, you listen), is information-laden (you take notes and study later), and allows for large amounts of material to be covered quickly. (We almost said "efficiently," but if most students aren't really listening after 15 minutes, it can hardly be called efficient, can it?)

Lectures can seduce students, even those who attend class regularly and take copious notes, into taking a passive role in the classroom. Some students have a second self, a "stenographer," whose only purpose is to write down everything a professor says. For them a full notebook creates a false sense of security. In reality indiscriminate note-taking wastes a lot of time because it leaves all of the learning for later and invites forgetting. These student-stenographers do not understand that a lecture is a sophisticated intellectual encounter that requires learning and understanding, not just note-taking. It's not enough to say, "I'll write everything down and worry about what's important later." Improper note-taking encourages intellectual laziness in the classroom and gets in the way of active listening — and learning. Not surprisingly, poor note-taking skills often correlate with poor grades. Look at the students with good grades and you will probably find good note-taking skills, too.

This chapter provides you with a proven system for effective note-taking in lectures — one that you can use to prepare for class, get the most out of class, and draw on as you review material for tests.

Figure 4.1 Learning and Forgetting

Psychologists have studied human forgetting in many laboratory experiments. Here are the "forgetting curves" for three kinds of material: poetry, prose, and nonsense syllables. The curves are basically similar. The shallower curves for prose and poetry indicate that meaningful material is forgotten more slowly than nonmeaningful information. Poetry, which contains internal cues like rhyme and rhythm, is forgotten less quickly than prose.

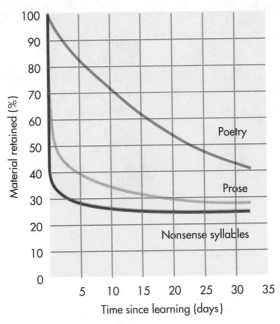

SOURCE: Used with permission from Wayne Weiten, *Psychology: Themes and Variations* (Pacific Grove, Calif.: Brooks/Cole, 1989, p. 254. Based on data from D. van Guilford, Van Nostrand, 1939).

A SOUND APPROACH TO NOTE-TAKING IN LECTURES

While the lecture system invites inefficient learning, you can do certain things to make it work for you. To see what an organized, planned approach can accomplish, we should first examine the nature of forgetting. Forgetting plagues us all, so it can help us to understand how and why we do forget.

As an undergraduate I was dismayed to find myself studying material over and over again, rereading chapters that seemed almost new, laboring over notes that were only a month old. Some years after college I learned something unforgettable about forgetting. I read an experiment (discussed in Pauk, 1989) involving people who were tested at various intervals after reading a textbook chapter. Researchers discovered that most forgetting takes place in the first 24 hours and then tapers off (see Figure 4.1). Apparently, if you can overcome the forgetfulness of that first 24 hours, you can greatly improve your chances of retaining the material.

Any effective study system must overcome forgetting with respect to both lecture and textbook materials. Let's see what an organized, planned approach to the lecture is and what it can do. We will divide the method into three phases: before, during, and after the lecture. Our objectives will be (1) increased on-the-spot learning, (2) longer attention span, (3) better retention, and (4) improved notes for later study, particularly at exam time.

The instructor isn't the only one who needs to prepare for a lecture. Stay abreast of the readings. Get your own ideas flowing again by reviewing notes from last time. What questions were left unanswered? Where should today's session begin?

Before the Lecture: Reading and Warming Up

If a lecture is a sophisticated, demanding, intellectual encounter, then logic would suggest you need to be ready intellectually. You wouldn't go in cold to give a speech, interview for a job, plead your case in court, or compete athletically. For each of these situations you would prepare in some way and set out with attention focused. So always prepare for class, especially when you are not asked, apparently, to do anything more than listen and take notes. Active listening, learning, and remembering begin *before* the lecture.

1. Do the Assigned Reading. Many students blame lecturers for seeming disorganized or confusing, when in fact the student has not done the reading that the lecture required for full understanding. Some instructors explicitly assign readings for each class session and refer frequently to readings; others will simply hand out a syllabus and assume you are keeping up. Either way, doing the assigned readings helps you to listen well, and active listening in turn promotes good reading. So keep up with your reading and most lectures will come alive — that is, the lectures will answer questions you may have had as you read. If you go into a lecture without having done the reading, the material will be unfamiliar and perhaps overwhelming.

2. Warm Up for Class. If you have read well and taken good notes, this should be quite easy. Warm up by quickly referring to the underlinings in your readings (see Chapter 5) and/or to the recall columns in your previous class notes. This gets you ready to pay attention, understand, and remember.

During the Lecture: Taking the Right Kind of Notes

Now that you're ready for class, you need to develop your listening and note-taking skills.

1. Identify the Main Ideas. Good lecturers always present certain key points in their lectures. The first principle of effective note-taking is to identify and write down the four or five most important ideas that the lecture is built

What are the key ideas? What's known? What's unknown? A professor often evaluates students' participation as much by their questions as by their answers.

around. Although some supporting details may be important as well, your note-taking focus should be on the main ideas. These may be buried in detail, statistics or anecdotes, or problems to solve, but you need to locate and record them for later study.

As you listen to any lecturer, keep these two frames of thinking in mind: general material (main idea) and specific information (supporting details). Every good lecturer is trying to express one or several main ideas. This is your general frame of reference. If the psychology lecture you were attending were on learning curves, you would likely formulate a main idea statement like the following: "There are three learning curves presented in this study." Then you would be alert for the specifics that would explain this general statement: "prose, poetry, and nonsense syllables."

Lecturers sometimes announce the purpose or offer an outline, thus providing you with the skeleton of main ideas and details. Some change their tone of voice or repeat themselves at each key idea. Some ask questions or promote discussion. These are all clues to what is important. Ask yourself, "What does my instructor want me to know at the end of today's session?"

Certainly not everything needs to be written down. Because of insecurity or inexperience, some first-year students try to write everything down — they stop being a thinker and let the stenographer take over. Don't fall into this trap. Be an **active listener**, always searching for main ideas and for the connections among them — those general assertions that must be supported by specific comments. After a week's practice, as you get to know your instructors, you will have better, and *shorter*, notes.

Unfortunately some of your instructors may teach in a manner that makes it difficult to take good notes. You can still use the same techniques, however, to organize the lectures for your own use. Even though some of your professors may not teach as you would like them to, you are ultimately responsible for making sense of what they said.

When a lecture is disorganized, you must strive to organize what is being said into general and specific frameworks; and where this order is not apparent, you need to take notes on where the gaps in the lecture's organization lie. After the lecture you may need to consult your reading material or your peers in order to try to fill in these gaps.

2. Leave Space for a Recall Column. In addition to helping you listen well, notes provide an important study device for tests and exams. This is the

Figure 4.2 Sample Page for Note-Taking

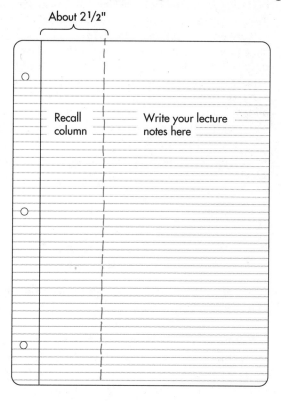

second principle of effective note-taking. In anticipation of this, treat each page of your notes as part of an exam-taking system.

On each page of notepaper draw a vertical line to divide the page into two columns (see Figure 4.2). (Looseleaf is a good choice, but write on one side only.) The column on the left, about 2½ inches wide, is called the "recall column" and remains blank while you take notes during class in the column on the right. The momentarily blank recall column, you will discover, is an incredibly powerful study device that reduces forgetting, helps you warm up for class, and promotes understanding in class. It also lets you review efficiently right after class. This recall column is essentially the place where you can sift through your note material to determine main ideas and important details.

EXERCISE 4.1   **Determining Main Ideas and Major Details**

Read the following excerpt from a psychology lecture on memory. Using any system that you are comfortable with, identify the main ideas and the supporting details on a separate sheet of paper. Then share your notes with your peers and instructor.

Today we will continue our discussion of memory and treat the idea of distributed practice—an important aspect of memory. This is the practice of learn-

ing a little bit at a time, as opposed to a lot at a time. Cramming for a test is an example of the opposite kind of practice known as massed practice. Distributed practice is what you need to develop as you study for your classes.

Further, what you learn tends to be remembered easily if you can attach it to similar knowledge. This is the third term I want to discuss today—the depth-of-processing principle. That is, information is stored in the brain on various levels. If it is stored superficially, the material cannot attach itself to rich associations. If it is stored deeply, the knowledge finds a series of associations to attach itself to. Storing material deeply allows for retention of it, while, as you would guess, storing superficially tends to lead to forgetting.

After the Lecture: Filling in the Recall Column, Reciting, and Reviewing

Now that the class is over, you still have some important work to do—if you want to combat forgetting.

1. Write the Main Ideas in the Recall Column. This is where the blank recall column becomes important. For 5 or 10 minutes quickly review your notes and select key words or phrases (or make up some) that will act as labels or tags for main ideas and key information covered in the notes. Highlight the main ideas, and write them in the recall column beside the material they represent.

2. Use the Recall Column to Recite Your Notes. Now cover the notes on the right and use the tags in the recall column to help you recite out loud a brief version of what you understand from the class you have just participated in. If you do not have 5 or 10 minutes after class to review your notes, find some time during the day to review what you have written. You might also want to ask your instructor to glance at your recall column to see if you have noted the main ideas.

3. Review the Previous Day's Notes Before the Next Class Session. As you sit in class the following day waiting for the lecture to begin, use the time to review quickly the notes from the previous day. This will put you in tune with the lecture that is about to begin and will also prompt you to ask questions about material from the previous lecture that may not have been clear to you. These "engagements" with the material will pay off later, when you begin to study for your exam.

Why is this process so powerful? First, you are encountering the same material in three different ways: (1) active listening and writing, (2) reading and summarizing in the recall column, and finally (3) saying aloud what you understand from class. Your whole person—mind and body—is involved. All of these actions promote learning.

Recitation is a particularly effective guard against forgetting. The very act of verbalizing concepts gives your memory sufficient time to grasp them. That is, you move material from short-term memory to long-term memory, where you can call upon it as needed. Strictly speaking, we never really forget anything; we just lose control of it somewhere in our minds. Having a good memory really means having an organized method of capturing

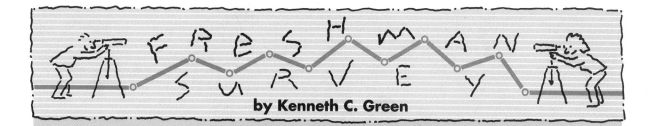

FRESHMAN SURVEY

by Kenneth C. Green

High School Grades and Academic Skills

Faculty often complain that today's students are less well prepared for college than they were two decades ago. Are they right?

As the accompanying figure shows, between 1966 and 1990 the proportion of entering freshmen reporting A or A− high school grade point averages climbed from 15 to 23 percent. The proportion of students reporting C or C+ averages dropped from 30 to 19 percent.

Do the higher grades mean that today's freshmen are better prepared for college than the freshmen of twenty years ago? Today many students believe that their grades are inflated, that high marks do not always accurately measure what they have learned or what they know. In Fall 1986, for example, nearly half (48.7 percent) of entering freshmen agreed that "grading in the high schools has become too easy."

Would you say that grading in your high school was too easy? What kind of grading policies do you think are right in college? Based on your grades in high school, what kinds of grades do you think you will earn in college? Why?

High School Grades of Entering Freshmen, 1966–1990

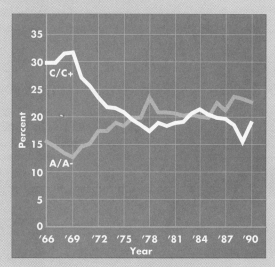

SOURCE: Higher Education Research Institute, UCLA

and recalling whatever our mind encounters, and recitation bolsters this practice.*

Now you may want to object, "I have three classes in a row and no time for recall columns or recitation between them. What can I do?" The rule of thumb is to recall and recite as soon after class as possible. In the case of successive classes review the most recent class first. Never delay recall and recitation longer than one day because by then you will have forgotten too much material. It will take you much longer to review, make a recall column, and recite. With practice you can fill in recall columns in 5 or 10 minutes

*In addition to recitation's power to combat forgetting, it also has value in preparation for the actual writing of a test or exam. (See Chapter 6.)

when material is still fresh. Recitation need only take a few more minutes. Done faithfully, these two activities are great aids to understanding and remembering.

EXERCISE 4.2   Using a Recall Column

Suppose the information in this chapter had been presented to you as a lecture rather than a reading. Using the system described previously, your lecture notes might look like those in Figure 4.3.

Look over the sample notes. Then cover the right-hand column. Using the recall column, try reciting in your own words the main ideas from this chapter. Uncover the right-hand column when you need to refer to it. If you can place the main ideas from the recall column in your own words, you are well on your way to mastering this note-taking system for dealing with lectures. Share your results with your peers and instructor. Does this system seem to work? If not, why not?

EXERCISE 4.3   Comparing Notes

Pair up with another student and compare your class notes for your study skills class. Are your notes clear? Do you agree on what is important? Take a few minutes to explain to each other your note-taking system. Agree to use a recall column during the next class. Afterward share notes again and take turns reciting what you learned to each other.

LEARNING: A COMPLEMENTARY PROCESS

Now that you know what to do to make the lecture system work as well as possible on your end, let's examine four things your professors can do to make their lectures clearer and to help you listen actively. Ideally, where feasible, your professors will follow these practices. Whether they do these things or not, remember the things you can do to maximize your learning:

1. **They:** Always refer specifically to any reading that relates to a forthcoming lecture; pose specific questions in advance to help you read well.

   You: Always read in preparation for class.

2. **They:** Always begin with an outline and/or a statement of purpose that helps you know what is important.

   You: Always search for important ideas.

3. **They:** Plan pauses in every lecture at 10- to 15-minute intervals for questions, illustrations, and learning activities; this helps rein in wandering minds.

Figure 4.3 Sample Lecture Notes

	Sept. 21 _How to take notes_	
	Problems with lectures	Lecture <u>not</u> best way to teach. Problems: Short attention span (may be only 15 minutes!). Teacher dominates. Most info is forgotten. "Stenographer" role interferes with thinking, understanding, learning.
	Forgetting curves	Forgetting curves critical period: over ½ of lecture forgotten in 24 hours.

	Solution: Active listening	Answer: Active listening, really understanding during lecture. Aims—
		    (1) immediate understanding
		    (2) longer attention
		    (3) better retention
		    (4) notes for study later

	Before: Read
	    Warm up
		<u>BEFORE</u>: Always prepare.
		    Read: Readings parallel lectures & make them meaningful.
		    <u>Warm up</u>: Review last lecture notes & readings right before class.

	During: main ideas	<u>DURING</u>: Write main ideas & some detail. No stens. What clues does prof. give about what's most important? Ask. Ask other questions. Leave blank column about 2½" on left of page. Use only front side of paper.

	After:
	   Review
	   Recall
	   Recite
		<u>AFTER</u>: Left column for key recall words, "tags." Cover right side & recite what tags mean. <u>Review/Recall/Recite</u>

You: Use active listening and note-taking activities to keep your attention level high.

4. **They:** Stop lecturing with 5 or 10 minutes left in class to let you make recall columns, recite, or discuss for better retention and understanding.

You: Review, recall, and recite as soon after class as possible, and review again just prior to the next class.

Following the "before/during/after" system will maximize learning even when the teaching is not ideal. If you use this three-phase method for each

How should we define this problem? What are our resources? The success of a roundtable depends on every participant's interest and perspective.

day's classes, you will be actively learning on a daily basis and preparing for effective study later. Of course you must be flexible in how you apply the system. When you encounter other, nonlecture styles (question–answer sessions, group discussions, workshops, seminars, and so on), always be ready to adapt your note-taking methods. In fact, group discussion is becoming a popular way to structure college learning, often replacing the traditional lecture format. In these discussion groups you must still keep in mind the two basic types of information — general and specific — and take the same types of notes as you do in lectures.

Assume, for example, that you are taking notes in a problem-solving roundtable of four students in your class. To determine general and specific bits of information, you would likely ask yourself the following questions: "What was the problem? What views were offered? Which were best?"

EXERCISE 4.4   Applying an Active Listening and Learning System

Examine the study schedule on page 31 in Chapter 2, and then answer the following questions:

1. Where do you see evidence of plans to use the recall column?

_____

_____

_____

2. What problems will the student have in performing review/recall/recite as soon after class as possible?

_____

_____

_____

3. How can these problems be solved?

_____

_____

_____

Share your answers with other students in a small group.

JOURNAL

Compare or contrast your present style of lecture note-taking with the approach suggested in this chapter. In which courses are you having the most success in terms of taking what you regard as satisfactory notes? Why? Decide which of the suggestions you will implement immediately.

REFERENCES AND SUGGESTIONS FOR FURTHER READING

Pauk, Walter. *How to Study in College*, 4th ed. Boston: Houghton Mifflin, 1989. See Chapter 5, "Forgetting and Remembering."

Sotiriou, Peter Elias. *Integrating College Study Skills: Reasoning in Reading, Listening, and Writing.* Belmont, Calif.: Wadsworth, 1989. See Part 3, "Taking Lecture and Study Notes."

Usova, George M. *Efficient Study Strategies: Skills for Successful Learning.* Pacific Grove, Calif.: Brooks/Cole, 1989.

CHAPTER

5

A Sound Approach
to Textbooks

Kenneth F. Long

A Sound Approach to Textbooks

I *'ve read this same para-graph five times and I still don't understand it. How does the professor expect me to be ready to discuss this chapter tomorrow when I can't even get through it? I did everything I know to help me concentrate. Turned up the stereo to drown out noise. Put a bag of chips next to the bed. Stretched out so I'd be relaxed. Highlighted practically every word on the page. There's gotta be a better way to study. Can't someone just drill a hole in my head and pour it in?*

What typically happens when you start to read those four chapters assigned for class two days away? You intend to start reading at 7:00 P.M., but when it's time to get to work you visit the bathroom (5 minutes), make a quick call to a friend (6 minutes), go get an apple (4 minutes), and then sit down to read, but only after clearing your desk, sharpening pencils, and arranging some notes (5 minutes). It is almost 7:30 and you haven't read a word yet! Then you start reading and quickly tune out. You continue to read, but your mind is constantly wandering. Each time you catch yourself drifting off, you have to flip back a page or two to find where to start reading again.

This situation reflects two common problems students encounter when reading textbooks: procrastination and short attention span. The result is not only an uncompleted assignment but, more seriously, a feeling of defeat — a sense that reading for study is something they *cannot* do. When this happens over and over again, it's no wonder students come to dislike reading. No one likes repeatedly having to do what they don't do well.

Make no mistake about it, textbook reading is tough work, and you almost certainly need to improve at it. Studies have shown that, as a typical first-year student, your attention span for textbook material is only about 5 minutes. That's not long enough! You need to be able to focus on your reading for at least 15 minutes at a stretch for immediate academic survival — and even more as you progress.

Where to begin? Perhaps we should start by considering how reading a textbook differs from reading for pleasure. Reading a newspaper or favorite magazine for news or entertainment is generally easy because it's relaxing, and relaxing because it's easy. In your own mind, and in the writer's, what you actually learn from the newspaper or magazine is often of secondary importance. Similarly most novels are frankly devoted to providing pleasure and entertainment, appealing not only to the intellect but to the imagination and emotions. Certain themes are ever popular — power, sex, and adventure. In short the best-selling novel is written with you, the reader, in mind, and its ultimate message is "Relax, enjoy."

The well-written textbook is also crafted with you in mind, but its appeal is almost purely to the intellect, and its message is "Wake up!" This is why it's so demanding, and also why your professor is justified in requiring that you read it. If you are going to learn from your textbook reading, you must assume a great deal of responsibility, just as you must take responsibility as an active listener in the classroom.

Don't despair. You can learn how to take advantage of procrastination, dramatically lengthen your attention span, and hence improve your reading skill. If you apply a system like the one suggested for dealing with lectures in Chapter 4, it can become (as it must become) a very manageable task.

It's a lot like jogging. At first you may not be able to run a mile. However, with planning and perseverance, a mile soon becomes only a warmup, and running, which was once boring and frustrating, becomes enjoyable and exhilarating. This chapter tells you how to get the most out of your textbooks — and how to enjoy doing so.

EXERCISE 5.1 What's Your Current Reading Attention Span?

Select a textbook from one of your courses. Begin reading a portion of the textbook, timing yourself with a clock or stopwatch. Determine your attention span (the number of minutes you read before your mind begins to wander) and the number of words read. Don't prepare to read by skimming or using other techniques; just read. Try this activity three separate times for the same chapter. Report your scores here:

Attention span (minutes): 1. ~~20~~ 15   2. __20__   3. __30__

Total number of words: 1. __120__   2. __200__   3. __300__

We'll be referring back to these figures shortly.

A PLAN FOR READING TEXTBOOKS

The following planned approach to textbook reading will increase your reading speed, promote understanding, and facilitate study for tests and exams. This system is based on two basic principles, each embodied in specific activities: (1) planning before reading and (2) marking, reviewing, and reciting.

Planning and Reading

Planning to read is an undemanding but important activity that can fit nicely into your procrastination time. The purpose is to create "advance organizers" in your mind by quickly surveying the pages to be read and looking for headings or key words or sentences that suggest what the reading is about. Sometimes chapters conclude with lists of main points, summary paragraphs, or questions. These are particularly useful in creating advance organizers, so read them as part of your planning. Creating advance organizers is similar to getting an overview of a trip by glancing at a map before you leave to get a general idea of your ultimate destination and to highlight route markers along the way.

If your instructor specifically informs you about connections between readings and classroom instruction, reconsider these clues before you read. Use any or all of this to warm up your mind and create a general plan for reading. Ask yourself questions like "Why am I reading this?" and "What do I want to know?"

EXERCISE 5.2 Prepared Reading

Take up the same textbook you used in the previous exercise. Read the next portion of the chapter, timing yourself with a clock or stopwatch. This time, before you read, plan by doing some of the activities just described and report your results here:

Attention span (minutes): _____

Total number of words: _____

How do these scores compare with the scores in the previous exercise? How much improvement was there? You should be able to read for a longer time and read more words per minute. With practice you will continue to improve. Share your results with your peers and instructor.

1. Measure the Reading Assignment. Measure the assignment and divide it up according to your own attention span and reading speed. Recall that a first-year student's attention span for reading textbooks is typically as short as 5 minutes, at a rate of far less than one page per minute. So let's say you can read about one or two pages in 5 minutes. You can either accept the reality of your current rate and make plans accordingly, or you can deny it and take your chances. If you choose the latter course, most likely your mind will soon be wandering, and more time will be wasted. Accept your current attention span as measured in the preceding exercises. Measure the assignment, warm up with some planning activities, and then read.

2. Read a Specific Amount in a Short Period, and Know What You Have Read. Try to read a page or two in 5 minutes, increasing the rate as you become more comfortable with the system. An effective warmup alone will lengthen your attention span and boost your reading speed, and practice will increase them even further. Some students report a doubling of capacity very quickly. Surprisingly, faster reading speed can also aid concentration and comprehension. Soon you should be able to divide a fifteen-page textbook reading assignment into four intense sessions of 10 minutes each.

Marking, Reviewing, and Reciting

Within each of these intense 10-minute sessions you should follow certain procedures.

1. Use Your Pencil as You Read. During the actual reading underline, circle, or draw arrows to important material and/or write notes in the margin. This is a part of active reading. Use your markings to point out key ideas and connections. Doing this will force you to concentrate as you seek out important ideas and supporting details. See how main ideas and supporting details inform what you read.

Don't be afraid to mark up your textbooks. Sure, they cost a lot, but it's a foolish economy to keep them clean and neat for resale. If you read a chapter one week without marking it, you'll find you've all but forgotten it a few weeks later. At test time you'll have to reread that unmarked text as though it were brand-new. The only alternative to marking is taking notes, but that is quite time-consuming. Read well, mark well, and transform your text on a regular basis into a study device that facilitates review.

The sample pages in Figure 5.1 discuss some ideas about improving memory. See how the reader marked the pages with underlinings and marginalia. Note that the underlining is selective and that much material is passed over. This shows that the reader consciously searched for what was important—the main ideas of the excerpt and the key supporting details. Note also that the marginalia state connections between important ideas. What the reader has done here is analogous to what you did in Chapter 4 when you divided your lecture note page into columns and used the recall columns to recite. Here the marginalia serve as the recall column while the underlined text provides supporting detail. The reader has created a means to review the text quickly and efficiently before an examination. When your reading results in pages like these, that will be proof that you have read well the first time.

EXERCISE 5.3   The Well-Marked Page

Photocopy Figure 5.2, which shows the next two pages of the book reproduced (and marked) in Figure 5.1. Then read and mark the two pages using your own underlinings and marginalia.

Compare your underlinings with those of your peers. Are you picking out the main ideas? Are you noting connections? Should you be underlining less or more for effective later review? Pointed, serious discussion with willing, equally serious partners is a great way to practice using a well-marked-up textbook. It lightens the workload, too.

Figure 5.1 Sample Marked Pages

(handwritten) How improve memory?

How can we improve memory?
Why do we sometimes forget?
Why do we sometimes think we remember something, when in fact we are wrong?

At one point while I was doing the research for this book, I went to find an article that I remembered reading, which I thought would very nicely illustrate a particular point I wanted to make. I was pretty sure I remembered the author, the name of the journal, and the date of the article within a year. So I was certain it would not take me long to find the article.

About four hours later I finally located it. I was right about the author, but I was wrong about the journal and the year. Worst of all, I discovered that the results the article reported were quite different from what I remembered. (The way I *remembered* the results made a lot more sense than the *actual* results!)

Why does my memory—and probably yours as well—make mistakes like this? And is there any way to improve memory?

IMPROVING MEMORY BY IMPROVING LEARNING

"I'm sorry. I don't remember your name. I just don't have a good memory for names." "I went to class regularly and did all the reading, but I couldn't remember all those facts when it came time for the test."

When people cannot remember names or facts, the reason is generally that they did not learn them very well in the first place. To improve your ability to remember something, be very careful about how you learn it.

Distribution of Practice

You want to memorize a part for a play. Should you sit down and study your lines in one long marathon session until you know them? Or should you spread your study sessions over several days? Research indicates that **distributed practice**—that is, a little at a time over many days—is generally better than **massed practice**, the same number of repetitions over a short time. One reason is that it is hard to maintain full attention when you repeat the same thing over and over at one sitting. Another is that studying something at different times links it to a wider variety of associations.

(handwritten) Distribution — over time

Depth of Processing

Once again, how well you will remember something depends on how well you understood it when

(handwritten) Depth — associations

"*Alas! poor Yorick. I knew him, Horatio.*" Hamlet delivers some two dozen soliloquies (solo speeches) of hundreds of words each. (In comparison, the Gettysburg Address is 266 words.) Actors generally use distribution of practice to learn their parts, memorizing a little daily over weeks. They also associate their lines with emotional motivations, physical movements, cues from other actors, and their own memories to help them remember.

IMPROVEMENT, LOSS, AND DISTORTION OF MEMORY   295

SOURCE: Pages reproduced with permission from James W. Kalat, *Introduction to Psychology*, 2nd ed. (Belmont, Calif.: Wadsworth, 1990).

Figure 5.1 *(continued)*

you learned it and how much you thought about it at the time. According to the **depth-of-processing principle** (Craik & Lockhart, 1972), information may be stored at various levels, either superficially or deeply, depending on the number and type of associations formed with it.

[margin note: Repetitions –shallow]

At the most superficial level, a person merely focuses on the words and how they sound. If you try to memorize a list by simply repeating it over and over, you may recognize it when you see or hear it again, but you may have trouble recalling it (Greene, 1987). Actors and public speakers who have to memorize lengthy passages soon discover that mere repetition is an inefficient method.

[margin note: Associations]

A more efficient way to memorize is to deal actively with the material and to form associations with it. For example, you read a list of 20 words. At a slightly deeper level of processing than mere repetition, you might count the number of letters in each word, think of a rhyming word, or note whether the word contains the letter *e*. Such activities require a more active involvement on your part and establish more connections among the words on the list and other items in your experience. At a still deeper level of processing, you might consider the meaning of each word and try to think of a synonym for it. According to this theory (and according to many experimental results), the deeper the level of processing, the more you will remember. *(How can you use this principle to develop good study habits?)*

[margin note: Deeper associations → meaning]

The depth-of-processing principle resembles what happens when a librarian files a new book in the library. Simply to place the book somewhere on the shelves without recording its location would be a very low level of processing, and the librarian's chances of ever finding it again would be slight. So the librarian fills out file cards for the book and puts them into the card catalog. To fill out just a title card for the book would be an intermediate level of processing. To fill out several cards—one for title, one for author, and one or more for subject matter—would be a deeper level of processing. Someone who came to the library later looking for that book would have an excellent chance of finding it. Similarly, when you are trying to memorize something, the more "cards" you fill out (that is, the more ways you link it to other information), the greater your chances of finding the memory when you want it.

[margin note: Association like multiple listings]

You can improve your memorization of a list by attending to two types of processing that are largely independent of each other (Einstein & Hunt, 1980; McDaniel, Einstein, & Lollis, 1988). First, you can go through the list thinking about how much you like or dislike each item or trying to recall the

[margin note: Remembering lists: two types of processing ① Each item]

last time you had a personal experience with it. That will enhance your processing of *individual items.* Second, you can go through the list and look for relationships among the items. That will enhance your processing of the *organization* of the list. You might notice, for example, that the list you are trying to memorize consists of five animals, six foods, four methods of transportation, and five objects made of wood. Even sorting items into such simple categories as "words that apply to me" and "words that do not apply to me" will enhance your sense of how the list is organized and therefore your ability to recall it (Klein & Kihlstrom, 1986).

[margin note: ② Relation-ships organization]

Concept Check

4. *Here are two arrangements of the same words:* **a.** *Be a room age to the attend hall will over party across be there 18 you after wild in the class must.* **b.** *There will be a wild party in the room across the hall after class; you must be over age 18 to attend.* Why *is it easier to remember b than a—because of processing of individual items or because of processing of organization? (Check your answer on page 312.)*

**Self-Monitoring
of Reading Comprehension**

What is the difference between good readers (those who remember what they read) and poor readers (those who do not)? One difference is that good readers process what they read more deeply. But how do readers know when they have processed deeply enough? How do they know whether they need to slow down and read more carefully?

Good readers monitor their own reading comprehension; that is, they keep track of whether or not they understand what they are reading. Occasionally in reading, you come across a sentence that is complicated, confusing, or just badly written. Here is an example from the student newspaper at North Carolina State University:

[margin note: Keep track of under-standing]

He said Harris told him she and Brothers told French that grades had been changed.

What do you do when you come across a sentence like that? If you are monitoring your own understanding, you notice that you are confused. Good readers generally stop and reread the confusing sentence or, if necessary, the whole paragraph. As a result, they improve their understanding and their ability to remember the material. When poor readers come to something they do not understand, they generally just keep on reading. Either they do not notice their lack of understanding or they do not care.

296   <small>CHAPTER 8: MEMORY</small>

Figure 5.2 Sample Unmarked Pages

The same is true for whole sections of a book. A student who is studying a textbook should read quickly when he or she understands a section well but should slow down when the text is more complicated. To do so, the student has to monitor his or her own understanding. Above-average students can generally identify which sections they understand best; they single out the sections they need to reread. Below-average students have more trouble picking out which sections they understand well and which ones they understand poorly (Maki & Berry, 1984).

[margin note: Under standing]

Actually, most people—including bright college students who get good grades—could improve their comprehension through better self-monitoring (Glenberg, Sanocki, Epstein, & Morris, 1987; Zabrucky, Moore, & Schultz, 1987). Many educators recommend that a reader pause at regular intervals to check his or her understanding. The Concept Checks in this text are intended to encourage you to pause and check your understanding from time to time.

A self-monitoring system you can use with any text is the SQ3R method: Survey, Question, Read, Recite, and Review.

- *Survey.* Read the outline of a new chapter and skim through the chapter itself to get a feeling for what the chapter covers. (Skimming a mystery novel would ruin the suspense. Textbooks, however, are not meant to create suspense.)

[margin note: outline]

- *Question.* Write a list of what you expect to learn from the chapter. You might include the review questions in the chapter, questions from the Study Guide, or questions of your own.

- *Read.* Study the text carefully, take brief notes, and stop to think about key points. (The more you stop and think, the more retrieval cues you form.)

- *Recite.* Reciting does not mean simply repeating without thinking. It means producing correct answers. Use what you have read to answer the questions you listed.

- *Review.* Read the chapter summary, skim through the chapter again, and look over your notes.

A similar system is the SPAR method: Survey, Process meaningfully, Ask questions, and Review and test yourself. Both SQ3R and SPAR rest on the principle that readers should pause periodically to check their understanding. Start with an overview of what a passage is about, read it, and then see whether you can answer questions about the passage or explain it to others. If not, go back and reread.

Encoding Specificity

A new book titled *Brain Mechanisms in Mental Retardation* arrives in the library. The librarian places it on the appropriate shelf and fills out three cards for the card catalog: one for the author, one for the title, and one for the subject, *mental retardation*. I happen to read a section in this book on the physiological basis of learning. Three years later I want to find the book again, but I cannot remember the author or title. I go to the card catalog and look under the subject headings *physiology* and *learning*. But the book I want is not listed. Why not? Simply because the librarian filed the book under a different heading. Unless I use the same subject heading the librarian used, I cannot find the book. (Had the librarian filled out several subject cards instead of just one, I would have had a better chance of finding it.)

A similar principle applies to human memory. (Note that I say *similar*. Your brain does not actually store each memory in a separate place, as a librarian stores books.) When you store a memory, you attach to it certain retrieval cues, like file cards. These retrieval cues are the associations you use both when you store a memory and when you try to recall it. Depending on your depth of processing, you may set up many retrieval cues or only one or two. No matter how many cues you set up, however, it helps if you use those same cues when you try to find the memory again.

[margin note: Human memory of information]

The encoding specificity principle states that your memory will be more reliable if you use the same cue when you try to retrieve a memory as you used when you stored it (Tulving & Thomson, 1973). Although cues that were not present when you stored the memory may help somewhat to evoke the memory (Newman et al., 1982), they are less effective than cues that were present at the time of storage.

Here is an example of encoding specificity (modified from Thieman, 1984). First, read the list of paired associates in Table 8.3. Then turn to Table 8.5 on page 301. For each of the words on the list there, try to recall a related word on the list you just read. *Do this now.*

The answers are on page 313, answer C. Most people find this task difficult and make only a few of the correct pairings. Because they initially coded the word *cardinal* as a type of clergyman, for example, the retrieval cue *bird* does not remind them of the word *cardinal*. The cue *bird* is effective only if

SOURCE: Pages reproduced with permission from James W. Kalat, *Introduction to Psychology*, 2nd ed. (Belmont, Calif.: Wadsworth, 1990).

Figure 5.2 (continued)

TABLE 8.3

Clergyman	—	Cardinal
Trinket	—	Charm
Social event	—	Ball
Shrubbery	—	Bush
Inches	—	Feet
Take a test	—	Pass
Baseball	—	Pitcher
Geometry	—	Plane
Tennis	—	Racket
Stone	—	Rock
Magic	—	Spell
Envelope	—	Seal
Cashiers	—	Checkers

cardinal is somehow associated with that cue at the time of storage. In short, you can improve your memory by storing information in terms of retrieval cues and by using the same retrieval cues when you try to recall the information.

Encoding Specificity: Context-Dependent and State-Dependent Memory

Almost anything that happens during an experience may serve as a retrieval cue for that memory. The environment at the time is likely to be associated with the experience and thus to become a retrieval cue. It may then be easier to remember the event in the same environment than in some other environment—an instance of context-dependent memory. For example, Duncan Godden and Alan Baddeley (1975) found that divers who learn a word list while 4.5 meters underwater remember the list much better when they are tested at the same depth underwater than when they are tested on the beach.

One's physiological condition at the time can also serve as a potent retrieval cue. A state-dependent memory is a memory that is easier to recall if a person is in the same physiological state he or she was in when the event occurred. Someone who has an experience while under the influence of alcohol, nicotine, or some other drug will remember that event more easily when under the influence of the same drug again (Lowe, 1986; Warburton, Wesnes, Shergold, & James, 1986).

All sorts of influence may lead to state-dependent memories. For example, the physiological condition of your body is different at different times of day. Other things being equal, your memory is slightly better when you try to recall an event at the same time of day at which it occurred (Infurna, 1981). (You may have noticed that when you wake up in the morning you sometimes start to think about the same thing you were thinking about the morning before.)

A person's mood may also contribute to state-dependent memory, although the evidence for mood-dependent memory is weak. Evidence is stronger for a related phenomenon: When someone is happy, he or she is more likely to think of happy events and words associated with happiness; a person who is sad is more likely to think of unhappy events and words associated with sadness (Blaney, 1986).

When you are trying to recall an event that happened first thing in the morning or when you were sick or when you were in some other distinct physiological state, trying to reconstruct how you felt at the time may strengthen your memory by opening up your access to state-dependent memories.

Mnemonic Devices

When you know that you will have to remember certain information at a future time—such as tasks you must tend to on Thursday or items you need to buy at the grocery store—what can you do to make sure you will remember?

One strategy is to repeat the list over and over again. That is the way Ebbinghaus memorized his lists of nonsense syllables. It may work fairly well for you, though you will probably forget at least part of the list.

A better strategy is to write out the list. Unless you lose the list, you need not worry about forgetting any of the items. Even if you do lose the list, you are likely to remember more items than if you had never written it out (Intons-Peterson & Fournier, 1986). (This is one reason it pays to take notes during a lecture.)

But what if you have no pencil and paper handy? Someone says, "Quick, we need supplies for the party. Go to the store and bring back ginger ale, ice, cups, instant coffee, napkins, hot dogs, paper plates, and nacho chips." One way to remember is to take the initials of those items—GICINHPN—and rearrange them into the word PINCHING. Now you just have to remember PINCHING and each letter will remind you of one item you need to get.

Any memory aid that is based on encoding each item in some special way is known as a mnemonic device; the word *mnemonic* ("nee-MAHN-ik") comes

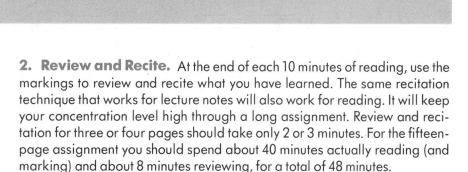

How to Read Fifteen Pages of Textbook in Less Than an Hour

It takes practice — but it can be done!

Pages 1–3	Read and mark	10 minutes
	Review and recite	2 minutes
Pages 4–7	Read and mark	10 minutes
	Review and recite	2 minutes
Pages 8–12	Read and mark	10 minutes
	Review and recite	2 minutes
Pages 13–15	Read and mark	10 minutes
	Review and recite	2 minutes
Review and recite for all fifteen pages. Answer aloud the questions, "What did I learn? How does it relate to the course?"		8 minutes
	Total	56 minutes

Done. Take a break — you've earned it!

2. Review and Recite. At the end of each 10 minutes of reading, use the markings to review and recite what you have learned. The same recitation technique that works for lecture notes will also work for reading. It will keep your concentration level high through a long assignment. Review and recitation for three or four pages should take only 2 or 3 minutes. For the fifteen-page assignment you should spend about 40 minutes actually reading (and marking) and about 8 minutes reviewing, for a total of 48 minutes.

Add 8 minutes for final review and recitation of the total assignment, reconnecting it to the purpose you established in your original warmup. Finish by answering aloud the questions, "What did I learn, and how does it fit into the course?" You now have completed 56 minutes of highly concentrated reading — a demanding, rigorous, and rewarding intellectual exercise.

Not even most professors read textbook-type material at a high level of understanding for much longer than an hour at a time. It's simply too fatiguing. All good readers punctuate bouts of reading with little pauses, or "breathers" for the mind. By planning these pauses and using them for review, you continually reinforce what you are learning, and you avoid becoming

Mastering the Précis

In this chapter we have been looking at techniques for increasing comprehension and recall of important material in your textbooks. Another technique for doing this is writing the précis.

A *précis* ("pray-see") is a written summary of the main ideas in a longer document. Being able to write an accurate précis is a skill that will be valuable to you not only in college and graduate school but also in many lines of work, including business, research, administration, teaching, and journalism.

A précis is particularly useful when you are expected to read a variety of materials on a subject and compare their main points. In college you will be writing such summaries mainly for study purposes. Later you may be writing them to condense and convey information efficiently to a business team leader, a client, or the general public.

A précis must be short. Generally it will include only the main ideas of the document and transitional phrases that show how the main ideas are related. The following describes the process of writing a précis as it might apply to an academic article.

1. *Read the article.* Underline and mark main ideas as you go. Work hard on reading well. Weak reading will result in an inaccurate précis.

2. *Analyze the article.* What is its purpose? Does it set out to *define* a particular concept, *compare* two points of view, or *prove* a certain idea? (See the "key task words" list in Chapter 6, beginning on page 103, for a summary of terms that describe the purpose of most writings.) Mark connections between main ideas. What is the overall main point (thesis) of the article? How well do the various secondary ideas support the main

point? Does the article accomplish its purpose? If the writer of the article holds some apparent attitude or bias, what is it?

3. *Select and condense.* Review the material you have underlined and mentally begin to put these ideas into your own words. You may want to number these underlinings now to reflect the order you think you will want to write them in the précis. What other main or connecting ideas does the article contain, apart from those you underlined? Jot some notes on those connections.

4. *Draft.* Begin your draft by writing one statement that states the author's purpose in writing the article and/or the author's main point. Continue with additional sentences that summarize the author's ideas in support of the main point and any other brief statements that will allow you to evaluate how well the author has achieved the purpose of the article.

5. *Rewrite.* Read over the draft. Supply missing transitions and connecting words (*so, but, therefore, because, although,* and so on). Look back over the article to see whether you have left out any main ideas. Make other revisions for completeness, clarity, and brevity. Rewrite the précis so that it will be easy to read the next time you look at it. Head it with the author's name, the title, source, and date of the article, and any other information you will need to locate the original material.

Try writing a précis of a chapter in this book or another textbook you are currently reading. Exchange your précis with that of another student and discuss how effectively each précis summarizes the information for the reader.

lost and feeling defeated. You develop and maintain a "can do" attitude about reading and about the course itself. Certainly you will be tired at the end of a reading session, so take a break, or study something else.

MAINTAINING FLEXIBILITY

With sincere effort you can improve your reading dramatically, but remember to be flexible. How you read should depend on the material. Begin early to assess the relative importance of assigned readings, and adjust your reading style accordingly. Some material may echo what you've read elsewhere and therefore warrant only quick review. In such cases skip quickly from idea to idea. Connect the whole to another important idea by asking yourself, "Why am I reading this? Where does this fit in?" When textbook reading is virtually identical to lecture material, you can save time by concentrating mainly on one or the other.

Remember that reading serious material with sound understanding and good recall is not something that one becomes adept at overnight. A planned approach, regularly applied, is the surest way to success. So always keep in mind the following rules for textbook reading:

1. Plan to read in your prime study time.
2. Use warmup time to prepare to read.
3. Set a specific number of pages to read within a specific amount of time.
4. Organize your work into short tasks for high concentration.
5. Underline, review, and recite for each section of reading.
6. Review and recite again for the whole reading.
7. Reward yourself.

EXERCISE 5.4 ## Handling Different Types of Reading

The nature and content of your academic reading depends on the subject matter involved. Review the required reading for all your classes. Where and when is it appropriate to do each different kind of reading? Investigate some locations around campus that you may want to use as places to study. Then fill out the chart on p. 92. (Two examples are provided.)

EXERCISE 5.5 ## Play It Again, Sam

Did you use a pen or pencil to mark this chapter as you read it? If not, read it again, making notes in the margins and underlining as you go. Share your underlinings and notes with your peers and instructor.

Class/Subject	Type of Reading Required	Ideal Time	Ideal Location	Why?
Calculus	*technical, equations*	*morning, early evening*	*my room, with calculator, math tables, and notebook*	*Need to be awake, attentive, and have resources nearby. Can do a little at a time—don't need a long period of uninterrupted time.*
European History	*lots of concentrated info— many dates, and references to events not explained in book*	*evening or weekend*	*library*	*Need to check other sources for further description of events mentioned in book. Need large blocks of time to complete reading sections and synthesize info about a particular historical period.*

JOURNAL

What do you think of the suggestions in this chapter for a "planned approach" to textbook reading? Does the chapter accurately describe some of your procrastination behaviors with respect to reading? What texts are you having the most trouble with, and why? What sort of help are you getting from the professors who assign these texts? What sort of help would you like? Which suggestions do you plan to try immediately?

SUGGESTIONS FOR FURTHER READING

Gross, Ronald. "Improving Your Learning, Reading, and Memory Skills." Chapter 6 in *Peak Learning*. Los Angeles: Jeremy R. Tarcher, 1991.

Phillips, Anne Dye, and Peter Elias Sotiriou. *Steps to Reading Proficiency*, 3rd ed. Belmont, Calif.: Wadsworth, 1992.

Smith, Richard Manning. *Mastering Mathematics: How to Be a Great Math Student*. Belmont, Calif.: Wadsworth, 1991.

Sotiriou, Peter Elias. *Integrating College Study Skills: Reasoning in Reading, Listening, and Writing*, 2nd ed. Belmont, Calif.: Wadsworth, 1989. See Chapters 3–8.

6

Making the Grade

▼▼▼▼▼▼▼▼▼▼▼▼▼▼▼▼▼▼

Strategies for Tests and Exams
Kenneth F. Long

**Academic Integrity:
Honesty in the Classroom**
Debora A. Ritter

Strategies for Tests and Exams

Three tests in the next two days! I am not going to live through this. Sure, I did everything it said in the chapters on how to take notes and how to read the textbook. Even looked over all the handouts and homework I got back. I should be ready. I think I'm ready. I even feel like I'm ready. (Ready as I'll ever be!) So why is my stomach doing flip-flops? Why am I biting my nails? Why can't I sleep? Why do they have to give tests?

This chapter focuses on one of the activities your studies culminate in — preparing for tests and exams. While grades do not necessarily reflect what you really know, they are the common method by which learning is evaluated. (If tests and exams generally make you feel very anxious, consult the "Stress Management" section of Chapter 15 for some tips on how to control these feelings.) Grades may also affect your chances of success in other areas like gaining entrance to graduate school or getting a good job.

Tests and exams come in many forms: essay, problem, short-answer, identification, multiple-choice, matching, and so on. By focusing on the four most frequently used types — essay, multiple-choice, true-false, and matching — we can get a good grasp on the strategies of study that can apply to all types.

You will learn something useful if you are reading this chapter on its own, but you will benefit even more if you have already read the preceding chapters on time management, note-taking in the classroom, and textbook reading. Together these chapters present a basic study plan that can help any college student get off to a strong start.

WHAT YOU SHOULD KNOW AND DO BEFOREHAND

The days and hours immediately prior to a test are critical. Knowing what to do and how to do it during this period can make a big difference. How much time do you need to prepare? The answer varies with the test and with each individual. But in every instance it is important to set aside enough time to study for the test and to know how to get the most out of that time. Good communication with your instructor, purposeful notes, well-reviewed texts, exam information, and refined time management all support your best efforts in the time just prior to the test.

1. Find Out About the Test

In order to use the right test-taking strategies, you should know several days in advance what type of test it will be and what kinds of questions will appear on it. It is at least inefficient, and possibly disastrous in terms of grades, to study for an essay exam when the format is multiple-choice or a mix of styles.

You also need to know how long the exam will last and how it will be graded. If you don't know, ask your instructor. This information forms the basis for your study strategy and for your work on the exam itself. For example, you may learn that a one-hour test will include a short-essay question worth 25 out of a possible 100 points. Knowing that, you should plan to devote about one-quarter of your preparation time to the short essay and to spend about 15 minutes on it during the exam. If you enter the exam without such a plan and find you can answer the short-essay question better than you can the other questions, you may be tempted to spend 25 or 30 minutes on it. The result may be that you "earn" the 25 points several times over but leave too little time for the rest of the test and end up with a lower grade than you deserved based on your knowledge and ability.

You should also obtain copies of old test questions, if they are available and if your professor allows it. Some professors may be willing to provide you with questions that reflect the kind of material that will be on the exam —

questions that will help you focus on the central ideas of the course. Students who have previously taken the course may also be able to show you copies of old tests. Reviewing and working through old tests helps you to identify important material and gives you an opportunity to practice under "game conditions." While old questions will give you some clue as to the way the professor writes exams, be careful not to assume that the "old questions" will be the same ones you encounter on your exam.

2. Study Throughout the Course

Students who don't study strategically and manage time well throughout the course cannot make the best use of the critical time just prior to an exam. In truth their problems begin in the first week of class. These students usually have to complete other assignments and fulfill various other commitments when they should be preparing for a test. The result is overload, panic, and underachievement. Clear, focused study time results only when you see well in advance what other responsibilities will converge with test preparation.

Similarly, if you have not taken an organized approach to the classroom and to textbook study, you are certain to be discouraged by pages and pages of unsummarized notes and many chapters of unmarked text, all bearing somehow on the test. What can be done? In the case of the textbook your only recourse is the lengthy process of rereading and marking. And the unsummarized lecture notes, some several months old, will have to be re-read, reunderstood, and rememorized.

Fortunately, by employing active daily study skills from the first week of classes, you can take the test under very different conditions. With good time management and a detailed weekly timetable, you can plan for tests and their relationship to other responsibilities well in advance. You can postpone all "extra" commitments, leaving ample free time just for study. You can reduce classroom notes regularly to recall columns and review and recite them in preparation for classes. You can reduce, review, and recite textbook readings in similar fashion. In each case you have identified and emphasized key concepts and terms.

Instead of an overwhelming accumulation of vaguely familiar material, you have a lean body of concepts and information. Regular recitation at the end of study sessions and again as a warmup for class has secured much of the material in long-term memory. While other students may be dealing with the material as though it were still all brand-new, for you it should be quite familiar. Now you can practice recalling information and refamiliarizing yourself with detail.

Let's see how all of this organized study pays off at exam time.

THE ESSAY EXAM

An essay exam requires focused, detailed study on selected topics that you think are likely to appear on the exam. As you prepare for an essay exam, you will want to concentrate mainly on key ideas, the evidence supporting these ideas, and their relationship to other key ideas. Essay exam questions generally focus on such broad questions rather than on details. They are generally graded in part according to how well organized your answer is.

The Basic System for Studying for Essay Exams

To study for an essay question, first select several pages of notes covering a body of information that you regard as a likely essay topic. Lay your pages of notes on the desk in front of you with each page covering two-thirds of the one before so that only recall columns show. (This is why we recommended in Chapter 4 that you write on only one side of the piece of paper.) Let the recall columns prompt you through a paraphrased recitation of the material at hand. When you get stuck, consult the supporting details to "boost" the recall column and then continue to recite. Work through the text chapters in similar fashion by using your markings to prompt recitation. When you can recite, you can feel confident you know the material. At this point you have little reason for anxiety.

This method of study trains your mind to respond to the test situation. The words in the test questions act like the words in the recall columns to prompt your thought processes and your written answer. This is exactly what you have been practicing all along in looking for and marking important material and reciting. So the essay exam situation is really nothing new. Moreover this system adapts easily to virtually any kind of study that requires review of material.

Another effective preparation technique is composing questions based on the material you are studying. Solid understanding is necessary in order to formulate questions, so practice at composing questions increases concentration. It is also a good idea, if time permits, to practice writing out answers to your questions.

EXERCISE 6.1   **Essay Strategies**

Using the information already presented in this section, develop and then answer two essay questions dealing with different material in this section or in a previous chapter. Share your questions and responses with your peers and instructor.

Improving on the System: Super Recall Columns and Mind Maps

You may want to refine the basic system further, especially for an exam covering large amounts of material. For example, let's say you have selected 100 pages of notes and supporting text. You divide these materials into ten more or less equal logical units. As you work through each unit, you continue to reduce each ten-page unit to one page, which will take the form of what is called a *super recall column* or *mind map*.

The best way to conceive a super recall column is to imagine that your instructor has allowed you to bring one page of notes into the exam with you. What would you put on that page? You would probably want it to contain recall information that surveys the course — a "super" recall column. A mind map is essentially a super recall column with pictorial elements added. Its words and visual patterns provide you with highly charged cues to "jog" your memory. The task of making the super recall column or mind map is

Figure 6.1 Sample Mind Map on Listening and Learning in the Classroom

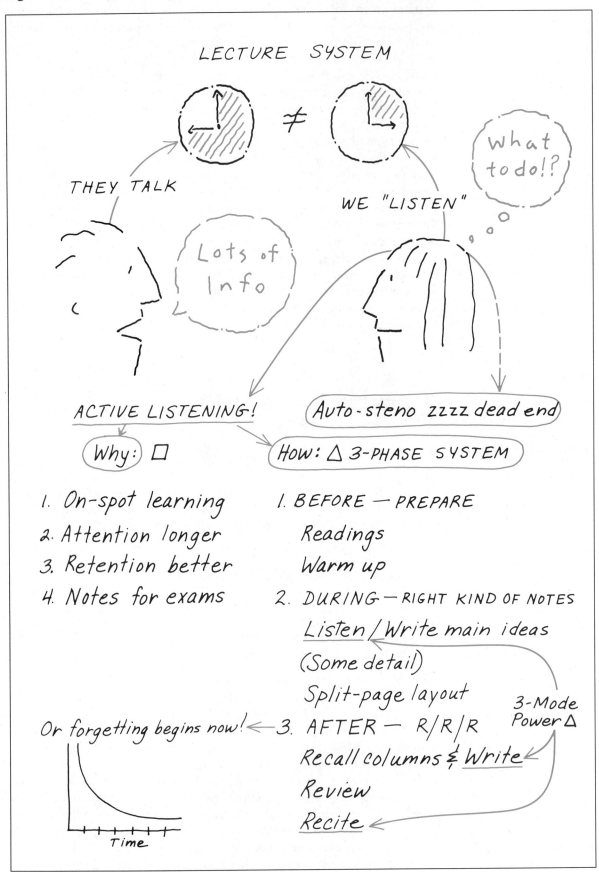

With the right exam strategy, you could be headed for the Dean's List.

itself a form of concentrated study. Practicing responses to the cues on the mind map is analogous to responding to the word cues in the questions on the exam. Chances are you will see exactly the same words on the exam that you have used in your mind maps. Even if they aren't the same, your study method represents an accurate rehearsal of the kind of thinking you'll have to do in the exam.

Figure 6.1 shows what a mind map might look like for Chapter 4, "Listening and Learning in the Classroom." Note the use of lists, arrows, and circles, all powerful aids to memory. When something can be visualized, it is easier to remember, and mind maps are highly visual. Visualizing the mind map during the test will help to release the flow of words you will need to answer the question, as will your previous recitation of the material.

Super recall columns and mind maps are particularly useful in the last hour, right before the start of the exam. Whereas notes and texts are too unwieldy to be of much use at this point, mind maps allow for quick, effective review. Of course nothing fights exam anxiety better than effective preparation.

Consistent daily study and the right exam strategy are the surest means to real learning and strong performance. Note that the strategies recommended here are not those of superficial memorization. Too often, memorization reflects only shallow understanding. The mechanics of our in-depth system require you to apply yourself repeatedly and attentively to the material, focusing always on *understanding* the significant points in large amounts of written material. How else could you make recall columns or mind maps?

EXERCISE 6.2   **The Power of the Mind Map**

Review the mind map in Figure 6.1. Create a mind map for each of the essay questions you developed in the previous exercise. Use them to prompt a recitation of the material needed to answer each question. Put the mind maps away for a day. The next day, try to re-create the mind maps from memory. You should find your retention of the material has increased. Share these maps with your peers and instructor, and see how theirs differ.

Three Principles for Taking Essay Exams

Following all of the previous suggestions won't be enough if you don't then perform well on the exam itself. Here are three principles for taking essay exams and ways to implement them.

1. Use Exam Time Well. Quickly survey the entire exam and note the questions that are easiest for you. To build confidence and start the recall process, answer these questions first. But be careful. Knowing certain material very well may tempt you to write brilliantly for 30 minutes on a question worth only 10 points, leaving little time for a harder question worth 30 points. This is how to get a C when you are quite capable of achieving a B or an A. Avoid this costly error by knowing ahead of time the basic exam structure, the point allotments, and the types of questions. Then govern yourself during the exam according to a plan for choosing questions and allocating the right amount of time for each. Also be sure to wear a watch to the exam. If you forget to do so, ask the professor to periodically call out or write the time or the time remaining on the board.

2. Write Focused, Organized Answers. Many well-prepared students write fine answers to questions that have not been asked. This problem stems either from not reading a question carefully or from hastily writing down everything you know on a topic in the hope that somehow the question will be answered. This is like shooting at a target with a shotgun, never completely missing, perhaps, but rarely hitting the bull's-eye. Instructors agree that shotgun answers are frustrating to read because of their lack of focus and organization. A simple seven-point strategy will help you stay focused and organized:

1. Read the entire question carefully.
2. Take the time to read it again and underline key words. This forces you to read the question accurately. The underlined words will stimulate recall of relevant information.
3. Brainstorm. Write down all the ideas you can think of in response to what the question asks. Then read over your notes, underline the most important points, and use them in your answer. If you do this extra writing on the exam paper, be sure to cross it out if you do not want it counted for credit.
4. Use the underlined words in the question and in your written brainstorming to construct a brief outline. This ensures good organization.
5. Begin your answer by rewriting the question or problem. This reinforces your focus.
6. Write the rest of the answer according to your outline. If new ideas come to mind as you write, add them at the end.
7. Make sure each answer begins with an introduction and ends with a conclusion.

Here is a sample question from a psychology test, selectively underlined to focus the question.

Modern educational psychology has discovered a great deal about how students learn, and this has led to the development of several powerful study techniques. Identify three such techniques and explain how and why they work.

Figure 6.2 shows how an outline for answering the question might be written during the actual exam. Commentary is provided on the right. While writing the essay our hypothetical test-taker remembers an additional important idea — visualization and mind maps — and adds that at the end of the essay.

3. Know the Key Task Words in Essay Questions. Essay questions often use certain task words such as *discuss* or *define*. Help yourself to focus more quickly and avoid misinterpretation by becoming familiar with them now. Don't feel you must memorize the exact definitions of these terms, and don't "lock up" on the exam if you can't define them precisely. A general familiarity will do. Perhaps your instructor will tell you which of these terms (what kinds of tasks) will appear on the test. Why not ask? Here are some of the most frequently used terms and their meanings.

Key Task Words

Analyze To divide something into its parts in order to understand it better, then to see how the parts work together to produce the overall pattern. Analyzing a problem may require you to identify a number of smaller problems that are related to the overall problem.

Compare To look at the characteristics or qualities of several things and identify their similarities. Instructions to compare things often are intended to imply that you may also contrast them.

Contrast To identify the differences between things.

Criticize/Critique To analyze and judge something. Criticism can be either positive or negative, as the case warrants. A criticism should generally contain your own judgments (supported by evidence) in addition to whatever authorities you might invoke.

Define To give the meaning of a word or expression. Definitions should generally be clear and concise and conform with other people's understanding of the terms. Giving an example of something sometimes helps to clarify a definition, but giving an example is not in itself a definition.

Describe To give a general verbal sketch or account of something, in narrative or other form.

Diagram To show the parts of something and their relationships in pictorial form, such as a chart. You are usually expected to label the diagram, and you may be asked to explain it in words as well.

Discuss To examine or analyze something in a broad and detailed way. Discussion often includes identifying the important questions related to an issue and attempting to answer these questions. Where there are several sides to an issue, a discussion involves presenting this variety of sides. A good discussion explores as much of the relevant evidence and information on a topic as it can.

Enumerate To respond in the form of a concise list or outline rather than in great detail.

Evaluate To judge the worth or truthfulness of something. Evaluation is similar to criticism, but the word *evaluate* places more stress on the idea of making some ultimate judgment about how well something meets a

Figure 6.2 Sample Essay Exam Outline

Introduction

Brief statement of topic or question and the approach.

Modern educational psychology has a lot to offer the student who wants to learn how to study more efficiently.

A simple direct restatement begins the answer with a focus on *how.*

Define efficiency. Describe forgetting as the problem.

The answer will build on two key concepts: efficiency and the problem of forgetting.

4 Advance organizers (conclusion)

3 Recitation

1 Recall columns

2 Super recall columns

5 Multiple-choice strategies (conclusion)

The techniques are first listed without numbers, in the order remembered. Then the techniques are numbered in the order that seems most logical for presenting them in the written answer. The first three techniques will appear in the body of the answer. The last two will be mentioned in a concluding paragraph, just to show that there are more than three.

Conclusion

Brief summary—final thoughts and perspectives.

certain standard or fulfills some specific purpose. Evaluation involves discussing strengths and weaknesses.

Explain To clarify or interpret something. Explanations generally focus on *why* or *how* something has come about. Explanations often require you to discuss evidence that may seem contradictory and to tell how apparent differences in evidence can be reconciled.

Illustrate On an essay examination, to give one or more examples of something. Examples help to relate abstract ideas to concrete experience. Examples may show how something works in practice. Providing a good example is a way of showing you know your course material in detail. Sometimes the instruction to illustrate may be asking you to literally draw a diagram or picture. If you're uncertain of the intention, ask the instructor.

Interpret To explain the meaning of something. For instance, in science you may be asked to interpret the evidence of an experiment, that is, to explain what the evidence shows and what conclusions can be drawn from it. In a literature course you may be asked to interpret a poem, that is, to explain what a specific passage or the poem as a whole means beyond the literal meaning of the words.

Justify To argue in support of some decision or conclusion; to show sufficient evidence or reason in favor of something. Whenever possible, try to support your argument with both logical reasoning and concrete examples.

Label To point to and name specific parts of a figure or illustration.

List To present information in a series of short, discrete points. See also enumerate.

Narrate To tell a story, that is, a series of events in the order in which they occurred. Generally, when you are asked to narrate events, you are also asked to interpret or explain something about the events you are narrating.

Outline To present a series of main points in appropriate order, omitting lesser details. Also, to present some information in the form of a series of short headings in which each major idea is followed by headings for smaller points or examples that fall under it. An outline shows the correct order and grouping of ideas.

Prove To give a convincing logical argument and evidence in support of the truth of some statement. Note, however, that academic disciplines differ in their methods of inquiry and therefore also differ in what they require in statements of proof.

Relate To show the relationship between things. This can mean showing how they influence each other or how a change in one thing seems to depend on or accompany a change in the other. In showing how things relate, it's often a good idea to provide an example.

Review To summarize and comment on the main parts of a problem or a series of statements or events in order. A review question usually also asks you to evaluate or criticize some aspect of the material.

Summarize To give information in brief form, omitting examples and details. A summary should be short yet cover all of the most important points.

Trace To narrate a course of events. Where possible, you should show connections from one event to the next. Tracing a sequence of events often points to gaps in the sequence that you may need to fill in by logical suppositions about what might link one event to the next.

EXERCISE 6.3   Keying on Task Words

Essay questions may require quite different responses depending on their key task words. Write brief answers to the following. Focus on what each task word is asking you to do, and tailor your responses accordingly.

1. Define the purposes of this course, chapter, or book (pick one).

   _____
   _____
   _____
   _____

2. Evaluate the purposes of this course, chapter, or book.

   _____
   _____
   _____
   _____

3. Justify the purposes of this course, chapter, or book.

   _____
   _____
   _____
   _____

Discuss your responses with your peers and your instructor.

THE MULTIPLE-CHOICE EXAM

Studying for multiple-choice exams is different from studying for essay exams. However, preparing for multiple-choice exams still requires purposeful notes, well-reviewed texts, and active daily learning. Whereas an essay exam requires focused, detailed study on selected topics (excluding a lot of material altogether), the multiple-choice exam requires a light review of nearly everything covered. Thus you should plan to review the material several times before the exam. Use your notes and text markings, aided by regular recitation, to quickly reread large amounts of material.

Take advantage of the many cues that multiple-choice questions contain. With careful reading you will find that the right answer is frequently apparent. Two suggestions will be helpful here: First, question those choices that use absolute words such as *always*, *never*, and *only*. These choices are often incorrect. Second, read carefully for terms like *not*, *except*, and *but*, which may come before the choices. Look at the following sample multiple-choice question on writing an essay exam:

1. In answering an essay question it is wise to do all of the following except:
   a. review your notes before the exam
   b. write out study maps to synthesize the material
   c. always memorize specific details at the expense of main ideas
   d. both a and b

Do you see how choice d would seem to be acceptable if you had not read the "except"? Also, did you notice the use of the qualifier "always" in choice c?

Some questions will be puzzlers. Skip over these questions as you first work quickly through the exam, but mark them so that you can find them easily later. When you have finished answering all of the obvious questions, return to the puzzlers. You will discover that you now know the answers to some of them. Why? Because a multiple-choice exam is a review of interrelated material, and information given in question 46 may contain or suggest the answer to question 10. This technique lets the nature of the exam work in your favor.

For the few puzzlers that remain, try another strategy. Since you can't find the right answer, try eliminating those that are clearly wrong. Usually at least one of the choices is far-fetched, another unlikely, and a third a "maybe." Eliminate as many choices as you can so as to increase the odds in your favor, and then make the best guess possible. You can often reduce your choices to two, so that your odds for correctly answering the question are 1 out of 2 rather than 1 out of 4 or 5.

Following these strategies can often mean a difference of 5 or 6 percent, which in turn can be the difference between a B or a C grade. Light, quick review of material (several times if necessary) and good exam room strategy make multiple-choice exams that much easier.

A word of caution: Make sure you know the scoring system. If, for example, there is a built-in factor to penalize you for guessing (number right minus a percentage of number wrong), it is not wise to guess. When in doubt, ask the professor what the scoring procedure will be.

THE TRUE-FALSE EXAM

You will find that true-false questions are often used in examinations. True-false questions contain only two choices, rather than the four or five you often find in a multiple-choice question, so your chances for selecting a correct answer are better. Like the multiple-choice question the true-false question tests your understanding of detail more than your mastery of general concepts.

Here are some hints for answering the true-false question:

1. Be sure that every part of the question is correct. For the question to be true, every detail within it must also be true.

2. Check to see how qualifiers are used. As with the multiple-choice question, true-false questions containing words like *always, never,* and *only* are usually false. Conversely the inclusion of less definite terms like *often* and *frequently* suggest the statement may be true. Note how the use of *always* makes the following statement false, while the use of *often* makes it true:

_____ 1. True-false questions always test specific information.

_____ 2. True-false questions often test specific information.

The first statement is suspect, because if you can think of even one example to counter the claim, the statement is automatically false. By contrast the second statement allows for a few exceptions and is thus more likely to be true.

3. As with the multiple-choice question, read through the entire exam to see if information in one question will help you answer a question whose answer you are unsure of.

THE MATCHING EXAM

Matching questions are still used on objective exams, particularly those that use a combination of objective questions: multiple-choice, true-false, and matching. Unlike these other two types of objective questions, the matching question is the hardest to answer by guessing. With the matching question, you need to know your stuff. Often matching questions test your knowledge of definitions as well as names and events. In one column you will find the term, in the other the description of it.

Before answering the matching-question part of the exam, review all of the terms and descriptions. See if a pattern emerges — perhaps terms on one side and definitions on the other, people in one column and descriptions of them in the other, or a combination of both. Match up those terms you are sure of first. As you answer each question, cross out both the term and its description. This will enable you to see more clearly which choices remain.

Here is an example of part of a matching test on this chapter:

_____ 1. essay question	a. often the most difficult objective question to answer
_____ 2. multiple-choice question	b. requires knowledge of general concepts
_____ 3. true-false question	c. only provides two choices
_____ 4. matching question	d. usually presents four or five choices per question

Do you see how this set of matching questions asks you to match up a term with a description of it? Now go back to these four questions and answer them, crossing out each correct match that you determine.

EXERCISE 6.4   Designing an Exam Plan

Use the following guidelines to design an exam plan for one of your courses:

1. Find out what the characteristics of the exam are: What material will be covered? What type of questions will it contain? How long will it be? How many questions will there be? What is the grading system?

2. Based on these characteristics, determine what type of studying is necessary.

3. Establish how much time and how many study sessions you will need to complete your studying.

4. Create a study schedule starting one week before the test. Indicate the length of each study session, the material to be covered, and the study techniques to be used.

Share your responses with other students and with your instructor. See how their responses are similar to or different from yours.

A variation of this exercise: Make up a hypothetical exam for the class. It may be essay, multiple-choice, or true-false. Show your questions to the professor for comment. You might also want to include sample answers.

MAINTAINING FLEXIBILITY AND SELF-DISCIPLINE

In the chapters on time management, learning styles, classroom notes, textbook reading, and exams, we have presented a general system for strategic study. Because no one study system can apply to all situations, however, you need to be flexible. Manage your time in accordance with daily needs. Even if you don't follow your schedule to the letter, it will keep you consciously in control of changing circumstances and objectives. Not all lectures are true intellectual encounters. Some may be badly organized, dull, or just a rehash of textbook material. Some assigned readings may have little bearing on your test or your grade. In fact, in some grading systems tests may be inconsequential as well. All of these possibilities can call for changes in strategy. So can your other responsibilities, your social needs, even your mood. Experienced students maintain focus on study but constantly adjust to accomplish exactly what they want to accomplish.

Of course knowing how to do something and doing it are two different things. Each semester I teach a class of first-year students, telling them what I have told you here. Since the system makes sense, most of these students try it and succeed. But there are always a few who don't. Typically they are the same ones who miss classes, ask for extensions on assignments, cram for exams, and write desperate, shotgun answers. These students often appear tired and uninterested.

I always wonder what's gone wrong. Have they fallen victim to their own new freedom? Without Mom and Dad around, are they staying up too late or not getting up early enough? Are they following an "in" crowd that always puts socializing ahead of everything else? Since there's no one around to tell them what to do, are they simply doing what pleases them most of the time? Or are they trying to do too much — working, raising a family, and going to college?

For most students college is a wonderful, challenging experience. Because the work is demanding, you need to manage your freedom responsibly. Effective study skills can facilitate success both in the classroom and out of it. But no study system can replace rigor, energy, commitment, perseverance, and regular application. These are the hallmarks of a mature self-discipline. Together with a dash of luck and a reasonable amount of native intelligence, they can guarantee success.

EXERCISE 6.5   An Essay Exam

Treat the following as an essay exam question. Use techniques (such as mind maps or outlines) and information from this section and previous chapters to organize and write your answer:

How soon is a student likely to forget lecture material even when full notes are taken? How much is likely to be forgotten? How can this problem be alleviated? Based on your own experience and your reading here, what is your opinion of recitation as a study technique?

Share your response with your peers and instructor.

JOURNAL

Think back on how you went about studying for quizzes and exams in high school. Describe when you studied (how far in advance of tests), where you studied, how much you studied, and how you went about it. Consider whether you studied alone or with a partner or group. If you've been using these same basic approaches in your studying in college, how have they worked? What former study behaviors have you already changed or are you considering changing? What suggestions from this section are you going to attempt to use?

SUGGESTIONS FOR FURTHER READING

Buzan, Tony. *Use Both Sides of Your Brain*. New York: Dutton, 1974.

McKowen, Clark. *Get Your A out of College: Mastering the Hidden Rules of the Game*. Los Altos, Calif.: Crisp Publications, 1979.

▼▼▼▼▼▼▼▼▼▼▼▼▼▼▼▼

Academic Integrity: Honesty in the Classroom

ife gets so complicated. My English professor tells us to bounce ideas off each other. But yesterday in my history class, two people were dropped from the class and will get F's because they worked together on something. I say do your own work in college. If you don't do it yourself, you can't be learning much. But what about this business of study groups, group projects, all that. . . . Isn't that cheating, too? Where do you draw the line?

DEBORA A. RITTER *is assistant director for resident student conduct at the University of South Carolina, Columbia. She has worked on student activities, residential programs, and student discipline since 1984. She consults with private industry on topics ranging from conflict resolution to date rape. Now working on a Ph.D. in educational leadership, she is exploring the role of values in higher education. She also gathered the exercises and activities for this entire text and wrote many of them herself.*

"I find it very rewarding to help students clarify their values and use them to make sensible choices about their behavior," she says. "While most of my freshman year memories are pleasant ones, I remember worrying about all the unwritten rules regarding behavior and classroom work that were never explained to me. I hope this chapter raises your awareness of the existence and purpose of these rules."

Frank was up late and studying in the dining room when a fraternity brother asked him what he was studying and who the instructor was. When the brother returned from the basement a short time later, he offered Frank a file with old notes and tests from the same course and the same instructor. Frank fell all over himself thanking the guy, amazed and grateful for how much help this would be. Frank went back to work feeling refreshed, confident, and equipped to prepare systematically and efficiently.

Darnell was tired when he left the classroom. It had been the hardest test he'd ever taken. He was glad he'd studied hard and hadn't needed to use the "cheat sheet" he had put together in his panic the night before. Now he felt embarrassed that he had been that desperate. As he walked down the hall he searched his pockets for his "equalizer," intending to throw it away. But it wasn't in his pocket. Then he realized Dr. Thomas had followed him into the hall. She was walking toward him with the tiny piece of paper in her hand. "Darnell, we need to talk," she said.

Karen and Beth were the best guards in the conference. When they were in the backcourt together, it seemed they couldn't be beat. Unfortunately, regardless of how good they were on the court, at least half the pair wasn't cutting it in the classroom. It looked like academic ineligibility was about to break up the dream team. Karen was reluctant, but she thought if she didn't let her teammate see her test, Beth would fail and playoff prospects would dim. She told herself, "It's only a psychology course," as she slowly moved her elbow to reveal the answer column.

Terrence was thrilled with himself and his little plan. The way he looked at it, he could ace this 500-level literature course, boost his GPA, and buy time to work on his law school applications. It would all take a weekend at most. He'd take the book titles to the library, look up the literary criticism on hand, translate it into his own words, get it typed, and submit instant book reviews according to the professor's schedule. If he finished it all early enough in the semester, he figured he could bluff his way through any questions that came up in class.

EXERCISE 6.6   Cheating or Fair Game?

Do any of the preceding scenarios depict "cheating"? Would your friends, parents, or professors judge them differently than you do? Fill in the blanks below with your opinions, and your predictions about the opinions of others.

Scenario 1: Frank

Your opinion: ⎯⎯⎯⎯⎯⎯

Friend's opinion: ⎯⎯⎯⎯⎯⎯

Parent's opinion: ⎯⎯⎯⎯⎯⎯

Professor's opinion: ⎯⎯⎯⎯⎯⎯

Scenario 2: Darnell

Your opinion: ⎯⎯⎯⎯⎯⎯

Friend's opinion: ⎯⎯⎯⎯⎯⎯

Parent's opinion: ⎯⎯⎯⎯⎯⎯

Professor's opinion: ⎯⎯⎯⎯⎯⎯

Scenario 3: Karen and Beth

Your opinion: ⎯⎯⎯⎯⎯⎯

Friend's opinion: ⎯⎯⎯⎯⎯⎯

Parent's opinion: ⎯⎯⎯⎯⎯⎯

Professor's opinion: ⎯⎯⎯⎯⎯⎯

Scenario 4: Terrence

Your opinion: ⎯⎯⎯⎯⎯⎯

Friend's opinion: ⎯⎯⎯⎯⎯⎯

Parent's opinion: ⎯⎯⎯⎯⎯⎯

Professor's opinion: ⎯⎯⎯⎯⎯⎯

Now ask one of your friends or classmates his or her opinion of each scenario. Did it match what you predicted?

This section discusses how academic integrity is defined, how to decide whether an activity constitutes misconduct, why students sometimes choose to cheat, and what steps you can take to avoid the temptation to resort to academic dishonesty. (See also Chapter 13, "A Personal System of Values.")

ACADEMIC HONESTY AND THE MISSION OF HIGHER EDUCATION

Higher education evolved in America with a strong commitment to the "search for truth," uncovering new knowledge and solving problems to benefit society. The commitment to truth was accompanied by the concept of **academic freedom**, which is the freedom of faculty and students to pursue whatever inquiry they feel is important and to speak about it in classrooms without fear of censorship.

Does Cheating Hurt the Individual?

Cheating confounds the process by which a student demonstrates his or her understanding of class content. It also prevents accurate feedback because the grade and the instructor's comments apply to someone else's work.

Academic misconduct also sabotages the quality of a person's education. Education inspires pride in accomplishment and ability. What confidence in ability will a person have whose work is not his or her own?

What's the long-term effect of taking what looks like "the easy way" through college exams and papers? It's bad if it gets you into a habit of attempting "shortcuts" in jobs, relationships, and even more demanding graduate education. What sort of personal life and career lie ahead for the person whose major skill is cheating?

Honesty and integrity are crucial to the search for truth and academic freedom. Imagine where our society would be if researchers reported fraudulent results that were then used to develop new machines or medical treatments. The integrity of knowledge is a cornerstone of higher education, and activities that compromise that integrity damage everyone.

A second mission of higher education is, of course, to disseminate knowledge through teaching. As students you participate in a learning cycle that includes receiving information, actively demonstrating your understanding, and receiving feedback that confirms or corrects your understanding. Now imagine if one of these steps were missing. Suppose your instructor gave your final exam without providing course instruction. Or your instructor taught but didn't give any tests or require any assignments, so that grades were based on what the professor assumed you had learned. Or your instructor taught and gave tests and assignments but didn't grade them or return them to you with comments.

Each part of the teaching cycle is necessary. Tampering with any of the components breaks down the teaching/learning process.

WHAT IS ACADEMIC DISHONESTY?

Most colleges and universities have academic integrity policies or honor codes that define clearly enough cheating, lying, plagiarism, and other forms of dishonest conduct, but it is often difficult to know how those rules apply to specific situations. For example, is it really lying to tell an instructor you missed class because you were "not feeling well" (whatever "well" means) or because you were experiencing that conveniently vague and all-encompassing malady, "car trouble"? Some people would argue that car trouble includes anything from a flat tire to trouble finding a parking spot!

Lying and Cheating

The University of South Carolina 1990 *Student Policy Manual* defines **lying** as "deliberate misrepresentation by words, actions, or deeds . . . for the purpose of avoiding or postponing the completion of any assignment, duties, test . . . or program." Are you familiar with the definition your school uses?

EXERCISE 6.7   **Discovering Your School's Academic Code**

Investigate the academic integrity standards for your school. Where did you find them? What specific behaviors do they prohibit? What procedures are followed when a student is suspected of violating the standards? Record three or four of the code's key rules here:

1. _____

2. _____

3. _____

4. _____

Institutions vary widely in what language they use to define, and in how specifically they define, the broad term *cheating*. For instance, one university's code of student academic integrity defines **cheating** as "intentionally using or attempting to use unauthorized materials, information, notes, study aids or other devices . . . [including] unauthorized communication of information during an academic exercise." This would apply to all of these:

► Looking over a classmate's shoulder for an answer
► Using a calculator when it is not authorized
► Procuring or discussing an exam without permission
► Copying lab notes
► Duplicating computer files

Does your school or your professor prohibit any of these activities?

EXERCISE 6.8   **Professors' Thoughts on Academic Honesty**

Ask one of your professors about his or her standards regarding academic integrity (you might even ask for his or her opinion about the behaviors listed in the last exercise). Share the results with classmates, and compare the similarities and differences you find.

Plagiarism Versus Referencing

While lying and cheating are considered wrong just about everywhere, plagiarism is especially intolerable in the academic culture. **Plagiarism** means taking another person's ideas or work and presenting them as your own. Just as taking someone else's property constitutes physical theft, taking credit for someone else's ideas constitutes "intellectual theft."

Rules for referencing (or "citing") another's ideas apply to the papers you write more so than to your responses on a test. After all on a test you are *supposed* to show how well you can remember the work of authorities! On written reports and papers, however, you *must* give credit any time you use (1) another person's actual words, (2) another person's ideas or theories — even if you don't quote them directly — and (3) any other information *not* considered common knowledge (for instance, the fact that there are twelve months in a year is common knowledge, but specific information about the process used in ancient times to develop a twelve-month calendar needs to be cited). You will want to check with your professors about how to cite material they've covered in classroom lectures. Usually you do not need to provide a reference for this, but it is always better to ask first.

Students are sometimes confused about how to represent material from written sources accurately and honestly. Read the excerpt below, which is part of a critique by Mark Twain of the famous author James Fenimore Cooper and his novel *The Deerslayer*. Then read the examples of student writing that follow, which illustrate the difference between plagiarism and correct referencing of work.

> *Cooper's gift in the way of invention was not a rich endowment but such as it was he liked to work it, he was pleased with the effects, and indeed he did some quite sweet things with it. In his little box of stage properties he kept six or eight cunning devices, tricks, artifices for his savages and woodsmen to deceive and circumvent each other with, and he was never so happy as when he was working these innocent things and seeing them go. A favorite one was to make a moccasined person tread in the tracks of the moccasined enemy, and thus hide his own trail. Cooper wore out barrels and barrels of moccasins in working that trick. Another stage-property that he pulled out of his box pretty frequently was his broken twig. He prized his broken twig above all the rest of his effects, and worked it the hardest. It is a restful chapter in any book of his when somebody doesn't step on a dry twig and alarm all the reds and whites for two hundred yards around. Every time a Cooper person is in peril and absolute silence is worth four dollars a minute, he is sure to step on a dry twig. There may be a hundred handier things to step on but that wouldn't satisfy Cooper. Cooper requires him to turn out and find a dry twig, and if he can't do it, go and borrow one. In fact, the Leatherstocking Series ought to have been called the Broken Twig Series.**

Example 1

INCORRECT: Although Cooper was not richly endowed in the area of invention, he did try some sweet things whose effects were quite pleasing.

---

*Anne Ficklen, ed., *The Hidden Mark Twain: A Collection of Little-Known Mark Twain* (New York: Crown Books, 1984).

This version is unacceptable because you may not simply change the order of another writer's words in an attempt not to plagiarize. The main idea must be preserved and rephrased in your *own* words and must include a reference to the source from which you borrowed it.

> CORRECT: *Twain notes that Cooper used but a few creative effects, and these appeared over and over again throughout the book.*[1]

In this version the phrasing is original, and the superscript number at the end of the passage leads the reader to the footnote or endnote where you provide the author's name, publication title, year of publication, and other information. This also allows the reader an opportunity to find more information on the topic.

Example 2

> INCORRECT: *Twain supports my view of Cooper's brilliant creativity: "Cooper's gift in the way of invention was . . . a rich endowment . . . and indeed he did some quite sweet things with it."*[2]

An ellipsis (. . .) is used when intervening words from the original quoted sentence or passage are omitted. However, as in this example, using the ellipsis to omit words and thereby change the meaning of the passage is misrepresentation, and thus unethical.

> CORRECT: *Twain offers only partial support for my view of Cooper's brilliant creativity: "Cooper's gift in the way of invention was not a rich endowment but . . . indeed he did some quite sweet things with it."*[2]

In this example the use of a direct quote correctly expresses the original author's material. Remember that quotes that run more than five lines should be set off in a separate paragraph, with indentations on both margins and without quotation marks.

EXERCISE 6.9 Paraphrasing and Referencing

In the space provided below and on p. 118, try correctly paraphrasing and referencing the last part of Twain's passage. Convey his opinion of Cooper's use of the "broken twig effect":

_____

_____

_____

_____

_____

_____

_____

Share your version with a classmate and discuss your use of paraphrasing.

Does Cheating Hurt the Academic Community?

The person who obtains a grade unfairly jeopardizes the basic fairness of the grading process. This makes other students cynical and resentful as they lose confidence in the system. This is especially important when grades are curved, because cheating then has an even more direct effect on every student in the class.

Frequent dishonesty within a college devalues the quality of any degree that school awards. Alumni, potential students, graduate schools, and employers learn to distrust degrees from schools where cheating is widespread. When this happens, everyone connected with the school loses.

Other Outlawed Behaviors

Most academic codes or policies outlaw lying, cheating, and plagiarism. In addition many schools prohibit other activities. For instance, the University of Delaware prohibits **fabrication** (intentionally inventing information or results); the University of North Carolina outlaws **multiple submission** (earning credit more than once for the same piece of academic work without permission); Eastern Illinois University rules out **tendering of information** (giving your work or exam answer to another student to copy during the actual exam or before the exam is given to another section); and the University of South Carolina prohibits **bribery** (trading something of value in exchange for any kind of academic advantage). Most schools also outlaw helping or attempting to help another student commit a dishonest act.

Some outlawed behaviors do not seem to fall within any clear category. Understanding the mission and values of higher education will help you make better decisions about those behaviors that "fall through the cracks."

EXERCISE 6.10   Making Decisions About Academic Behavior

Review the behaviors listed below. Put a Y for yes by any you think constitute cheating, an N for no by those you think are legitimate shortcuts, and a question mark (?) by those that could be either, depending on the situation.

_____ 1. Taking an exam in place of another student or having someone take an exam in your place

_____ 2. Rewriting passages (so they sound better) of a paper you're typing for a friend

_____ 3. Having someone write a paper to submit as your own work

_____ 4. Discussing your outline/ideas for a paper with a friend in your class who is writing on the same subject

_____ 5. Allowing another student to copy from you during an exam

_____ 6. Changing your lab results to reflect what you know they should have been, rather than what you got

_____ 7. Turning in the same paper to two different classes

_____ 8. Studying from old exams

_____ 9. Getting questions or answers from someone who has already taken the same exam

_____ 10. Borrowing an idea for a paper without footnoting the source

_____ 11. Working on homework with other students

_____ 12. Including a few items, which you didn't really use, on a bibliography

_____ 13. Changing a few answers on a graded exam and resubmitting it for a higher grade

_____ 14. Reading just the abstracts of articles, rather than the entire article, when doing research for a paper

_____ 15. Asking someone to proofread your draft of a paper

Compare your answers with other students in a small group. How do your decisions relate to the mission and values of higher education? Of those behaviors that everyone agrees are cheating, which are the most serious? The least serious?

REASONS FOR CHEATING

It might surprise you to learn that academic misconduct occurs frequently in higher education, though local estimates vary. Consider the following figures: One school reported that over 81 percent of students surveyed in a

The drive to succeed at any cost can exact a very heavy price, as Michael Milken, the "Junk Bond King," learned only too well. As head of the junk bond department for the Wall Street firm Drexel Burnham Lambert, he was involved in illegal activities. As a consequence, in 1990, Milken was sentenced to ten years in prison; his firm filed for bankruptcy.

year committed some type of academic cheating (Gohn, 1984). Most surveys report the frequency at around 25 percent of students. Nor are entering freshmen strangers to academic dishonesty. A 1987 national survey reported that 30.4 percent of freshmen had cheated on a test, and 52.7 percent had copied another student's homework (1987 *ACE-UCLA Freshman Survey*). At the same time, most students don't necessarily *plan* to cheat or engage in academic dishonesty. So what causes them to cheat?

Ignorance of the Rules

Many students never know exactly what constitutes cheating. This may not be surprising, especially if you and your classmates had different opinions about the scenarios at the beginning of this section. In one study conducted at the University of South Carolina, 20 percent of students responding to a survey thought buying a term paper did not constitute cheating. Forty percent thought using a test file (a collection of actual tests from previous terms or years, usually kept by an organization or club) was acceptable behavior. Sixty percent thought getting answers from someone who had taken an exam earlier in the same semester or in a previous semester was proper conduct. Yet each of these behaviors is considered unacceptable by at least some professors. While there may not be absolute agreement about what is acceptable and what is not, students seldom ask their instructors for clarification. Unfortunately, when caught violating the academic code, pleading ignorance of the rules is a weak defense.

Success at Any Price

Students often don't see the connection between their current classwork and their subsequent careers. Getting a decent grade becomes more important than developing skills and cultivating talents that can be used in a job or career. Yet good grades not supported by true learning will not take you far in the workplace. Imagine saying to your boss, "You can't fire me because I'm incompetent — I had a 4.0 average!"

People who overestimate the importance of grades may come to think it's important to succeed *at any cost.* In some ways this is a reflection of today's competitive society, but it also may be the result of pressure from parents, peers, or teachers; of the competition for admission to a graduate or professional school; or of simple test anxiety. "Success at any cost" may be accompanied by a strong fear of failure, another poor excuse for dishonesty.

Lack of Preparation

A very common cause of cheating is the student's own lack of preparation. Students experience a variety of demands on their time: class load, outside jobs, co-curricular activities, and time spent with friends or family. Ineffective management of all these activities can leave a student unprepared for a test or paper. Instead of explaining their situation to a professor and attempting to negotiate a later deadline, students may simply assume the professor won't listen and resort to dishonesty. While honesty may not always result in the extension of a deadline, it will maintain self-pride and integrity.

Even if you're well prepared, you may find yourself succumbing to pressure from family or friends. You may need to be more assertive with your friends and choose to stay home and study some nights instead of socializing. Or you may need to tell your family you have to study this weekend instead of visiting. At these times it may help to keep your long-term goals in mind. A few nights spent at home or in the library is a small price to pay for being well prepared for the future.

Other Reasons

Factors in the environment may also make cheating seem more or less acceptable: Knowledge that peers are cheating, ads in the media for term paper mills (companies selling mass-produced term papers for profit), the existence of test files, identical exams used semester after semester, and classrooms left unsupervised during tests — all may give the impression that academic honesty is not very important.

Students are also more likely to cheat if they are not disciplined when cheating is discovered. In general professors and administrators bear some responsibility for cheating if they do not (1) explain their standards, (2) provide an environment conducive to academic honesty, and (3) respond with swiftness and severity to incidents of dishonesty. However, final responsibility lies with you.

REDUCING THE TEMPTATION TO CHEAT

If you are discouraged or depressed by all this talk about cheating, take heart — there are some things you can do to avoid cheating in the first place or stop once you have started.

1. Improve Self-Management

Most students prefer to earn their grades honestly and resort to dishonesty only when they're falling behind, out of time, overwhelmed, or otherwise unprepared. The most effective method to assure academic integrity is to be well prepared for all quizzes, exams, projects, and papers. This may mean *un*learning some bad habits (such as procrastination) and building better time management and study skills, as described in Chapters 2–6.

2. Seek Help

You may want to seek help on campus. Find out what is available for assistance with "methods" — study skills, time management, and test-taking — and take advantage of it. If your methods are in good shape but the content of the course is too difficult, consult with your professor or teaching assistant. As a student you are also a consumer and should "get what you pay for." That means getting a solid education in exchange for your money and hard work. Also check into the possibility of working with a tutor on difficult subjects.

3. Withdraw from the Course

Consider cutting your losses before it's too late. Your school has a policy about dropping courses, and you may choose this route and plan to retake the course later. Some students may choose to **withdraw** from all their classes and take some time off before returning to school. This may be an option if you find yourself in over your head, or if some unplanned event (a long illness, a family crisis) has caused you to fall behind with little hope of catching up. Again, see what your school's policy is about withdrawing for a period of time.

4. Reexamine Goals

You may need to stick to your own realistic goals instead of feeling pressure from parents or friends to achieve impossibly high standards. What grades do you *need*, and what grades do you have the potential to earn? You may also feel pressure to enter a particular career or profession. If this isn't what you want, your frustration is likely to appear in your lack of preparation and your grades. It may be time to sit down with your parents and tell them you need to choose your own career.

If you are generally unhappy or unstimulated by your courses, consider a change of majors. Your first step should be to visit the career center on your campus. You may decide to try a different major, or you may become more excited about your present one (see Chapter 11).

KNOWING THE RULES

Even if you have never cheated and have no desire to do so, you can protect yourself from being wrongly accused. Specific rules governing academic behavior can vary, so learn about the academic code at your school early in your academic career. Your professor may not discuss academic integrity guidelines at the beginning of the semester; one survey (Nuss, 1982) reports less than half take the time to do this. When this happens, don't assume — ask him or her what behaviors are acceptable and unacceptable, and stay within those guidelines. Don't hesitate to ask questions as situations arise.

You can also guard against becoming unwittingly involved in an incident of cheating. Remember to do the following:

1. Keep your answers covered and your eyes down, and put all extraneous material away during tests.
2. Refrain from discussing exams with others unless it is specifically permitted.
3. Tell friends exactly what is acceptable and unacceptable if you lend them a term paper.

4. Ask for assistance to ensure you cite others correctly in your work.
5. Make sure your typist understands he or she may not make any changes in your work.
6. Refuse to assist others who enlist your aid in cheating.
7. Help your friends resist the temptation to cheat.

Cheating can have serious consequences, not the least of which is being suspended from your school. If you are failing a class, the F on your transcript may say you didn't learn. That can be remedied—sometimes by taking the class again or by doing well in a similar class. However, a notation of academic dishonesty on your transcript will not be so easy to remedy.

Consider the "big picture"—you are in college for the long-term goal of preparing yourself to be a knowledgeable, productive person. Don't compromise *your own* standards. Take pride in knowing you honestly *earned* every grade you received. It's clear you don't *have* to cheat—there are many ways to avoid it. And with something as important as your college education, honesty *is* the best policy.

EXERCISE 6.11 **Sharing What You've Learned**

With a small group of students develop a broad "marketing" plan that would ensure all students know about the academic integrity standards at your school, understand their importance, and know the purpose behind them.

JOURNAL

This section notes that 20 percent of the students responding to a survey thought that buying a term paper did not constitute cheating, 40 percent thought using a test file was okay, and 60 percent thought that getting answers from someone who had taken an exam earlier was acceptable. What are your reactions to these responses? What is your own position? How do you personally define cheating? What would another student have to do in order for you to report him or her for an infraction of your own institution's code with respect to academic dishonesty?

REFERENCES AND SUGGESTIONS FOR FURTHER READING

Cahn, S. M. *Saints and Scamps: Ethics in Academia.* Totowa, N.J.: Rowman and Littlefield, 1986.

Gohn, Lyle A., and Sarah S. Hicks. Personal correspondence from the University of Arkansas, December 3, 1984.

Hesburgh, T. *The Hesburgh Papers: Higher Values in Higher Education.* Kansas City: Andrews and McMeel, 1979.

Kuh, G. D., and E. J. Whitt. *The Invisible Tapestry: Culture in American Colleges and Universities.*

ASHE-ERIC Higher Education Report No. 1. Washington, D.C.: Association for the Study of Higher Education, 1988.

Morrill, R. L. *Teaching Values in College*. San Francisco: Jossey-Bass, 1980.

1987 *ACE-UCLA Freshman Survey*. Cooperative Institutional Research Program of the American Council on Education and the University of California, Los Angeles.

Nuss, Elizabeth M. "Enhancing Academic Integrity." *The Judicial Files*. Newsletter of American College Personnel Association Commission XV, Campus Judicial Affairs and Legal Issues. August 1982.

▼▼▼▼▼▼▼▼▼▼▼▼▼▼▼▼▼▼▼

Professor and Student: Partners in Learning

A. Jerome Jewler
John N. Gardner

Professor and Student: Partners in Learning

*S*he's so smart, how can I talk to her? Walks in and starts talking about her passion for geology, then asks us questions about things I've never even thought about. We have to have a conference with her during office hours to talk about how we're doing. Alone. And mine is today. I'm doing all right in the course, I think. But what in the world am I going to say to her?

Nothing in college is more important than what happens in the classroom. For one thing, if you don't pass, you won't be around to do all the other things that college has to offer. It's that simple. So this chapter focuses on the classroom and the people who manage it: your college professors. It has been said that teaching is one of the most complex and demanding professions on earth, and most college professors would agree.

In his classic work *Zen and the Art of Motorcycle Maintenance* Robert Pirsig claims that a university has two personas. One he calls the "other university," which consists of those aspects and features of university life that most people think of: buildings, grounds, boards of trustees, administrators, athletic contests, and much more. But this is not the "real university," according to Pirsig. The real university, he claims, is simply that great body of knowledge that is passed on from one generation to the next.

To many college professors grading is simply a necessary process by which the transmission of knowledge is ensured. They would much rather always focus on the learning itself, but they need a process by which they can verify that students are progressing. Ultimately they feel they have done their job only when they know that they have helped their students gain new knowledge and insights.

This chapter discusses how college professors differ from high school teachers, what professors spend their time doing, and how you can go about finding the good professors.

DIFFERENCES BETWEEN PROFESSORS AND HIGH SCHOOL TEACHERS

Strangely enough, your college professors probably never took a single course in teaching, whereas your high school teachers probably were required to take several such courses in order to qualify for their jobs. That may have its disadvantages as far as you are concerned, but it has one great advantage as well.

If nothing else, a good college instructor knows his or her subject. For example, your history professor is a historian who has spent years studying a specific period in the evolution of civilization and who is probably teaching that period to you. If that professor has a Ph.D., then he or she has written a lengthy dissertation — the equivalent of a book — about a particular aspect of history that has never been studied in such detail before. If you wonder why professors love their subjects, don't forget that they have already spent many years nurturing that love in undergraduate and graduate work.

Another important difference between high school teachers and most professors is that the latter probably won't spend much time in class teaching you what you can read about in the assigned textbooks. This is one reason you will need to take good lecture notes. Chances are the questions you will have to answer on quizzes and exams will be based on both the text and the lectures. In fact, your professors may often disagree with or question information in the text to emphasize that there is more than one way to interpret facts, events, theories, and so on. This is what critical thinking is all about.

Perhaps your high school teachers periodically looked over your notebooks to see that they were neat, took attendance daily, and checked to be

"He Said, 'I Am Really Tired'"

From the first day of class in my U.S. Constitution course, the instructor came in, stood at the lectern, and read his notes. I did not care too much about what he said (and most people cared even less), especially his opinions, because I had no empathy with him (it wasn't because he was boring). How can you have a feeling for, or care about, a lecture robot? No one can be empathetic with a machine. But one day he came, and went to the lectern like usual. But instead of lecturing like always, he said, "I am really tired," and walked to a chair in the back of the room and sat down. He told us about a dream he had the night before. He had dreamed he was giving a lecture in class, but there were only two students present. As he went to leave, he found that his shoes were nailed to the floor. He talked about his past (he had taught at a prison, and was scared of his students at first). He also gave us his feelings about the area. It was great. Now the classes are better, even though he still lectures, because it's more personal. I can have empathy with a person who I know has funny dreams, gets scared, and is tired.*

How do you think you would have responded to what this professor did? What is it you *most* want in a professor? What do you *least* want?

*This excerpt by Mark Gauss. From Rob Anderson, *Students as Real People* (Rochelle Park, N.J.: Hayden Book Company, 1978), pp. 73–74.

certain you were keeping up with your work. Don't expect all professors to follow suit. They will expect you to take care of yourself.

In high school your teachers filled you with information accumulated by others. While your college professors may do some of the same, they will also be introducing knowledge of their own, accumulated in many cases through original research. College professors must keep abreast of developments in their fields by reading relevant publications and attending meetings and conferences in their fields. They may also do some form of research, the results of which may be published in books or as articles in scholarly journals or presented as formal papers at professional meetings. You will find yourself doing such research, most often based on library resources, in many of your college courses when you write term papers. If you supplement this "secondary research" with "primary research" — interviews, surveys, new interpretations of existing facts — you will find yourself discovering new information and uncovering new ideas.

UNDERSTANDING YOUR PROFESSORS

Although it's difficult to generalize further about college professors, we can safely assume that most of them believe in the value of a liberal education. "Liberal" refers to the ability of education to free your mind; the goal of a liberal education is to free you from the biases and prejudices that may have characterized you before you came to college.

Formative Reading?

For more than twenty years, the *Chronicle of Higher Education* has kept track of best-selling books on a variety of college campuses. Many of your current professors were college students or young teachers twenty years ago. What were they reading when the *Chronicle* compiled its listing in January 1971?

1. *Love Story* (Erich Segal)
2. *Everything You've Always Wanted to Know About Sex* (David Reuben)
3. *The Greening of America* (Charles A. Reich)
4. *The Sensuous Woman* ("J")
5. *Future Shock* (Alvin Toffler)
6. *Crisis in the Classroom* (Charles E. Silberman)
7. *Civilisation* (Kenneth Clark)
8. *Knots* (R. D. Laing)
9. *The Prophet* (Kahlil Gibran)
10. *The Godfather* (Mario Puzo)

Compare that list to the list for January 1991:

1. *The Authoritative Calvin and Hobbes* (Bill Watterson)
2. *All I Really Need to Know I Learned in Kindergarten* (Robert Fulghum)
3. *The Plains of Passage* (Jean M. Auel)
4. *Foucault's Pendulum* (Umberto Eco)
5. *The "Late Night With David Letterman" Book of Top Ten Lists* (David Letterman et al.)
6. *Wiener Dog Art: The Far Side Collection* (Gary Larson)
7. *Where's Waldo?* (Martin Handford)
8. *The Bonfire of the Vanities* (Tom Wolfe)
9. *Misery* (Stephen King)
10. *The Civil War* (Geoffrey C. Ward et al.)

Comments, anyone?

What Do Your Professors Expect from You?

Your professors want you to grow intellectually and will probably demand more of you than your high school teachers did. Most college professors believe students entering college are woefully underprepared. As a result they'll challenge you to raise your standards, which means you'll have to study more hours for each course in college than you did in high school.

To most professors a college education is more than a means to a job and a lifetime of financial security. To them anything that stimulates and challenges the mind is worthwhile. They have a higher opinion of educated persons because such people are interested in more things: painting, theater, music, sculpture, dance, history, human behavior, social issues, travel, reading, films, government and the law, and any other topics that affect the way we live today. No matter what their specialty, most professors are interested in issues that transcend their academic disciplines. They would like to see you become this sort of person, and they may take a personal interest in you as a student, especially if they see such qualities emerging in you.

Deep within nearly all college professors is the desire to use their knowledge and experiences to help others. If you asked any of your professors why they chose to teach, they would likely mention this as a major reason.

What Do College Professors Do?

One of the common myths about college professors is that they lead easy lives of quiet contemplation, interrupted only by a few hours of classroom teaching each week. Nothing could be further from the truth. While the average professor spends only between 6 and 15 hours in the classroom each week, he or she probably works 60 hours or more a week.

To keep current in their field, professors read. Such reading necessitates updating of classroom lecture notes, and notes take far longer to prepare than to deliver in class. Professors may spend time conducting experiments, doing research, reviewing manuscripts for journals and textbook publishers, and writing books and articles. They may be called upon to speak to local and professional groups, and they may consult for a private corporation or government agency.

While they're not doing these things, you will probably find them advising their students — helping them to plan academic programs for the coming term, reach career decisions, deal with personal problems, or find ways to improve their coursework. The majority of professors consider meetings with students to be a part of their job as an educator. In fact, the most effective professors put a high priority on the time they can spend advising students.

In the time that's left professors perform administrative duties, serve on academic committees, and become involved in special campus projects. And, of course, they grade papers, tests, reports, and the like. What's more, like most adults they may hold responsibilities as parents and providers and devote part of their time to their families.

EXERCISE 7.1   A Professor's Ideal Student

In the eyes of most professors, who is the ideal student? List the qualities and behaviors you believe professors want in their students.

_____

_____

_____

_____

_____

_____

_____

_____

_____

_____

Compare your response with that of several classmates. Ask one of your teachers what he or she wants in a student.

Most professors are busy people who enjoy contact with their students. That's one reason they chose to become teachers.

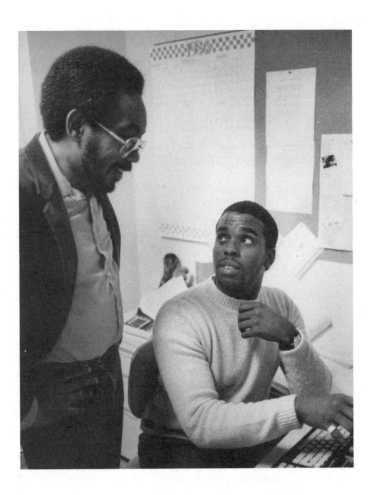

How Can You Make the Most of the Student—Professor Relationship?

You should make it a point to come to class regularly and on time — your professor wants you in class. If you have to miss a class, you'll need to ask another student for the notes; it's okay to do so as long as the student agrees and you don't make a habit of it. But remember, learning is easier when you are there every day. Save your cuts for emergencies; you will have them.

You should also sit near the front of the classroom. A number of studies indicate that students who do so tend to earn better grades. That should come as no surprise, since sitting up front forces you to focus on the lecture, to listen, and to participate in class discussions and ask questions.

Although it may make you nervous to challenge professors if you don't agree with some of their statements or simply don't understand what they mean, we encourage you to speak up anyway. A good professor will appreciate your questions and comments, will probably engage you in a polite discussion, and may even admit to seeing things from your point of view, so long as you really know what you're talking about.

In addition, you should never hesitate to see your professor out of class when needed. Professors are required to keep office hours expressly for the purpose of conferring with students. In other words, seeing you is one of their assigned duties. Again, while you may be hesitant to approach a professor for an appointment, you should take the risk if you have something you need to discuss. You can make an appointment by calling the professor's office. Doing so will ensure that the professor is available when you show up.

Good professors will welcome you into their offices, especially when they know in advance that you are coming. If you have trouble contacting the professor during office hours, approach him or her at the end of class. We repeat: Seeing your instructor outside class is worth making an extra effort.

ACADEMIC FREEDOM IN THE CLASSROOM

To a professor the classroom is a place where ideas may be exchanged in an atmosphere of free speech. Academic freedom lets professors raise questions without risk of losing their jobs. While it doesn't give them total immunity from external pressures and potential reprisals, it does allow them more latitude than your high school teachers had.

The Right to Free Expression

Although academic freedom has its origins in the Middle Ages, it continues to be a burning issue among those individuals who have seen this freedom threatened during their lifetime. We have only to recall the government witchhunt for communist sympathizers in the 1950s, the brutal treatment of civil rights marchers in the 1950s and 1960s, or the attacks on Vietnam War protestors in the 1960s and 1970s to understand how precious is the freedom to speak out for what we believe in, whether it be in a classroom discussion about economic policy or at a public rally on such current issues as abortion and gay rights. What matters as much as what we believe is our right to proclaim that belief to others without fear of reprisal.

Colleges and universities have promoted the advancement of knowledge by granting scholars virtually unlimited freedom of inquiry, as long as human lives, rights, and privacy are not violated. Such freedom is not always possible in other professions and may be still another reason your professors chose teaching as a career.

Some of your professors may surprise or even anger you with their ideas. They may insult a politician you admire or speak sarcastically about the president. In college, as in life, you must tolerate opinions vastly different from your own. You need not always accept them, but you should learn to evaluate them for yourself, instead of basing your judgments on what others have always told you.

Do professors say controversial things just to get a reaction from you? Possibly—they may believe they have to provoke you to get you to think critically. You won't have to agree with them to earn high grades, but you must begin to understand their views, examine them rationally, and be prepared to defend your own views if you still believe you are correct.

Tenure and Rank

Academic freedom is related to tenure. **Tenure**, which provides lifetime employment at the institution at which it is granted, is awarded to professors who have proved themselves as educators in terms of teaching skills, research that contributes to the body of knowledge in their field, and service to the university and to the community at large. Because all processes are subject to human error, tenure status and effectiveness in the classroom are not always related. In fact, some of your best professors may not yet have received tenure. Although nontenured faculty have academic freedom, tenured faculty theoretically have more of it. A tenured faculty member may be

discharged only for a serious crime, for insubordination or incompetence, or as part of a bona fide reduction in staff. Since insubordination and incompetence are difficult to prove, dismissals for such reasons are rare.

Not all professors hold equal rank. At the lowest level are instructors and lecturers. Then come assistant professors, associate professors, and "full" professors. This hierarchy won't matter much to you unless you begin seeking references for graduate study. In that case you might want to choose from your full professors, especially if they are well known in their field. Your college catalog will reveal the rank of your professors; it may also indicate whether an individual holds a "chair" (a position funded by an outside source and generally renewed annually) or is a "professor emeritus" (an individual who has retired but who may still teach a class or two).

Knowing how to address your professors is quite another matter — some faculty may be sensitive to how you address them. Most have earned a **doctoral degree** and therefore should be addressed as "Dr. _who_ ." You can also use "Professor _X_ " as a means of address. In fact, using either of these is a fairly safe bet. If your professor isn't a "doctor," it's doubtful he or she will mind your use of the term! What's most important is that you learn the names of your professors on the first day of class and feel comfortable addressing them by name and proper title. They'll appreciate your efforts.

EXERCISE 7.2   Your Ideal Professor

In the space provided on the next page, list the qualities and behaviors you believe you should find in a good professor. Get ideas for your list from others in your class.

Consult your list as you write a few paragraphs about your ideal professor. If any of your professors exhibit the qualities you have listed, explain why these qualities are important in terms of what you are learning in his or her class. Share your writing with other students in your class.

FINDING THE GOOD PROFESSORS

Before you can find the right professors, you have to have some idea what you're looking for. What qualities did you choose in Exercise 7.2? If you used words like *sincere, caring, fair, challenging, spontaneous, dramatic, enthusiastic, knowledgeable, involved, acknowledging, organized, clear,* and *humorous,* you're in agreement with most students and former students. According to national surveys "clarity and organization" come first, followed by "an interesting presentation." Then come the qualities that indicate the professor is a human being: "approachable," "understanding," "caring," and so on. Good professors, in the eyes of students, are like good coaches. They challenge students and work them hard, but like the good coach, they also show they care about each student's success.

If you're lucky enough to have these kinds of professors, you'll probably want to let them know at the end of the term not only how much you enjoyed their classes but how much you learned. Although a good professor may work to keep class lively, he or she never lets entertainment get in the way of high standards.

This brings us to two questions: (1) What is a good teacher and (2) How do you find him or her at your college or university? Several studies of teaching confirm that students learn best when the teacher involves them in the learning process. Teachers who follow this rule will encourage you to discuss material in class, will send you to the library to discover information on your own, and then provide time for you to share that knowledge with your classmates. Such teachers will have you solve problems or answer questions in small discussion groups and present your solutions or advocate your position to them and to the rest of the class. These kind of teachers will make a genuine effort to know each of you in some way.

Joseph Lowman of the University of North Carolina claims that students want a teacher who appears to have strong interest in them as individuals, who acknowledges their feelings about class assignments and policies and may even encourage them to express such feelings, who seems eager for them to express personal viewpoints, and who somehow lets them know that their understanding of the material is important to him or her. If you're in such a class you will feel the teacher knows about you and cares about your learning. You will therefore be highly motivated to do your best.

Three Kinds of Teachers

Research on effective teaching suggests that all teaching styles can be divided into three groups. First, there is the "teacher-centered" teacher, who believes "the main reason this course is worthwhile is because I am teaching it." Such teachers are said to have a "charisma," and many students actually learn more because of the teacher's unique approach and delivery of information. Second is the "content-centered" teacher, who believes "my main task is to cover everything I am supposed to cover in this class, from A to Z." Such teachers make certain they discuss everything they feel is important in a particular course. Third is the "student-centered" teacher, who believes "the best learning takes place when I get students to participate in the learning. Since every student is an individual, I need to know my students well before I can be certain they are learning."

Admittedly most teachers combine elements of all three styles, but often one quality predominates. Which of the types do you like most? Which least? Why?

Engineering professor Jack V. Matson auctions a T-shirt at the final exam. Which kind of professor is he?

Perhaps one of the best descriptions of the outstanding teacher comes from Dr. Elliot Engel of North Carolina State University:

Great teachers always know their subjects well, devoting a lifetime to being students of them. But they also know their students well, studying them almost as diligently as they do their specialty. Great teaching fundamentally consists of building a bridge from the subject taught to the student learning it. Both sides of that bridge must be surveyed with great care if the subject matter of the teacher is to connect with the gray matter of the student. But great teachers transcend simply knowing their subjects and students well; they also admire both deeply. . . . These teachers are humbled by the sense of renewal whenever their students learn. They know that this has all been done before and is forever to be done again. . . . This sense of renewal should make all teachers aware that the occupation most similar to teaching is farming. We cultivate our particular crops in the fall and harvest them in the spring. We boast of the sprouts which burst into vibrant bloom and sigh over those that withered on the vine, believing (like a farmer) that luck had too much to do with the blooms and our own failure with the blights. . . . A society *blighted by a dearth of great teachers soon finds itself in danger of growing nothing but blooming idiots.* *

So know your professors, respect their needs, and look for those who will respect yours. How do you find the best ones? You may not be able to during your first semester, but you can begin by asking other students. Through the grapevine you'll soon discover which professors to avoid and which to try for. And don't be surprised if you're warned to stay away from the easy ones. What good is a high grade if it doesn't mean anything? Find out if the student body publishes a guide that evaluates professors. Ask who's won teaching awards. Visit a professor before you register for his or her class; by asking about the course, you'll probably learn much about the professor, too.

What if you get a bad professor? First, check to see if you are beyond the point in the semester when you can drop the course without a grade penalty. Most colleges allow such a period during the early part of the term. Or arrange a meeting with the professor to see if you have misunderstood his or her approach or philosophy. Getting to know the professor may help you cope with the way the course is taught.

If, however, you get no satisfaction from talking with the professor and are having serious problems that cannot be resolved, you can share your concerns with higher levels of authority, provided you follow the prescribed "chain of command" (professor, department head, dean, and so on). Keep in mind, however, that professors' freedom to grade is a sacrosanct right, and no one can make them change their grades against their will. Above all, whether you have a good or bad professor, accept your responsibility to learn and to fulfill your academic obligations. Try hard not to let a "bad" professor sour you on the rest of college, and remember that even a bad course will be over in a semester.

EXERCISE 7.3   Interviewing a Professor

Choose a professor to interview — perhaps your favorite instructor or one you'd just like to know better. Make an appointment beforehand so he or she has some uninterrupted time to talk with you. Prepare your questions before you go, but also be ready to "go with the flow" of your conversation. Consider asking some of the following questions:

1. What were you like as a freshman?
2. When did you decide to be a professor? Why?
3. How has your academic career brought you to this point?
4. What do you like most about your job? What do you like least?
5. What has been your most important professional experience so far?
6. Do you have a philosophy of teaching?
7. What do you expect from your students? What should they expect from you?

*From a column in the *Dickens Dispatch*, the newsletter of the North Carolina Dickens Club, January 1989.

8. What are some of your research interests?
9. What else do you do in addition to your teaching and research activities?
10. What are your plans for the future?

Write an essay about what you learned from your professor and also what surprised you the most about him or her.

JOURNAL

How are your college professors different from your high school teachers so far? How are you reacting to those differences? Describe one or two of your professors. What do you think of them? Did reading this chapter help you better understand any of your professors? Explain. What further questions do you have about your professors or how to deal with them? Which of these might you raise in class?

REFERENCES AND SUGGESTIONS FOR FURTHER READING

Lowman, Joseph. *Mastering the Techniques of Teaching.* San Francisco: Jossey-Bass, 1984.

Pirsig, Robert. *Zen and the Art of Motorcycle Maintenance: An Inquiry into Values.* New York: Morrow, 1974.

▼▼▼▼▼▼▼▼▼▼▼▼▼▼▼▼▼▼▼

An Information Age Introduction to the Library

Charles C. Curran

An Information Age Introduction to the Library

I went to the library for the first time last week to look up something I was really curious about. I'm not even sure how to tell you my question. I couldn't find anything in the catalog, and the librarians all looked busy with people who seemed to know what they wanted. I knew I'd sound stupid asking, so I just wandered around awhile and came out. I don't know. Maybe I wasn't so curious after all . . .

CHARLES C. CURRAN *is professor of library and information science at the University of South Carolina, Columbia.*

"I was bewildered by college," he admits, "and the main reason for my confusion was that I could not even describe my problem. There I was, a freshman in the Duquesne University library. I had a major assignment and no strategy—no inkling that mine was an information management problem I had never learned how to handle. Thirty years in the information business have convinced me that students who want to survive and thrive must have a solid plan for dealing with information problems. I have developed and tested such a plan, and it works. In this chapter I share it with you."

Many beginning students willingly accept the challenge of learning to use the college or university library. In the old days this was not true—students would often moan and groan at the idea of a "library lesson." By contrast today's students are more serious about succeeding. They understand that the better they are able to find and manage information, the better they will do in college.

This chapter is for those students who have reached this level of appreciation for the role information plays in our lives. The chapter is also for those who accept the idea that information is the new and valuable currency—the medium of exchange in this, the **Information Age**. Finally this chapter is for those who understand that being more "information literate" will help them succeed in college and beyond.

INFORMATION LITERACY

Knowing how to get information and how and when to trade it is what information literacy is all about. Information literacy is composed of a number of subskills that include knowing (1) when information might be useful, (2) where to get information, (3) how to get information, (4) what to do with information when you get it, and (5) how to communicate information. Information literacy is a survival and a "thrival" skill because information-literate people know how to amass and communicate information, the medium of exchange in the world of ideas. If you believe that information is power, you will have no trouble seeing the analogy of information *as a commodity*. As an information manager your mission is to promote survival, excellence, and self-reliance—both in college and beyond. Useful information is power, and knowing where and how to get that information is a powerful skill in its own right. The skills you are about to practice won't solve all your problems, but they will help you address every college assignment that involves some need for information.

EXERCISE 8.1   Retrieval, Organization, and Presentation

This exercise involves you, your professor, and the staff at your college or university library. Each of you will have a different role to play. You will be executing an assignment. After alerting the library staff your professor will give you the assignment, monitor your progress, and evaluate the results. Librarians will read the assignment sheet and have advance knowledge of your imminent arrival in the library, know what you need, and be ready to help you.

A word of advice about dealing with librarians: Most librarians who work "in full view," such as those at a reference desk, really like helping you. That's why, of all the library jobs they could have picked, they chose public service. And they also like it when a professor gives them advance notice about assignments so they can be ready for the inevitable barrage of questions. It is in your best interest to get in the habit of asking librarians for help. Knowing how to make the best use of their talent can make a big difference to you. Make sure your library staff knows that you are working the following exercise.

GETTING STARTED

Okay, here we go. Remember, you are seeking to become information literate, and information literacy involves retrieval, organizational, and communication skills. You need a framework for this, and that framework will consist of (1) a topic to be researched, (2) some information to be retrieved, interpreted, and organized, and (3) a 5-minute oral presentation to your class.

The presentation should have some structure. We suggest the following structure or outline for the presentation and recommend also that you use this outline as a test of relevancy for retrieved pieces of information:

> A. *Definition:* What is this topic about? What does it mean?
>
> B. *Importance:* Why is this topic important? How important is this topic? What would happen if this problem were not addressed or if no one knew about it?
>
> C. *Effect:* How does this influence my thinking? Does my research tell me something I did not know? Have I changed my mind as the result of reading this? What is there about this information that contributes to my understanding of the topic?
>
> D. *Reaction:* What do I want to say? What insight do I wish to report? What is important enough that I want to tell others? How does this information make me *feel*?

Not only does the preceding serve as an outline for the 5-minute presentation, it provides a test of relevancy. When we find a book or article, the test of whether it is relevant or useful is whether it fits, or does not fit, the outline. We will consider using it if it fits and put it aside if it does not.

During the course of your search you will find lots of material. You will also discover that some sources you might expect to be rich in relevant information are not so at all. Do not be confused or discouraged by this. You will have some hits and some misses. Part of becoming information literate involves knowing how to sort out an abundance of information and also knowing what to do when you reach a dead end. Remember, insofar as the *sorting* of information is concerned, material that answers the questions raised in your outline should be

Tips for Your 5-Minute Oral Presentation

1. Assign each group member a speaking role and category.
2. Select the strongest points from each category.
3. Study those points, and list them on 3 × 5 note cards.
4. Make sure your talk has a *beginning* and an *end*. Don't just stop.
5. *Tell* the class what you know; *do not read* to them.
6. Address your whole audience, not just the instructor.
7. Find friendly faces — this reduces nervousness.
8. Accept that you'll be nervous, and make it work for you.
9. *Practice* your talk. Check timing and audience contact.
10. Imagine doing a super job. Believe it: This works!
11. Repeating number 5: Do *not* read your stuff; *tell* it.

placed in your *usable category*; material that appears not to answer your outline questions should be placed in your *unusable category*.

SELECTING A TOPIC

Examine the following list. Pick three topics that really interest you, and on a sheet of paper print your name and list your three topics in order of interest to you.

AIDS	Hypnosis	Prejudice
Adoption	The KKK	Racism
Autism	Love	The Reformation
Burnout	The Mafia	Schizophrenia
Capital punishment	Marriage	Scuba diving
Drug use	The occult	Single parents
The future	Palimony	Terrorism
Gambling	Paranoia	Values
The Great Depression	Penology	Venereal disease
Herpes	Pop Art	Witchcraft

Give the sheet to your instructor. He or she will match it against those of your classmates, grouping you with one or two other students on a topic for which you all showed a preference. The two or three of you will now work as a group.

THE JOB OF THE GROUP

The job of your group is to locate, assemble, inspect, evaluate, organize, and communicate some information about the topic you have been assigned. But what exactly do we mean by *locate, assemble,* and so on?

However big or small the library, a reference librarian can help you use it.

Locate means find and place your hands on.

Assemble means collect.

Inspect means look at, read, and understand.

Evaluate means decide whether the information you have gathered is pertinent: Is it helpful in explaining your topic? Does it fit your outline?

Organize means put it in order, preferably according to your outline.

Communicate means transfer information (in other words, tell someone about your findings).

DRESS REHEARSAL: THE RESEARCH PROCESS

Let's walk through the research process using the topic AIDS to illustrate the necessary steps. Since the very first thing you have to do is *define* (step A in your outline), a good strategy is to go to sources that define and present basic information. Encyclopedias provide this kind of basic information, and good ones offer reliable help.

Don't let anyone tell you that encyclopedias are trivial sources, or "baby" sources fit only for grade-schoolers. Encyclopedias often get a bum rap because they are misused by some elementary school teachers who tell their students, for example, to "go to the encyclopedia and do some research on *fish*." So the students "research" their topics by copying directly from an encyclopedia. The teachers accept the plagiarized "reports," award A's, and later complain that their students never graduate from encyclopedias. They absolve themselves from blame. Your college and university instructors know that authoritative encyclopedias provide very useful basic information and helpful leads to additional sources. That's why we start with encyclopedias. Once you've consulted encyclopedias, both general and specialized, you move on to periodicals, books, and "opinion" pieces. Let's look at each source category.

Source Category 1: General Encyclopedias

Source: *Encyclopedia Americana.* Danbury, Conn.: Grolier, 1989.

When using any multivolume encyclopedia, *always* consult the index volume (usually the final volume in the set). You will be tempted to go to the A volume if

your topic is *automobiles*. But look at all the stuff you will miss if you don't check the index: transportation, Detroit, combustion engines, Henry Ford, and more. None of these begins with *A*, and if you consult only the *A* volume, you'll miss them. Simply put, your chances of finding what you need will be greatly enhanced if you check the index.

So what does the index volume of the *Encyclopedia Americana* list under *AIDS*?

Index vol. 30
Page 13: AIDS (Acquired Immune Deficiency Syndrome) (med.) 1 - 365
        Africa 1 - 283
        Drug Addiction and Abuse 9 - 413
        Zaire 29 - 741L

Note that the *AIDS* entry refers you to Volume 1 (the *A* volume) but also to two items of potential value that are *not* in the AIDS article in Volume 1: one in Volume 9 and one in Volume 29. Observe, however, that the *Africa* entry is also in Volume 1, so the bulk of what you need may be in the *A* volume.

Okay, you've found the information. Is it relevant? Remember, the test of relevance or usefulness is: Does the information address the outline? The information in the encyclopedia is relevant to your purposes because your search is assignment-driven, and the outline describes your assignment. In the following outline, which is based on the model on page 142, we'll record information that we believe matches what the coded outline calls for. If we can match a unit of information with one or more of the outline items, we have found material that will help us with our assignment.

A.	*Definition*	". . . a progressive degenerative disease of two major organ systems, the immune system and the central nervous system." (p. 365)
B.	*Importance*	". . . death results . . . from infections . . . 10–20 million people worldwide . . ."
C.	*Effect*	—
D.	*Reaction*	—

Note that we have responded for you with respect to *Definition* and *Importance*. *Effect* and *Reaction* are left blank because we are not sure how to respond for you, or even if you feel the need to respond to the information you read. What we do know is that if you want to be sure you have found something you can use, you can employ this method to build your assignment.

You need a definition for *AIDS*. Does this provide it? Yes? Then this is useful. Does this article suggest implications for humankind? Does it provide *Importance* data? If you think the answer is yes, then this is useful. And so on, using your outline as a guide.

Source Category 2: Subject Encyclopedias

Source: *McGraw-Hill Encyclopedia of Science and Technology*, 6th edition. New York: McGraw-Hill, 1987.

General encyclopedias provide "general" basic information. Subject encyclopedias often provide more in-depth information, and they may presuppose some prior knowledge. So we *graduate* from the general to the specific when we consult encyclopedias devoted to one main subject area, such as science, art, religion, psychology, or history. Here's what the *McGraw-Hill Encyclopedia of Science and Technology* index volume lists for AIDS:

Index vol. 20
Page 131: AIDS see Acquired immune deficiency syndrome
Page 125: Acquired immune deficiency syndrome (AIDS) 1 - 89-90*

The index volume entry on page 125 refers you to Volume 1, pages 89–90. The asterisk simply means this is an article title. Under this heading you will find eleven additional references to material on AIDS; these can be found in volumes 1, 9, 11, 14, 16, and 19.

Now, let's run through the outline.

A.	*Definition*	". . . an apparently lethal disease . . . which has become identified with increasing frequency since 1980."
B.	*Importance*	People appear to become infected from intimate sex or from contaminated needles.
C.	*Effect*	—
D.	*Reaction*	Adding to the tragedy is the fact that even babies can be victims. We have to *do* something!

The *Definition* and *Importance* material comes from a reading of the articles. The *Reaction* material comes from the heart and expresses a desire for the tragedy to end. This may be how you would react. Remember, you have an assignment requiring you to discover and communicate some information. The four outline points give you a filter for all the data you are about to collect. The outline is your test of relevance for this assignment.

Source Category 3: Periodical Indexes, General
Source: *Readers' Guide to Periodical Literature*. September 25, 1989. New York: H. W. Wilson.

This issue of the *Readers' Guide*, which is an index or a key to finding information in magazines, has two items of potential interest. One comes directly to you under the heading *AIDS (disease)*, the other through a cross-reference to *HIV VIRUSES*.

Page 3: AIDS (Disease)
Fending off AIDS with deep sleep? [research by Suzan E. Norman] K. Fackelmann. *Science News* 136:13 Jl 1 '89

See also
HIV viruses

Page 68: HIV VIRUSES
Do sperm spread the AIDS virus? [research by Virginia Schofield] J. L. Marx. il *Science* 245:30 Jl 7 '89

It is *very* important that you understand a couple of points here. First, *different* sources refer to your subject in *different* ways. You cannot always expect to find what you want in source B under the term you have used successfully in source A — the terms may not be standard. Second, you really have to watch for cross-references. They can appear in obscure places, such as at the end of a series of listings under the original heading you are looking up. If you miss them, a whole cache of information can go unnoticed. If you see and consult them, you enrich your search. For example, "See also *Antibodies*" is a cross-reference telling you that the articles on antibodies also contain information relevant to whatever it is you are searching — in this case AIDS.

Now let's see if these periodicals that the *Readers' Guide* listed provide us with any useful information.

Article 1
First, there is the "Fending Off AIDS" article, which describes Norman's research. It was written by Fackelmann, and it appears in *Science News*, volume

136, on page 13, of the July 1, 1989, issue. Does your library have that periodical? If so, it will be listed somewhere. In some libraries it will be on the computer; in others it may be on sheets of microfiche or reels of film, in the card
catalog, or in a separate print booklet. (This would be a good time to get ac-
quainted with a librarian and observe how helpful the library staff can be. Tell
the librarian you have a magazine citation to locate and ask how to do it.)

So you check the library's list and discover the magazine has a call number,
like Q 679 .L45 or maybe 365. Your library will contain a chart or map that tells
you where the Qs and the 365s are. Go where the notice tells you to and look for
your title.

Let's run our outline check on the article about sleep.

A. *Definition*	—
B. *Importance*	Maybe there's a connection between getting a good night's sleep and health.
C. *Effect*	I don't see this as "cure related."
D. *Reaction*	My grandmother knew this. Apparently there *is* a link between sleep and health.

Note that there's nothing here under *Definition*. Some pieces of information will
build upon foundations (definitions) you have supplied from other sources, such
as encyclopedias.

Article 2
Second is the article about sperm. We are directed to this article by the cross-
reference *AIDS See also HIV VIRUSES* in the *Readers' Guide* entry for the previous article.

A. *Definition*	—
B. *Importance*	AIDS carriers may be able to have children safely if sperm are shown not to carry the AIDS virus. There seems to be conflicting evidence about this issue.
C. *Effect*	It looks like research is making some tentative discoveries.
D. *Reaction*	—

Source Category 4: Periodical Indexes, Subject
Source: *Social Science Index*. New York: H. W. Wilson.

There are many special-subject periodical indexes you can consult. Your library may have a list of them, and you can *guess* which ones might relate to your topic. A better strategy would be to ask a librarian for help. Indicate that you have already used the *Readers' Guide*, and now you want to find a subject index on your topic. For this topic you could use *Social Science Index* to find two articles.

Article 1
Source: *Social Science Index*, Vol. 14. New York: H. W. Wilson, April 1987-March 1988

Page 46: AIDS (Disease)
A framework for preventing AIDS. W. W. Darrow. *Am J Public Health* 77:778-9 Jl '87

Look on page ix of the *Index* and you'll see that the cited periodical abbreviation stands for *American Journal of Public Health*.

A.	*Definition*	—
B.	*Importance*	AIDS is a problem with many dimensions, not just medical ones. Consider the plight of the sufferer, the tasks faced by those who give medical assistance, and the social implications.
C.	*Effect*	—
D.	*Reaction*	—

Article 2
Source: *Social Science Index*, Vol. 16, No. 2. New York: H. W. Wilson, Sept '89

Page 16: AIDS (Disease)
Government Policy
Implications for public policy: Towards a pro-family AIDS policy. E. A. Richardson. bibl *Marriage Fam Rev* 13: No. 1-2 187 228 '89

Note that we have consulted a different volume of the index. We point this out to you because we have observed that students sometimes look in a particular year's worth of index entries only, under the belief that if there is anything on their topic, it would be in *that* volume only. Look for the years of coverage for the index and you'll see that coverage starts all over for each new volume. Page vi of the *Index* tells you that the abbreviated journal title stands for *Marriage and Family Review*.

A.	*Definition*	—
B.	*Importance*	—
C.	*Effect*	—
D.	*Reaction*	Scenarios for the future are chilling and intense. Impact on heterosexuals will increase; people will divorce less frequently and have fewer partners; testing will become mandatory; and casual intimate behavior will lessen.

Computer Access to the Library

Even if your school library has already converted its card catalog to an online computerized catalog, we still recommend that you do the exercise in this chapter as it's written — as a manual search. Doing so will teach you a lot about finding your way around the library. After you complete the exercise, learn how to use the computerized catalogs as well. As you do, consider the following:

► A great deal of information and references in print may not yet be on the computer indexes. Don't take the computer index as the final word about what's available. Ask a librarian which sources the computer may not contain.

► Computerized catalogs and indexes exist for specific areas of interest. Here are several of the many useful indexes:

ERIC (for education)

PsycLit (for psychology)

Life Sciences Collection

General Science Index

Newspaper Abstracts

Editorials on File

► The more specifically and precisely you know what you are looking for in a computer search, the more effective it will be. If computerized index headings don't quite match what you're looking for, ask a librarian for help.

► Your school may have indexes on what is called CD ROM. These are like music compact discs in appearance and operation. ROM (Read-Only-Memory) means that you can "read" or view information from the disc but cannot erase that information. CD ROMs may contain many years of periodical citations from many indexing sources. Find out how to use them.

► You may have free access to part or all of your library's computerized reference facilities, or you may have to pay a service fee of up to $50 or more in order to use some services.

► You may be able to access computerized library catalogs from computers located outside the library. If you own your own computer, you might even be able to view library catalogs via modem connection over the telephone.

Source Category 5: Books

For a topic like AIDS, because it is a relatively recently discovered disease — more recent than typhus, for example, or polio, about which much has been written — you are going to find that periodicals supply the bulk of useful information. The book collection will be helpful, however, and should be checked.

The key to a library's book collection is its catalog. The key to the catalog is the list compiled by subject authorities. This list tells you what subjects to check.

We don't want to lecture you on the intricacies of library science here, but we should point out that sometimes the subject you have in mind is called something else by the people who determine the subject headings that libraries use. If you think of a subject one way but the books and periodicals are listed under other subject headings because the subject authorities thought another way, you may not find what the library has to offer on your topic. Here's an example: You need something for your abnormal psychology course, so you approach the catalog,

The computer is a terrific information-gathering tool; now if it could only write your paper for you . . .

computer, or periodical index thinking *abnormal psychology*. However, the subject authorities who construct the lists of official ("legal") terms thought, *Psychology, pathological*. So what? Well, the person who checks a catalog for *abnormal psychology* may come away empty-handed — nothing may be listed under that "illegal" heading. Since the subject authorities determined that the term used for abnormal psychology is *Psychology, pathological*, it's under that ("legal") subject heading that you'll find most of the relevant books in the library's catalog.

In many libraries the subject authority list is the *Library of Congress Subject Headings*, which will normally be prominently displayed near the catalog. Another good strategy would be to ask a librarian for help at this point. And remember to watch for cross-references to broader, related terms.

On page 79 of the *Library of Congress Subject Headings* for 1989 (12th ed.), you will find this heading:

AIDS (Disease)

You will also see some entries prefaced by capital letters:

BT (broader term)

RT (related term)

NT (narrower term)

This means that the subjects so tagged are also relevant to your search and can be pursued in the catalog. Again, ask a librarian on duty to explain the potential of these associated terms.

AIDS (Disease) is a "legal" term, so let's go to the library's book catalog. This may be in a computer, a card catalog, or some other format. Under *AIDS* there are a number of titles, two of which are listed here, along with our outline/ relevance information.

Book 1

AIDS: The New Workplace Issue; AMA Management Briefing. New York: American Management Association, 1988.

Noting the call number — RC 607 .A26 A365 — you check the location and retrieve the book.

A.	Definition	—
B.	Importance	AIDS is not just a health issue, it's also an economic/business one.
C.	Effect	Personal views and the law might be in conflict, and management needs to be aware of the law.
D.	Reaction	As long as hiring and termination decisions are made on the basis of testing results, some people may seek to escape testing. This could be dangerous.

Book 2

AIDS: The Women. Pittsburgh: Cleis Press, 1988.

This is a collection of essays, several of which are highly likely to fit with your outline. Again you check the call number and retrieve the book.

A.	Definition	—
B.	Importance	Few women are prepared for the challenges that caring for AIDS victims presents.
C.	Effect	I have become aware of — and compassionate about — what AIDS victims and their loved ones go through.
D.	Reaction	What a complicated, gut-wrenching issue AIDS is!

Source Category 6: Opinions and Points of View

Source: *Editorials on File*. July-December, 1987.
> Index = Acquired Immune Deficiency Syndrome (AIDS) Leaders quit presidential panel 1152-1157

Nobody sees and reports things entirely objectively. Each observer—reporter brings a whole collection of experiences, attitudes, biases, and preconceived notions to the process of perception and transfer of information. The good ones try to control for these contaminants; the poorer ones overlook or disguise their biases. One kind of reporting that makes no attempt to disguise its point of view is the editorial. An editorial is an unabashed personal opinion written by a newspaper or magazine editor. Sometimes it is useful to see collections of editorial comment on an issue, and that is why *Editorials on File* is a useful source of information. As you might suspect, this volume is a compilation of editorials from newspapers from all over the country.

A.	Definition	—
B.	Importance	—
C.	Effect	Some panel members claim lack of support from the Reagan administration.
D.	Reaction	As long as there is political bickering and in-fighting among doctors, we cannot have much of a national response to the AIDS crisis.

In the preface of these kinds of sources, you can usually find instructions that will help you read and decipher the entries and find the cited material. Ask a librarian for help. Mention that you are interested in "current opinion" about your topic. The librarian may recommend that you consult government documents or newspaper indexes, or even that you contact a local person who is an authority on your topic.

Additional Resources

The research procedure you just read about outlines a plan of action that should help you find some information on just about any topic. The more experience you gain in seeking, retrieving, analyzing, and reporting information, the more you will refine your own personal strategies. The specific encyclopedias, periodical indexes, book catalogs, and "opinions" titles mentioned here may not help you with each and every topic you search, but others might. Once you are familiar with the general *categories* of information sources, then you can look for alternative choices within those categories. For example, a library may have as many as ten general encyclopedias, fifteen periodical indexes or abstracts, and several "opinion" and "current awareness" items, like *The New York Times Index*, *Keesing's Record of World Events*, or *Facts on File*.

You will probably find that the *librarian* is the most important source. Never hesitate to ask for assistance. When you do, you help librarians do the job they were trained and hired to perform — to assist *you*. In dealing with librarians, be prepared to answer the type of questions a librarian might ask you, such as the following:

1. What is your topic?
2. Can you tell me a little about your topic?
3. How much information do you need?
4. Is this for an assignment?

DOING THE ACTUAL EXERCISE

Now you are ready to begin work on your *real* assignment. (Refer back to pages 142–144.) You have a topic, you have a partner or two, and you have an outline that you are going to use to determine whether the information you retrieve is relevant. *You can use the worksheets that follow to record your findings, or you can make your own.* If you make your own, perhaps on 3 × 5 cards, then you can later arrange them in whatever order you wish and use them as notes for your 5-minute presentation. And don't forget: *Ask for help often!*

Once you have recorded information on the following worksheets, we suggest you copy them so that each group member can have a set of worksheets. The question may come up: Does each of us have to do a separate search, or may we do just one and then copy the same information on each set of worksheets? We suggest you each do individual searches on your team's topic. That way your group will have, say, six *Readers' Guide* articles instead of only two. Most important, you will each gain *personal* survival experience if you each contribute your own search to the project. This will supply the added benefit of giving you the valuable experience of paring and sorting a large collection of sources into a *manageable* number for your presentation.

And speaking of *management*, it is extremely important that your group practice your presentation so that you can deliver it in the assigned time limit. Your instructor will be doing you no favors if, in a misdirected attack of niceness, he or she permits you to ramble on beyond the time limit. Why? One of the features of the Information Age is that there is lots of it, and people are constantly being bombarded with messages, only some of which are important. The unimportant information is *noise*, and people will tune it out. This becomes significant when you realize that *60 percent* of you are going to make your living creating, processing, and transferring information. In this kind of arena you cannot afford to have people tune you out. What and how well you communicate is going to determine how successful you will be.

TOPIC _____

Source Category 1: General Encyclopedia

Title _____

Term Used in Index _____

Index Page _____

References to This Term	**Vol.**	**Page**
_____	_____	_____
_____	_____	_____
_____	_____	_____

Any cross-references to related terms? _____

A. _Definition_ _____

_____

_____

B. _Importance_ _____

_____

_____

C. _Effect_ _____

_____

_____

D. _Reaction_ _____

_____

_____

Source Category 2: Subject Encyclopedia
(Ask a librarian for location.)

Title _____

Term Used in Index _____

Index Page _____

References to This Term	**Vol.**	**Page**
_____	_____	_____
_____	_____	_____
_____	_____	_____

Any cross-references to this term? _____

A. _Definition_ _____

_____

_____

B. _Importance_ _____

_____

_____

C. *Effect* _____

_____

_____

D. *Reaction* _____

_____

_____

Source Category 3: Periodical Indexes, General

Title and Date _____

Term Used in Index _____

Index Page _____

Any cross-references to this term? _____

Article 1

Article Title _____

Magazine Title _____

Vol. _____ Page _____ Date _____

Call Number (Ask a librarian to help you use the serials list.)

_____

Location in Library _____

A. *Definition* _____

_____

_____

B. *Importance* _____

_____

C. *Effect* _____

_____

D. *Reaction* _____

_____

_____

Article 2

Article Title _____

Magazine Title _____

Vol. _____ Page _____ Date _____

Call Number _____

Location in Library _____

A. *Definition*　＿＿＿＿＿＿＿＿＿＿＿＿＿＿＿＿＿＿＿＿

　　　　　　　　　＿＿＿＿＿＿＿＿＿＿＿＿＿＿＿＿＿＿＿＿

　　　　　　　　　＿＿＿＿＿＿＿＿＿＿＿＿＿＿＿＿＿＿＿＿

B. *Importance*　＿＿＿＿＿＿＿＿＿＿＿＿＿＿＿＿＿＿＿＿

　　　　　　　　　＿＿＿＿＿＿＿＿＿＿＿＿＿＿＿＿＿＿＿＿

　　　　　　　　　＿＿＿＿＿＿＿＿＿＿＿＿＿＿＿＿＿＿＿＿

C. *Effect*　＿＿＿＿＿＿＿＿＿＿＿＿＿＿＿＿＿＿＿＿

　　　　　　　　　＿＿＿＿＿＿＿＿＿＿＿＿＿＿＿＿＿＿＿＿

　　　　　　　　　＿＿＿＿＿＿＿＿＿＿＿＿＿＿＿＿＿＿＿＿

D. *Reaction*　＿＿＿＿＿＿＿＿＿＿＿＿＿＿＿＿＿＿＿＿

　　　　　　　　　＿＿＿＿＿＿＿＿＿＿＿＿＿＿＿＿＿＿＿＿

　　　　　　　　　＿＿＿＿＿＿＿＿＿＿＿＿＿＿＿＿＿＿＿＿

Source Category 4: Periodical Indexes, Subject

Title and Date ＿＿＿＿＿＿＿＿＿＿＿＿＿＿＿＿＿＿＿＿

Term Used in Index ＿＿＿＿＿＿＿＿＿＿＿＿＿＿＿＿＿＿

Index Page ＿＿＿＿＿＿＿＿＿＿＿＿＿＿＿＿＿＿＿＿＿

Any cross-references to this term? ＿＿＿＿＿＿＿＿＿＿＿

Article 1

Article Title ＿＿＿＿＿＿＿＿＿＿＿＿＿＿＿＿＿＿＿＿

Magazine Title ＿＿＿＿＿＿＿＿＿＿＿＿＿＿＿＿＿＿＿＿

Vol. ＿＿＿＿＿　Page ＿＿＿＿＿　Date ＿＿＿＿＿

Call Number ＿＿＿＿＿＿＿＿＿＿＿＿＿＿＿＿＿＿＿＿

Location in Library ＿＿＿＿＿＿＿＿＿＿＿＿＿＿＿＿＿＿

A. *Definition*　＿＿＿＿＿＿＿＿＿＿＿＿＿＿＿＿＿＿＿＿

　　　　　　　　　＿＿＿＿＿＿＿＿＿＿＿＿＿＿＿＿＿＿＿＿

　　　　　　　　　＿＿＿＿＿＿＿＿＿＿＿＿＿＿＿＿＿＿＿＿

B. *Importance*　＿＿＿＿＿＿＿＿＿＿＿＿＿＿＿＿＿＿＿＿

　　　　　　　　　＿＿＿＿＿＿＿＿＿＿＿＿＿＿＿＿＿＿＿＿

　　　　　　　　　＿＿＿＿＿＿＿＿＿＿＿＿＿＿＿＿＿＿＿＿

C. *Effect*　＿＿＿＿＿＿＿＿＿＿＿＿＿＿＿＿＿＿＿＿

　　　　　　　　　＿＿＿＿＿＿＿＿＿＿＿＿＿＿＿＿＿＿＿＿

　　　　　　　　　＿＿＿＿＿＿＿＿＿＿＿＿＿＿＿＿＿＿＿＿

D. *Reaction*　＿＿＿＿＿＿＿＿＿＿＿＿＿＿＿＿＿＿＿＿

　　　　　　　　　＿＿＿＿＿＿＿＿＿＿＿＿＿＿＿＿＿＿＿＿

　　　　　　　　　＿＿＿＿＿＿＿＿＿＿＿＿＿＿＿＿＿＿＿＿

Article 2

Article Title _____

Magazine Title _____

Vol. _____   Page _____   Date _____

Call Number _____

Location in Library _____

A. *Definition*   _____

_____

_____

B. *Importance*   _____

_____

_____

C. *Effect*   _____

_____

_____

D. *Reaction*   _____

_____

_____

Source Category 5: Books

Library of Congress Subject Headings
Ask a librarian for the name of the subject authority list in your library. It may not be the *LC* list. Check.

Page on which your term is listed _____

"Legal" terms for your topic

_____

_____

_____

Use these subjects when searching for your topic in the library's catalog.

Book 1

Author _____

Title _____

Call Number _____

Location _____

A. *Definition*   _____

_____

B. *Importance*   _____

_____

_____

C. *Effect* _____

_____

_____

D. *Reaction* _____

_____

_____

Book 2

Author _____

Title _____

Call Number _____

Location _____

A. *Definition* _____

_____

_____

B. *Importance* _____

_____

_____

C. *Effect* _____

_____

_____

D. *Reaction* _____

_____

_____

Source Category 6: Opinions and Points of View

Title and Date _____

Term in Index _____

Page to Which I Am Referred _____

A. *Definition* _____

_____

_____

B. *Importance* _____

_____

_____

C. *Effect* _____

_____

_____

D. *Reaction* _____

_____

_____

EVALUATION CHECKLIST

Here's a checklist you may use to evaluate your group or other groups.

Speaker _____

Criteria	Comment
Speaker "knew" topic.	_____ _____
Speaker organized presentation well.	_____ _____
Speaker *talked* to us; he or she did not read to us.	_____ _____
Speaker had full audience contact (not just front row or *me*).	_____ _____
Speaker showed evidence of practice and effort devoted to this project.	_____ _____

JOURNAL

This chapter argues that information is power. Reflect on your personal, working, and academic life. How do your possession and use of information in these three domains give you power, such as the ability to influence people or events? How helpful was Exercise 8.1 in teaching you how to deal with your librarians and find your way around the library? Did it improve your ability to retrieve, evaluate, and use information? How can you further improve these skills?

SUGGESTIONS FOR FURTHER READING

Gates, Jean K. *Guide to the Use of Libraries and Information Services*, 6th ed. New York: McGraw-Hill, 1988.

Kessler, Lauren, and Duncan McDonald. *The Search: Information Gathering for the Mass Media*. Belmont, Calif.: Wadsworth, 1992.

Naisbitt, John, and Patricia Aburdene. *Megatrends 2000: Ten New Directions for the 1990's*. New York: Morrow, 1990.

Roth, Audrey J. *The Research Paper: Process, Form, and Content*, 6th ed. Belmont, Calif.: Wadsworth, 1989.

Toffler, Alvin. *Previews & Premises*. New York: Morrow, 1983.

Wurman, Richard S. *Information Anxiety*. New York: Doubleday, 1989.

Writing for Success

Carolyn Matalene

Writing for Success

So what is my point in this paper? If I knew that, I'd be able to write. But I don't know it and I can't write. Not a word. And the more I stare at that blank computer screen, the more I can't write. No wonder; I don't have anything much to say anyway. I didn't come to college to be a writer. My major's accounting, for crying out loud. Accountants don't write . . . do they? This is the electronic age. Now if I could put my ideas down on tape and hand that in, that would be cool.

THE NIGHT WAS DARK AND STORMY.
THE DARK NIGHT WAS STORMY.
IT WAS STORMY THAT DARK NIGHT.
IT WAS A DARK AND STORMY NIGHT.

CAROLYN MATALENE *is an associate professor of English at the University of South Carolina, Columbia. In her own inimitable way she offers three profiles of herself. So take your pick.*

1. Stuffiest: "Directed the freshman English program for four years and since then has taught in China, Liberia, and most recently in Finland on a Fulbright. For the past five years she has been writing coach at The State *newspaper, Columbia, S.C., and has been on the faculty of The Poynter Institute for Media Studies in St. Petersburg, Florida."*

2. Somewhat less stuffy: "An award-winning teacher, she has also published Worlds of Writing, *a collection of articles by writing teachers who work with writers in professional settings."*

3. Just little ol' me: "I like teaching writing at home and abroad, to freshmen and seniors, to graduate students and professionals. I not only get to learn about everything in the whole world, I also get to watch writers grow and learn and change as people. Students who are confident as writers stand taller and talk louder and try harder because they know they have more power to effect change. To me, nothing is more exciting and rewarding than helping students discover themselves as writers."

Unfortunately many college students (and even some of their professors) feel uneasy about writing. Some students are so fearful of having to write that they will actually refuse to sign up for courses that require papers.

Yet not being asked to write means being short-changed as a student, because writing is at the center of what a college education is all about. Being educated means being skillful with language — able to control language instead of being controlled by it, confident that you can speak or write effectively instead of feeling terrified. When successful people explain how they rose to the top, they often emphasize their skills as communicators: "I could write better than anyone else, and the boss liked that," or "I was the only person who could explain things simply." Again and again the essence of success lies in being an effective speaker and writer, being able to explain issues clearly and to convince others.

This chapter presents a gradual program for easing you into the role of writer. If you follow along, do the exercises, and incorporate some of the suggestions into your regular study practices, you will not only *feel* better about writing, you'll *be* better at it too. You'll get better grades and know why you are getting them.

GETTING STARTED — PERSONAL WRITING

If you really do feel fearful about writing, perhaps you need some "therapy." That's what the next exercise is all about.

EXERCISE 9.1   Your Composing Process (or What's Wrong with It)

Take some time right now to write about your composing process or, if you prefer, what's wrong with your composing process. Get your pen moving on the page, write as fast as you can, and don't correct anything. You are writing this only for yourself. No one else will read it, so let it all hang out: "I hate to write because . . ." Fill a page — or several pages — with what you do when you write and how you feel about it. Make yourself keep writing — and writing fast — for at least 15 minutes.

What did you find out? That you really do hate to write? Or that it's not so bad once you get into it? Did you have some ideas that surprised you or that you didn't expect to have? That is one of the major reasons for writing — to discover what you actually think and feel. Perhaps that sounds strange. After all, how could you not know what you think and feel? Easy — by proceeding semiconsciously, by reacting instead of acting, by staying in neutral. Writing forces you to kick your mind into gear, to engage with ideas, to wrestle with language, to express your thoughts and feelings in words. When you write, *you* have to be the agent. Thus writing is extremely valuable as a technique of self-discovery, of therapy, and finally, of learning.

The writing you just did — *personal writing* — can help you sort out your thoughts and feelings. Perhaps you already know this and keep a diary — many people do because they have found that writing to themselves helps them cope. It can help you, too. Quickly filling a page or two with thoughts, feelings, problems, worries, frustrations, hopes, and dreams usually makes you feel better, often helps you sort out your feelings ("I really do like my roommate"), and may help you solve problems. Give it a try, especially when you are feeling really down, or really angry.

GETTING INVOLVED — PRIVATE WRITING

Personal writing can be great therapy, and it may help you stay in college — or stop berating your roommate — but of course it won't get you through college. To succeed as a college student, you have to deliver according to rules you didn't make. Some students misunderstand the rules when they come to college. They believe that they can "get an education" the way they get a new car or a new job. They think that if they "learn" what's in the book and become repositories of information, then they will become educated. They are wrong. The truth is, you can't "get educated" because education isn't an event that happens or a commodity that you purchase. Rather, it is a process that you take part in for the rest of your life by becoming a learner. Being a *rememberer*, or a passive knower, may get you through some of your exams, but you won't really succeed unless you become a *learner*. A learner does more than remember. A learner synthesizes and evaluates, questions and considers, sees relationships, and draws conclusions. A learner develops an interior voice and exhibits purpose and control.

If you want to be a learner, not just a fact-rememberer, take the next step as a writer: Move on from *personal* writing, which is mostly about your feelings, to *private* writing, which is mostly about your thoughts. (Of course the two can't be completely separated, but writing about your history course is probably less personal than writing about your roommate.) *Private writing* is writing that you undertake as a way of learning, that you practice as a technique for studying, that only you see because it is not intended to communicate knowledge or information to anyone but yourself. Private writing works as a medium for you to communicate with yourself as a learner, asking your own questions about what you read and hear, questioning your own answers, and eventually becoming fluent in the language of a discipline. Of course you will also have to produce *public writing*: the essays, exams, research papers, and critical analyses for your courses. In public writing you must go through the process of revision and editing; your writing must be finished and polished. By contrast, private writing can remain unfinished, exploratory, inconclusive—a way of remembering facts and terms even if their meaning is not yet clear to you.

In order to become an active participant in any field of learning, you have to master the language of that field. In any course you take, you need to write as well as read, speak as well as listen. Some students start out thinking that reading is enough. And certainly readers can be active learners if they engage with the text, ask questions, make connections and comparisons, evaluate—if, in a word, they think. If you've read Chapters 4–6, you already know that in order to really learn something, either in class or from a textbook, you need to combine listening and reading with a faithful system of taking and reviewing notes.

I would like to suggest another, complementary strategy to the steps suggested in the earlier chapters. For each of your courses use one section of your course notebook for *reading notes*. Take your sociology text, for example, and read a portion, perhaps a chapter. Don't underline or highlight every sentence. Instead read thoughtfully and then close the book. Now, in your reading notebook, write a brief summary in your own words of what you read: What is the chapter really about? Next, write some of your own reactions, comments, and thoughts: What does this chapter make you think of? What can you relate it to? What examples from your own experience can you think of that would prove the major points? Or what examples can you think of that would disprove those points? What questions do you have? What seems strange? What seems unclear or hard to understand? If you could ask your professor some questions about this material, what would they be?

Write. And write some more. Don't worry about spelling or sentence structure, just write as fast as you can. Remember, no one is going to read this but you. As you write, you will have more ideas; that's the fun of writing, the infinite creativity language allows its users. So enjoy it. Read another chapter and write again. If you hate the text, say so and explain why. By writing, you are now painlessly increasing your chances of remembering the material because you are involved in it. You are also becoming literate in the field you are reading about; you are making the language of the subject your own. You are engaged. And that is the essence of what any professor wants from any student — not agreement, but engagement with the subject.

EXERCISE 9.2   Engaging with the Subject

Write your thoughts about the chapter so far. What is it about? What do you think of what you have read? What questions does it raise for you?

RESPONDING — PROCEDURES OF THOUGHT

You can write in response to anything — a chapter in a textbook, a novel or a part of a novel, a poem, a lesson, a lab session, a lecture. And when you do write in response to what you are studying, you learn a lot more. Research shows that students who engage in extended writing about a topic are capable of more complex thoughts and are better able to see relationships among concepts. When you write in response to a text or a topic, your mind inevitably performs the mental procedures that all humans use to analyze experience and to learn systematically. You try different ways of looking; you practice *procedural* knowledge.

There are a number of common *procedures of thought* you can use as you respond to reading by writing. The first and most important is simply to read for the main idea: What is the main, central, or most important idea presented in this section or chapter? Once you have answered that question, you can choose from a number of analytical strategies to organize your thoughts and your writing.

Comparison and Contrast

One way to respond to a text is to draw comparisons: "What this chapter seems to be saying is *like* what we studied last week in this way." or "This chapter is *different* from what we have studied so far in these ways." Spend some time in your notebook comparing and contrasting, writing about similarities and differences. You can compare concepts or events or terms or people. Comparison is perhaps the most powerful learning tool at your disposal. Some learning specialists think that comparing is the basis of all learning, that new understanding results from matching — or comparing — the unfamiliar with the familiar, or new information with information we already have. (We can't avoid comparing, it seems, a new friend with an old one, this teacher with that one, tonight's dinner with last night's, and so on.) Another good reason for thinking in terms of comparison is that comparison questions frequently turn up on exams: Compare the economic development of Chile with that of Argentina; compare Wordsworth's theory of poetry with Pope's; compare treatments for dyslexia. Try writing some comparisons of your own *before* the exam.

EXERCISE 9.3   Comparing

Select a course you are now taking. Do some private writing (or perhaps write a note to a close friend) comparing it to a related course you took in high school. How is it similar? How is it different?

Cause and Effect

In some courses — especially history — thinking in terms of cause and effect is important: This caused the uprising; these were the major causes of World War I; these were the major effects of Roosevelt's domestic policies. Focusing on cause and effect is also a common and powerful way to structure our experience, one that we rely on again and again as we try to solve problems, effect change, and achieve new understanding. Human beings are human partly because they are always asking questions: What would happen if we mixed nitrogen and glycerine? What will be the effects of a tax cut? Competency test? A lower speed limit?

EXERCISE 9.4   Cause and Effect

What "caused" you to decide to go to college, or to this college in particular? What have the "effects" been so far? Write privately about this cause–effect relationship.

Narration

Another important thought procedure for writing in any historically oriented course is getting the order of events straight: This is what happened; this is the story of . . . Writing that presents a sequence of events is called a narrative, and of all of the different ways of structuring writing, the narrative seems to be our favorite. Being able to tell yourself the story of an event or a discovery or a work of literature is an effective way to remember it.

EXERCISE 9.5   Narration

In private writing summarize what happened in one of your classes today. Narrate exactly what happened, in the order it happened. Make it sound like a story. What points was the teacher making? How did you and other members of the class respond? How did this particular class session fit into the course as a whole?

Theories and Opinions

In a course that involves learning the theories of "major thinkers," such as Marx or Darwin or Freud, it is important that you do some writing in which you explain what the thinker thought — in your own words: This is what Freud thought about infantile sexuality; this is what Marx thought about surplus value. Feel free to write down what *you* think: "This is my interpretation of Nietzsche's phrase 'God is dead.'" or "This is my opinion of Churchill's foreign policy." You will also discover that sometimes your professor will disagree with the author of a textbook. Write about that: "Samuelson says this, but my instructor disagrees and says this instead. But I think they both are wrong because . . ." Now you are getting practice in keeping straight who thinks what or which ideas belong to whom. And that, of course, is what academic discourse is all about.

You don't have to be serious all the time either. You might write about what would happen if Freud went to Jung for treatment or what Matthew Arnold would say about the poetry of e.e. cummings or how Mozart would react to the Beatles, or Beethoven to U2. Or you could write a letter to your mother telling her how complicated or strange or interesting or unusual your philosophy course is and how you feel about that.

EXERCISE 9.6   Theory or Opinion

Choose a theory you have heard about recently in one of your classes or read about in your general reading. Or choose an opinion you heard someone express recently on the radio or television or in person. In private writing or a note to a close friend, try to clarify your understanding of what that person meant. In what respects do you agree or disagree? Why?

Explanation and Argumentation

The final thought procedure is explanation and argumentation: This is what ought to be done; this is the best course of action. One of the best ways to make sure you understand a principle or a theory or a historical event is to write a pretend letter to someone who is not in your course. In the letter you should explain clearly to this open-minded but ignorant person what the issue is, why it matters, and why any truly educated person should know about it. You will start to sound like an expert, and sounding like an expert is also what academic discourse requires. Experts are often convinced that their version or solution is the right one, so explaining and arguing are two more useful writing responses that you can practice.

EXERCISE 9.7   **Explanation and Argumentation**

In private writing or a note to a close friend, argue for one of the following: (1) in favor of something you think should happen on campus that isn't happening now, or against something that is happening that you think should stop; or (2) against taking a particular class, and for taking a different class instead.

The Essayist Attitude

As you write privately about your reading or about your classes, you will be developing what has been called "the essayist attitude." That is, you will be engaging in thinking about what you are perceiving. Writing about what happened in class today or what you learned from the discussion or what you didn't understand or what changed your mind will help you to examine your life as student. It will also help you to become more comfortable with the philosophical approach. As you learn to adopt the essayist attitude, you will probably get better at writing the essays required in freshman English. And all the while you will be improving your communication skills.

GETTING CONTROL – FROM PRIVATE TO PUBLIC WRITING

Now that you've acquired some specific analytical skills and practiced using them in your private writing, you're ready to apply them to your public writing — essays, reports, exams, and so on. The transition from private writing

Stop, Read, and Listen!

How well informed do you keep about what's happening in the world? If you're not sure, answer the following questions:

1. Do you listen to National Public Radio? When you're getting dressed in the morning, do you tune in to "Morning Edition"? When you're exercising after class, do you listen to "All Things Considered" on your headset? Do you listen to your campus station? What other good local or national radio information programs do you listen to regularly?

2. Do you read your campus newspaper? Do you read the local paper every day? On Sunday do you set aside some time to read a good national paper, such as *The New York Times, The Washington Post,* or the *Los Angeles Times*?

3. Do you read a magazine or two every week? Along with *Time* or *Newsweek,* do you read *Rolling Stone, The New Yorker, Sports Illustrated, Harper's, Vogue, Vanity Fair, Esquire,* or *The Atlantic*? Do you read any of the many specialized magazines on computers, sports, cars, boats, and so on? Do you go to the open periodical room in your library and let yourself do some random reading every now and then?

4. Do you ever read some good current nonfiction? Have you ever tapped the wealth of living writers helping us make sense of our world — among them John McPhee, Joan Didion, Jane Kramer, Tracy Kidder, Garry Wills, Mark Singer, Lewis Thomas, Roger Angell, Tom Wolfe, Michael Herr, Annie Dillard, Paul Theroux, Russell Baker, and Frances Fitzgerald?

The more you know about what's going on, the more you'll have to say, both in and outside class. The more you read, listen, and inform yourself in general, the better you'll write.

to public writing terrifies many students, but the more you practice private writing, the less you will need to worry about exams and papers. You will gain confidence as a writer because you will be developing a composing process that works for you.

Writing to Study for Exams

In addition to the strategies discussed in Chapter 6, you can prepare for a test or exam by writing. You might start your review by jotting down individual words—all of the special words or terms that were used in a given course, such as *Manifest Destiny* or *Mutual Assured Destruction* or *epanalepsis* and *anadiplosis.* Then you can write a paragraph about each one, defining the term, explaining it, giving some examples, and so on. By doing this you are preparing yourself for that favorite exam mode of so many in-

structors, the "ident." Professors are fond of asking you to "briefly but ade-quately identify any ten of the following." If you are studying for a literature course, you might write down all of your (or the professor's) favorite lines or phrases from the works you have read: "Call me Ishmael." "Do I dare to eat a peach?" "Let me not to the marriage of true minds admit impediments." (If you can't remember any such lines, refer back to your books.)

After you have warmed up on some terms or lines, try writing a summary of the entire course for that pleasant but ignorant imaginary person you wrote to before. Explain what this course is really about, why it matters, what the essence is, and why everyone should take it. Next, try to "psych" the professor. What questions are obviously and inevitably going to be on the exam? What questions did the professor say would appear on the test? Write them down. Then write the answers.

Writing to Organize

Write the answers? "That's going too far. I'll do that in the exam but not now," most students say. You may think that writing the answer to an anticipated tough essay exam question represents a rather grim way to study. It might also seem that your creativity and spontaneity would suffer if you wrote the answer down ahead of time and that your answer would sound boring. Fair enough. But at least get in the habit of *outlining* the answers to some of the exam questions you have imagined. Then you will be ready to outline the answers during the exam before you start to write. While the outline ranks as one of the most despised study tools and least-liked means of preparation for writing ever required of innocent students by sadistic teachers (anyone who likes outlines or outlining is probably not to be trusted!), it is an extremely useful vehicle. Call it planning instead of outlining if you like, but whatever the word, the key issue is *organization*. And organizing, or building a structure, is the essential transformation that must occur between the writing you do *for your own learning* and the writing you do *to show that you have learned*. Your papers and exams will be read and judged by someone else — a reader who is an expert.

Writing to Communicate

The composing process refers to the stages a writer goes through in order to achieve results that are worth being read. Private writing can just flow as a stream of consciousness, wandering out of the main channel, stopping and starting. But public writing, because it must provide readers with a structure, doesn't happen so spontaneously. In private writing the focus is on the first stage of the composing process, *invention*. During the invention stage (some call it prewriting) writers concentrate on thinking, on questioning and connecting and generating and gathering and analyzing and evaluating. Of course private writing also means drafting, since words and sentences do appear on the page; but the drafting is fast and free, with little concern for grammar, syntax, sentence structure, and so on. When you engage in public writing, however, the drafting must yield more structured discourse; somewhere along the way, either on paper or in your head, planning must take place.

Moving from private to public writing requires you to focus on structure. If you have been studying all along — and studying, you should realize by now, means reading *and* writing — then you have been practicing invention all along. When exam time comes or when the paper assignment is given, you have available an abundance of content that you must now shape into the proper *form*. A successful piece of public writing will be based on a plan, an organizational principle, a structure so clear that a reader could outline it if need be.

Establishing Structure. The obvious technique for success in public writing — but one that many students never figure out — is to look for the tip-offs to an appropriate overall structure in the question or the assignment itself as explained in Chapter 6. Are you being asked to *compare* two things? To *explain* the effects of something? To *summarize* a theory? To *relate* what happened? To *interpret* a text or an event? Remember to focus on the structure words in the question or the assignment and do what they tell you, not something else.

The next step is to write a plan (an outline) that corresponds to the task. In an essay exam you will need to write the plan quickly, but you must take the time to do it. The plan will help you focus on the question asked instead of drifting and also help you budget your remaining time. For a term paper or a critical analysis you might spend a major portion of your time on the plan. Figuring out what you are going to say and how you are going to say it — that is, establishing your structure — is hard work, but it's well worth it.

Some writers, however, cannot or will not or do not plan before they write. They just plunge into writing — the same way you do in private writing. Their writing "grows from the top." The problem with this approach is that, if an idea or plan or project fails, it's much easier to discard a plan — a page with some words and arrows and circles on it — than to throw away an entire draft of hard-won sentences. Writers who do not plan, who write by drafting (and some excellent writers do proceed this way), insist they don't really throw away sentences; it only looks that way for a while. Eventually everything gets used, but maybe in a different place.

Whether you plan before you write or plan while you write doesn't matter in the long run if you are accomplishing effective writing. What does matter is that the writing you hand in goes through the transformation from private to public and has a clear structure apparent to readers.

Maybe you are not quite sure about what the word *structure* really means when applied to writing. Don't be alarmed; you're not alone, because structure is hard to explain. When applied to writing, structure means the conceptual "skeleton" that holds the writing together. In carefully structured discourse each sentence relates to the main idea of the paragraph, each paragraph relates to the idea of that section, and each section relates to the plan of the whole. Think of structure as a hierarchical or pyramidal diagram, like the flowchart of a corporation or the chain of command in the military. Readers expect writing to be structured hierarchically. They also expect — and insist upon — writing that moves up and down the different levels on the pyramid, from abstract to concrete, from general to specific, from assertion to proof. Readers find such writing both readable and convincing. When writing remains on the same level, readers lose interest.

In fact levels of generality is what our unpopular friend the outline is all about. An outline is a diagram that shows hierarchical structure; the main points (I, II, III, and so on) are general or abstract. They are supported or proved by less general or more specific statements (A, B, C, and so on). These in turn are supported by even more specific information (1, 2, 3, and so on), and even further down the abstraction ladder are the specifics or the details (a, b, c, and so on) that make writing believable and colorful and memorable. So try not to hate the outline; instead try to keep its structure in your mind's eye as you write, and remember that good writing does not stay at the same level of generality or abstraction all of the time. Hearing only about the decisions of the generals during a battle won't tell us everything about what happened; we need information from the front as well as from headquarters. This is a metaphoric way of saying that good writing offers us information from a variety of levels; good writing "moves" between the abstract and the concrete, between the general and the specific, between making assertions and proving them.

EXERCISE 9.8   Being Specific

Make up a generalization about the students at your school, such as "The problem with students here is apathy," "The students here are high achievers," or "Students today are too materialistic." Now provide a number of specifics to prove or support your statement. What does it take to convince your classmates that your generalization is accurate?

Why You Need a Computer . . . and How to Buy One

The Center for Scholarly Technology at the University of Southern California reports that in 1990, 14 percent of all U.S. community college students and 29 percent of all private university students owned their own personal computers. Those students have a great advantage over students who do not have computers.

A computer will help you become a better writer and raise your grades on written work. Word-processing programs make it easier to organize ideas, type them out, revise, and make corrections. Many programs will also check your spelling. Computers are useful in math, science, and business courses, as well as in other areas. Ask your instructors in these and other departments about the uses of computers. Whatever line of work you follow after college will almost certainly require some knowledge of computers.

Attached to a device called a "modem," computers can send and receive documents and information over the telephone. You may be able to use your computer to find out what books are available in the library or get information from a wide variety of on- and off-campus "bulletin boards" and reference sources including entire encyclopedias. You can also exchange "electronic mail" with other computer users.

Before you purchase your own computer, you should do several things. Take an introductory workshop on personal computers and talk with the instructor about your needs. Get friends to show you their computers. Then visit computer stores and ask for a demonstration. Be sure not to buy until you've shopped around and asked a lot of questions.

When you are ready to make that purchase, buy what other students and faculty on your campus are using so you can get help learning how to use the computer and can share equipment in an emergency. An Apple Macintosh computer or a computer that is "compatible" with IBM personal computers is your best bet.

Keep in mind, too, that most schools offer special student prices on computer hardware and/or program software. Compare these prices with those at the computer stores. Also, printers and other add-on equipment may be cheaper at discount outlets. Look in magazines that advertise discount sales.

A top-of-the-line computer system can run into the thousands of dollars, but you don't need to spend that kind of money. You can get a good, reliable computer, screen, and keyboard for under $1,000, a dot matrix printer for under $300, and a decent word-processing program package for under $75.

Drafting. *Drafting* (that is, writing it down) may be the stage in the composing process that induces the greatest terror. Those of us who plan before we write do so not because we are virtuous but because planning makes us feel braver as we face the blank page or the empty screen. Panic, it seems, is part of the process for most writers. As with the fear you feel at the top of the ski run or on the high dive or at center stage, you have to learn to deal with it. Many would-be writers intensify their own panic to the level of paralysis by trying to do two tasks at once, two tasks that can only be achieved separately. They try to get it down and gef it right at the same time.

Thus, for every thought the right brain sends out, the left brain pounces on it and says, "That's stupid! You dummy! Nobody would want to read that!" The writer writes a word, crosses it out, writes a sentence, and then crumples the page. It's called writer's block. The internal editor functions as a nagging and judgmental critic. That editor must be told to be quiet for awhile. Speak to your negative critic firmly: "Shut up! I don't have to listen to you. I will call on you later. Right now I need to take some risks, and I am too inspired to worry about your misplaced concerns."

As John McPhee, a talented professional writer, says, "You've got to put bad words down. And then massage them." What he means is his first draft, and your first draft, will probably be terrible, but only after you have something on paper can you work out the kinks. Perfectionism applied too early in the process prevents many intelligent people with interesting things to say from ever becoming capable or competent writers. In fact an important reason for engaging in private writing is that writing for yourself, quickly and furiously, will make you feel easier about drafting. You will not be embarrassed to express outlandish ideas on paper; you will be comfortable with sloppy phrasing. Messy prose can always be tidied up, revised, and edited. Blank pages can't be turned into anything.

Revising and Editing. After you have completed the first sloppy draft, it's time to unleash your internal editor. Try to read what you have written as a reader rather than as the writer. Of course, if you are writing within the time constraints of an examination, you must speed up the entire composing process. You can't revise your answer; there isn't time. (That's why the plan matters so much.) The best you can do is to proofread carefully, add a few words, correct the obvious errors, and turn it in. But essay exams are only one kind of public writing — a special, hurried kind that *requires* you to turn in first drafts. Many college students don't seem to understand this and turn in first drafts as final versions for all of their writing assignments. Not surprisingly, they tend to get C's — or worse.

If you want to get A's on your papers, you have to hand in final versions, not first drafts. That means putting your rough first draft through the process of revision, making it clearer, better organized, more tightly focused, more interesting, and livelier. You have to make your writing work for a reader who is in fact an expert — your professor. Some professors will offer to read a draft of your paper and make suggestions before the final version is due. *Always* take them up on this. Their criticisms and suggestions are the blueprints for your A.

Revising (getting the big plan right) and *editing* (tinkering with the words and sentences to make them say what you want them to say) are essential elements of the writing process. Professional writers invest extraordinary amounts of time and energy in revising and editing. So, as an amateur, you should certainly invest some. Actually, revising can be rewarding; turning an ordinary paper into a highly respectable one feels good — though it usually feels best after you are done. And editing — searching for just the right word and changing weak sentences into powerful ones — offers pleasures, too.

Some writers give their first drafts to someone else to read. The truth is, everybody needs an editor. Professional writers have professional editors. Finding a good editor for your own writing, though, can be tricky. Your roommate, your girl- or boyfriend, or your mom may like you so much that they are too kind. You need an editor who reads well and who has the courage to say to you — in a kindly way and only when asked — "No, I can't follow your argument. No, it doesn't make sense." You want an editor who

Writer Louise Erdrich (Tracks, The Beet Queen) and her husband, Michael Dorris (A Yellow Raft in Blue Water, The Broken Cord), also a writer, collaborate closely on their work. Erdrich says, "We're probably a lot harder on each other than other editors are with writers because we really have more at stake in each other's work. . . . I started out being very wary of collaboration and working together, but . . . I would really look at the work and I'd realize that it was better for the efforts."*

doesn't gush or flatter but who can be an honest critic, someone who wants you to succeed but who knows clarity from chaos, good writing from bad.

Most of us, after finishing a first draft and even a final draft, have little ability to accurately judge our own writing. We tend to over- or underestimate its worth. We give the piece an F if we are pessimists or an A if we are optimists, and lifelong optimists may turn into gloomy pessimists late at night. Writing, after all, is one of the most complex mental tasks we try. Not surprisingly, we aren't always good at judging our own creations. The editor who didn't experience the pain or the pleasure you invested in your draft may be a better judge of its worth than you are.

When you think your draft is as good as you can make it in the time available, summon up the English teacher editor from your subconscious. Let this purist worry about punctuation and spelling. If you are writing on a word processor — and you certainly should be — run the spelling check to catch the typos. (Not being able to type in the late twentieth century means you can't use a computer; that's like not being able to drive. Quick, take a typing course!)

*Michael Schumacher, "A Marriage of Minds." Writer's Digest (June 1991), p. 31.

When at last you hand in your great work, you probably will feel it still isn't perfect. That's okay — nothing is. The ultimate point is not the *product* anyway, but the *process*: What has this piece of writing done for you as a learner? How have you changed because you wrote it? As Robert Pirsig concluded in his novel *Zen and the Art of Motorcycle Maintenance*, "The real motorcycle is a cycle called yourself."

Writing, private or public, is finally not about grade points. Writing is really about you, about the richness of your life lived in language, about the fullness of your participation in your community and in your culture, about the effectiveness of your efforts to achieve change. The person attuned to the infinite creativity of language leads a richer life. So can you.

JOURNAL

Take stock of where you are now in your private, personal, and public writing. What are your strengths and weaknesses? What are your goals? If you could change anything about your writing process, what would it be? How important do you think your competence as a writer is to your future success?

SUGGESTIONS FOR FURTHER READING

Goldberg, Natalie. *Living the Writer's Life.* New York: Bantam New Age, 1990.

Gordon, Karen Elizabeth. *The Transitive Vampire: A Handbook of Grammar for the Innocent, the Eager, and the Doomed.* New York: Times Books, 1984.

Kobler, Helmut. *Campus Computing: How to Use Computers to Study Smarter, Earn Cash, and Even Improve Your Social Life at College.* Berkeley, Calif.: Lyceum, 1990.

Williams, Joseph M. *Style: Ten Lessons in Clarity and Grace,* 3rd ed. Glenview, Ill.: Scott, Foresman, 1989.

Woolever, Kristin R. *About Writing: A Rhetoric for Advanced Writers.* Belmont, Calif.: Wadsworth, 1991.

Zinsser, William. *On Writing Well: An Informal Guide to Writing Nonfiction,* 4th ed. New York: Harper & Row, 1990.

Zinsser, William. *Writing to Learn: How to Write and Think Clearly.* New York: Harper & Row, 1988.

10

The Liberal Arts and Critical Thinking

H. Thorne Compton

Foster E. Tait

The Liberal Arts and Critical Thinking

I think I'm going to major in business. Or maybe journalism. Pharmacy sounds good too. Something I can use. I mean, what's the use of history or English once you're out of school? For that matter, what good is psychology? Or philosophy? Or anthropology? What's the logic in taking that stuff anyway?

H. THORNE COMPTON *is chairman of the theatre, speech, and dance department at the University of South Carolina, Columbia.*

"When I started college," he says, "I was certain I wanted to be a journalist, and I imagined I would take a lot of courses in college on how to write exciting, investigative essays for newspapers. Instead I found myself taking required courses in European history, logic, French, and biology. I was frustrated, even angry. But my academic advisor had no sympathy. 'How are you going to be a writer,' he said, 'when you don't know anything to write about? If you want to write about human beings, you study the human species. That's what the liberal arts are about.'

"That was the first time I had really paid attention to the phrase 'liberal arts,' and I had no idea what it meant. But gradually I found I was learning more to think about and also learning how to think in different ways.

"While I eventually changed my career goal, I never gave up needing to understand 'the human species.' Today I see more clearly than ever how the liberal arts are the foundation for the rest of college learning."

FOSTER E. TAIT *is an associate professor of philosophy at the University of South Carolina, Columbia.*

"As director of advising in the philosophy department," he says, "I speak individually with over a hundred students at least twice a year. I find that a consistent academic problem with our majors concerns the organization of papers and the ability to draw correct conclusions from research. I experienced similar difficulties in college and learned that facts by themselves are not nearly as important as being able to use them correctly. I wish I had been able to study logic early in college. I also wish I had had a course in my freshman year dealing with the value and purpose of higher education."

What are the liberal arts? Where do they come from? Why do they matter? And what are the patterns of thought that you should bring to bear in any branch of the liberal arts? These are the central questions to be answered in this chapter.

WHAT ARE THE LIBERAL ARTS?

The "liberal" in "liberal arts" has nothing to do with politics — it comes from a Latin root word *liber*, which means "to free" (*liberate* comes from the same root). An art (from the Latin root *ars*) is a skill or ability. The **liberal arts** are those skills or abilities or understandings that set us free. We are liberated by understanding ourselves, and to do that we must understand our culture and environment. The liberal arts, then, are those studies that give us such understanding. These subjects focus on, among other things, how human beings think, behave, and express themselves.

The Liberal Arts in College

The liberal arts college is the ancestor of all of our modern colleges, universities, and professional training programs. Pythagoras, the ancient Greek mathematician and philosopher, can be considered the founder of the liberal

arts. He taught music, astronomy, geometry, and numbers theory as the four core subjects every educated person should know. These subjects were supplemented in the Middle Ages by three more — logic, grammar, and rhetoric — to comprise what were then accepted as the "seven liberal arts." Only in recent times has training in law, medicine, engineering, and even business administration (subjects once taught within the context of the liberal arts) been separated from a broad liberal arts environment. The liberal arts core is still central to a college or university education.

The liberal arts program is normally organized around several groups of disciplines that integrate knowledge from a variety of perspectives to form a **liberal education**. These usually include the following:

- ► **The arts**. The academic disciplines that explore and represent human thought and behavior in creative works. Creating works of art is a way of both coming to understand and expressing ideas and feelings.
- ► **The humanities**. The academic disciplines that study human thought and experience through the written record of what people have thought, felt, or experienced in a variety of cultures. Subject areas include languages, literature, philosophy, history, and religion.
- ► **The social sciences**. The academic disciplines that study human beings and their behavior from a variety of perspectives: as individuals (psychology), within social groups (sociology), within cultures (anthropology), or even as economic or political entities (economics and political science).
- ► **Quantitative studies**. The academic disciplines that create systems for describing the physical world or human behavior in abstract or mathematical terms. Subject areas include mathematics, statistics, and computer science.
- ► **The physical and biological sciences**. The academic disciplines that study the physical world, its inhabitants, and the symbolic relationships within it.

While colleges and universities are normally broken up into subject departments like history, English, and music, these subjects are all closely interrelated. For example, psychologists study human behavior, but in order to do so, they must understand and appreciate creations of the human mind — literature, fine arts, music, drama, and so on — which represent outward expressions of our inner behavior. They must also understand something about human biology and about the social systems that regulate human behavior and the way those systems evolved. In other words, to understand human behavior we must understand culture, the human environment, and the scientific and social forces that affect humans.

Most schools require a foundation of liberal arts courses during the freshman and sophomore years. These courses also transmit certain essential communication, thinking, and research skills.

EXERCISE 10.1   The Liberal Arts at Your School

Consult your college catalog to see what program is required of you. Write down what classes, if any, you are required to take in each of the five liberal arts areas. Do your school's requirements include each major area of the liberal arts — arts, humanities, social sciences, quantitative studies, and physical or biological sciences? What courses do you hope to take to broaden your knowledge and satisfy the requirements? Are there any areas you particularly want to explore even though they are not required?

The Liberal Arts in the Workplace

Many professional programs are now demanding more and more from the liberal arts components of their degrees. Like everyone else, practicing professionals must strive to understand and get along with others. Perhaps even more than most people they must communicate effectively and be able to respond to change.

Even most "nonprofessional" jobs require that you interact with co-workers or clients. As the president of one of our state's largest banks said, "Banking is not a money business, it's a people business. Banks don't create money, they must *persuade people* to put money into the bank." Knowing how the society works, knowing what the cultural conceptions of the people with whom you work are, knowing how to communicate effectively — all make you better at any job.

Several years ago *Time* magazine featured the computer as its "Man of the Year." At that time it was predicted that the home computer would become as ubiquitous, and as essential, as the dishwasher. A number of huge companies, with fantastic technology and extensive market research, sank billions of dollars into the home computer market. The product was truly remarkable and was produced at a reasonable price, yet within two years many of the companies were either out of the home computer market or out of business entirely. The problem was that while the computer was an amazing machine, it didn't do anything in the home that most people needed done or couldn't do more easily themselves. The decision most people had to make was not whether it would be nice to have a computer, but whether buying a computer was more important than buying snow tires or getting the heater fixed. Many computer companies now employ people with liberal arts backgrounds to figure out how to both sell and use the product.

EXERCISE 10.2   The Liberal Arts and Careers

In what ways might your studies in the liberal arts improve your ability to succeed at a career? Identify one potential career for yourself. Then select at least four of the following liberal arts disciplines, and explain how each might bear on your success in this career. Be prepared to discuss in class.

Career: _____

Liberal Arts Disciplines

Anthropology   Political science
Biology   Psychology
Chemistry   Sociology
Economics   Religion
Foreign languages
History   Other: _____
Literature
Mathematics   Other: _____

The Liberal Arts Beyond the Workplace

Just as the workplace has grown more complex and demanding, so has living and coping outside the workplace. As a parent, as a citizen, as a human being you will be faced with an enormous number of hard decisions when you leave college. You may be asked to vote on issues like the location of toxic waste disposal facilities in your community. To make a good decision you must synthesize a large quantity of often contradictory information presented by scientists and experts on both sides of the issue. Or you may be asked to decide whether your child should go to school with children who are infected with AIDS. Again you have to separate the real information from the propaganda and decide whom or what to believe. Such issues are extremely complex not only because they involve scientific and technical problems but also because the human dimension and the political and social consequences are so difficult to assess. You *will* have to make these decisions, and a broad education that sees the relationships among the scientific, social, political, cultural, and human dimensions will help you do so wisely.

But there's more. Most of us think that after college we will find a challenging, satisfying job in which we will work with interesting, creative people and make a significant contribution to society. In truth much of your working life is going to be spent doing the routine, frustrating, repetitious tasks that are a part of every job. You will spend a lot of time worrying about making mortgage payments, getting your children's teeth straightened, and dealing with the "dull gray stuff" of adulthood. This makes it even more important that there be something in your head besides what you *do* — that there be an aspect of yourself that is what you *are*.

You may know people who seem to live only for work and who have no identity or ideas outside of work. Your college education, especially in the liberal arts, should help you develop a self that transcends your job skills and allows you to be a thoughtful, creative, and fulfilled person outside of the work environment. That's a good goal to think about and work toward while you are in college.

A social worker friend of ours majored in history. We asked her once if history was a good major for social workers and she replied that it was "because it gives me something to think about when I'm going crazy." That may now seem a very limited "use" for your major, but it could become a very important one.

What can a liberal arts education give you? It can give you the tools you'll need to make the decisions you'll face throughout your life.

There is much about yourself and your life that you will spend a lifetime trying to understand — this is true of most people. Being able to put these problems into a context, knowing that people over the centuries have endured the same tragedies and uncertainties, having the ability to experience these feelings through the arts or see them examined by thinkers in psychology, philosophy, or theology, connects you to other people, to your culture, and to your species. This removes the sense of isolation and empowers you, according to Hamlet, to "take arms against a sea of troubles." While Hamlet may not have been too successful at resolving *his* conflicts, his eventual willingness to confront his fears and problems made him, in the end, a hero. Studying about how that student prince, home from school on vacation, dealt with some wrenching dilemmas might make *your* life seem a bit more comprehensible.

EXERCISE 10.3   Uses of the Liberal Arts

Choose one of the following issues:

1. Military spending
2. Effect of recycling on the environment
3. Mainstreaming retarded children into regular classrooms

Suppose you were a public speaker for an organization whose purpose was to influence people's thinking on this issue. Which of the following liberal arts disciplines might help you understand the issue and inform others about it? How would each discipline be useful? For the purposes of your topic, are there any disciplines that you think would definitely not be useful? Make notes for each discipline. Be prepared to discuss your notes and additional thoughts in class.

Anthropology _____

_____

Biology _____

_____

Chemistry _____

_____

Economics _____

_____

Foreign languages _____

_____

History _____

_____

Literature _____

_____

Mathematics _____

_____

Political science _____

_____

Psychology _____

_____

Sociology _____

_____

Religion _____

_____

_____ _____

other _____

_____ _____

other _____

CRITICAL THINKING

The liberal arts not only give you "something to think about," they also help you with the process of thinking more critically. One of the differences between high school and college that troubles some students is that college professors expect something different of them. As one of our students put it,

"In high school when the teacher asked you a question, he knew the answer and wanted to see if you knew it too. In college, they ask you questions that *no one* knows the answer to just to see what you will say." That's essentially true. In your earlier education you were building a knowledge base. It was important to learn facts and concepts and their applications. To make sure you were learning the "facts," you were most often tested on what you *knew*. Unfortunately this process implied that there was usually a "right" and a "wrong" answer and that being wrong was bad. When in doubt about an answer, you may have learned that it was best just to *keep quiet*.

Being Willing to Take Risks

While there are still a lot of facts to learn in college, much more emphasis is placed on using the knowledge as a foundation from which to explore new ideas and concepts. That's why teachers do ask questions "no one knows the answer to" — they are more interested in your learning the process of generating new ideas than in your rehashing old ideas. In short they're interested in **critical thinking**.

This takes courage, especially for students who have been trained not to be "wrong" and who are afraid to take risks in thinking and learning. The psychologist and philosopher Rollo May tells us in his book *The Courage to Create* that creating anything new implies risk and destruction. Just as a bird must painfully tear its way out of the egg, destroy what has been its source of security and protection, and emerge completely vulnerable in order to grow and finally to fly, we must be willing to risk and even to give up our secure womb of ideas and self-concepts in order to grow and learn. That can be especially frightening in a high pressure place like college.

The process of moving from security through helpless uncertainty can be very painful. In retrospect some of the ideas and identities we try on seem ridiculous, but they are an integral part of growth to adulthood.

Thinking with What You Know

In the classroom we are often so terrified of failure that we cannot think or learn at all. We can combat these fears by doing two things in our thinking process: (1) acknowledging what we do know and learning to use it and (2) learning to analyze and think critically.

Imagine that you have been trapped in a nuclear power plant that is in the midst of a meltdown. Everyone else has evacuated the plant, fleeing catastrophe. You stumble into the control room and approach the control panel, desperate to save your own life and perhaps the lives of many thousands in the area. You know absolutely nothing about nuclear power or the functioning of this plant, but you realize you have to do *something*. On the control panel are two switches and two dials, as in Figure 10.1. The switches are labeled "Containment Grid" and the dials are labeled "Temp." and "Stress System." One of the switches is up, the other down. The Temp. dial is turned all the way to the right, the Stress System dial all the way to the left. What do you do?

Before you panic, stop and think about what you *do* know. You may know nothing about nuclear power, but you do know some very simple things that may help. You know, for instance, that in your experience switches are normally *on* when they are up and *off* when they are down. This tells you that on the containment grid (whatever that might be!) something is turned off that perhaps should be turned on (or vice versa). Likewise dials are normally *on* when turned to the right and *off* when turned to the left. Again something is

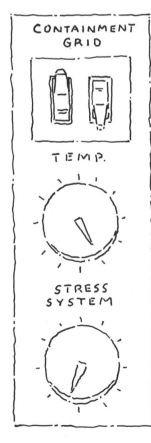

Figure 10.1 Nuclear Power Plant Control Panel

off that perhaps should be turned on. Now you might decide to turn all of the switches on or turn all of them off. Or you might decide that if what is happening now is bad, maybe if you reversed the switches something good would happen. Suddenly you have a lot of options. You might proceed from this point (if you have time) by trying to figure out what the labels on the switches and dials mean. Of course none of this may work, but since you *have to do something*, you have started a course of action that is rational and is based on what you know. The key is acknowledging what you do know and letting yourself think.

The same strategies of using what you do know to make an intelligent guess about something you don't know also apply to the classroom test situation. Let's say you have a pop quiz in history and your teacher asks you to comment on the importance of labor unions in the United States from 1900 to 1950. You somehow missed that chapter of your text, but instead of panicking, you react as you might have in the nuclear power plant and start reviewing what you do know. You know that for a long time strong laws have governed labor conditions in the United States. You know that there are health and safety laws, child labor laws, minimum wage laws, and so on, most of which have been enacted in the twentieth century. You also know from your political science class that in modern American politics most laws have resulted from strong constituent demand. You know from your economics course that the average wage of industrial workers rose sharply and steadily in the first five decades of the twentieth century. You reason that since most legislation is the result of constituent demand, and since employers seldom raise wages except in response to economic forces, somehow workers were able to pressure their employers and the government into enacting reforms. The growth of labor unions into an important political and economic force in the twentieth century seems to be a reasonable explanation.

PATTERNS OF THOUGHT

Sound reasoning requires two things: (1) choosing certain starting information (*premises*) that you consider true and relevant to the problem and (2) extending this information through logical argument to reach some *conclusion*.

Deductive Versus Inductive Thinking

The two main patterns of reasoning are deductive and inductive thinking. A *deductive argument* is one that begins with one or more general statements as premises, from which more specific statements must logically follow. The following are valid deductive arguments because if the premises are true, then the conclusions must also be true.

1. All dachshunds are dogs.
2. All dogs are canines.
3. Therefore my dachshund is a canine.

1. This month is October.
2. November follows October.
3. So next month must be November.

In each of these arguments the conclusion is more specific than at least one of the premises. For example, in the second argument, one premise is that

November always follows October. The conclusion is that this year, also, November will follow October. Of course, if a premise is wrong, a deductive argument can also be wrong.

1. All dachshunds are cats.
2. All cats are felines.
3. Therefore all dachshunds are felines.

An *inductive argument* is one that uses one or more specific premises to reach a more general conclusion.

1. A bag contains 100 marbles.
2. Ninety-nine marbles have been drawn from the bag that was thoroughly shaken between draws.
3. All the marbles drawn thus far have been green.
4. The remaining marble is probably green.

Notice the word "probably" in statement 4, the conclusion of this example. While deductive arguments can be judged valid or invalid, inductive arguments are never proved with absolute certainty. Because they involve making guesses about general patterns based on limited information, their conclusion is never absolutely certain. However, some inductive arguments are stronger than others. In the previous example, had the sampling been limited to drawing two or three green marbles, we would be much less certain that the other marbles in the bag were green.

EXERCISE 10.4   Deductive Versus Inductive Arguments

Identify whether each of the following is a deductive or an inductive argument. If it is deductive, is it valid and true? If it is inductive, is it strong?

A. 1. All of the marbles in this bag are blue.
   2. I draw two marbles from the bag.
   3. The marbles I draw are blue.

B. 1. I burnt my toast this morning and went without breakfast.
   2. Then I missed my bus and was late for English.
   3. Then I left my wallet somewhere.
   4. I guess this isn't my lucky day.

C. 1. Over half the people in this room are musicians.
   2. Therefore you're probably a musician.

D. 1. A unicorn is a horselike creature with a single horn.
   2. This horselike creature has no horn.
   3. Therefore this creature is not a unicorn.

E. 1. San Francisco had a major earthquake in 1906.
   2. San Francisco had another large quake in 1989.
   3. The next large San Francisco earthquake should come around the year 2072.

Empirical Versus Nonempirical Thinking

Both deductive and inductive logic are useful in the sciences, though certain branches of science may lean more toward one type of argument or the other. For instance, the science of mathematics is largely *nonempirical* — that is, much of what mathematicians study is not directly related to what one can observe directly in the physical world. Rather than amassing observations from the world and drawing inductive conclusions from them, mathematicians often take deductive steps, using what they call axioms and postulates (or premises) to deductively prove certain theorems (or conclusions). If you have studied plane geometry, you are familiar with the remarkable power of deductive mathematics, as discovered by the Greek mathematician Euclid.

The *empirical* sciences apply principles of deductive and inductive reasoning to observations of physical reality. On that basis they state rules or predictions about the physical world. One of the more spectacular scientific predictions was made by the astronomer Edmund Halley, for whom the comet was named. Halley observed his comet in 1682 and recorded data concerning its motion through our solar system. He also studied the work on motion and gravitation published by the physicist–mathematician Isaac Newton. In 1705, based on Newton's theories and his own observations, Halley concluded that the comet returned at approximately 75-year intervals and that the comet therefore would return sometime in December 1758. Halley died in 1743, but 15 years later, on Christmas Day 1758, the comet appeared. Halley's observations allowed him to predict the comet's return to within one month — 53 years in advance of that arrival. Thus the motion of comets, which had previously been considered erratic and even mysterious, was described in a system of laws that could predict their behavior. Halley's work actually reflects several valid deductive and strong inductive arguments. His conclusions regarding the general behavior of the comet were inductive; his prediction of its return was deductive.

Progress in the empirical sciences (both physical and social) relies heavily on inductive reasoning. Prediction is an essential part of testing the validity of inductive conclusions in these fields. The better a theory predicts future behavior, the stronger it appears to be.

EXERCISE 10.5 Would Columbus Fall Off the Edge of the World?

Contrary to the myth that Columbus set out on his voyages to "prove" the world was round, and long before Magellan's ship sailed all the way around the world, many thinkers already were convinced on the basis of empirical observation and inductive reasoning that the earth was in fact a globe.

Suppose you had been among those thinkers. What evidence from your general knowledge of science and everyday observations might you have been able to use to build an inductive argument to support the view that the world was round? What evidence might you have mustered to argue that it was flat? How convincing do you think the arguments might have been to other serious thinkers? To other contemporaries?

Critical Frameworks

Within an academic discipline scholars generally share some ideas about how to think. For instance, they more or less agree on what broad questions they are trying to answer and on what smaller questions are likely to help them answer the larger ones.

Some questions are more productive than others. One broad question that psychologists frequently ask is to what extent human behavior is due to "nature or nurture"; that is, to what extent is behavior inherited versus learned? It is not generally very productive to pose this question as an absolute choice between heredity or environment, because the answer usually proves to be some combination of the two. A somewhat smaller question focusing on language might be, Is there something about human biology that makes us uniquely suited to the use of language? A further question that might help to answer that question is, To what extent are other animals capable of creating and using symbols? For instance, can other primates, such as gorillas, learn and create language? How different are they from humans in this respect?

Within a discipline scholars must also agree somewhat about what methods are appropriate for answering certain questions. Physicists or psychologists test their theories and hypotheses by predicting the outcomes of highly controlled experiments. Sociologists often rely on surveys of opinion. By contrast, historians or literary scholars may have little recourse to controlled experiments or may find the whole concept of surveys irrelevant to their needs.

Members of a discipline also often agree about what theories or frameworks of ideas are most worth discussing. Even when a theoretical framework does not directly answer a question, it may stimulate thought and research. At other times the same theories can hinder one from seeing a problem from a more productive perspective.

One theoretical framework through which social scientists and historians frequently view the world is that of the *dialectical process*. According to this model, change occurs when two different entities or ideas come together and their interaction leads to a new entity or idea. In the language of dialectics a *thesis* meets its *antithesis*, and from this meeting a *synthesis* is formed. (The thesis and antithesis are not necessarily opposites in every sense, just different ideas that interact in some meaningful way.) The synthesis may be a combination of the thesis and antithesis (a kind of compromise), or it may be something completely different, but it would not exist without the interaction of thesis and antithesis. Dialectical thinking has inspired a great deal of intellectual activity in the last two centuries in the areas of political and economic theory, including the writings of Marx and other nineteenth- and twentieth-century economists, historians, and political scientists.

Another framework for conceiving how things change is the *evolutionary model*. According to this model change comes about mainly through small increments spread over many moments in time, rather than through large collisions at certain crucial moments. Our notions of biological and geological change generally conform with this way of thinking.

Large ideas like dialectics and evolution may originate in one area of study and then become important in other areas as well. For instance, Freud's pioneering studies in psychology borrowed heavily from physical science and engineering concepts such as hydraulics. Einstein's scientific theory of relativity has influenced many areas of thought. Most recently, concepts derived from computer technology have provided new ways of thinking about the human brain.

As you embark on a new discipline, perhaps by taking an introductory course, try to identify and understand the thinking strategies and patterns that scholars and researchers find useful in that field. Learn what major questions they think are most important and what lesser questions guide their research. Discover what broad theories or concepts underlie their way of thinking.

EXERCISE 10.6 Critical Thinking Within the Disciplines

Look over your notes and readings from one of your introductory courses, such as history, literature, psychology, sociology, science, or economics. In a small group discuss the following questions:

1. What two or three large questions seem uppermost in the minds of scholars in this discipline? What smaller questions also concern them?

2. What methods do scholars in this field use to generate information and understanding? What methods, if any, do they exclude? In what ways do the methods seem appropriate to the questions? Are there other methods they might use?

3. What general theories, concepts, and metaphors seem to prevail in this discipline? Are any of these borrowed from another field?

SOME COMMON FALLACIES IN CRITICAL THINKING

Fallacies are patterns of incorrect reasoning. Learning to identify some common fallacies like the following should help you to avoid being misled by specious arguments and to remove them from your own writing and thinking.

▶ *Argument directed to the person: argumentum ad hominem.* The *ad hominem* fallacy means attacking a person's beliefs or reputation rather than his or her arguments. When strong emotions are involved, people often get caught up in disparaging their opponent's character rather than examining their argument.

▶ *Appeal to authority: argumentum ad verecundiam.* This fallacy involves the presentation of someone as an authority who isn't really an authority on the topic. Advertising abounds with *ad verecundiam* reasoning: Sports stars who are not doctors or nutritionists urge us daily to eat a certain cereal; glamorous models tell us that a certain transmission will help our cars run better. What expert knowledge do these people possess?

▶ *Appeal to force: argumentum ad baculum.* Galileo Galilei (1564–1642) adopted the Copernican theory that the earth was not the center of the universe. This theory contradicted centuries of church teachings, which held that everything revolved around the earth. For this reason Galileo was condemned for heresy by the Inquisition and threatened with burning at the stake if he didn't change his position. The argument used by the Inquisition was basically this: "Your ideas disagree with our ideas, so you must be wrong. If you don't admit this, we'll kill you." Galileo did change his position publicly, but the argument posed against his views was hardly legitimate.

▶ *Appeal to pity: argumentum ad misericordiam.* This fallacy involves an appeal to pity. For example: "Please, officer, don't give me a ticket because if you do I'll lose my license, and I don't deserve to lose my license because I have five little children to feed and won't be able to feed them if I can't drive my truck." Appeals to pity often arise in arguments that engage our sense of justice. One of the appeals of popular Marxism as an explanation of social forces has certainly been *ad misericordiam.* The poverty and misery of great masses of people during the period of industrial development in Europe seemed to support the truth of a theory that promised an end to the misery.

▶ *Argument from ignorance: argumentum ad ignorantiam.* Arguments noted in this fallacy state, "My position is correct because it hasn't been proved incorrect." For example, dozens of books detail "close encounters" with flying saucers and beings from outer space. Almost all of these books describe the person who has had the encounter as beyond reproach in terms of integrity and sanity. And, the description goes on, although witnesses have had their statements questioned by government investigators and unrelenting reporters, critics could not *disprove* their claims. But it is a fallacy to regard something as proved because it has not been disproved.

▶ *False cause.* The false cause fallacy asserts that if one event follows another, the first event must have caused the second event. This kind of thinking persists in all of us. For example, someone blows smoke on you in an elevator. You become ill that evening and place the blame on the smoker. Yet the cause might be the deviled crab you ate at that charming restaurant on the dock. It's difficult to establish causal relations. Certainly a single encounter with something isn't sufficient for assuming a causal relation.

▶ *Hasty generalization.* Statisticians realize that inductive conclusions about the real world cannot be made on the basis of one or even a few samples. Avoid hasty generalizations in your thoughts and in your writing. Premature generalizations about your experience (about people you meet, courses you take, or your own abilities) may lead you to limit your own opportunities to grow. First steps are often shaky, and first reports are often wrong.

EXERCISE 10.7 Recognizing Fallacies

Identify any of the fallacies just discussed in the following examples:

1. Generations of diehard Red Sox fans had come and gone without ever seeing their team win the World Series. There was no way all their hopes and suffering could have been for nothing. By 1990 it was inevitable that the Boston Red Sox would finally win the World Series.

2. William F. Buckley, Jr., is one of those patrician types who always sound like they have nothing better to do than sit around and compare the taste of English Breakfast and Earl Grey tea. You're not going to take his political ideas seriously, are you? The man to listen to when it comes to politics is definitely Clint Eastwood. He really takes charge!

3. If the only way I can convince you to study 3 hours a day for your economic theory course is to assure you get an F if you don't study that much, well, so be it!

4. Most of our troubles today really stem from the fact that we lost the war in Vietnam. A few years after we pulled out of there, oil prices went crazy, the Ayatollah Khomeini took over Iran, huge numbers of Americans were being held hostage in Iran, and there was nothing we could do about it. Not only that, but inflation was suddenly running wild.

5. Extrasensory perception is definitely real. Psychics have been challenging the scientists for years to prove it isn't real, and the most they've been able to do was uncover a few tricksters. No one has ever been able to prove that psychic communication is impossible. Also Shirley MacLaine has written some wonderful things about it.

6. National health insurance is a terrible idea. For one thing Ralph Nader is in favor of it, and he's one of those consumer advocate types who's always complaining about something. For another thing look at Sweden. They have national health insurance and half the Swedes are still depressed.

7. It's not worth complaining when something you buy is defective. The very first time I wrote to a company asking for a refund they never even answered my letter.

EXERCISE 10.8 Identifying False Arguments in the Media

Now that you're familiar with some common false arguments, apply your knowledge to the media. In the next week expose yourself to at least two types of media (television, radio, newspapers, or magazines), and find two examples of fallacious argument in each. Write these up in a short report. Describe the medium, quote the message, and explain the fallacy.

ANALYSIS AND CRITICAL THINKING

Strategies for clear and careful thinking are often based on a process called analysis. *Analysis* as a scientific term means separating a chemical or compound into its constituent parts and studying the individual parts to see how they form the whole. The term means the same thing when we apply it to thinking. When we analyze an idea, we first must understand the parts of the idea and then see how those parts interact to form the complete idea.

Suppose someone alleges that *the rise in the number of violent crimes is caused by the increase in violence in TV programs.* This seems like a rather simple idea with which we could either agree or disagree. When we begin to analyze the statement, however, we find that things become very complicated. Let's use this example to explore three basic steps of analysis.

1. *Define the terms.* Our first step is to define our terms. Which crimes are considered "violent"? Is destruction of property a crime of vio-

lence, or do people have to be physically harmed? These are important questions, for under one definition writing graffiti or cutting into a line might be crimes of violence, while armed robbery would not. What does "violence" consist of on a TV show? Does it have to involve actual physical aggression in which bodily harm takes place, or can it be subtle and psychological? Under one definition the National Basketball Association playoffs might be considered harmfully violent while Alfred Hitchcock's classic thriller *Psycho* might not.

2. *Examine the premises.* Our next step is to examine the ideas on which the statement is based — the "premises" — and determine whether they are true. Once *violent crimes* is defined, we have to find out whether there has been a real increase in these crimes. Have these crimes actually happened more often, or are they simply reported more frequently? Has there actually been an increase in "violence," as you have defined it, on TV, or has television just been more closely watched for such things in recent years?

3. *Examine the logic.* After determining whether the premises are true, we now need to examine the logic of the statement itself. We cannot really understand the statement unless we realize that some hidden assumptions must be considered. The first assumption is that there is an actual causal link between what we see and what we do. The second assumption is that the same people who watched the "violent" TV shows committed the "violent" crimes. The first assumption *might* be true but can only be proved through scientific experiment and the use of statistical data. Even if the second assumption can be proved true, we might argue that people who are naturally violent watch these TV programs, and thus the programs are a reflection rather than a cause of the crimes.

This kind of analysis or critical thinking is an essential tool for learning — no matter what field you choose to study.

Born in the U.S.A.

The question "Why do men do better than women on SAT mathematics tests?" has led some people to jump to the conclusion that there might be a possible physiological basis for this difference.

An equally interesting fact is that the number of successful women in science and mathematics who were born outside the United States is very much higher than the number of successful American-born women. A typical example is a woman physicist who emigrated from Europe to New York as a high school student and found she was considered peculiar because in America "girls were not supposed to be smart." She had not encountered this pressure in Europe.

The top women who have had successful careers in America in my own field of nuclear physics have nearly all been born outside the United States. In many countries, like France and Italy, the number of women in science is incomparably greater than in the United States. In my recent contacts with Soviet Jewish immigrants to Israel and the United States, I have been impressed by the large number of women mathematicians, physicists, and engineers. One of these women was the only woman with a tenured position in a leading American university mathematics department for several years. Recently they hired another woman as a full professor—she was born in China.

I have been told that European Catholic countries have more women in science than Protestant countries do because the Virgin Mary serves as a role model, indicating that women can be important and rise to high positions. The Protestant culture has no corresponding figure.*

Mathilde Krim (Ph.D., genetics), founding co-chair of the American Foundation for AIDS Research. Nationality? Swiss. What explains the relative strength of European and Asian-born women in mathematics and the sciences?

Does this professor's information cast doubt on the idea that men are somehow more suited physiologically to mathematics than are women? Why do you suppose men do better than women in math on the SAT? How could you test your explanation?

What do you think of the professor's speculation about the role of the Virgin Mary? What further questions or research might help to test this explanation?

*Adapted, with permission, from Harry J. Lipkin, "Women in Math and Science," UME Trends (American Mathematical Society, October 1990).

EXERCISE 10.9 An Analysis

Conduct an analysis on one of the following statements similar to that just described. What additional information, definitions, and so on would you need in order to decide whether the statement is true, false, or uncertain? How might you go about acquiring missing information?

1. Automobiles are great for individuals but terrible for society.
2. Capital punishment is the best way to control murder.
3. There must be some physiological difference that makes men better than women at math.
4. The fact that women live longer than men is just another indication of their physiological superiority.
5. Democracy doesn't really work in America because so few people bother to vote.

As you accumulate knowledge, actively seek to understand. The result of your college education should not be a data bank of useful information, but an integration of knowledge and understanding that allows you to think and create independently. Your diploma is not a certification that you know all you need to, but an indication that you have the tools and the knowledge to begin to learn, to grow, and to create.

EXERCISE 10.10 Your Thoughts on the Liberal Arts

Write a statement of several paragraphs on one of the following topics:

1. Some students initially see little use for liberal arts course requirements. What, in general, are the liberal arts requirements on your campus? How do you feel about them and about the argument made for the liberal arts in this chapter? Are you in favor of any change in the liberal arts requirements on your campus? Support your position.
2. You are probably already aware that content in your classes is interrelated. Describe the relationship as you have already experienced it. Include at least two examples of how information or concepts from one of your classes complements your learning in another.
3. People often think of artists — especially poets — as existing outside the "real world." Yet two of America's most famous poets worked in traditional professions: William Carlos Williams was a physician, and Wallace Stevens was a corporate lawyer and vice president of a major insurance company. Most of

their professional friends did not even know they were poets. Identify some-one you admire who has worked at a traditional profession and also pur-sued an outside artistic or intellectual interest. What does that person's life suggest about the value of a background in the liberal arts?

JOURNAL

How are you being introduced to the liberal arts? How are you finding college different from high school in terms of the kind of "thinking" de-manded of you? Do you notice any of the fallacies described in this chapter in your own thinking or in the thinking of others around you? What other problems do you experience when it comes to thinking either creatively or logically? What might you do to improve your powers of reasoning?

SUGGESTIONS FOR FURTHER READING

Bloom, Allan. *The Closing of the American Mind*. New York: Simon & Schuster, 1987.

Booth, Wayne C. *The Knowledge Worth Having*. Chicago: University of Chicago Press, 1967.

Conway, David A., and Ronald Munson. *The Elements of Reasoning*. Belmont, Calif.: Wadsworth, 1990.

Gray, William D. *Thinking Critically About New Age Ideas*. Belmont, Calif.: Wadsworth, 1991.

Jarrell, Randall. *A Sad Heart at the Supermarket*. London: Eyre and Spottiswoode, 1965.

Kahane, Howard. *Logic and Philosophy*, 6th ed. Belmont, Calif.: Wadsworth, 1990.

May, Rollo. *The Courage to Create*. New York: Norton, 1975.

McPeck, John E. *Critical Thinking and Education*. New York: St. Martin's Press, 1981.

Oliver, James Willard, and James L. Stiver. *Introduction to Logic*, 4th ed., rev. Apex, N.C.: Contemporary, 1987.

———. *Workbook for Introductory Logic*, 4th ed., rev. Apex, N.C.: Contemporary, 1987.

Sagan, Carl. *The Dragons of Eden*. New York: Random House, 1977.

C H A P T E R

11

▼▼▼▼▼▼▼▼▼▼▼▼▼▼▼▼▼

Major, Career, and Academic Advisors

Getting the Most from Your Academic Advisor
John N. Gardner
A. Jerome Jewler

Choosing a Major and Planning a Career
Linda B. Salane

Getting the Most from Your Academic Advisor

I met with my academic advisor today. I was sort of looking forward to this, but I was relieved that he actually seemed glad to see me. His office was a total wreck — books on the floor, stacks of paper everywhere, a cup of cold coffee on the desk. But he really wanted to help me plan my courses. Talked about my major and how I was doing. I talked, he listened mostly. Cleared up some things I wasn't sure about. I think I can trust this person.

When life was simpler, and colleges and universities offered structured academic programs in the liberal arts and sciences with few options or choices, many young people completed college without benefit of an academic advisor.

That was also a time when many faculty believed that their only responsibility to students was to teach them, and that matters of choosing courses, dealing with stress, and providing career information were best left to others on the campus. This gave professors a great deal of time in which to prepare their lectures and conduct their research. It also left many students in the dark about decisions that often would affect their chances of success in college.

In this section we'll explain why most college students today need an academic advisor, what an academic advisor does, and what students need to do in order to get the most from their relationship with academic advisors.

THE NATURE AND IMPORTANCE OF ACADEMIC ADVISING

The idea of academic advising is certainly not new, but never before in the history of higher education has it been regarded as so essential. There's good reason for this; with so many programs and so many choices, even faculty and staff must check and double-check academic requirements and regulations to be certain students are making the right choices. So many students pursuing higher education today are the first in their families to do so that it's even more important that there be someone to whom they can turn for advice. In broader terms, if faculty and staff believe that college should help students develop holistically — that is, vocationally, emotionally, physically, spiritually, culturally, and socially as well as intellectually — the academic advisor can be the focal point for such development.

We already know that when a student has one person on campus who cares about his or her survival, that student stands a better chance of graduating than the student who lacks this significant other person. Through a mounting body of evidence colleges and universities have come to realize that poor academic advising is one major reason students drop out of college. For this reason academic advising has become one of the most important ingredients for student success. Although your "significant other person" may be a professor, a staff member, an upperclass student, or a counselor, it might also be none other than your academic advisor.

What Is Academic Advising?

Academic advising is a dynamic process for obtaining the critical information you need to make the most important decisions about college, decisions affecting your academic major, career goals, elective courses, and secondary fields of study. Academic advising is also a one-to-one, highly personal, out-of-class form of learning. Academic advising includes periodic assistance in scheduling courses that you will take the following term and is inextricably related to the process of career planning and decision making. But beyond decision-making and scheduling considerations, it represents a relationship between two human beings who care about, understand, and respect each other.

That's your academic advisor on the right, cleverly disguised as a fire hydrant.

A more holistic view of academic advising sees the advisor as a person to whom you can turn for any sort of problem, especially if the problem is affecting your ability to successfully complete course work. Such problems might include a learning disability; a personal problem that causes stress, insomnia, or anxiety; perceived unfair treatment by a professor; indecision about choice of major or career; an ethical or moral dilemma; inability to keep up with course work due to any number of reasons, including excessive employment hours; or poor grades that may lead to suspension from the institution.

Even if you have no serious problems, you may want to talk with your advisor for any number of reasons: to get advice on applying for a job, to get a reaction to a piece of writing or a project, to ask for the names of books in a given field that might be helpful to you, to share some good news about grades or job interviews, or to check on academic rules and regulations.

Why Is Academic Advising So Important?

Schools provide advising in part because it helps them to retain students. But there is also evidence that students who receive good academic advising are much more likely to be satisfied with their college experience. Academic advising is critical because it contributes to the important process of planning for college, for careers, and for life. An academic advisor often becomes your most important mentor at college. Furthermore advisors can help you find other sorts of needed information, assistance, and counseling and may serve as a reference when you apply for graduate school or a job.

What Do Academic Advisors Do?

At a minimum your **academic advisor** informs you about your degree requirements and options and gives you approval to register for courses each term. Ideally academic advisors also help you explore life goals and vocational goals, select academic programs, and choose and schedule courses.

Academic advising should be a process whereby you communicate regularly with someone you respect about a broad range of concerns. The process should be linked to career planning and may include personal counseling. It may also include an "early warning system" through which the college monitors your academic progress as a freshman and sends frequent grade reports during your first semester to your advisor. He or she then contacts you and refers you, as needed, to other counseling and support resources to assist you with academic difficulties. This approach is often called "intrusive academic advising" and is designed with your well-being in mind. You should not worry if you are called in to meet with your academic advisor because you are having problems with your studies. The purpose of such a meeting is not to criticize you but to help you cope with the academic problems you may be experiencing.

Academic advising may also include a process that monitors your class attendance during your first semester and alerts you if you miss too many classes. Later the process will include your advisor making sure that you have met all the requirements for graduation and certifying that you are eligible to receive your diploma.

EXERCISE 11.1   Academic Advising at Your School

Explore the academic advising process at your institution. To find out about it, you may have to contact your advisor, the advisement center, your department head, or another campus resource. Knowing how to locate resources is an important skill to develop in college!

Try to answer these questions and others you may have:

1. What types of people serve as academic advisors on your campus?

2. In what ways are they expected to help you?

3. How does a student get assigned to a particular advisor? Does a student normally have the same advisor throughout college? How can a student go about arranging for a different advisor if necessary?

4. What other counseling and advising services can your academic advisor help you find when you need them?

Who Are Academic Advisors?

At many colleges academic advisors are full-time faculty. At some schools, in the freshman and sophomore years, academic advisors may be educators whose sole professional responsibility is advising. At some institutions you'll find a combination of faculty and professional staff members as advisors.

Some institutions will assign freshmen immediately to faculty advisors in their intended field or discipline. At many large community colleges academic advising is done by counselors in the college counseling/advising center. These counselors are trained in and responsible for assisting students with both academic and personal issues. If you haven't declared a major, you may be assigned to an advisor who specializes in dealing with undecided students. You may be attending an institution that, as a matter of policy, does not assign freshmen to advisors in their intended major field, but does so for sophomores or juniors. Even if you are not assigned a faculty member from your major field, your advisor is expected to be familiar with the requirements of your major. You also have the option of talking to a faculty member in your major in addition to seeing your advisor. Your institution may have a "general college," "university college," or "lower division" in which all freshmen are administratively registered, housed, and advised.

EXERCISE 11.2   Who's Your Academic Advisor?

Find out and record the name of your academic advisor, along with his or her office location, phone number, and normal advising hours. If you have not already done so, arrange to meet this person.

Name: _____

Office location: _____

Phone(s): _____

_____

Hours: _____

Where and When Is Academic Advising Conducted?

One of the many differences between high school and college is that most college faculty have private offices where they can meet with you during their posted office hours. At many institutions academic advising takes place in advisement centers. These centers may also include offices for personal counseling, career planning and placement, financial aid, and study skills. Generally, at least once a semester, students are notified to sign up for appointments with their advisors to discuss the selection and scheduling of courses for the next term. This advising period may last up to two weeks and is usually widely publicized on campus. It is very important that you be aware of these periods and schedule a conference to discuss your course selections for the coming term.

Ideally academic advising is a process that involves more frequent interaction between you and your advisor. The nature and frequency of this relationship depend on how you and your advisor choose to pursue this opportunity. Like virtually everything in college, academic advising will be what you make of it.

EXERCISE 11.3 Advising Process and Schedules

To prepare for your basic academic advising sessions, do the following:

1. Find out when the academic advising process for next semester begins, and record the date here: _____

2. Record here what you need to do to prepare for the advising process (include any important dates):

   _____

   _____

   _____

   _____

   _____

Don't forget to transfer the important dates to your calendar so you'll be prepared!

How Is Advising Different from Other Types of Counseling?

Most colleges offer highly differentiated counseling services that include academic advising, career counseling and placement, financial aid planning, academic skills assistance, personal tutoring, and personal counseling. Each type of counseling is usually performed by someone with expertise in that specific area. At very small colleges counseling may be provided by a small number of counselors filling multiple roles. Academic advising, of course, focuses primarily on the knowledge and information you need to make wise decisions about academic choices and options. It is different from, but closely related to, career counseling. Academic advising may or may not include some elements of personal counseling. Making important academic decisions may also require assistance on personal and social issues that can influence and shape the kind of person you want to become. For this reason a competent advisor is not only a good listener but one who can refer you to other kinds of counseling services on campus.

RELATING TO YOUR ADVISOR

Advising is likely to be much more successful for you if you take the relationship seriously and work hard to make it meaningful. You need to take responsibility for keeping your advisor informed of your progress or problems. At the very minimum you should make an appointment to meet at least once a term to discuss plans for the next term. You might ask for advice on course prerequisites, interesting courses to take, and good professors to study under. Discuss any major decisions—such as adding or dropping a course, changing your major, or deciding to transfer or withdraw from school— before making them. You may also need to discuss personal problems with your advisor. If he or she can't handle these, ask for referral to a professional on campus who can. Your advisor should be someone you can always turn to. Even if he or she doesn't know the answer immediately, the advisor should know who to call to get you the help you need. Will your advisor respect your request for confidentiality on such matters? That's something you will need to clarify.

Your advisory sessions will be more productive if you are already familiar with your college catalog (see Appendix A, "How to Read Your College Catalog"). Make up a list of questions before your appointment and also arrive with a tentative schedule of courses for the coming term. At many colleges your entire academic record will be stored in an online data base that your advisor can access on a personal computer during your advising sessions. At others the department office will have your academic records on file for use in the advising session.

EXERCISE 11.4   Questions to Ask Advisors

Read the following description of Frank, a first-year student:

Frank has had an average first semester at college. He has excelled at English and history but has been pretty disappointed with his performance in biology and calculus. He was always a good student in high school, so he is somewhat baffled by his performance in those two classes. He thinks it may be because his job keeps him up late at night, so he's not alert for his morning classes (which happen to be calculus and biology). On the other hand, it may be the teaching styles of those two classes—loads of students, lots of lecture, and little personal attention. Anyway, those two classes aren't that important to him, since he's decided to switch majors from pre-med to philosophy. He isn't sure what kind of job he'll get, or how he'll tell his parents, but he knows the philosophy classes his roommate, Joe, is taking sound a whole lot more interesting! Which reminds him that his roommate also seems pretty interesting. How does Joe have time to get involved in so many things? Frank feels like all his time is spent studying, working, and going to class. High school was sure a lot more fun. . . .

1. Frank has an appointment with his academic advisor tomorrow. What questions would you suggest Frank ask?

   _____

   _____

   _____

   _____

   Compare your suggestions with those of other students in your class.

2. Now spend some time reviewing your school term so far. Jot down some of the issues you're experiencing, or questions you have, so you'll remember to speak with your advisor about them.

_____

_____

_____

_____

Is Your Advisor Right for You?

The key word here is *trust*. You will know if you have the right academic advisor if you have established good rapport with this person. Do you feel comfortable with him or her? Does your academic advisor seem to take a personal interest in you? Is the advisor available during posted office hours? Does the advisor keep scheduled appointments with you? Do you get accurate information? Does the advisor listen actively? Is the advisor polite? Does the advisor provide enough time for you to accomplish what needs to be done? Does he or she either make an effort to get you the information you request or tell you where you can find it yourself? If so, congratulations.

But what if your academic advisor is a dud? You could discuss your lack of satisfaction with your advisor as tactfully as possible. But since this may be awkward, a better approach might be to ask for another advisor. Students have a right to do this, yet many students fail to exercise this right simply because they feel it's not their prerogative to do so. To find a better advisor, you might consider asking one of your professors, perhaps one with whom you have developed a personal rapport or whom you respect. Get his or her agreement; then make the change officially. *Never* stay in an advising relationship that isn't working for you.

How Do Faculty Feel About Academic Advising?

For many faculty academic advising is a highly rewarding form of teaching. In fact professors who consistently advise students claim that these one-on-one sessions help them "take the pulse" of students with regard to the college experience and thereby help them teach more effectively in the classroom. Although dedicated faculty enjoy advising students, academic advising is not without its frustrations, particularly when students don't take it seriously, fail to sign up for sessions, miss appointments, attempt to circumvent established procedures, or come poorly prepared for the session and expect the advisor to do all the work. Fortunately such students are few. As students *you* are responsible for learning how to be prepared for advising sessions. Admittedly the level of personal interest your advisor takes in you and his or her level of commitment to the advising process will vary.

Advisors may be frustrated by other things, too. At some institutions, particularly large, research-oriented universities, the academic advising process is not held in very high regard by faculty because it takes time away from their research. At many colleges advising loads are unevenly distributed. Frequently the best advisors bear the heaviest loads but are not proportionately rewarded. Many colleges still do not have enough advisors,

What Are You Looking for in Your Academic Advisor?

Not all students want the same thing from their advisors. As the accompanying figure, which records results of a recent study of students at Harvard, shows, men and women tend to look for different qualities.

When asked about advising, men want an advisor who "knows the facts." Or "if he doesn't know the data, he knows where to get it or to send me to get it." Or one who "makes concrete and directive suggestions, which I'm then free to accept or reject."

Women, in contrast, want an advisor who "will take the time to get to know me personally." Or who "is a good listener and can read between the lines if I am hesitant to express a concern." Or who "shares my interests so that we will have something in common." The women's responses focus far more on the importance of a personal relationship.*

What do you plan to look for in your advisor? What can you do to ensure that you get the advisor who is best for you?

*Richard J. Light, The Harvard Assessment Seminars, First Report (Cambridge, Mass.: Harvard University Graduate School of Education and Kennedy School of Government, 1990).

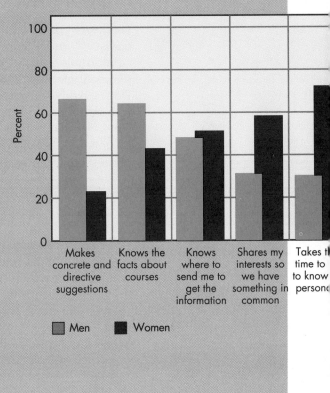

What Students Want from Their Academic Advisor (percentage indicating "very important")

which means that what advisors there are may not have enough time to give this important process the attention it deserves. At some colleges there are no tangible rewards for academic advising, such as reduced workloads or additional pay, and no special recognition, not even a thank you from the administration. And at many colleges there isn't even formal training for advisors.

We don't really know how effectively academic advising is being performed because it is rarely evaluated by students. We do know, however, from student interviews nationally that it can serve as positive reinforcement for students as they face the many challenges of earning a college degree. We also believe that a great number of faculty and staff are enthusiastically

committed to the advising process and to the students they advise. Colleges and universities have made enormous strides since the mid-1970s in improving the condition of academic advising, and it is now being taken very seriously at many schools. A number of advisors are now being trained, evaluated, and rewarded. The process of personalizing academic advising will more than likely continue, and more and more students like yourself will have the opportunity to benefit from it. Be certain that you do.

EXERCISE 11.5 **Preparing to Meet with Your Advisor**

Thinking ahead to your advisement session for next semester, what questions do you have for your advisor in each of the following areas? Record those questions here.

1. Your major and potential career:

_____

_____

_____

2. Other majors and potential careers:

_____

_____

_____

3. Classes you need next semester:

_____

_____

_____

4. Order of classes you need to take:

_____

_____

_____

5. Difficulty level of classes you may be taking next semester:

_____

_____

_____

6. Electives you might be interested in:

_____

_____

_____

7. Schedule problems:

_____

_____

_____

8. Teaching styles of specific professors:

_____

_____

_____

9. General campus information:

_____

_____

_____

10. Information about scholarships, internships, cooperative education, or other enhancements:

_____

_____

_____

11. Other questions or issues (don't forget the notes you recorded for Exercise 11.4):

_____

_____

_____

Throughout the rest of this quarter or semester use this worksheet to record other questions for your advisor as you think of them. The night before your appointment, review the list for any additions or deletions. To make good use of your appointment time and not forget anything, take this list with you.

JOURNAL

What has your academic advising experience been like to date? Describe your satisfaction or your lack thereof with the academic advising you have received. Comment on the characteristics and personality of your academic advisor. Also describe what attempts you have made to develop a relationship with him or her and how successful they have been.

REFERENCES AND SUGGESTIONS
FOR FURTHER READING

The NACADA Journal. c/o Roberta Flaherty, Executive Director, National Academic Advising Association, 446 Bluemont Hall, Kansas State University, Manhattan, KS, 66506-5322.

O'Banion, Terry. "An Academic Advising Model." *AAJ Journal.* March 1972.

Winston, Roger B., Jr., et al. *Developmental Academic Advising: Addressing Students' Educational, Career, and Personal Needs.* San Francisco: Jossey-Bass, 1984.

Choosing a Major and Planning a Career

*G*ot the results of my career inventory today. It said I ought to go into the funeral business! And me, a marketing major! What can you sell to dead people?! But the career counselor said it all made sense because funeral directors deal mostly with the survivors, and they have to know how to run a business. It doesn't mean I have to be a funeral director! In fact, I'm thinking of changing to management anyway, now that I found out there's nothing wrong with changing your major. But I guess I should do it early.

LINDA B. SALANE *is vice president for financial and institutional planning at Columbia College in Columbia, South Carolina. She describes herself as "a creative, flexible risk-taker and a natural planner who keeps her eyes open for career opportunities." Her academic background in sociology, student affairs, business, and higher education has prepared her for many career paths. She has worked in production planning, social work, residence life, women's education, business consulting, career development, budgeting, personnel, and strategic planning. She has developed her own plan rather than follow the plans of others, and in this section she strongly encourages you to do the same.*

When most people think of career planning, they think of choosing among career fields, deciding on a job, or changing employers. For first-year college students the most immediate decisions may be choosing an academic major, selecting elective courses, and finding activities to get involved in at college to prepare for a career. For many years college freshmen have indicated that the primary reason they attend college is to be able to get a better job. And every year too many graduating seniors are disappointed with the job offers they receive. Obviously many students are making uninformed choices about their careers and ending up disillusioned.

That doesn't have to happen to you. If you make your decisions based on your personal priorities and on the realities of the job market, your decisions can lead to an array of exciting career fields. Not only will you understand the rationale underlying your choices, but you will also be in a position to change direction as your priorities change. Of course, you should also be well-informed about the variety of courses and majors available to you on your campus. If you're not already familiar with your college catalog, see Appendix A, "How to Read Your College Catalog."

For some students choosing a major is a simple decision, but most students who enter college straight out of high school don't know which major to select or which career they may be best suited for. If you find yourself facing such decisions right now, stop and ask yourself the following questions:

1. What kind of work do I want to do?
2. Which career fields offer opportunities for this kind of work?
3. What role will college play in my future career plans?
4. Are there specific things I can do to enhance my chances of getting a job when I graduate?
5. Do my career goals complement my life goals and work values?

Career planning involves discovering how these questions relate to one another and finding the answers you'll need to make effective career choices. This section tells you how to answer these questions.

WORKPLACE AND WORK'S PLACE

Career planning can help you find your place in the world of work. You've probably met people who tell you how much they love their jobs and even marvel that they're being paid to do something they enjoy. You've probably

Sports . . . physiology . . . psychology . . . ? Start your search for your major with some thought to your major interests.

also met people who dislike what they do, count the days until Friday, and are always looking for another job. We might say that the latter group has a place to work while the former group has work that has a place in their total lives.

Career planning stresses the importance of knowing enough about yourself, your personal values system, and specific career fields so that you can consciously make the right decisions. To identify work that will be a vital part of your life, you need two kinds of information. First, you need information you can obtain from self-assessment: personality type, interests, values, aptitudes, skills, and goals. Second, you need information you can obtain through career research to determine which career fields will let you explore your interests, exercise your values, demonstrate your aptitudes, use your skills, and fulfill your personal goals.

MAJORS AND CAREERS

Before you actively begin planning your career, you need to realize several things about **majors** and their effect on careers. First, most college students think that a direct relationship exists between academic majors and specific career fields and that it's impossible to enter most career fields unless they major in the right area. In reality the relationship of college majors to careers varies. Obviously, if you want to be a nurse, you must major in nursing. Engineers major in engineering. Pharmacists major in pharmacology. There's no other way to be certified as a nurse, engineer, or pharmacist. However, most career fields don't require a specific major, and people with specific majors don't have to use them in usual ways. For example, if you major in nursing, history, engineering, or English, you might still choose to become a bank manager, sales representative, career counselor, production manager, or a number of other things.

Second, in most cases a college major alone is not enough to land you a job. There is tremendous competition in the job market, and you need experience and competencies related to your chosen field. Internships, part-time jobs, and co-curricular activities provide opportunities to gain experience and develop these competencies. Thus you should plan your college

212   Chapter 11

curriculum so that you can study what you enjoy, what you can do success-fully, and what will serve as groundwork for the future you want.

The most common question college students ask is, "What can I do with my major?" Career planning helps you focus on a more important question: "What do I *want* to do?" This question leads you to explore yourself and fields where you can achieve what you want.

As you attempt to determine what you want to do, the choice of an aca-demic major will take on new meaning. You'll no longer be so concerned with what the prescribed route of certain majors allows you to do. Instead you'll use your career goals as a basis for academic decisions about your major, your minor, elective courses, internships, and co-curricular activities. Consider these goals when you select part-time and summer jobs. Don't confine yourself to a short list of jobs directly related to your major; think more broadly about your goals.

FACTORS IN YOUR CAREER PLANNING

You are a unique and complex individual, a maze of characteristics. You have developed and will continue to refine an image of who you are. Some people have a very definite and complex self-image by the time they enter college, but most of you are in the process of defining (or perhaps redefining) yourselves. Often you see yourself as a puzzle. To begin understanding this puzzle, you need to consider each piece of the puzzle — interests, skills, aptitudes, personality characteristics, life goals, and work values — sepa-rately and then consider the impact each has on the others.

Interests

Interests develop from your past experiences and from assumptions you formed in previous environments. For example, you may be interested in writing for the college newspaper because you did it in high school and loved it or because you'd like to try something new. Throughout your life your interests will develop and change. Involvement in different courses or activ-ities may lead you to drop old interests as you add new ones. It's not unusual for a student to enter Psychology 101 with a great interest in psychology and realize halfway through the course that psychology is not what he or she imagined or wants to pursue.

EXERCISE 11.6　**What Are Your Interests?**

How do you identify what you're interested in? Take standardized inventories or tests through the counseling services at your school. Also try the following:

1. Read through your college catalog and check each course that sounds inter-esting. Ask yourself why they sound interesting.

2. Make a list of all the classes, activities, and clubs you enjoyed in high school. Ask yourself why you enjoyed these things.

Bring these materials to class so that you can discuss these thoughts.

Skills

Skills are things you do well. To claim something as a skill, you must have proof that you are indeed good at it. You can't claim to be a good writer, for example, unless you really do write well. You measure your current level of skill by your past performance. Note the reference to "current level of skill." Skills, like interests, can be developed. You may be a poor writer now, and you may choose to work on that skill. By using resources available to you at college and by practicing, you can become a better writer.

EXERCISE 11.7   What Are Your Current Skills?

Use the following list to help you determine your best skills. First, place a check mark next to the skills you presently have. Then identify and circle the five skills you are most confident about, those about which you could say to anyone, "I am good at this." Finally, place an X next to the skills you would like to develop in college.

_____ writing	_____ socializing	_____ getting results
_____ reading	_____ making a team effort	_____ being neat
_____ conversing	_____ explaining	_____ keeping records
_____ reporting information	_____ helping others	_____ being accurate
_____ interviewing	_____ teaching	_____ asserting self
_____ being creative	_____ entertaining	_____ taking risks
_____ making machines and mechanical things work	_____ public speaking	_____ negotiating
_____ applying technical knowledge	_____ being sensitive	_____ selling
_____ building things	_____ learning	_____ winning
_____ repairing things	_____ analyzing	_____ being friendly
_____ operating tools	_____ evaluating	_____ motivating
_____ observing	_____ handling money	_____ managing
_____ listening	_____ planning	_____ directing others
_____ coming up with ideas	_____ problem solving	_____ adapting
_____ cooperating	_____ scheduling	_____ encouraging
_____ being tactful	_____ following through	_____ other: _____
		_____ other: _____

Select two or three of your strongest skills. Suppose you were asked to prove you possessed these skills. How would you do this?

Aptitudes

Aptitudes are inherent strengths. They may be part of your biological heritage, or they may have developed through early learning. Aptitudes are the foundation for skills, so high aptitudes generally indicate the potential for higher skill levels. Remember that through practice and the use of available resources, you can improve a skill. For example, if you have an aptitude for writing and couple that aptitude with practice, you'll probably become a better writer than someone who doesn't have a strong writing aptitude. Although high motivation and hard work alone may not entirely compensate for low aptitude, aptitude coupled with high motivation and hard work breeds success. We all have aptitudes we can build on. Build on *your* strengths.

EXERCISE 11.8   What Are Your Aptitudes?

Read the following aptitude areas. Place an X next to those you know you are weak in. Place a question mark (?) next to those you are not sure about. Place a check mark next to your strongest aptitudes. Are they in the same family as the skills you previously checked?

_____ 1. *Abstract reasoning.* People with strong aptitudes in abstract reasoning can interpret poetry, solve scientific problems in their heads, and solve logic problems.

_____ 2. *Verbal reasoning.* People with strong verbal reasoning can talk through problems easily or can understand the problems more easily when they hear them described than when they see them on paper.

_____ 3. *Spatial relations.* People with strong aptitudes in spatial relations are able to understand the physical relationships between two- and three-dimensional objects or designs.

_____ 4. *Language usage.* People with strong aptitudes in language usage are able to write and speak effectively.

_____ 5. *Mechanical ability.* People with strong mechanical ability are able to physically manipulate the parts of a machine to make it work.

_____ 6. *Clerical ability.* People with strong clerical ability are able to do detailed general office work efficiently and to organize records or accounts.

_____ 7. *Numerical ability.* People with strong numerical ability are able to solve arithmetic problems easily.

_____ 8. *Spelling.* People with strong aptitudes in spelling are able to understand and remember patterns and details.

Select two or three of your strongest aptitudes. Suppose you were asked to prove you possessed these aptitudes. How would you do this?

Personality Characteristics

What makes you different from others around you? Obviously each of us is physically unique, but we're all psychologically unique, too. The personality characteristics you've developed through the years make you *you*, and those characteristics can't be ignored when making career decisions. The quiet, orderly, calm, and detail-oriented person probably will make a different work choice than the aggressive, outgoing, and argumentative person. Many psychologists believe that working in an occupation consistent with your personality can make you feel more successful in and satisfied with your work.

EXERCISE 11.9 What Are Your Personality Characteristics?

What ten words would you use to describe yourself? Write them down:

1. _____   6. _____

2. _____   7. _____

3. _____   8. _____

4. _____   9. _____

5. _____   10. _____

Ask at least three people who know you well (your parents, your spouse, your brother or sister, a close friend) to write down ten words they would use to describe you. How do the lists compare?

Life Goals and Work Values

Most people want two things from life: success and satisfaction. Each of us defines these words in our own way, and one person's perception of success and satisfaction may be quite different from another's. Defining these concepts is complex and very personal. Two things influence our conclusions about success and happiness: (1) knowing that we are achieving the life goals we've set for ourselves and (2) finding that we value what we're receiving from our work.

EXERCISE 11.10   What Are Your Life Goals?

The following list includes life goals some people set for themselves.* This list can help you begin to think about the kinds of goals you may want to set. Place a check mark next to the goals you would like to achieve in your life. Next, review the goals you have checked and circle the five you want most. Finally, review your list of five goals and rank them by priority (1 for most important, 5 for least important).

_____ the love and admiration of friends

_____ good health

_____ lifetime financial security

_____ a lovely home

_____ international fame

_____ freedom within my work setting

_____ a good love relationship

_____ a satisfying religious faith

_____ recognition as the most attractive person in the world

_____ an understanding of the meaning of life

_____ success in my profession

_____ a personal contribution to the elimination of poverty and sickness

_____ a chance to direct the destiny of a nation

_____ freedom to do what I want

_____ a satisfying and fulfilling marriage

_____ a happy family relationship

_____ complete self-confidence

_____ other: _____

EXERCISE 11.11   What Are Your Work Values?

The following list includes typical work values, reasons people say they like the work they do.† It can help you begin to think about what you want to receive from your work. Read each definition and place a check mark next to the items you'd like to have as part of your ideal job. Next, review the items you've checked and circle the ten items you want most. Finally, review your list of ten items and rank them in order of importance (1 for most important, 10 for least important).

_____ *Help society.* Do something to contribute to the betterment of the world.

_____ *Help others.* Be involved in helping other people in a direct way, either individually or in a small group.

_____ *Have public contact.* Have a lot of day-to-day contact with people.

_____ *Work with others.* Have close working relationships with a group as a result of my work activities.

_____ *Compete.* Engage in activities that pit my abilities against others where there are clear win-and-lose outcomes.

*Adapted from Human Potential Seminar by James D. McHolland, Evanston, Ill., 1975. Used by permission of the author.
†List reprinted with permission, from Howard E. Figler, *PATH: A Career Workbook for Liberal Arts Students* (Cranston, R.I.: Carroll Press, 1979). Copyright © 1979 by Carroll Press.

_____ *Make decisions.* Have the power to decide courses of action.

_____ *Hold power and authority.* Control other people's work activities.

_____ *Influence people.* Be in a position to change the attitudes or opinions of other people.

_____ *Work alone.* Do projects by myself, without any significant amount of contact with others.

_____ *Seek knowledge.* Engage myself in the pursuit of knowledge, truth, and understanding.

_____ *Hold intellectual status.* Be regarded as a person of high intellectual prowess, an acknowledged "expert."

_____ *Create (general).* Create new ideas and programs, not following an established format.

_____ *Supervise.* Have a job in which I'm directly responsible for the work done by others.

_____ *Experience change and variety.* Have work responsibilities that frequently change content and setting.

_____ *Be stable.* Have a work routine that is largely predictable.

_____ *Be secure.* Be assured of keeping my job and a reasonable financial reward.

_____ *Live at a fast pace.* Work in circumstances where there is a high pace of activity and work must be done rapidly.

_____ *Gain recognition.* Be recognized for the quality of my work.

_____ *Feel excitement.* Experience frequent excitement in the course of my work.

_____ *Find adventure.* Have work duties that involve frequent risk taking.

_____ *Profit materially.* Have a strong likelihood of accumulating large amounts of money or other material gain.

_____ *Be independent.* Determine the nature of my work myself; not have to do what others tell me to.

_____ *Be in the right location.* Find a place to live (town, geographical area) that allows me to do the things I enjoy most.

_____ *Control my own time.* Have work responsibilities that I can accomplish on my own schedule.

If you had difficulty with the preceding exercise, you might want to talk with a career counselor in your career planning and placement center. Career counselors are trained to help you identify your strengths and prioritize them according to what is most important to you.

WHAT ARE YOUR CAREER CHOICES?

You might be surprised to learn that the federal government lists more than 31,000 career fields. How many can you name? If you're like most college students, your list begins to get sketchy beyond thirty-five or fifty occupations. Most students admit they don't know much about occupations. Few have accurate information about typical on-the-job activities, necessary skills, occupational outlook, salary range, methods of entry, or related fields — even for their most likely occupational choice. Obviously you can't make a good choice if you don't know what your choices are.

Dr. John Holland, a psychologist at Johns Hopkins University, has developed a system designed to help you identify potential career choices. He separates people into six general categories based on differences in their interests, skills, values, and personality characteristics — in short, their preferred approaches to life. His categories include the following:*

▶ *Realistic.* These people describe themselves as concrete, down-to-earth, and practical — as doers. They exhibit competitive/assertive behavior and show interest in activities that require motor coordination, skill, and physical strength. They prefer situations involving "action solutions" rather than tasks involving verbal or interpersonal skills, and they like to take a concrete approach to problem solving rather than rely on abstract theory. They tend to be interested in scientific or mechanical areas rather than cultural and aesthetic fields.

▶ *Investigative.* These people describe themselves as analytical, rational, and logical — as problem solvers. They value intellectual stimulation and intellectual achievement and prefer to think rather than to act, to organize and understand rather than to persuade. They usually have a strong interest in physical, biological, or social sciences. They are not apt to be "people-oriented."

▶ *Artistic.* These people describe themselves as creative, innovative, and independent. They value self-expression and relations with others through artistic expression and are also emotionally expressive. They dislike structure, preferring tasks involving personal or physical skills. They resemble investigative people but are more interested in the cultural-aesthetic than the scientific.

▶ *Social.* These people describe themselves as kind, caring, helpful, and understanding of others. They value helping and making a contribution. They satisfy their needs in one-to-one or small-group interaction using strong verbal skills to teach, counsel, or advise. They are drawn to close interpersonal relationships and are less apt to engage in intellectual or extensive physical activity.

▶ *Enterprising.* These people describe themselves as assertive, risk-taking, and persuasive. They value prestige, power, and status and are more inclined than other types to pursue it. They use verbal skills to supervise, lead, direct, and persuade rather than to support or guide. They are interested in people and in achieving organizational goals.

▶ *Conventional.* These people describe themselves as neat, orderly, detail-oriented, and persistent. They value order, structure, prestige, and status and possess a high degree of self-control. They are not opposed to rules and regulations. They are skilled in organizing, planning, and scheduling and are interested in data and people.

*Adapted from John L. Holland, *Self-Directed Search Manual* (Psychological Assessment Resources:1985). Copyright © 1985 by PAR, Inc. Reprinted with permission.

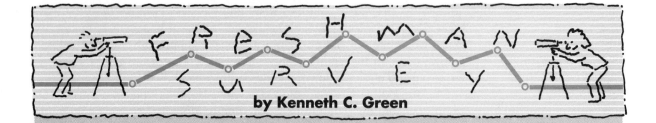

by Kenneth C. Green

Engineering and Computer Science

Freshman interest in engineering careers and majors fell sharply in the early 1970s, just after the first Apollo moon walk and the termination of funding for the American supersonic transport airplane project (an American version of the Concorde) and other large government contracts. Potential engineering students received ample televised coverage of unemployed engineers in Seattle, Long Beach, and St. Louis, cities where aerospace and defense contractors have large plants. Consequently these students opted for other fields and careers.

Freshman interest in engineering careers rose again after 1975. This increase reflected a return of men into engineering as well as a growing (if still small) number of women coming into this field. Later in the 1970s rising interest in technical careers such as engineering and computing was further stimulated by declines elsewhere in the economy; science and technology were the only "hot spots" in an otherwise slow job market between 1977 and 1982.

In the mid- to late-1980s, however, student interest in engineering dropped surprisingly, about one-fourth, from a peak of 12 percent in 1982 to 8 percent in 1990. In this same period there was an even more significant decline in the proportion of entering freshmen planning to pursue computing majors and careers as programmers or systems analysts. These declines are surprising because the job market remains very strong for people with technical skills. As a group technical majors command the highest salaries of all students earning bachelor's degrees, and the demand for technical graduates will remain strong well into the twenty-first century.

Why the apparent declining interest in technical careers? Special analyses of the UCLA

Freshman Interest in Technology Careers, 1966–1990

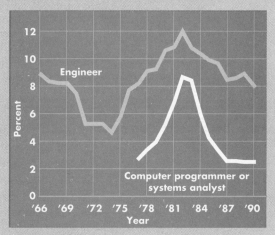

SOURCE: Higher Education Research Institute, UCLA

Freshman Survey data suggest that the drop is largely due to the movement of the B students into and then out of the technical fields. The dire state of the economy in the late 1970s and early 1980s prompted many science-capable B students to consider technical careers. As employment options improved in other sectors, many of the B students who were challenged by the science and mathematics requirements of their majors moved into less academically demanding fields.

The recent decline in freshman interest in computer science is also due, in part, to increasing student familiarity with the technology. More students have had contact with computers and have come to realize that they can be skilled and sophisticated computer users without becoming programmers.

EXERCISE 11.12 The Holland Categories

Look back over Holland's list of categories. Which category most accurately describes you? Write it here:

1. _____

Now look back over the other categories. Which of the remaining categories most nearly fit you? Write your second and third choices here:

2. _____

3. _____

In choosing several categories that seem to best describe you, don't let one or two factors keep you from making a choice. Choose the ones that contain the *most* true statements about you.

Holland's system organizes career fields into the same six categories. Career fields are grouped according to what a particular career field requires of a person (skills and personality characteristics most commonly associated with success in those fields) and what rewards particular career fields provide for people (interests and values most commonly associated with satisfaction). As you read the following examples, see how your career interests match the category as described by Holland.

► *Realistic.* Agricultural engineer, barber, dairy farmer, electrical contractor, ferryboat captain, gem cutter, heavy equipment operator, industrial arts teacher, jeweler, navy officer, health and safety specialist, radio repairer, sheet metal worker, tailor, fitness director, package engineer, electronics technician, computer graphics technician, coach, PE teacher

► *Investigative.* Urban planner, chemical engineer, bacteriologist, cattle-breeding technician, ecologist, flight engineer, genealogist, handwriting analyst, laboratory technician, marine scientist, nuclear medical technologist, obstetrician, quality control technician, sanitation scientist, TV repairer, balloon pilot, computer programmer, robotics engineer, environmentalist, physician, college professor

► *Artistic.* Architect, film editor/director, actor, cartoonist, interior decorator, fashion model, furrier, graphic communications specialist, jewelry designer, journalist, medical illustrator, editor, orchestra leader, public relations specialist, sculptor, telecommunications coordinator, media specialist, librarian, reporter

► *Social.* Nurse, teacher, caterer, social worker, genetic counselor, home economist, job analyst, marriage counselor, parole officer, rehabilitation counselor, school superintendent, theater manager, production expediter, geriatric specialist, insurance claims specialist,

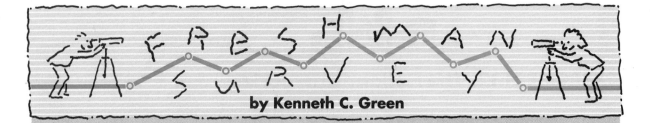

FRESHMAN SURVEY

by Kenneth C. Green

Popular Business

Between 1972 and 1990 the proportion of first-year students planning business careers more than doubled, as the first figure shows. Although interest in business careers has declined by one-fourth since the peak in 1987, it is still the most popular career choice among college students. The percentage of first-year students planning to major in business increased from 14.3 percent in 1966 to 24.6 percent in 1987, and then dropped to 18.6 percent in 1990.

Women's interest in business has grown even more dramatically, as the second figure shows. Between 1966 and 1985 the proportion of women planning business careers increased six-fold. Indeed, in some business specializations women now outnumber men. For several years more women than men have stated a preference for accounting majors and careers.

Freshman interest in the business major remains high despite the rising chorus of corporate leaders who say they want to hire well-read, well-trained people who have been well prepared in the *liberal arts*! That students in the mid- and late-1980s did not accept this message seemed to be their way of saying that they doubted the vocal CEO's were working the campus recruitment circuit themselves. Instead they assume, wrongly at times, that many college recruiters want business majors.

Ironically many students today do not recognize training in *science* as a resource for business careers. Yet to work in pharmaceutical sales and marketing or many other technical fields, college graduates must have a strong background in the sciences, along with strong writing, presentation, and interpersonal skills. Others fail to see how skills acquired as literature or social science majors apply to the business world.

While business offers many opportunities—both as a major and as a career—do *not* assume that you must study one to pursue the other. Indeed, each year tens of thousands of liberal arts graduates find good jobs and begin

Freshman Interest in Business Careers, 1966–1990

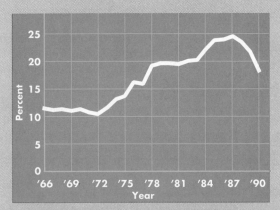

SOURCE: Higher Education Research Institute, UCLA

Freshman Interest in Business Careers, by Sex, 1966–1990

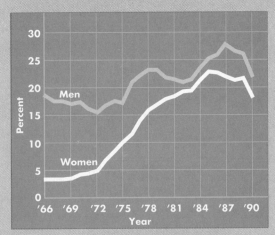

SOURCE: Higher Education Research Institute, UCLA

promising careers in hundreds of thousands of large corporations and small businesses. Your career options will not be determined exclusively by *what* you study; rather, career opportunities ultimately depend on *how* you capitalize on the opportunities available to you in college.

Figure 11.1 Holland's Hexagonal Model of Career Fields

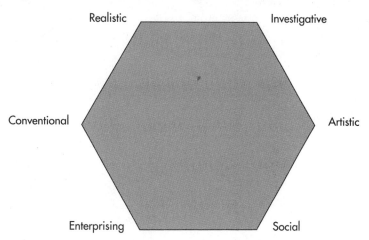

minister, travel agent, guidance counselor, convention planner, career specialist

► *Enterprising.* Banker, city manager, employment interviewer, FBI agent, health administrator, industrial relations director, judge, labor arbitrator, personnel assistant, TV announcer, salary and wage administrator, insurance salesperson, sales engineer, lawyer, sales representative, marketing specialist, promoter

► *Conventional.* Accountant, statistician, census enumerator, data processor, hospital administrator, instrument assembler, insurance administrator, legal secretary, library assistant, office manager, reservation agent, information consultant, underwriter, auditor, personnel specialist, data base manager, abstractor/indexer

At first glance Holland's model may seem to be a simple method for matching people to career fields, but it was never meant for that purpose. Your career choices ultimately will involve a complex assessment of the factors that are most important to you. To display the relationship between career fields and the potential conflicts people face as they consider them, Holland's model is commonly presented in a hexagonal shape (see Figure 11.1). The closer the types, the closer the relationships among the career fields; the farther apart the types, the more conflict between the career fields.

EXERCISE 11.13   The Holland Hexagon

See where your first, second, and third choices in Exercise 11.12 are located on the Holland hexagon. Are they close together or far apart? If they're far apart, do you feel they do in fact reflect a conflict in your goals or interests? How has the conflict affected you so far? Write a brief statement about this. Discuss your categories and your written response with another member of the class.

Looking for an unusual major? Try bagpiping at Carnegie-Mellon University. Requirements include bagpipe instruction, and music theory, composition, and history. Aerobic exercise may also be recommended.

Holland's model can help you address the problem of career choice in two ways. First, you can begin to identify many career fields that are consistent with what you know about yourself. Once you've identified potential fields, you can use the career library at your college to get more information about those fields. Find out the following information:

► Daily activities for specific jobs
► Interests and abilities required
► Preparation required for entry
► Working conditions
► Salary and benefits
► Employment outlook

Second, you can begin to identify the harmony or conflicts in your career choices. This will help you analyze the reasons for your career decisions and be more confident as you make choices.

College students often view the choice of a career as a monumental and irreversible decision. Some feel haunted by the choice as they decide on a college major. Others panic about it as they approach graduation and begin to look for a job. They falsely assume that "the decision" will make all the difference in their lives. In its broadest sense a career is the sum of the decisions you make over a lifetime. There is no "right occupation" just waiting to be discovered. Rather, there are many career choices you may find fulfilling and satisfying. The question to consider is, "What is the *best* choice for me *now*?"

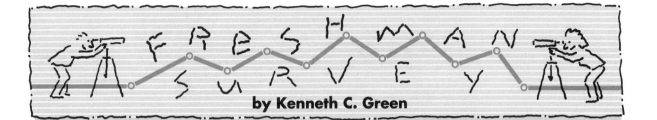

by Kenneth C. Green

Declining Majors in the Humanities

The humanities have declined in freshman popularity over the past two decades, with English and the fine arts especially hard hit. For example, between 1966 and 1990 the proportion of freshmen planning to major in English fell from 4.4 to 1.3 percent. (English actually dropped as low as 0.8 percent in 1982!)

Although many students indicate that they would prefer to major in literature, they also feel they need to study business to be competitive in the job market. However, some corporations prefer liberal arts majors to business students as management trainees, even though the former group may have comparatively little formal training in "business skills." You may be surprised to learn that in some organizations liberal arts majors actually have a better track record for performance and promotion than their peers who majored in business as undergraduates. For example, a twenty-year study of AT&T employees reveals that liberal arts majors advanced faster than other, nontechnical managers (that is, individuals who were not initially hired as engineers or researchers).

What advantages or disadvantages do you see in these fewer numbers for those who major in English and other liberal arts fields? Why do you think some corporations would prefer to hire liberal arts graduates over business majors?

TIME FOR ACTION

In selecting a major, ask yourself these questions:

1. Am I interested in learning about the field?
2. Do I have the skills necessary for success?
3. Am I gaining skills, information, and perspectives that will be helpful in my career choices?

After choosing a major, begin to learn about other academic opportunities in your department. Talk with your advisor about **minors, internships, independent study, study abroad, exchange programs,** and other options that might broaden your academic experience.

As we said earlier, for some people there is a direct correlation between the major and the career; for others the choice of a major is best based on subject interest, not career considerations. If your major is not directly related to your career choices, plan to use work experience or campus activities to gain entry into your first job—many students are hired as bank management trainees or investment analysts based on their experience as treasurer of a student union committee rather than on their finance major.

Involvement in campus activities and part-time jobs are important in two ways. First, these experiences serve as the basis of a resume, which you will write to get your first job after college. Second, through these experiences you develop confidence in your career choice. It is better to discover that you

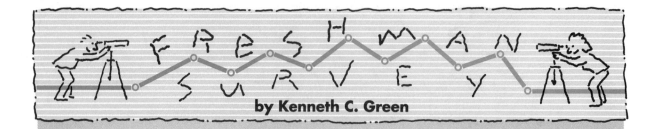

by Kenneth C. Green

Falling Interest in Science

Of all the traditional liberal arts fields, the sciences have shown the most severe decline in student popularity. Between 1966 and 1990 the proportion of freshmen planning to major in mathematics dropped by 80 percent while interest in physical sciences majors (for example, chemistry and physics) fell by half, as shown in the accompanying figure. Only the biological sciences have maintained a relatively stable "market share" of freshman interest; however, this probably reflects freshman interest in premed studies rather than any intrinsic interest in biological science. (What historical events might explain the briefly increased interest in biological sciences in the mid-1970s?)

Conventional wisdom might suggest that interest in science majors among first-year women should have *increased* over the past two decades, as women presumably received more encouragement to pursue "nontraditional" majors and careers. However, the UCLA Freshman Survey data suggest that women's interest in science majors dropped from 8.8 percent in 1966 to 5.0 percent in 1990. How would you explain this decline?

Freshman Interest in Science Majors, 1966–1990

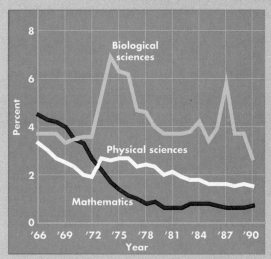

SOURCE: Higher Education Research Institute, UCLA

hate inventory control *before* you graduate and accept a fabulous, high-paying job as an inventory control trainee.

Throughout this section you have done exercises aimed at gathering information about yourself and about the world of work and clarifying the most important issues involved in your choice of career and academic major. Here are a few other activities that may help:

► *Career exploration.* Once you've selected possible career fields, talk with people working in those fields to get a clear idea of what life is really like as a social worker or accountant or office manager. Read what people in this field read. Visit local professional association meetings.

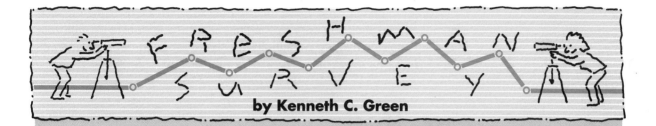

by Kenneth C. Green

A Teacher's Market

There has been growing discussion in recent years about the critical role of education to the nation's future, and students are once again thinking about teaching careers.

As the accompanying figure shows, teaching was an extremely popular career choice among young women two decades ago. But its popularity fell dramatically in the 1970s and the first part of the 1980s. Yet in recent years student interest in teaching careers has been rising. Why do you think freshman interest in teaching careers has been on the rise since 1985?

Although the numbers are up, current levels of interest in teaching are still far below those of the mid- to late-1960s — and well below the numbers required to meet future needs. Even though teaching is becoming a popular career choice again, it seems unlikely that we will have enough new teachers in the next ten or fifteen years.

You may wish to think about education as a major or minor and about teaching as a career: Demand is very high and salaries have improved dramatically in recent years.

Freshman Interest in Teaching Careers, by Sex, 1966–1990

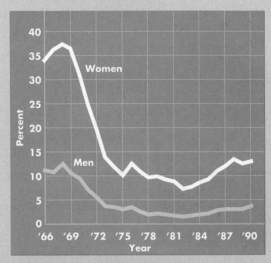

SOURCE: Higher Education Research Institute, UCLA

▶ *Choice of major.* Talk with faculty members about the skills and areas of expertise you'll develop in studying the disciplines they're teaching. Ask if they're aware of careers or jobs in which the skills and knowledge they teach can be utilized.

▶ *Connection between major and career.* Ask employers if they look for graduates with certain majors or academic backgrounds for their entry-level positions.

▶ *Skill development.* Get involved in work experiences or campus activities that will allow you to develop skills and areas of expertise useful to your career plans. Find a summer job in that area, or volunteer as an intern. Keep a record of skills you have demonstrated.

By identifying and evaluating your interests and skills, obtaining career information, and assessing the role of goals and work values in your life, you turn career planning into an effective decision-making process. Career planning isn't a quick and easy way to find out what you want to do with your life, but it can point you to potentially satisfying jobs. Career planning *can* help you find your place in the world of work. Take advantage of it.

EXERCISE 11.14 Planning Your Resume

Using the forms on pages 229–230, prepare your resume first as it would look today. Then, drawing on what you have learned from this section, career experts, and faculty advisors, prepare a second resume as you would like it to look when you graduate.

JOURNAL

Reread the five basic questions about you and the career planning process on page 211 and answer them accordingly. If you are still undecided about your major and career choice, that's fine; just answer the questions as best you can.

SUGGESTIONS FOR FURTHER READING

Bolles, Richard N. *What Color Is Your Parachute? A Practical Manual for Job Hunters and Career Changers*. Berkeley, Calif.: Ten Speed Press, 1992.

Carney, Clarke G., and Cinda Field Wells. *Discover the Career Within You*, 3rd ed. Pacific Grove, Calif.: Brooks/Cole, 1991.

Carney, Clarke G., Cinda F. Wells, and Don Streufert. *Career Planning: Skills to Build Your Future*. New York: Van Nostrand, 1987.

Dictionary of Occupational Titles (DOT). Washington, D.C.: Bureau of Labor Statistics.

Directory of Directories. Detroit: Gale Research. Published annually.

Encyclopedia of Associations. Detroit: Gale Research. Published annually.

Figler, Howard. *The Complete Job-Search Handbook*. New York: Holt, Rinehart & Winston, 1979.

———. *PATH—A Career Workbook for Liberal Arts Students*. Cranston, R.I.: Carroll Press, 1979.

Harris-Bowlsbey, Joann, James D. Spivack, and Ruth S. Lisansky. *Take Hold of Your Future*. Towson, Md.: American College Testing, 1982.

Holland, John. *The Self-Directed Search Professional Manual*. Gainesville, Fla.: Psychological Assessment Resources, 1985.

Jackson, Tom. *The Perfect Resume*. Garden City, N.Y.: Anchor Books, 1981.

Kennedy, Joyce, and Darryl Laramore. *Career Book*. Lincolnwood, Ill.: VGM Career Horizons, 1988.

Occupational Outlook Handbook, 1986–87 ed. Washington, D.C.: U.S. Department of Labor, 1987.

Salzman, Marion, and Nancy Marx Better. *Wanted: Liberal Arts Graduates*. New York: Doubleday, 1987.

Stair, Lila B. *Careers in Business: Selecting and Planning Your Career Path*. Homewood, Ill.: Irwin, 1986.

My Current Resume

(Date: _____)

_____
(Your name)

EDUCATION:

_____
_____
_____

Highlights of Education:

_____
_____
_____

WORK EXPERIENCE:

_____
_____
_____

Highlights of Work Experience (include your accomplishments):

_____
_____
_____

CO-CURRICULAR ACTIVITIES:

_____
_____
_____

Highlights of Co-curricular Activities (include your accomplishments):

_____
_____
_____

HONORS AND AWARDS:

_____
_____
_____

My Ideal Resume at Graduation

(Date: _____)

_____
(Your name)

EDUCATION:

_____
_____
_____

Highlights of Education:

_____
_____
_____

WORK EXPERIENCE:

_____
_____
_____

Highlights of Work Experience (include your accomplishments):

_____
_____
_____

CO-CURRICULAR ACTIVITIES:

_____
_____
_____

Highlights of Co-curricular Activities (include your accomplishments):

_____
_____
_____

HONORS AND AWARDS:

_____
_____
_____

C H A P T E R

12

▼▼▼▼▼▼▼▼▼▼▼▼▼▼▼▼▼

The New Diversity

**Women: The Majority
of First-Year Students**
Sue V. Rosser

Minorities: The Coming Majority
Laura I. Rendón

**You're Never Too Old
to Go to Class**
Dorothy S. Fidler

Women: The Majority of First-Year Students

All this talk about sexism in the classroom got me thinking. All of my professors are men. And my academic advisor kind of looked at me when I said I might major in geology. My boyfriend's advisor told him *it* was a great choice! My psych professor told us that women were not often used as subjects in experiments because they "messed up the data." Maybe something's messed up all right, but I don't think it's me.

SUE V. ROSSER *is director of women's studies and professor of family and preventive medicine at the University of South Carolina, Columbia. She believes that the first year is particularly crucial for students as they develop attitudes about education, majors, and careers.*

"It was due to the influence of one professor, his outstanding teaching, and his pushing me to go into science during my first year, that I chose my current career," she says. Rosser feels that including information about women in our college curriculum can have a strong positive impact on the lives of women students. She says, "With the significant issues and problems facing our nation today, we cannot afford to waste the resources of over half the population."

Were you aware that women were not permitted to enroll in institutions of higher education in the United States until 1833, when Oberlin College began to admit women and African-Americans? Did you know that although several women's colleges were established in the middle of the nineteenth century, it was only when publicly funded, land grant universities were founded later in the century that coeducation became prevalent? Or that only in the last twenty-five years have most men's colleges, such as Harvard and Yale, become schools for men and women, fully integrating degree programs, residences, and curricula? During the past two decades, however, changes in the role of women in society have reversed the pattern of male dominance. Women are now the majority of college students, approximately 54 percent.

Unfortunately many aspects of the classroom environment have not yet changed to reflect the needs of this new majority. Although the changes that are needed may not be completed in our lifetime, it is heartening to see what has taken place in just the last few years. Sexist language, classroom behavior, and curricular content are currently undergoing changes that should ultimately remove sexism from the classroom.

If you are a female, you may be wondering what we're talking about. You may feel that you have never been discriminated against in the classroom, either personally or sexually. If you are a male, you may be skeptical about the idea that classroom environments favor your gender. If this is the case, I would like to share with you my own experiences of growing up and attending college in a "man's world."

When I entered college at the University of Wisconsin–Madison in 1965, it was an exciting time to be a student. As part of the baby boom generation, our class represented the largest, most qualified group to enter the university. Our college years were times of student activism over issues such as the Vietnam War, civil rights, and the women's movement.

As an undergraduate I was not really aware of discrimination against me as a woman. It never occurred to me until many years later that women's history and accomplishments and other information about women were absent from the courses I took. For example, my literature classes included only books written by men, and my psychology professor stated that women were not used as subjects in experiments because they didn't fit the model and

"messed up the data." However, I just accepted this as the way things were. I didn't really wonder why information about women was also missing from my courses in art history, biology, and political science.

Only one of my professors during the entire four years was a woman, but three of my teaching assistants were women. Although most of my male professors were nice to me, particularly since I was a good student, I did notice that a few of them seemed to take the male students a little more seriously, especially when the discussion turned to future plans and careers. One time I dropped a course rather than risk a bad grade from the teaching assistant who refused to accept my polite excuses for why I couldn't go out with him.

All of these experiences, and similar ones I had in graduate school, just seemed like a normal part of a woman's life in our society. It was not until 1975, when I became involved with women's studies, that I began to recognize the difference that the absence of women from the curriculum, the lack of female role models, and a "chilly climate" in the classroom for women can make in the college experience.

In this section we'll examine **sexism** in terms of how men and women may be treated differently in the classroom and how and why information about women should be included in the curriculum. Whether you are a man or a woman, this information may help you to assess more clearly what you are learning as well as what is happening in the classroom.

LANGUAGE

Although generally unintentional, the use of the male gender in language tends to color meaning. When terms such as *he* and *mankind* are used, people rarely visualize women. Such generic use of the masculine term also implies that being male is the norm in society, when in actuality using masculine nouns and pronouns to refer to all people excludes more than half of the population! Sexism in language takes a variety of forms beyond usage of the generic pronoun. **Gender referencing** ("the doctor gives *his* patient" but "the nurse gives *her* patient") permeates classroom language and writing and suggests career stereotypes. **Labeling** has often been used as a

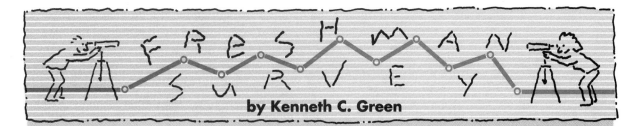

FRESHMAN SURVEY

by Kenneth C. Green

Grades and Self-Assessment

What does the accompanying figure show about the high school grades of women entering college? Would it surprise you to learn that women generally have less self-confidence in their academic preparation than men, despite the fact that they have higher grades? How would you explain the discrepancy between the women's higher grades and their lower self-confidence?

High School Grades of Entering Freshmen, by Sex, 1966–1990 (percentages reporting A or A⁻ grade point average)

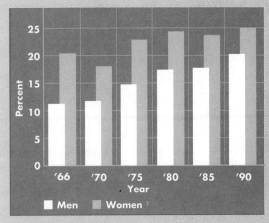

SOURCE: Higher Education Research Institute, UCLA

subtle form of discrimination against women and people of color ("boy" or "girl" for an adult; "credit to your race"). **Nonparallel terminology** ("men and ladies" or "the dentist and his doctor wife were in Hawaii") also conveys unequal status. **Stereotyping** may refer to roles (all women as housewives), to occupations (all truck drivers as men), to personality characteristics (stoic men versus passive women), and to physical, mental, and emotional characteristics (mathematical men and verbal women).

It is not difficult to replace such language with words appropriate for both men and women. Simply do the following:

1. Use plural nouns and pronouns ("help *children* develop *their* table manners" rather than "help the *child* develop *his* table manners").

2. Replace pronouns with articles ("every doctor has *a* preferred method of treatment" rather than "every doctor has *his* preferred method of treatment").

3. Eliminate the pronoun ("each social worker determines the best way *to handle* difficult clients" instead of "each social worker determines the best way *that she can handle* difficult clients").

4. Use genderless nouns ("the average citizen" rather than "the man on the street"; "sales*person*" for "sales*man*"; "student" instead of "coed").

Most instructors try to eliminate the barriers to learning raised by stereotypical, sexist, or racist language. However, because of varied backgrounds, some people have difficulty in recognizing such language. In their publication *A Guide to Nonsexist Language*, the Association of American Colleges suggests "two abbreviated rules to check material for bias: Would you say the same thing about a person of the opposite sex? Would you like it said about you? That's the bottom line. Use your own good sense on whether a joke, comment or image is funny or whether it unfairly exploits people and perpetuates stereotypes" (p. 1).

EXERCISE 12.1   Sexist Language

Decide whether each of the following sentences contains wording that should be changed because of unnecessary gender referencing, stereotyping, or other sexist language. Explain why you think the passage should be changed or left unchanged. Make your changes, if any, directly on the sentences below.

1. Studies of preindustrial cultures suggest that primitive man spent a greater part of each day resting than do most late-twentieth-century Americans.

2. Typically, a legal secretary earns much less than the lawyer she works for.

3. When the *Cadence* first put out to sea, she was as well manned as any great racing ship had ever been.

4. The athlete's training, his genetic inheritance, his sense of purpose and commitment, and his willingness to do as his coaches and trainers advise him all play a part in his success.

5. Four score and seven years ago, our fathers brought forth on this continent a new nation, conceived in liberty and dedicated to the proposition that all men are created equal.

6. Biologists compared the development of the fetus in the rat, the guinea pig, the goat, and man.

7. Ardery's thesis, which so pleased the American businessman, was that man was by nature an aggressive, hostile beast.

8. If you doubt mankind's ingratitude, just look at the state of Mother Earth.

9. The party we met at the border consisted of several refugees along with their wives and children.

10. His work as a male nurse during the Civil War affected Whitman deeply.

11. Each of us should do as she pleases.

CLASSROOM BEHAVIORS

Studies of classes containing both men and women have demonstrated that men talk more than women and exert more control over the topic of conversation. Men also interrupt women much more frequently than women interrupt men.

In addition to sexist language, sexism in nonverbal behavior or body language may encourage males to learn while discouraging females. Studies indicate that some faculty may make eye contact more often with men than women, nod and gesture more often in response to men's questions and comments than to women's, and wait longer for men than for women to answer a question before going on to another student. In certain situations women may be "squeezed out" from viewing a laboratory assignment or demonstration, may be asked simpler questions than men ("On what date did the United States enter World War II?" versus "What were the causes of World War II?"), or may be passed over in favor of men as student assistants.

EXERCISE 12.2 Interactions in the Classroom

Observe the gender composition (number of males and females) in each of the classes you are taking this semester. Take a watch with a second hand to class on a day that a large part of the period will be devoted to discussion to aid you in answering the following questions:

1. Do male or female students talk more frequently in class? (Be sure to count the number of times rather than relying on your impression.)
2. Do male or female students talk for a longer period of time when called upon?
3. Does the professor call more frequently on male or female students?
4. Does the professor wait as long for a female student to respond to a question as for a male student?
5. Do your answers to questions 1–4 vary depending upon the gender composition of the class?

CURRICULAR CONTENT

Sexism in course content may present an additional barrier to learning for female students. Information on the history, roles, experiences, and accomplishments of women has traditionally been absent from the curriculum. However, during the past two decades the new scholarship on women has produced extensive information about the roles, accomplishments, and experiences of women. Increased numbers of women in college and in the work force, the changing role of women in society, and the explosion of new knowledge demand that the male bias in the curriculum be eliminated.

Integrating information about women into the curriculum generally occurs in phases. In the first phase women are absent from the curriculum; in the final phase women are part of a **gender-balanced curriculum**. The model of integration developed by Peggy McIntosh (1984) of the Wellesley Center for Research on Women includes five phases.

Phase I: The Womanless Curriculum

This is the traditional curriculum, in which the absence of women is not even noted. In the study of history only men and the great events involving them are considered; for instance, presidents and battles are emphasized. Art history courses recently taught on many campuses also reflect this pattern — the most widely used art history text included no women artists until the 1986 version. English courses at this stage include few or no women authors. Likewise much psychological research and many psychology courses ignore women entirely; for example, many theories of human development are based on male subjects only. In most biology and other science courses, gender is not even considered to be an issue, since science is "objective." However, many experiments are run on male animal subjects only, while certain subjects of particular interest to women, such as childbirth and other women's health concerns, receive less funding for research. Responding to this problem, the National Institutes of Health issued new guidelines in December 1986, suggesting that proposals draw on both male and female experimental subjects and include topics of interest to women.

Phase II: The Curriculum with "Add-on" Women

In this phase heroines, exceptional women, or an elite few who are seen to have been of benefit to culture as defined by the traditional standards of the discipline are included in the curriculum but only as afterthoughts. This stage is characterized by the addition of women without any change in the basic syllabus or traditional framework of the course. History courses might include women such as Joan of Arc, Abigail Adams, or Betsy Ross. The nine women who have won a Nobel Prize in medicine or science certainly would be included at this stage. Literary anthologies have been passing gradually through this phase. For example, the 1977 edition of the *Norton Introduction to Literature* contained only 48 writings by women authors and 345 by men, whereas the 1991 edition contained 145 writings by women and 312 by men.

Phase III: The Curriculum in Which the Treatment or Absence of Women Is Regarded as a Problem or an Anomaly

In this phase women are viewed as victims, as deprived or defective variations of men, or as protestors. At this stage historians might ask why there have been no female presidents. People considering art history begin to ask

It was big news in 1990 when Mills College decided to continue its all-women's program. Since the 1960s, many formerly all-women's colleges have opened their doors to men — one more reason your college should strive for a gender-balanced curriculum.

questions like, "Why aren't there more women artists, and what is art anyway?" In English courses the question becomes, "Why aren't there any female Shakespeares?" In psychology the question becomes, "Why doesn't women's development fit the models of human development?" This soon leads to the question of what is wrong with psychological models that don't address half of the people in the world. At this stage many biologists point out some of the flaws in research studies that have supposedly proven superior mathematical ability in males.

Phase IV: The Curriculum in Which Women Are the Focus for Studies

This is the arena of women's studies, where women become the center of research and teaching. This phase acknowledges that since women have had half of the world's life experiences, those experiences need to be documented, studied, and considered as half of history. Focusing on women causes faculty to use all kinds of evidence and source materials that academic people are not in the habit of using. In this phase people doing art history research may begin to view certain types of crafts, quilts, and stitchery work (much of which has traditionally been done by women) as art. In English courses people look at what women have written — diaries, letters, novels — and examine how it differs from the writings of men. Psychologists begin to explore female models of development that emphasize different methods of ethical and moral decision making practiced by girls and women compared to boys and men.

Phase V: The Curriculum Redefined and Reconstructed to Include Us All

This is the ultimate goal toward which many are working: the gender-balanced curriculum. Granted, it will be a long time in the making and will probably not occur in our lifetime, but such a curriculum will help students understand that women are both part of and alien to the dominant male-defined culture.

In this final phase women are not separated out but are present in all disciplines. The idea is not to replace the womanless curriculum with the manless curriculum, but to include the knowledge about women in all introductory and advanced courses. Only when learning reflects the diversity of experiences, roles, and achievements in our *whole* population will it fully prepare us for the diversity in the world.

EXERCISE 12.3 Your Previous Learning

Use what you learned during high school to do the following:

1. List three women and three men who are famous because of their contributions to American history.

   _____   _____

   _____   _____

   _____   _____

2. List four male and four female authors and the pieces of literature they have written.

   _____   _____

   _____   _____

   _____   _____

   _____   _____

3. List three male and three female scientists and the discovery for which each is known.

   _____   _____

   _____   _____

   _____   _____

Compare your responses with those of others in your class. Do you think that your academic education up to this point has paid enough attention to both men and women? In what subjects do you think your previous education has been influenced by sexism? In what subjects has it not?

TOWARD A NONSEXIST CLASSROOM

Sexism in language and classroom behaviors, combined with the absence of information about the achievements, roles, and experiences of women from most college courses, leaves many female students feeling somewhat alienated from what they are learning. Sexism may be particularly severe for women who seek careers in science and engineering, which are not perceived as traditional arenas for women. *The Classroom Climate: A Chilly One for Women?* (Hall and Sandler, 1982) documents the ways in which the small inequities that occur in the classroom may have a major negative effect upon a female student's self-esteem, choice of major, and career plans. If

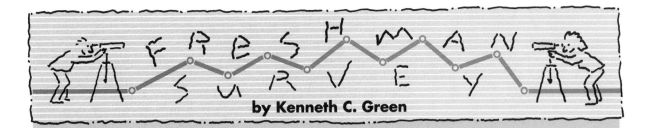

by Kenneth C. Green

Women Aim Higher

First-year students' degree aspirations have increased in recent years, as the accompanying figure suggests. Between 1980 and 1990 the proportion of first-year students planning to pursue some type of graduate degree rose by about one-fifth, from 49.3 percent to 60.7 percent. Interest in the doctorate gained by roughly half, from 7.9 to 12.4 percent.

Women's aspirations have risen even more dramatically. Between 1970 and 1990 the proportion of women planning to pursue a doctoral degree almost doubled, from 6.5 percent to 12.5 percent. Among the men, however, it's been an ebb and flow pattern. How would you explain these changes?

Aspirations for a Doctorate, by Sex, 1970–1990

SOURCE: Higher Education Research Institute, UCLA

these inequities are aggravated by such overt forms of sexism as **sexual harassment**, the effects on women are likely to be more severe. It may shock you to learn that 20–30 percent of all female college students experience some form of harassment ranging from sexist comments to direct solicitations for sexual favors to assault. Dropping the course, changing majors, or dropping out of college entirely may be reactions to sexual harassment.

Most colleges and universities have policies that make sexual harassment illegal. You should familiarize yourself with the policy of your institution so that you will understand your rights. You can usually find a copy of the policy in the dean of students office.

In addition the Association of American Colleges Project on the Status and Education of Women advises you to take the following steps to stop harassment:

1. Speak up and say no clearly at the time of an incident.
2. Keep records, such as a journal and any letters or notes received. Include names, dates, places, times, witnesses, and the nature of the harassment.
3. Tell someone such as a fellow student or co-worker.
4. Find a counselor who can give emotional support and information about the informal and formal procedures of the institution.

5. Consider writing a letter to the harasser. For legal reasons alone putting your complaint in writing is a wise move. It might also resolve the problem by making it clear to the other party that the remarks or behavior constituted sexual harassment. In some cases the harasser may not be aware that the conduct, though clearly intentional, was harassment. It is smart to seek legal counsel for assistance in writing such a letter. Ask your student affairs office for help in this regard. Your campus should have a designated individual to provide help in matters involving sexual harassment.

6. Report the behavior on the course evaluation form.

7. Consider reporting the incident to the person at your institution responsible for dealing with sexual harassment cases to determine whether you should pursue institutional, civil, or criminal action. On a given campus this person might be the affirmative action officer or the chief student personnel officer (for example, the vice president for student affairs). Or he or she might be located through the personal counseling center.

Other actions women and men can take to help faculty create a nonsexist classroom include the following:

1. Recognize features of your own speaking style and behavior that may contribute to sexism in the classroom, and change them.

2. Discuss your perceptions of classroom interactions with other students to see if their experience coincides with yours.

3. Give your professors positive feedback for their efforts to create a nonsexist learning climate.

4. Encourage the school newspaper or other student publications to write about sexism in the classroom.

5. Encourage student organizations to press for inclusion of classroom climate issues in faculty development programs, course evaluations, and official statements relating to teaching standards.

Most faculty and staff are eager to have all first-year students be as comfortable in their learning environment as possible. Overcoming sexism as a barrier to learning and including more information about women in curricular content are ways to begin to create an environment that is conducive to learning for *all* college students.

EXERCISE 12.4 **Comparing Your Experience**

On the basis of your personal experience, respond Y for yes or N for no to the following statements.

_____ 1. I find I have trouble picturing or including myself when I hear terms like *mankind*.

_____ 2. I think that males are superior to females in mathematical ability.

_____ 3. I often find myself being interrupted or ignored by other students.

_____ 4. I have been sexually harassed by an employer or professor.

_____ 5. A professor or another student has questioned whether I am serious about my chosen career.

_____ 6. I worry a considerable amount about how well my career plans will fit in with my plans for a relationship and/or family.

_____ 7. I have been questioned by my professor or advisor about my plans for marriage or family.

_____ 8. All of my classes include information about contributions made by famous people of my sex.

_____ 9. Several times when I was in high school, a teacher made comments to me about my clothes or physical appearance.

_____ 10. I find that I learn the names of the individuals of the opposite sex in my classes better than the names of the people of my own sex.

_____ 11. A factor in the choice of my major was that it is a traditionally appropriate field for a person of my sex.

_____ 12. At least half of the faculty members are of the same sex that I am.

Compare your responses with those of someone of the opposite sex. Compare the responses of males in your class with those of females. What patterns emerge? What, if anything, do you think should be done about them?

JOURNAL

What are your reactions to the statements about sexism on campus? Based on the classes you are taking, how prevalent do you think sexism is on your campus? Are you aware of sexist comments or behaviors on the part of your instructors or other students? How did these behaviors make you feel? Which phase of the curriculum as outlined in this section best describes the courses you have taken so far?

REFERENCES AND SUGGESTIONS FOR FURTHER READING

Andre, Judith. "Stereotypes: Conceptual and Normative Considerations." In *Women's Studies in the South*, ed. Rhoda E. Barge Johnson. Dubuque, Iowa: Kendall/Hunt, 1991.

Association of American Colleges. *A Guide to Nonsexist Language*. Washington, D.C.: Project on the Status and Education of Women, 1986.

Basow, Susan A. *Gender Stereotypes: Traditions and Alternatives*, 3rd ed. Pacific Grove, Calif.: Brooks/Cole, 1992.

Hall, Roberta M., and Bernice R. Sandler. *The Classroom Climate: A Chilly One for Women?* Washington, D.C.: Project on the Status and Education of Women, 1982.

McIntosh, Peggy. "The Study of Women: Processes of Personal and Curricular Revision." *The Forum for Liberal Education* 6, no. 5 (1984): 2–4.

Moses, Yolanda T. *Black Women in Academia: Issues and Strategies*. Washington, D.C.: Association of American Colleges Project on the Status and Education of Women, 1989.

Paludi, Michele A., and Darlene C. DeFour. "Research on Sexual Harassment in the Academy: Definitions, Findings, Constraints, Responses." *Initiatives* 52: 43–49, Fall, 1989.

Rosser, Sue. *Female Friendly Science*. New York: Pergamon Press, 1990.

———. *Teaching About Science and Health from a Feminist Perspective*. New York: Pergamon Press, 1986.

Shapiro, Amy H. "Creating a Conversation: Teaching All Women in the Feminist Classroom." *NWSA Journal* 3(1):70–80, 1991.

Minorities: The Coming Majority

I was so embarrassed once when my high school history teacher asked my opinion of the civil rights movement of the 1960s. Maybe it wasn't right to tell her in front of the class that, since I wasn't even alive then, I wondered why she considered me the expert. Because I'm black? If you're anything but white, people see you as different. They don't expect as much from African-Americans, and they think all Asians are walking Einsteins. When are they going to catch on to the fact that we're individuals just like anyone else?

LAURA I. RENDÓN *is an associate professor of higher education at Arizona State University, Tempe. She began her higher education at Laredo Junior College, Texas, in 1966.*

"At the time I didn't realize that I was one of the few Hispanics in the country enrolling in college," she says. "Today I am one of the few Hispanic women university professors. As a Mexican-American who has herself experienced the personal struggles minority and women students undergo in college, I wrote this section to help Asian, Alaska Native, American Indian, African-American, Hispanic, and other minority students succeed in college, and to help nonminority students learn more about their minority peers and understand better what it means to be a minority student on a predominantly white campus. In addition, I believe that what I have to say about ensuring personal success can work for anyone."

African-American, Hispanic, Asian, Alaska Native, American Indian, and other minority students are among the most talked-about student groups in the American educational system today. And with good reason. The "minority" population of the United States is growing so fast that the term *minority* is rapidly becoming outdated. According to *Education That Works*, a 1990 report issued by the Quality Education for Minorities (QEM) project, some 48 million Americans (20 percent) are Alaska Native, American Indian, African-American, or Hispanic. It is expected that by the year 2020 one-third of the nation will consist of these and other "minority" groups. By the last quarter of the twenty-first century, largely as a result of immigration and high birth rates for racial and ethnic minorities, these minorities are expected to be the majority in this country. If the projections hold, by the year 2000 minorities will make up more than 30 percent of the college-going population, and by 2025 nearly 40 percent.

This monumental population shift will have important effects on all of us. In some respects it is a change for which neither our nation nor our higher-education system is well prepared. To some individuals it may seem threatening, just as the arrival and growth of new religious or national minorities — Irish or Italian Catholics, German or Russian Jews, Eastern Europeans, and so on — seemed threatening to some earlier generations of Americans.

This section discusses how we can work together to make the college experience successful for everyone. Much of the advice I offer to minority students applies to all other students as well, especially those who have also had to deal with problems of economic disadvantage, less-than-ideal high school preparation, the strains of feeling culturally different, or the pressure of being the first in their family to go to college. Keep in mind, however, that not all minority students fit the same pattern. For instance, within any minority group, while many students have attended academically substandard high schools or come to college encumbered by numerous social and economic problems, there are also those who are quite well prepared and whose backgrounds are impressive by any standards.

GOOD NEWS AND BAD

In some respects this is a bright new era for minority Americans in general and for minority college students in particular. According to the 1990 QEM report minority students now form the majority in such large urban elementary and secondary school districts as New York City, Los Angeles, Chicago, Houston, San Antonio, Detroit, Albuquerque, and El Paso. In 1989 thirteen out of Boston's seventeen public high school valedictorians were born in foreign countries. More minority students who attend high school are graduating and more are enrolling in college. In 1986, 76.4 percent of African-American students graduated from high school, as did 59.9 percent of Hispanics, 60 percent of American Indians, and 83 percent of whites. In 1980, 80 percent of Asian males and over 70 percent of Asian females ages 18–24 were high school graduates, and between 1976 and 1986, college enrollments among Asian students increased by 125 percent (Suzuki, 1989).

Progress in education is paralleled by increasing numbers of minority individuals in the higher levels of national political, social, educational, and economic life. In politics, many people have enjoyed strong support from both white and nonwhite voters, including Jesse Jackson, twice a presidential contender; Henry Cisneros, former mayor of San Antonio; David Dinkins, mayor of New York City; and Virginia Governor L. Douglas Wilder, the first elected African-American governor in U.S. history.

Progress in education is reflected in the careers of such people as Native American Janine Pease-Windy Boy, president of Little Big Horn College in Montana; Elsa Gomez, a Puerto Rican and the first Hispanic woman to be named president of a four-year college (Kean College of New Jersey); and Lauro Cavazos, a Mexican-American from south Texas and former U.S. secretary of education.

In the arts author Alice Walker (*The Color Purple*) and filmmaker Spike Lee (*Do the Right Thing, Jungle Fever*) are examples of minority writers and artists whose work now receives national praise and recognition. In journalism Connie Chung and Charlayne Hunter-Gault are respected national television news correspondents. In another sphere of writing Ronald Takaki, a professor of ethnic studies at the University of California at Berkeley, recently

Table 12.1 College Degree Attainment, 1986–1987

Group	Undergraduate Enrollment	Percent of Total	B.A.	Percent of Total
White	8,552,000	79.2	841,280	85.0
Hispanic	569,000	5.2	26,990	2.7
American Indian/Alaska Native	84,000	0.7	3,971	0.4
African-American	995,000	9.2	56,555	5.7
Asian/Pacific Islander	394,000	3.6	32,618	3.2
Nonresidents	204,000	1.8	29,308	2.9
Total	10,798,000		990,722	

Group	Graduate Enrollment	Percent of Total	M.A.	Percent of Total	Ph.D.	Percent of Total
White	1,132,000	79.0	228,870	79.0	24,435	71.7
Hispanic	46,000	3.2	7,044	2.4	750	2.2
American Indian/Alaska Native	5,000	0.3	1,104	0.4	104	0.3
African-American	72,000	5.0	13,867	4.7	1,060	3.1
Asian/Pacific Islander	43,000	3.0	8,558	2.9	1,097	3.2
Nonresidents	136,000	9.4	29,898	10.3	6,587	19.4
Total	1,434,000		298,341		34,033	

SOURCE: U.S. Department of Education. Cited in QEM, *Education That Works: An Action Plan for the Education of Minorities* (Cambridge: Massachusetts Institute of Technology, 1990). Used by permission.

won a Pulitzer Prize nomination for his book *Strangers from a Different Shore: A History of Asian Americans*. Virtually every profession now includes an important core of minority men and women in its ranks.

But in some ways present conditions are not so bright. Precollege dropout rates for minority youths continue to be high, especially in inner-city schools. For most minorities the proportion of high school graduates enrolling in college is smaller than the proportion of white graduates. For example, in 1986 about 34 percent of white high school graduates entered college, compared to 29 percent for African-Americans, 29 percent for Hispanics, and 17 percent for American Indians. Furthermore very few minority students are transferring from community colleges to four-year institutions, where they could go on to earn bachelor's degrees. Finally, only small numbers of minority students are earning bachelor's, master's, and doctoral degrees (see Table 12.1).

Should only minority groups be concerned with these statistics? Definitely not. What happens to minorities profoundly affects the white population. According to a Hudson Institute report, *Workforce 2000* (1987), in the next twelve years more than four out of ten new entrants into the workforce will be nonwhite or immigrant. At the same time, a majority of new jobs will require some form of postsecondary education. Unless colleges attract more minority students, minority group members will lack the skills necessary to enter the workforce, creating labor shortages and jeopardizing our nation's economy. In short, unless more minority students stay in school, enroll in college, and earn degrees, we may have not only a poorer economy but a diminished quality of life. Minority issues affect all of us.

THE MAJOR GROUPS

What follows is a brief description, based mainly on information acquired from the 1990 QEM report, of the major groups that are currently considered minorities in this country. Keep in mind, however, that these groups are growing so rapidly that in many areas they now are the majority population.

Asian-Americans

Since the lifting of discriminatory immigration restrictions in 1965, Asians have become one of the nation's fastest-growing minority groups, currently numbering over 6 million, or over 2.5 percent of the total U.S. population (Suzuki, 1989). By 2000 the Asian population is projected to grow to nearly 10 million, or about 4 percent of the total U.S. population.

Asians are a very diverse group; the six largest Asian subgroups are Chinese, Japanese, Koreans, Asian Indians, Filipinos, and Vietnamese. All of these peoples have made major contributions to the economic and agricultural development of the American West and Hawaii.

Asian parents tend to place a great deal of emphasis on education, and Asian students have higher high school graduation rates than whites, prepare themselves better for college, and outperform white students on quantitative tests. At the same time, a large proportion do not speak English as their first language and need help in developing verbal skills. In addition, many Asian families still live in poverty, especially the Chinese in Chinatowns of New York, Los Angeles, and San Francisco, as well as Southeast Asians in several regions of the country.

In college, while Japanese and Chinese students may be overrepresented relative to their proportion in the general population, other, less affluent groups such as Filipinos and Southeast Asians (including Cambodians and Hmong refugees) are poorly represented. As a group Asian students score substantially below whites in verbal achievement, and the writing skills of Asian students in high school and college are substantially below those of white students. Consequently Asian students concentrate on high-level courses in mathematics and science and take fewer courses in English and social studies.

Alaska Natives/American Indians

Three distinct native groups (Eskimos, Aleuts, and American Indians) constitute 14 percent (7,500) of Alaska's population. There are twenty Alaska Native languages, and many students start school speaking little English. About 60 percent of these people live in rural areas, and students making the transition from villages to larger cities experience great difficulties adjusting to new, often hostile environments. Although various social problems continue to hamper them, these native groups have a rich history and cultures filled with tradition and spirituality. Unfortunately only about 2.7 percent of Alaskan teachers are Alaska Natives, which means teachers there often do not understand or value the native culture or languages.

Throughout the United States there are more than 300 American Indian tribes and at least 100 native languages. While American Indians have increased their high school graduation rates from 51 percent in 1970 to 60 percent in 1988, the high school dropout rate is still high, and few Indians are college graduates.

African-Americans

African-Americans are the largest nonwhite minority, comprising 12 percent of the population, and are drawn from a diverse range of cultures and countries in Africa, the Caribbean, and Central and South America. African-

"Is It Wrong to Mention a Person's Race?"

I had a job last summer as a "gofer" for a conference center outside Monterey, California. One of my duties was to pick up people at the local airport. It was interesting because people came to this place from every walk of life and every corner of the country.

Usually I would be in the office when they called for pickup, and I would ask them what I should look for. They would say things like, "I'm wearing a suit," or "I'm tall with glasses." Or they might mention the color of some piece of clothing. The one thing they almost never mentioned was race, so I had to study their name and listen to their voice for some hint of whether they might be, say, black or Hispanic. You'd be sur-prised how many people aren't what they sound like over the phone, or what their name suggests. I wasted a lot of time wading through crowds of tourists saying, "Excuse me, are you . . . ?"

I finally solved the problem by taking a sign with the visitor's name on it, and letting them find me! I felt pretty lame about it. I wish instead I could have asked them what they looked like beginning with their race, but my manager thought it was rude to ask these things of a stranger.

Is is wrong to mention a person's race? Of course I mean when it's relevant. And it is relevant sometimes, isn't it?

Americans continue to face severe economic and social problems stemming from the legacy of slavery and more than three centuries of repression and continuing discrimination.

In response to its exclusion from the mainstream white culture, the African-American community has developed a system of historically black colleges and universities, dating from the mid-nineteenth century — the only minority group in the United States to do so. As recently as a decade ago, these schools awarded nearly 70 percent of all bachelor's degrees received by African-Americans. However, many of these schools currently are experiencing financial difficulties even greater than those being felt by most predominantly white institutions.

Recently African-Americans have made gains in high school graduation and student retention rates and in test scores. Yet, despite the civil rights breakthroughs of the 1950s and 1960s, most of these students still attend essentially segregated schools. In 1980 about 64 percent were in predominantly minority schools and 33 percent were in intensely segregated schools, which are often underfunded and understaffed.

Currently a large concern is that fewer African-Americans are enrolling in college, especially African-American males. According to *Black Issues in Higher Education* (1990) the rate of African-American females ages 16–24 attending college rose from 29.2 percent to 32.3 percent between 1980 and 1988, while African-American males in the same age group slipped from 27 percent to 26.2 percent. The rate of African-American females ages 25–34 enrolling in college rose from 8.7 percent to 10.5 percent between 1980 and

Students at the University of Texas publish the newspaper Tejas in an undergraduate journalism course. The paper was begun outside class by a group of Hispanic students who disagreed with the dominant campus newspaper's coverage of Hispanic issues.

1988, while enrollment for same-aged African-American males dropped from 10.8 percent to 7.3 percent. In 1989 African-American females at historically black institutions outnumbered African-American males 120,412 to 79,462.

Mexican-Americans

Hispanics make up 12 percent of the U.S. population. Note, however, that the term *Hispanic* masks variations in language, setting, history, and geography. The roots of the Mexican-American community — one Hispanic subgroup — can be found in the colonies established by Spain and Mexico over ten generations ago in much of what is now the American Southwest. Mexican-Americans also include recent immigrants who applied for legal resident status or "amnesty" under the Immigration Reform and Control Act of 1986. Also called Chicanos, Mexicans, and Latinos, Mexican-Americans are the largest and fastest-growing Hispanic subgroup, now numbering some 12.6 million people. More than half live in California and Texas, with concentrations in seven other states as well.

In terms of college attendance and performance Mexican-Americans (and Puerto Ricans) are the least-educated and most underrepresented Hispanic group; Cubans are the most educated and most successful in society. Although, like African-Americans, Mexican-Americans have made gains in high school and college graduation rates, they face a number of obstacles. First, they often attend schools where minority children are the majority of the student body, which limits their exposure to the dominant culture. Second, many Mexican-Americans work as migrant and other poorly paid farm labor, which affects family life and hinders education at all levels. Finally, many Mexican-Americans are recent immigrants with minimal English language skills. It's no wonder Mexican-American students are plagued by high dropout rates and poor literacy skills.

Puerto Ricans

Puerto Ricans are U.S. citizens. There are 2.3 million Puerto Ricans on the U.S. mainland and 3.3 million in Puerto Rico itself. Students experience language difficulties because they grow up speaking Spanish on the Island and must learn English on the mainland. In many ways, however, the Islanders have it better than their mainland counterparts. Puerto Ricans live in racially integrated neighborhoods on the Island, but many are forced to live in racially segregated areas on the mainland. Island children are more likely to grow up with positive role models, whereas mainland children often have few images of success. On the Island affluent children attend private schools, whereas low-income children attend public schools. The Island has a high rate of college enrollment: Of Island high school graduates 83 percent go to college, as opposed to only 34 percent of those on the mainland. And large numbers of mainland Puerto Ricans drop out of high school: In 1985 only 46 percent of mainland Puerto Rican adults had completed high school. A major problem is how to coordinate educational programs for the thousands of students who move to and from the mainland.

EXERCISE 12.5 Your School's Ethnic Composition

Find out the percentage of your school's different populations (the admissions office or institutional/research office should have this information). In the chart below list the percentage of groups in your school's enrollment and the percentage of those groups in the state and county or city population.

Does each percentage in your school reflect the percentage in your area? Are you aware of any initiatives to increase the number of minority students and/or their graduation rate? What are these initiatives?

Group	Percent in School	Percent in State	Percent in City or County
Asian-Americans			
Alaska Natives/ American Indians			
African-Americans			
Mexican-Americans			
Puerto Ricans			
White Americans			

PROBLEMS FACING MINORITY COLLEGE STUDENTS

As the previous discussion should suggest, minority groups are very diverse. Yet in college they have many problems in common and must address numerous important issues that cut across racial/ethnic lines.

"That Corner in the Cafeteria"

When I think about my freshman year at a predominantly white university, these are the things I remember: "'Negro' students who graduate from your high school tend not to do well at this university; therefore, we encourage you to attend a summer precollege program," said a representative from the university. (I did.) "You'll do well here if you never take a math course," stated my advisor during the freshman orientation program. (I never did take a math course, and I paid for it!) Of the 300 students in Psychology 80, no one would sit next to me!

One day, by accident, I wandered into the commuter cafeteria, and there they were — black people! I was so glad to see them that I think I ran toward them. The group was composed primarily of upperclass students and two graduate students. "Hey, what's your aim in life?" hollered Jack, one of the graduate students, as I approached the group. I opened my mouth to respond, but I don't think anything coherent came out. Can you imagine how I felt when they told me that we were in a university of well over 20,000 students and that maybe, just maybe, there were a total of 50 black undergraduate and graduate students? Later I found out that 15 out of the 50 black students were freshmen!

As the semester progressed, I spent a considerable amount of time in the cafeteria and became better adjusted to the university. That corner in the cafeteria was my home away from home. Those black students were my family and support system. They reprimanded me for cutting class and applauded me for my achievements. There were no black faculty, as far as I knew.

Interaction with white students was fairly minimal. They appeared not to know what to say to me, and vice versa. Communication with white faculty members was a little different. They had the information; therefore, I did talk to them. My grades were not that fantastic, though, and it wasn't until my junior year that I became a serious student.

SOURCE: Francine G. McNairy, interim vice president for academic affairs, West Chester University of Pennsylvania. Reproduced, with permission, from Francine G. McNairy and Dan Romero, "Minority Students on Campus: Enhancing Cultural Growth and Understanding," in *College Is Only the Beginning: A Student Guide to Higher Education*, 2nd ed., John N. Gardner and A. Jerome Jewler, eds. (Belmont, Calif.: Wadsworth, 1989).

Preparation

Many minority students were poorly counseled in high school and received a substandard academic preparation in basic skills such as reading, writing, and math. Minority students have often been placed in nonacademic tracks and have not taken the courses that would best prepare them for college. Many have attended largely segregated, inferior, poorly financed, overcrowded schools. Many teachers in these schools are inexperienced, while others have simply "given up" on an overburdened system and do not expect their students to learn much or amount to anything. Often students who do not speak English as their first language have been placed in learning-disabled or remedial-learning groups, rather than given intensive instruction in English as a Second Language (ESL) programs.

Because of the shortage of minority teachers, most minority students have had few role models to identify with and have studied a curriculum that still largely excludes minority culture, language, and contributions in science, history, and the arts.

Money

Many traditional-aged minority students come from families that are unable to finance much of their college education. In fact, once in college and receiving aid or working while they attend school, many are obliged to use portions of these funds to help support the parental family. Also minority parents and students often lack information about the costs, benefits, and consequences of getting a college education.

The Two-Year/Four-Year Connection

While community colleges can often be the starting point on the road to a bachelor's degree, many minority students are enrolled in community colleges where transfer rates to four-year colleges remain low. Unless transfer rates increase, few of these students will earn bachelor's and graduate degrees. Many enroll in vocational/technical programs of study, but few are in high-tech programs that lead to higher-paying jobs.

Quotas

Some minority groups — particularly Chinese-Americans — are increasingly reporting quotas that discriminate against them and limit their numbers on campus in relation to nonminority students. In recent years the number of Asian students admitted to college has remained the same or decreased, although many more Asians, usually with higher combined SAT scores than white students, are applying to college.

Bias in Testing

The whole college admissions process is still influenced to a great extent by a national system of testing that favors the native speaker of English (and the student who grew up in a "standard English" environment) over other students, even in subject areas where command of English is not the primary concern. This affects not only admission per se but also the status of the minority student once on campus. Because of this cultural bias many American Indian and other minority students with poor English skills are miscategorized as special education students.

Lack of Minority Faculty

Minority students attending predominantly white schools find few professors of their own background on the college teaching staff. This puts minority students at a disadvantage when it comes to making contact with faculty, since minority students are less likely to share the backgrounds and connections that facilitate relations between white students and professors. Many such students feel they have no faculty to turn to who are concerned with their well-being on campus or who understand their interests or cultural perspectives.

Lack of Representation in the Curriculum

The heart of the curriculum continues to be dominated by a White Anglo-Saxon Protestant (WASP) male perspective, which teaches history, philosophy, sociology, and so on from a predominantly white, male, European

"This Class Wasn't Listed..."

One of the most thought-provoking classes I attended during my freshman year was not listed in the class schedule. Attendance was not mandatory, and grades were not given. It was a rally on minority educational issues, and I happened on it quite accidentally.

It was the first time I had seen so many African-American students in one place since being on the campus, and I was drawn to them by some sudden urge for companionship. But what I heard that day made it very difficult to make friends. Many speakers—students and faculty—some angry, some calm and serious, filed across a makeshift platform to accuse the school's administration of complicity in a host of problems affecting minorities in higher education. They blamed the administration's policies for contributing to declining minority college enrollment, for the dearth of faculty of color, and for inadequate minority programs. Meanwhile, those in the crowd shouted their approval for what was being said and waved large banners denouncing racism on the campus.

I was 27 at the time, an army veteran with a full-time job and a family of four, and feeling very proud of what I had accomplished. But as I listened that day, the euphoria, the sense of accomplishment, and the promise of being a freshman dimmed ever so slightly. I felt the hard work that I had done to make it to college was being belittled by a group of people who were saying I needed special consideration in order to succeed.

Yet, I also realized that I knew little about the educational issues that had brought them together. Thereafter I began to look more critically at things. I found I could no longer go to my classes without wondering why so few of my classmates and instructors were African-Americans and why the decision makers where I worked were seldom minorities. I began to wonder if individual effort alone was enough, or whether action through constant protest was the way to effect changes in the system.

Oddly, it was the memory of another out-of-class experience that helped me to gain a better understanding of the protesters, and of being a freshman, a student, and an individual. Many years before, while I was living in the West Indies, I had taken ill one week before a crucial examination that not only would allow or deny me entry to high school, but also, depending on my performance, would determine whether the government paid part or all of my tuition and expenses. Much to my surprise, my teacher visited me at my home with the notes from the days I had missed. She assured me that although I would miss the last week of class work, she was confident I would do well on the examination. Her interest in my welfare spurred me to study harder and I subsequently did extremely well.

In the end I concluded there was much in common between the vocal and demanding rallies of my freshman year and the quiet, bedside visit of my elementary teacher. Those memories make me ask myself whether I am doing enough for others. They also remind me that I am no less an individual for having had some help.

SOURCE: Clive McFarlane, San Francisco State University, class of '91.

perspective. Although ethnic and feminist studies are now included in some of the liberal arts curricula, for the most part minimal attention is given to them, and frequently they are completely ignored. Students do not often get to explore the interrelationships among white and minority males and females or to learn about the contributions of women and minorities to literature, history, art, philosophy, music, and so on. The fact that few college instructors are from minority groups contributes to this problem.

Some American Indian students have responded to this problem by choosing to attend tribal community colleges where, in addition to the courses offered by most community colleges, they find a welcoming learning environment, in which their languages and cultures are respected and tribal sovereignties are recognized.

Racist Attitudes and Behaviors

All minority groups have been stigmatized by racism, prejudice, discrimination, and other barriers to success in high school and college. Recently the incidence of overt racism has been increasing on campuses in the form of harassment, violence, physical assaults, and slurs and signs.

Minority students are frequently stereotyped by faculty and other students. At larger state universities African-American males tend to be dismissed academically because some of them have been recruited for the school's athletic program, and athletes are generally stereotyped as low academic performers. In contrast African-American females are perceived not as athletes, but as students, and academic expectations for them tend to be higher. In the same vein Asian-American students are expected to be industrious, conscientious, "well-behaved" overachievers, but even such apparently positive stereotypes are in some ways subtly damaging.

Some instructors put minority students on the spot by calling on them more often than on others or by asking them to speak for their group. Others almost never call on minority students because they feel these students aren't capable of participating in informed class discussions. Students and professors often make derogatory remarks about the English proficiency of Asian, Hispanic, and Indian students, while African-Americans, Hispanics, American Indians, and others may be resented for receiving what is perceived as preferential treatment in the awarding of financial aid.

Isolation

Social isolation is another problem, especially where there are few students of a given minority on campus. American Indian and other minority students from rural backgrounds also suffer feelings of isolation when they attend distant urban colleges. The problem is made worse by the imbalance in the number of males and females, particularly among African-American students. Even where other students go out of their way in trying to make a student feel welcome, a sense of isolation from home and one's own familiar culture frequently persists. And feelings of isolation are compounded when schools are located away from the urban or rural areas where minority students might be with people who speak their language and follow familiar patterns of communication, support, and culture.

EXERCISE 12.6   **Bias on Campus**

A. Have you witnessed any examples of racism, prejudice, or discrimination in your classes or on campus? If so, describe one such situation in a brief written report. Why do you think this constituted racism, prejudice, or discrimination? How did the situation affect you?

B. Talk with one or two upperclass students, professors, staff members, or administrators from cultural backgrounds different from your own. Ask them the questions in part A. Talk with them about how they think students on your campus can best respond to any form of discrimination or prejudice. What advice do they have for minority students about being successful at your school? Describe and discuss your findings with other members of the class. How does your own experience compare with that of the people you interviewed?

EXERCISE 12.7 An Inclusive Curriculum

The previous section, "Women: The Majority of First-Year Students," described five phases of development toward a nonsexist curriculum. We might construct a similar scheme for the inclusion of minorities in the curriculum:

Phase I. Ignore them completely.

Phase II. Focus only on outstanding or unusual examples of minority involvement — accomplishments that benefited the majority society.

Phase III. Treat the minority perspective as an issue or problem of society.

Phase IV. Focus exclusively on the minority perspective, separate from that of the majority (an entire book or special chapter or section).

Phase V. Include minority and majority perspectives throughout, assigning parallel and equal importance.

Review the syllabus and textbook(s) for one of your liberal arts courses. How are minority perspectives incorporated into this class? If they are not covered adequately, what can you do to broaden your understanding of minority perspectives related to this subject?

Be prepared to discuss the course and your ideas.

All these overt and covert forms of prejudice and discrimination hinder minority students in their social adjustment in college and their academic achievement. The majority of white colleges and universities have responded to these issues in a wide variety of ways. Common practices include the following:

- ► Offering courses in minority studies
- ► Hiring more minority faculty and counselors
- ► Bringing minority children from elementary and secondary schools to campus so that they will feel more comfortable about applying for admission later on
- ► Targeting some financial aid for minority students
- ► Incorporating counseling strategies in which counselors from one racial group are trained to counsel students of a different race
- ► Providing resource centers for the support of all students having academic difficulties
- ► Recognizing the legitimacy and needs of minority student organizations
- ► Developing racial awareness programs
- ► Creating ethical conduct standards
- ► Publicly declaring support for a truly integrated college or university

"Mi Casa Es Tu Casa"

I was born and raised in a southwestern state that claims a rich mixture of Hispanic, Indian, and Euro-American cultures. As I proceeded through high school, however, I found that most of the college-bound students taking "college-track" courses I was enrolled in were white students. When I attended the university, the trend continued. While my home state had almost 40 percent Hispanic citizens in the 1960s, the university enrolled about 12 percent Hispanics. The number of Native Americans, blacks, and Asian-Americans at the university was so small as to render them virtually invisible.

I remember my freshman year as one of feeling out of place. Many weekends during the year I would return home, some seventy miles away, to be with family and high school friends. I felt uncomfortable at the university. Looking back, part of the feeling was due to trying to fit into a predominantly non-Hispanic group in which I could be accepted only to a point. I learned that as a Mexican-American, I was accepted in some groups, but not in all, and that even those groups who did accept me did so conditionally. As more Hispanics enrolled in the university toward my junior and senior years, I also learned that for many of them, I was too "establishment" or too white and was not accepted by some members of Mexican-American ethnic organizations.

From my undergraduate experience I learned that minority students encounter a tremendous pressure in college to choose sides — either to become part of your ethnic group's identity or be acculturated into the establishment. I found that seeking my own identity meant not accepting either extreme; I wanted to create a bicultural identity and realized that I would not be understood by some.

I also remember that I knew little about my Hispanic heritage and culture. Much of what I studied and learned about in high school and college ignored the rich culture and history of my ancestors in the Southwest. I looked Hispanic, and at times I felt uncomfortable and out of place associating with my white peers. Sensing that some of our values were dissimilar, my friends simply attributed the disparity to personal, not cultural, differences. I remember, for example, inviting many of my friends to my home to sample Mom's cooking and to be part of the family. Seldom was that favor returned. At the time I surmised there was something wrong with me, but with time I have learned that others may not value a concept such as "mi casa es tu casa" (my house is your house) or the openness associated with my family.

SOURCE: By Dan Romero, associate director, Career Planning and Placement Center, University of California at Berkeley. Reproduced, with permission, from Francine G. McNairy and Dan Romero, "Minority Students on Campus: Enhancing Cultural Growth and Understanding," in College Is Only the Beginning: A Student Guide to Higher Education, 2nd ed., John N. Gardner and A. Jerome Jewler, eds. (Belmont, Calif.: Wadsworth, 1989).

Unfortunately many of these efforts are simply too limited or represent centralized efforts to problems that ultimately can be overcome only by fundamental changes in the attitudes and behaviors of countless individuals.

Nevertheless, as you move through your college career, I hope you will be involved in helping your school to improve its ability to serve *all* students. On the institutional level there is much to be done. On an immediate, personal level there is also a great deal you can do.

ENSURING PERSONAL SUCCESS

Being a college student is hard work, and college life is very demanding. No one gave me any advice on how to make it in college, so I want to share with you my list of important things I wish somebody had told me when I graduated from high school. While all students can benefit from my list, it is applicable especially to minority students.

1. *Develop an "I can do it" attitude, and stay in college.* You made it through twelve years of school, and you graduated from high school or earned your GED. These are highly significant accomplishments! You've already shown you're quite capable of studying, learning, and achieving. You may need a little help in some areas, but that's okay — your college has counselors, tutoring centers, and career centers to help you. Take advantage of them. Remain positive and forward thinking.

   Did you know that your freshman year is the most critical year of college? Studies show that students who are successful during the first year of college are more likely to continue their education than those who merely squeeze by or drop out thinking they will continue later. Make an effort to finish your freshman year and to make it successful and rewarding! Remember that alarming numbers of Hispanic, African-American, and American Indian/Alaska Native students are dropping out of high school and college. A closer look at Table 12.1 will reveal that very few minorities are earning college degrees. These dismal statistics can be turned around only if *you* graduate from college! It's hard work, but in the words of Jaime Escalante (subject of the film *Stand and Deliver* and the book *Escalante: The Best Teacher in America*), "You can do it!"

2. *Shoot for an A.* Grades are important. You may not want to think right now about getting a master's or doctoral degree, but chances are you will in the future. When you apply to graduate school, your undergraduate GPA will be very important in determining whether you gain admission. It's okay to make B's, maybe even a few C's, but you should set your goals much higher than that. Study hard, seek help when you need it, and try to do your very best. Your future employers may also review your college transcript, so be sure your academic record looks good.

3. *Form a study group.* Calculus professor Philip Uri Treisman is a prominent figure in the development of collaborative learning strategies to help African-American and Hispanic students succeed academically. In the middle 1970s he began to question why Chinese students at Berkeley outperformed African-American students in freshman calculus. He discovered that one very important factor was the Chinese students' reliance on study groups, informal mutual support networks for studying together and for pooling knowledge of teachers and other resources on the largely white campus. In brief the majority of Chinese students studied with partners or in groups, whereas virtually no African-American students in calculus did this. When Professor Treisman proceeded to organize African-American students into groups, they too succeeded at calculus.

   Get together with a group of fellow students to study together. For example, if you are taking a math class, don't try to solve math problems by yourself. Form a study group and practice solving the problems together. Talk about the steps you went through to solve the

The Best Teacher in America

Jaime Alfonso Escalante Gutierrez was born in 1930 in Bolivia and was educated in La Paz. Although he describes himself as "a somewhat undisciplined young man," he nevertheless excelled in school and went on to a teacher training college because his family could not afford to send him to engineering school. For twelve years as a high school teacher in La Paz, he gained a reputation for excellence, creating a team of science students that consistently won city-wide science contests.

In 1963 he and his family emigrated to the United States. Barred from teaching because he did not hold a U.S. degree, he worked as a cook and at other jobs while slowly earning night school credits at California State University, Los Angeles. After ten years, in 1974, he was finally hired to teach basic mathematics at Garfield High School, a predominantly Hispanic barrio school in East Los Angeles.

In 1978 he began teaching an advanced placement (AP) calculus course. Four years later, when all eighteen of his students passed the AP examination for college calculus (seven with perfect scores), the Educational Testing Service, which administers the test, concluded that some of his students had copied their answers and forced twelve of them to retake the test. All twelve passed a second time. With this incident, Escalante's program drew local, state, and national attention, including the dramatization of the story in the 1988 film *Stand and Deliver*. By 1988–89 over 200 students were enrolled in the AP calculus program.

Jaime Escalante believes that motivation is the key to learning. Here's what he has to say:

I do not recruit students by reviewing test scores or grades, nor are they necessarily among the "gifted" or on some kind of "high IQ track." . . . My sole criterion for acceptance in this program is that the student wants to be a part of it and sincerely wants to learn math. I tell my students, "The only thing you need to have for my pro-

gram — and you must bring it every day — is ganas [desire, or will to succeed]." If motivated properly, any student can learn mathematics. . . .

From the beginning, I cast the teacher in the role of the "coach" and the students in the role of the "team." I made sure they knew that we were all working together. In La Paz, . . . our "opponent" was the annual secondary school mathematics competition. . . . [Today] the AP test provides the formidable outside "opponent." . . . I have found it easy to focus student attention on this challenge and its very real rewards of possible college credits and advanced placement in college. . . .

I greatly admire the discipline of athletic teams. . . . I often use professional sports superstars as examples of successful self-discipline, outstanding performance, the will to win, persistence . . . , and other qualities. The walls of my room are covered with posters of sports figures in action. . . . Before class, my AP Team has "warm-ups" (hand clapping and foot stomping to the rock song "We Will Rock You," played over my Bose loudspeakers). They wear classy satin team jackets, caps, and tee-shirts; and their "practice schedule" is as rigorous as that of any championship football team. These are all part of my effort to make math fun, a team activity. . . .

I often break the students into groups to solve lecture problems. . . . After school, the students almost always work in teams. . . .

The key to my success . . . is a very simple time-honored tradition: hard work, and lots of it, for teacher and student alike. . . . When students of any race, ethnicity, or economic status are expected to work hard, they will usually rise to the occasion. . . . They rise, or fall, to the level of the expectations of those around them, especially their parents and their teachers.*

*Jaime Escalante and Jack Dirmann. *The Jaime Escalante Math Program* (Washington, D.C.: National Education Association, 1990), pp. 2–3, 6–9.

problems, and share study techniques that work for you. In other classes study for exams with your groups, comparing notes and reviewing the main points covered in class. If you can't find a study group, form one yourself. You will be surprised at the results!

EXERCISE 12.8 Forming a Study Group

Use the goal-setting process from Chapter 1 to form a study group for at least one of your courses this semester. As you do this, think about your strengths and weaknesses in a learning or studying situation. For instance, do you excel at memorizing facts but find it difficult to comprehend vague theories? Do you learn best by repeatedly reading the information or by applying the knowledge to a real situation? Do you prefer to learn by processing information in your head or by participating in a "hands-on" demonstration? (Refer to Chapter 3 for a review of learning styles.) Make some notes about your learning and studying strengths and weaknesses here:

Strengths: _____

_____

_____

Weaknesses: _____

_____

_____

In a study group how will your strengths help others? What strengths will you look for in others that will help you?

How you can help others: _____

_____

_____

How others can help you: _____

_____

_____

In your first study group session, suggest that each person share his or her strengths and weaknesses and talk about how abilities might be shared for everyone's maximum benefit.

4. *Visit with your instructors outside of class.* Several times during the semester you should make an appointment with your instructors. Introduce yourself, tell them about some things you have enjoyed in

class, and ask them questions about issues covered in class that you don't understand. Try to find at least one faculty member with whom you can maintain regular contact. This may be someone you trust and admire, someone who can serve as a role model or mentor.

5. *Take advantage of academic and student support services offered by your college.* In addition to tutoring, counseling, and career centers, your campus may have centers for African-American, Hispanic, Indian, and Asian students. Visit these places often. Introduce yourself to the directors and staff. Discuss any problems you may be having. Ask for help.

EXERCISE 12.9   Campus Resources

Find out about resources on your campus that can offer academic or other assistance to minority students and other special populations. List the names, purposes, and locations and phone numbers of those that could be of service to you.

Organization or Service	Purpose	Location and Phone
_____	_____	_____
_____	_____	_____
_____	_____	_____
_____	_____	_____
_____	_____	_____

6. *Participate in co-curricular activities.* Clubs and organizations offer you an opportunity to make friends, socialize, have fun, and get involved with the college and your community. Avoid simply coming to class and not socializing with anyone. Try to join at least one organization. Just be careful that you don't overlook your academic work in favor of your social or co-curricular life.

7. *Attend college full-time if you can.* Most students have to work. If you work, try to find a campus job, but don't work more than 20 hours a week. Go to your financial aid office and get information about college work study, grants, and scholarships (see Appendix B). Try to avoid taking out loans until you are ready to go to graduate school, so you won't have to repay the loan when you graduate. If you work full-time, you will not have the time and energy to devote to your studies, and it may take you longer to complete your degree. Give your study time top priority.

8. *Don't be afraid to take math and science courses or to go into math- and science-based fields.* Math and science are the areas in which minorities are *least* represented: Very few minority group members

work in science and engineering and as math and science teachers. By choosing not to take math and science courses you are excluding yourself from careers in computers, technology, medicine, and related health fields — all of which pay big bucks! Scholarships for minority students are particularly available to those pursuing math and science careers. Consult with your financial aid office, your academic advisor, and a career counselor about these options.

9. *Learn to take standardized tests.* Most Hispanics, African-Americans, and American Indians do not do well on standardized tests such as the ACT, SAT, or GRE. These tests may not reflect your culture, and many of you have never been trained to take these tests. Your college or some agency in your community usually offers test preparation sessions. Enroll in them, especially if you are planning to pursue a graduate degree.

10. *Select careers that carry long-term benefits.* When you choose what to do with your life, think about how that choice will affect you five to ten years from now, and not so much about how that choice will affect you today. Try to decide on your major program of study by the end of your sophomore year so that you can take the proper sequence of courses. If you are having trouble selecting a major, go to the counseling center or career center or talk to your academic advisor to get assistance.

    Try to get a graduate degree such as a master's degree, a doctorate, or a law degree sometime after you complete your bachelor's degree. If you like teaching, shoot for being a teacher, not a teacher's aide. If you like nursing, plan to be a registered nurse, not a health assistant. If you like dentistry, try to be a dentist, not a dental assistant. Prestigious, high-paying careers take a longer time to attain, but in the long run they will do more for you.

11. *Be the best in whatever you undertake.* Oprah Winfrey is absolutely on target when she says that "excellence is the best deterrent to racism." To succeed you must be good at two things. First, you must "know your stuff," that is, be highly competent in your field. Second, you must be able to get along with other people. Too many people are respected for what they know but detested because they can't work effectively with others. Don't let this happen to you. Others will define and respect you not only for your competence, but also for your personality.

12. *Be proud of your heritage and culture.* People of color are the fastest-growing population in the United States. By the year 2080 minorities will be the majority population in this country. Minority groups can become empowered only if they participate fully in the country's economic, scientific, and political future. In college you may hear racist remarks and witness or be the target of behaviors rooted in ignorance, bigotry, and hatred. Stand tall. Be proud. Refuse to tolerate such behavior, whether directed toward others or yourself.

    Take courses in African-American, Hispanic, Indian, and Asian studies. Help other minority students. Make friends with students from different racial and ethnic backgrounds. Get to know the minority faculty and administrators on campus. Become involved in staging events that sensitize students, faculty, and administrators to cultural diversity. Remember, if you are a minority student, *you* are now a role model. Other students can learn from your experience.

EXERCISE 12.10 Minority Excellence

For each of the following fields, identify a minority person who has achieved success. This might be someone famous or someone in your community. In a brief report or oral presentation, describe what these persons contributed to society.

Politics   Music/entertainment
Literature   Mass communications
Art   Math and science

JOURNAL

What are your general feelings about the opportunities for or difficulties facing minority students on your campus? What do you think of the author's advice about how minority students can be successful at your school? How does this advice compare with the twenty-one keys to success in Chapter 1?

REFERENCES AND SUGGESTIONS FOR FURTHER READING

Carrion, A. M. Puerto Rico: A Political and Cultural History. New York: Norton, 1983.

Elk, B. Black Elk Speaks. Lincoln: University of Nebraska Press, 1961.

Hudson Institute. Workforce 2000. Indianapolis, Ind.: Hudson Institute, 1987.

Kingston, M. H. The Woman Warrior. New York: Knopf, Random House, 1976.

Manning, K. Black Apollo of Science. New York: Oxford University Press, 1983.

Marger, Martin N. Race and Ethnic Relations: American and Global Perspectives, 2nd ed. Belmont, Calif.: Wadsworth, 1991.

Mathews, J. Escalante: The Best Teacher in America. New York: Holt, Rinehart & Winston, 1988.

Quality Education for Minorities Project. Education That Works. Cambridge: Massachusetts Institute of Technology, 1990.

Suzuki, B. H. Asian Americans in Higher Education: A Research Agenda for the 1990s and Beyond. Paper presented at conference sponsored by the American Council on Education, San Francisco, California, December 1989.

Wiley, E. "Institutional Concern About Implications of Black Male Crisis Questioned by Scholars." Black Issues in Higher Education 7, no. 9 (1990): 1, 8–9.

You're Never Too Old to Go to Class

*T*alk about frozen. I wasn't even sure my legs would get me down the hall and into the classroom. I know 43 isn't old, but next to a roomful of adolescent freshmen, I feel old! And what their looks say: "Well, she's going to ruin the fun in this course. Hey, she looks older than my mom. Always so serious about her work. Who does she think she is?" I'll tell you who I am: a hard-working mother and wife who wants to improve herself. It's great to be in school. I can't believe how well I'm doing.

DOROTHY S. FIDLER *is co-director of the National Resource Center for the Freshman Year Experience at the University of South Carolina, Columbia. She knows what it's like to be a returning student.*

"After fourteen years as a housewife," she says, "I returned to college to complete my education. On the night of my first class, I turned to a stranger sitting next to me and said loudly, 'What on earth am I doing here? I have a baby at home in diapers and she probably needs to be changed right now.' I literally had to hang onto the desk to stay seated until the professor began speaking." Her persistence culminated in a Ph.D. in psychology. Since then she has directed and taught in a program for returning students and has engaged in research on how to help entering students of all ages.

All over the country adult students (usually defined as those over 25 years of age) are enrolling in college courses in record-breaking numbers. Some observers predict that by the end of the 1990s, one out of every three college students will be over 25 years old; others predict one out of two. Educators are watching this trend with great interest, for they recognize that older students are changing the face of higher education as campuses adapt to meet their demands.

Younger and older students can learn from one another. Each sees the other as a reflection of him- or herself at a different stage of life. At the beginning of college younger students often feel threatened by older classmates, and older students fear they can't compete with bright young teenagers fresh from college preparatory classes. Yet after several weeks older students find that their high motivation enables them to compete for good grades, and younger students learn to appreciate the multiple roles of spouse, parent, and employee that many adults fill in addition to being students.

CHARACTERISTICS OF OLDER STUDENTS

Most educators and younger students heartily welcome older students for the many assets they bring to the classroom, such as a high level of motivation. Because professors enjoy teaching students who really want to learn, you will surely be appreciated.

Another plus that you as an adult bring to college is your real-life experience: working in the community, holding a job, raising children, or managing a household. Not only do these practical experiences enrich the theoretical concepts presented in the classroom, they provide a vast resource of material for written assignments and classroom discussions.

Research suggests a third asset for older students: a definite increase in verbal skills. In recent studies hundreds of individuals took tests of learning ability at ten-year intervals. Results of these tests showed that, contrary to popular belief, learning ability does not decline with age. In fact verbal ability actually increases as one grows older.

So you're smarter now that you're older, with better verbal skills, heightened motivation to learn, and a wealth of experiences. As more and more adults enroll, colleges increasingly will value these assets.

EXERCISE 12.11 Does Age Matter?

Not all college students these days are 18–22 years old. As a matter of fact, many colleges report the median age of their students as over 25. When you share a classroom with students much older or younger than you, does the age difference have any effect on the way the professor teaches, the learning taking place, or individual attitudes of students about what happens in the classroom? What are the effects, and how do they affect your satisfaction with the class?

In spite of these assets you may feel a great deal of anxiety as you begin your college career. This is a venture that literally can change your life! You will learn new skills that can open the door to new opportunities, new goals, and new directions for yourself. You may experience spurts of intellectual growth and personality development. You may begin to reevaluate long-held beliefs and values. And any apprehension that you feel at the beginning of such a challenge is genuine — virtually all adult students are apprehensive.

One of your tasks is to learn how to make your anxiety a positive rather than negative force. Note that while *anxiety* is merely a label used to describe a feeling, the feeling itself is caused by heightened levels of adrenaline in your body. When you wish to perform well, adrenaline levels rise to meet the challenge. Thus increased adrenaline generally improves performance — up to a point (some researchers suggest that too much adrenaline might "blow the circuits" and worsen performance).

You usually apply different labels to describe the feelings associated with different levels of adrenaline in your system. For example, if your adrenaline level is only slightly raised, you may label this physiological state as "feeling excited." If the adrenaline level becomes moderately high, you may say you're "a little worried or apprehensive." If your adrenaline level is very high, you'll probably label this feeling as "intense fear" or "dread."

Fortunately you can alter the level of adrenaline and thus the label you use to describe your feeling. A variety of stress-reduction techniques will reduce the amount of adrenaline to a manageable level. One such technique is to relabel the feeling itself. Relabeling "apprehension" as "challenging excitement" improves your outlook and your ability to cope. It may even reduce the actual amount of adrenaline in your bloodstream! You may want to practice this technique of relabeling as you face the challenge of beginning college. (See Chapter 15 for more help with managing stress.)

HELPFUL HINTS FROM ADULT LEARNERS

The following list provides additional ways to help you reduce stress and successfully meet the challenges in your new college environment. Select ideas that may apply to your particular situation. These hints are bits of wisdom passed on by others who are old hands at being older students.

"Out to Lunch"

The following journal entry was written by a 32-year-old freshman on the first day of classes:

I was so restless for the past month thinking about what going to college would be like. Every day I got a little more excited. As the time grew nearer I lost my appetite, I found myself daydreaming and basically "out to lunch" a great deal of the time. My thoughts centered around: Would I do well? Am I smart enough? Can I handle the change from having been out of school for fourteen years and definitely out of shape when it comes to brain power? Do I even remember what it is like to study? Will I be adequate?

Well, what it boils down to is that I have been psyching myself up and out. I have questioned my own ability to the point to where I am suffering from extreme anxiety tension.

Don't be too hard on yourself—it's only natural to feel apprehensive, but remember, you have a lot to offer.

1. *Enroll part-time.* As in any new venture, getting started is the hardest part. Returning to an academic setting is a time of great change for you. Small colleges and large universities alike have subcultures: a new language (for example, semester, quarter, grade point ratio), new regulations, new expectations. In learning the lingo and becoming part of the college culture, you may undergo a bit of culture shock. Some researchers argue that any change (even positive change) is stressful. Learning to gauge the optimal amount of change for you is part of learning stress management. Too much change can lead to physical and psychological stress, which in turn can lead to physical illness. Enrolling as a part-time student and taking only one, two, or three classes reduces some of the stress. A reduced course load allows you the extra time to relax and enjoy the challenge of learning. After adjusting to the new culture, you may want to increase your course load and become a full-time student.

2. *Take a course in how to study.* Many colleges offer courses in study skills. Most adults have not studied since high school and have very rusty study habits. Studying isn't the same as reading for pleasure. How to organize material meaningfully to aid memory retention, how to study for different kinds of exams, how to read textbooks and take notes in class—these are processes you can learn with the help of other chapters in this book. (See Chapters 3–6 and 9.) But a complete course in study skills can help you additionally to become a more efficient student.

"My House Is a Disaster Area"

The following is from one adult student's writing:

My greatest difficulty in going back to college has been scheduling my time. One has to schedule so many activities in a limited time period and the following is on my schedule: time for my son, time for studying, time for housework and cooking, and time to relax. There never seems to be enough time to do everything, so I have to do things that I think are most important first.

I always take time to help my son with his homework, read to him, and play with him because I think he should be first in my list of priorities. Studying comes next on my time schedule. I have discovered if I get behind in my studies, it is nearly impossible to catch up, and I study every day. Although I should cook more and prepare better meals, we have been eating out a lot. A woman and a small child can eat out almost as cheaply as she can cook. We also have more soup and sandwiches than we did before. My house is a disaster area and I hate to live in a messy house, but I avoid looking at messy bedrooms by simply closing the bedroom doors.

Washing the dishes is my hardest task, so I buy paper plates and paper cups. Having time to relax has been my most difficult task. This is something I have not been able to do. The only time I relax is when my son goes to sleep, but sometimes I use this quiet time to study.

I will continue taking up time with my son because he is young only once, and I know he needs me. Studying is still very important to me, so I will continue to put study time before housework and cooking because I believe I can make up for that by cooking good meals when I have more time, by getting help with the housework, and by thoroughly cleaning my house on the weekend.

Going back to school has been a wonderful experience.

How well do you think this mature student is managing her time? What priorities has she set? How well are they working? What might you do differently?

3. *Look for review courses.* If you learned French or algebra years ago, you've probably forgotten a lot of it. You may need to review basic math, language, or writing skills before beginning upper-level courses. Fortunately, relearning once-familiar material is much easier than learning new material. There are several ways to review basic skills. You may try studying on your own or attending adult education courses offered by the local public schools. Many colleges offer courses that review math, grammar, and writing skills.

4. *Learn good time management techniques.* Time allocation is the single most critical problem you will face. A college education requires a serious time commitment regardless of age, but for a mature student with prior commitments, time pressures are relentless. Because demands from family, job, friends, and school often coincide, you may well have serious conflicts. Such conflicts require you to set priorities and carefully allocate your time. As you set priorities for what's essential in your own life, your values may shift. Things that were important before college may fade into the background as new priorities emerge. (See Chapter 2 for more on time management.)

EXERCISE 12.12 Assessing Your Basic Skills

List your strengths and weaknesses in areas such as reading, writing, and math and in study skills such as listening, taking notes, and studying for tests. Determine what kind of help you need, and find out where you can obtain that help on your campus. Look for noncredit classes and labs that offer review of high school courses. Visit the offices that offer these review courses and/or labs and sign up for tutoring or review sessions.

EXERCISE 12.13 Surviving and Succeeding as an Adult Student

A. *For adult students:* Many of you must juggle work and family responsibilities with class attendance and study demands. List some strategies that may be useful in coping with the time crunch.

_____

_____

_____

_____

_____

_____

Share your list with another adult student (or several others). Are there some similarities? Are there additional good suggestions?

B. *For traditional students:* Imagine that your mother or father is a single parent paying your tuition and supporting your younger brother and sister. Your parent does not have a college degree. Twice she or he has applied and been turned down for a promotion at work, a promotion needed to make ends meet. Over the years the company's prerequisites for certain jobs have changed, so that new people hired for your parent's job and for subordinate positions are required to have a college degree, and now the boss has begun to pressure her or him to complete a college degree. Pretend that you are the parent, and discuss your feelings; then list some problems that she or he may encounter and some strategies for coping with those problems.

_____

_____

_____

_____

_____

_____

5. *Be realistic about expectations.* Some students unrealistically expect to make all A's simply by attending class. The following rule of thumb may help you set realistic goals and allot adequate time for study: On an average you should plan on at least 2 hours of outside preparation for every hour in the classroom to obtain a grade of C. By this rule a class of three 50-minute sessions per week requires at least 6 hours of preparation per week. Depending on your own special abilities and past experiences, you may need more or less time to maintain a passing grade. If you expect A's in every class, you may need to spend even more time reading, outlining, studying, and writing papers. Many adults push themselves to get A's in every course. Remember that such high expectations may cause you to make undue sacrifices in other important areas of life.

SUPPORT SYSTEMS ON CAMPUS

As alien as the college environment might initially seem, never forget that you don't have to face it alone. Support and encouragement to pursue goals can come from several sources. You should be able to find encouragement from all of the following sources on your campus.

Peer Support Groups

Developing friendships in a peer group helps students stay in school. If you become friends with at least one other student you can confide in, study with, and call in emergencies, you'll be more likely to enroll in college classes again next year. For example, you can exchange lecture notes if you miss a class or entrust your friend with your cassette recorder to tape a lecture if you know ahead of time you're going to miss it. By simply sharing thoughts over coffee together, you can monitor your own reactions to the college environment. Forming a study group is one of the best ways to give and receive peer support. (See "Ensuring Personal Success" on p. 258 and Exercise 12.8 on p. 260.)

Some colleges offer special orientation programs designed to foster peer support groups among adult learners. These orientations also deliver information on the availability of special courses, services, facilities, and organizations for adult students, as well as on-campus child-care facilities. In addition several large universities reserve sections of courses for adult students only. These sections sometimes feature a unique curriculum adapted to the needs and interests of older learners.

Classes, orientation programs, and student organizations designed for adult learners provide opportunities for you to meet other older students who share your interests and concerns. If no such services exist on your campus, you might place an ad in the college newspaper and form your own group. After all, younger students have many ways of forming mutual support groups: fraternities and sororities, student organizations, dances, intramural sports, and roommates. And there's no doubt that peer support is an important factor in your staying in school.

Faculty/Academic Advisors

Finding a good advisor is another critical factor in your college education. Some universities now designate special academic advisors for mature students. Such advisors must be attuned to the conflicting demands of job, home, and school as well as to the course scheduling problems of adults who work full-time. Information about weekend and evening courses, knowledge of the registration process, and recognition of mature students' time constraints are hallmarks of an excellent adult advisor. If there is no special advisor for mature students on your campus, ask your favorite faculty member to help you select courses, schedule classes, and plan your college career.

Administrator/Ombudsman

The "royal runaround" in administrative procedures probably exists in some form on every college campus. Bureaucratic red tape is a major hurdle to older students with limited time and lack of experience in dealing with such challenges. Campus procedures were originally established to serve faculty, administrators, and younger students. In order to adapt procedures to serve adult learners as well, many campuses now have an administrator designated as advocate or ombudsman for adult students. In large universities adult advocates are often found in the division of student affairs or in continuing education programs, which schedule evening or weekend classes. The larger the campus, the more likely you are to need help from an administrator who understands procedures, knows how to get things done, and is sympathetic to your special needs.

Some colleges and universities are just beginning to change to meet the needs of mature students. If you encounter obstacles rather than encouragement, remember that a college education requires persistence as well as intelligence!

Student Services

Research on students who stay in school versus those who drop out shows that the more support services a student uses, the more likely he or she is to reenroll. Thus you should seek out and use the student services on your own campus. If you need help in selecting a major, visit the career planning or academic advisement center. If you have a personal problem that interferes with your studies, seek help from the counseling center. If you need help with study skills, look for an academic skills development center. Active use of such student services will improve your own chances of survival in this new subculture of academia.

On many campuses student support services may not exist or may not be available on nights and weekends. If a vital support service is not available to you, consider requesting that it be made available. Some colleges are still adjusting to adults as a new clientele and will welcome formal petitions to extend support services to older students.

EXERCISE 12.14 Campus Resources

In your class, work together to discover special services offered for older students on your campus. Each student should volunteer to look into one area and share his or her discoveries with the rest of the class. Each should interview a staff member from one of the services to find out what kinds of problems they deal with and what assistance they offer.

After completing your research, you may decide to invite someone from one of these offices to speak to your group on a topic relevant to all of you, such as stress management, time management, or study skills.

Support from Spouse or Partner

If you're currently married or living with a significant other, his or her support for your educational goals is crucial. An actively supportive partner will willingly adjust household routines and family responsibilities to accommodate exam schedules. A nonsupportive partner who interferes with study time will greatly reduce your chances of success in the classroom. If your partner feels threatened by what you are doing, he or she may attempt to sabotage your college career. At the first signs of such conflict, you would be wise to seek counseling or, at the very least, to sit down with your partner and attempt to resolve your problems. If you cannot resolve the conflict, you may have to choose between forfeiting your education and leaving your spouse. These are tough choices, but you're poised at the beginning of a period of great intellectual and personal development. Adjustments in relationships between partners often go hand in hand with enormous growth. The pursuit of a college education is no exception.

FINANCIAL AID FOR ADULT STUDENTS

Lack of financial resources is one of the biggest hurdles facing adult students. Like much else about higher education, financial aid eligibility and procedures were designed for younger students who are dependent on their parents. Older students often do not meet the eligibility criteria established for younger students. And yet an adult with adequate income to support a

family may not also be able to pay tuition for college courses. On campuses across the nation administrators of financial aid programs recognize the unique circumstances of mature students. But cutbacks in state and federal student aid have delayed progress in meeting the needs of adult learners.

In spite of this gloomy outlook for financial aid, you'll want to check out all the resources on your own campus. For example, some states allow free or reduced tuition to individuals over 60 years old enrolled in state-supported schools. If you're employed, your company may pay your college tuition to encourage you to upgrade job skills or complete a degree. You may qualify for a loan or scholarship from a local or national civic club or women's organization. (For more on financial aid see Appendix B, "How to Manage Your Money and Obtain Financial Aid.")

WHY COLLEGE IS WORTH IT

You may be feeling guilty about the money you're spending on your own education, especially if you are using family resources to pay tuition costs. Perhaps a look at the reasons older students enroll in college courses can help alleviate those guilt feelings. For both men and women, whether married or single, any one of the following reasons is legitimate grounds for making this financial investment in yourself.

Self-Fulfillment

The ultimate reason you choose to attend college is for self-fulfillment. This is the single most legitimate reason for you to make this investment in yourself — taking courses for the pure pleasure of learning is its own justification. Expanding your horizons through the study of genetics, political science, anthropology, literature, art history, or psychology represents the epitome of self-fulfillment and personal development.

Job Advancement Skills

Some adults take a few specific courses to acquire skills for job advancement and promotion in their present careers. Others enroll in degree programs to obtain credentials in the marketplace. Older women, for example, often seek a college degree as a way to enter the job market for the first time. Many working women and men seek a degree to implement a career change. Of course reasons that lead directly to financial gain are simple to justify, but the reasons that fill deep human needs are just as legitimate.

The Need to Grow to Full Potential

Some adults seek a college education to fill a vacuum in a stage of adult development. For example, some women and men feel a loss of identity, a sense of stagnation or isolation during certain stages of adulthood, as familiar roles erode. A mother whose children have grown and left home may experience the "empty nest syndrome." A man or woman who has recently retired or lost his or her role as breadwinner may also feel out of kilter.

Some psychologists suggest that stages of disequilibrium are necessary for further development — the discomfort can cause the person to grow and develop. For some adults, seeking a college education fills a void and reduces isolation or stagnation.

If you have never experienced serious bouts of isolation or stagnation, and your development has been rather smooth and uneventful, you can still expand your horizons and grow through a college education. Learning new concepts or new philosophies can trigger a period during which you question long-held beliefs. Long-cherished values may erode in the face of new information. If so, be assured that you may be on the brink of a new and more advanced stage of development.

Of course a college education is not a panacea; it offers no guarantees that you'll reach your goals. But for whatever reasons you decide to continue your education — to fill a void, to expand horizons, to enter the job market, or to advance in the marketplace — those reasons are valid because they're *your* reasons. You can get rid of any guilt about using time, energy, and money to pursue your goal, because you're making a new investment in yourself. This investment also benefits those around you as you strive to attain your fullest potential.

YOUR CONSUMER IMPACT ON HIGHER EDUCATION

Because you're making an investment in yourself and the stakes are high, you need to approach a college education as a good consumer. You should have a real interest in the quality of classroom instruction and the availability of student support services suitable for adult learners. You are here because you want to be. You are probably paying your own way, and you undoubtedly want your money's worth.

This consumer approach is typical of adult students and has the potential for altering institutions of higher education for the better. Already many colleges and universities are changing to meet the demands of adult learners. By their sheer numbers older students are changing programs and procedures, and depending on how prevalent and how vocal adult students become, they may have a lasting positive impact on the quality of higher education.

Be proud of your accomplishments! Along with your own growth and personal development, you and many others like you offer to institutions of higher education across the nation the promise of a period of renewed growth and revitalization. It's a worthy challenge and a worthy cause.

EXERCISE 12.15 Preparing for Change

How do you expect to change (intellectually, socially, spiritually, vocationally, and emotionally) as a result of going to college? Do you expect your relationships with your spouse or significant other and your friends to change? How?

_____

_____

_____

_____

_____

Share these thoughts with your spouse, significant other, or close friend. For more information about how people (especially older students) change throughout the life span, consult the books by Erikson, Friedan, and Sheehy suggested as further reading.

EXERCISE 12.16 Life-Tasks

Developmental psychologists study differences in life-tasks across age groups. For example, first-graders must learn to tolerate separation from their care-givers, to work quietly at their desks, and to raise their hands before speaking. Of course they also must learn many other tasks before becoming successful first-graders. Likewise college students, both younger and older, must learn many new life-tasks. List ten life-tasks that you feel you must master now. Then rank-order your list (1 for the most important task, 10 for the least important).

1. _____

2. _____

3. _____

4. _____

5. _____

6. _____

7. _____

8. _____

9. _____

10. _____

Compare your life-tasks with those of students in your age group as well as those who are younger or older. Do you find any differences by age in the listing and ranking of life-tasks?

EXERCISE 12.17 Drawing Your Lifeline

On a sheet of poster-sized paper, draw your "lifeline" — a pictorial or symbolic representation of important milestones in your life. Concentrate on those factors in your history that affected your decision to attend college. Don't worry about the quality of your drawing, since that's not the point of this exercise. Add a few words or numbers if they seem necessary.

Present and explain your lifeline drawing to the class.

JOURNAL

Many adult students know that their study skills are a little rusty and fear the competition for grades with younger students whom they see as better prepared. At the same time, many students attending college straight out of high school appreciate the experiences and insights older students bring to class. If you are an adult student, offer a bit of advice to traditional-age students who share classes with you. If you are a traditional-age student, give some advice to adult students. Consider sharing what you've written with someone from the opposite group and asking for a response.

SUGGESTIONS FOR FURTHER READING

Astin, A. W., W. S. Korn, and E. R. Berz. *The American Freshman: National Norms for Fall 1990.* Los Angeles: Cooperative Institutional Research Programs, University of California, Los Angeles, 1990.

Beal, Philip E., and Lee Noel. *What Works in Student Retention.* Iowa City, Iowa, and Boulder, Colo.: American College Testing Program and National Center for Higher Education Management Systems, 1980.

Erikson, Erik. *Childhood and Society.* New York: Norton, 1964.

———. *Identity: Youth and Crisis.* New York: Norton, 1968.

Friedan, Betty. *The Feminine Mystique.* New York: Dell, 1962.

Josselson, R. *Finding Herself: Pathways to Identity Development in Women.* San Francisco: Jossey-Bass, 1989.

Lenning, Oscar T., Philip E. Beal, and Ken Sauer. *Attrition and Retention: Evidence for Action and Research.* Boulder, Colo.: National Center for Higher Education Management Systems, 1980.

Paulsen, M. B. *College Choice: Understanding Student Enrollment Behavior.* ASHE-ERIC Higher Education Report No. 6. Washington, D.C.: The George Washington University, School of Education and Human Development.

Sheehy, Gail. *Passages: Predictable Crises of Adult Life.* New York: Dutton, 1974.

Upcraft, L., and J. N. Gardner. *The Freshman Year Experience.* San Francisco, Calif.: Jossey-Bass, 1989.

A Personal System of Values

Richard L. Morrill

A Personal System of Values

*I*t freaks me out to hear some people talk about what's important to them. I mean, would you believe she would rather die than miss a frat party? Or that he feels guilty if he misses church? And two of my other friends think nothing of spending the night together three or four times a week. When I got to college, I thought everybody would more or less feel the way I do about lots of things. We did in high school. Not here!

RICHARD L. MORRILL *is president of the University of Richmond in Virginia. "As president of a university," he says, "I find that the issue of values continues to be central in the experience of most freshmen. For many students the challenges are indistinct and tend to pass quickly, but for others a lengthy and sometimes troubling process of adjustment is set in motion. Experience has taught me that, whatever else, a clear understanding of values and how they function is a crucial first step in making the best ultimate decisions in the values realm.*

"I suppose some of my interest in the field comes from my own experiences in college. I had been brought up in a conservative home in which standards of personal behavior were tightly enforced. When I arrived at college, I confronted ways of living that contradicted the ways I had been reared. As I met others with different ideas about everything from alcohol to personal relationships, it was time to think through the basis for my own positions. Undoubtedly some of my continuing interest in values dates to these early personal challenges."

Discussions about values often generate more heat than light because the very word *values* means different things to different people. For some the word refers to specific positions a person holds on controversial moral issues such as capital punishment. For others it refers to whatever might be most important to a person, such as a good job, a fancy car, or the welfare of the family. For still others it refers to abstractions such as truth, justice, or success. In this chapter we offer a definition of values and explore ways to discover your values and apply them to the college experience.

DEFINING VALUES

Perhaps we can best define a *value* as an important attitude or belief. Let us include in the definition the idea that a value commits us to taking *action*, to doing something. In other words when we truly hold a value we act on it. We do not necessarily act in response to other feelings. For instance, we might watch a television program showing starving people in Africa that gives us a feeling of sympathy or regret but take no action whatsoever. If our feelings of sympathy cause us to raise funds to help those suffering, then those feelings qualify as values. Action does not have to be overtly physical. Action may involve thinking and talking continually about a problem, trying to interest others in it, reading about it, or sending letters to officials regarding it. The basic point is that when we truly hold a value, it leads us to *do* something.

Let us also define values as those beliefs that we have accepted by *choice*, with a sense of responsibility and ownership. Much of what we think is simply what others have taught us. Many things we have learned from our parents and others close to us will come to count fully as our values, but only once we fully embrace them for ourselves. One must personally accept or reject something before it can become a value.

Finally let us make the idea of *affirmation* or *prizing* an essential part of values. We are proud of our values and the choices to which they lead. We also find ourselves ready to sacrifice for them and to establish our priorities

around them. Our values draw forth our loyalties and commitment. Because they hold sway over us, our values can also be a source of self-condemnation when we fail to fully realize them in our daily lives. In other words a real aura of pressure or "oughtness" surrounds the values we have chosen.

DISCOVERING VALUES

You probably already have at least a fair sense of what your values are. Yet one of your key tasks in college is to more consciously define your own approach to life and articulate your values. College is an opportunity to locate and test those values by analyzing their full implications, comparing them with the values of others, and giving voice to your beliefs.

No one is neutral, or without values, though values are held with varying degrees of clarity and commitment. Identifying your values is at once simple and complex. One way to start is by asking yourself directly what your most important values are. You began doing this in Chapter 11 in relation to a potential career. Let's continue in a broader vein.

EXERCISE 13.1   Prioritizing Your Values

Consider the following list of twenty-five values.* Rank-order these values (1 for the most important value, 2 for the second-most important value, and so on down to 25 for the least important one). (Note: If you have difficulty with this part of the exercise, you may need practice at **values clarification**. The more often you reflect on your values and confirm or change their priorities, the easier this type of exercise will become.)

_____8_____ 1. companionship

_____2_____ 2. family life

_____7_____ 3. security

_____6_____ 4. being financially and materially successful

_____14_____ 5. enjoying leisure time

_____12_____ 6. work

_____3_____ 7. learning and getting an education

_____13_____ 8. appreciation of nature

_____22_____ 9. competing and winning

_____4_____ 10. loving others and being loved

_____1_____ 11. a relationship with God

_____5_____ 12. self-respect and pride

_____17_____ 13. being productive and achieving

_____18_____ 14. enjoying an intimate relationship

_____15_____ 15. having solitude and private time to reflect

*List used with permission from Gerald Corey and Marianne Schneider Corey, *I Never Knew I Had a Choice*, 4th ed. (Pacific Grove, Calif.: Brooks/Cole, 1990).

_23_ 16. having a good time and being with others

_19_ 17. laughter and a sense of humor

_11_ 18. intelligence and a sense of curiosity

_21_ 19. opening up to new experiences

_20_ 20. risk taking and personal growth

_24_ 21. being approved of and liked by others

_16_ 22. being challenged and meeting challenges well

_10_ 23. courage

_4_ 24. compassion

_25_ 25. being of service to others

Look at your top three choices on the list. What was the source for each of these values? We usually "learn" values from important people, peak events, or societal trends. List each value and try to indicate where you "learned" it.

Value   **Source**

1. _____   _____
                                     _____

2. _____   _____
                                     _____

3. _____   _____
                                     _____

Review the values and their sources. Can you detect an overall pattern? If so, what does the pattern tell you about yourself? Were there any surprises?

EXERCISE 13.2   Evidence of Values

Another way to start discovering your values is by defining them in relation to some immediate evidence or circumstances. In the space below list fifteen items in your room (or apartment or house) that are important or that symbolize something important to you.

_____   _____   _____

_____   _____   _____

_____   _____   _____

_____   _____   _____

_____   _____   _____

Now cross out the five items that are least important — the ones you could most easily live without. Of the remaining ten, cross out the three that are least important. Of the remaining seven, cross out two more. Of the remaining five, cross out two more. Rank-order the final three items from most to least important.

What has this exercise told you about what you value?

Another way to begin discovering your values is by looking at some choices you have already made in response to life's demands and opportunities. For example, consider some of your reasons for deciding to attend this particular institution. Many students will say that they chose a certain college because of its academic reputation. How much do you value your school's reputation? And more precisely, what does the word *reputation* mean to you? Are you interested in the prestige that comes from enrolling in the college? Does this signify an interest in high achievement and in meeting demanding standards? Obviously a value such as prestige can run in several directions, one being social prestige, another reflecting commitment to intellectual distinction. Finding the values that stand behind your choices requires continual exploration of the implications of those choices.

Many students say they have chosen a college because it offers the best opportunity for a good job in the future. Is this true for you? The choice to seek education in terms of its employment benefits suggests any number of possible values. Does this mean that economic security is one of your top values, or does it suggest that you are defining personal success or power in terms of wealth? And once again, what are the implications of the choice? How much are you willing to sacrifice to achieve the goals connected with this economic value? Does the achievement you are seeking bring fulfillment on a short- or long-term basis? How will your obligations to family and to society relate to this particular value?

By asking such questions about each of your supposed values, you can gain a fuller understanding of them and of the rest of your commitments. What are the reasons behind your choices? Are they made on the basis of your true values?

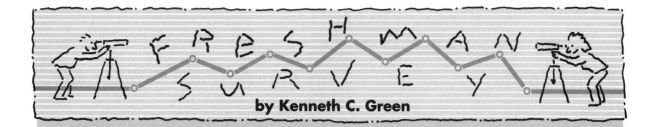

by Kenneth C. Green

What's Essential?

The accompanying figure shows dramatic shifts over the past two decades in the life goals of entering freshmen. Each year since 1967 the UCLA Freshman Survey has asked students to indicate the importance of "being very well off financially" and "developing a meaningful philosophy of life." How would you interpret the results in the figure?

One striking aspect of these dramatic shifts in values during this period has been the changes in goals among first-year women. In 1967 first-year men were almost twice as likely as first-year women to identify "being very well-off financially" as an important life goal (54.2 percent for men, 30.0 percent for women). By 1990 the gap between men and women on this issue had narrowed from 24 to 7 percentage points (77.7 percent for men, 70.3 percent for women).

Changes in Freshman Life Goals, 1967–1990 (percentage indicating "essential" or "very important")

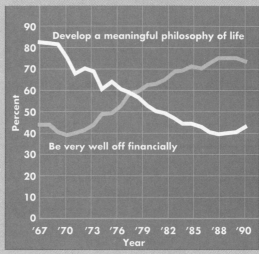

SOURCE: Higher Education Research Institute, UCLA

In exploring your values, you may also ask how you became committed to this value in the first place and how it relates to other values. Conflict in values is a frequent, sometimes difficult problem. How far are you willing to go in service to this value? What sacrifices do you accept in its name? How do the values you have chosen provide you with a meaning for your future? Few of us ever stop trying to give a sharper and clearer account of exactly what our values mean and what implications they have for ourselves and those around us.

The previous exercises present ways to begin identifying values. Of course this is not a one-time task — even seemingly strongly held values may change with time and experience. Thus you should not only develop a sense of your present values but also gain some sense of how they are evolving in a variety of areas: personal, moral, political, economic, social, religious, and intellectual. A major problem for most of us is sorting out how our own values resemble or contrast with those of our parents.

EXERCISE 13.3 Your Values and Your Parents' Values

The process by which we assimilate our parents' values into our own value systems involves three steps: (1) choosing (selecting freely from alternatives after thoughtful consideration of the consequences), (2) prizing (cherishing the value and affirming it publicly), and (3) acting (consistently displaying this value in behavior and decisions). List three values your parents have taught you are important. For each, document whether you have completed the three-step process to make their value yours.

Value	Choosing	Prizing	Acting
1. _____	_____	_____	_____
	_____	_____	_____
2. _____	_____	_____	_____
	_____	_____	_____
3. _____	_____	_____	_____
	_____	_____	_____

If you haven't completed the three steps, does it mean you have *not* chosen this value as your own? Explain your thoughts about this.

_____

_____

_____

_____

Let's turn our attention now to two special areas in which college is likely to affect your values: personal values and intellectual values.

COLLEGE AND PERSONAL VALUES

Almost all students find that college life challenges their existing personal and moral values. The challenge typically comes through friendships and relationships with new people whose backgrounds, experiences, goals, and desires run counter to their own. This clash with diversity can be unsettling, threatening, exciting; it can also produce positive change.

Students differ one from another in everything from sleep and study habits to deep philosophical beliefs about the purposes of life. First-year students are often startled at the diversity of personal moralities to be found on any campus. For instance, some students have been taught at home or in church that it is wrong to drink alcohol. Yet they may find that friends whom they

Bye-Bye, Miss American Pie?

The American dream: The basic cultural pattern of the American middle class has been a generational investment in rising aspirations and economic mobility — parents sacrifice for their children so the next generation will live better. Parents hope that their children will equal or surpass them economically. Over the past forty years this upward mobility has been reflected in three unique symbols of the American experience:

► Purchasing a home

► Sending one's children to college

► Owning two cars and trading them in every four to five years

Today a growing number of students sense they may not be able to match the economic attainments of their parents. College, home, and even cars seem increasingly out of reach. Many students believe that the middle-class life of the twenty-first century may require them to be wealthy, at least by their current understanding of the term. Most acknowledge that it will take two working parents to provide their children with the comforts that one working father once could provide.

respect and care about see nothing wrong with drinking. Likewise students from more liberal backgrounds may be astonished to discover themselves forming friendships with classmates whose personal values are very conservative.

How do you react when you do not approve of some aspects of a friend's way of life? Do you try to change his or her behavior, pass judgments on the person, or withdraw from the relationship? Often part of the problem is that the friend demonstrates countless good qualities and values that make the conduct itself seem less significant. In the process your own values may begin to change under the influence of a new kind of relativism: "I don't choose to do that, but I'm not going to make any judgments against those who do." A similar pattern of response often develops regarding sexual involvements. People become friends with others whose behavior and values differ from their own, and the result is personal turmoil.

In such cases one can always recommend tolerance, since tolerance for others is a central value in our society and one that often grows during college. Yet it is easy to think of cases in which tolerance becomes indulgence of another's destructive tendencies. It is one thing to accept a friend's responsible use of alcohol at a party, and quite another to fail to challenge a drunk who plans to drive you home. Sexual intimacy in an enduring relationship may be one thing; a never-ending series of one-night stands is quite another. Remember, the failure to challenge destructive conduct is no sign of friendship.

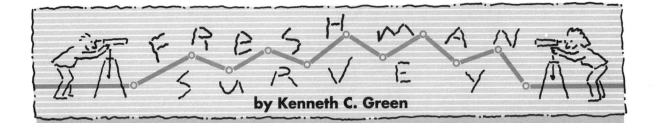

FRESHMAN SURVEY

by Kenneth C. Green

Where Are You Politically?

Popular wisdom has it that students in the 1960s were very liberal and in recent years have become very conservative. Is it true? Not really. The accompanying figure suggests that students' political preferences shifted from liberal to middle-of-the-road over the past two decades, rather than from left to right.

In Fall 1990, 24.4 percent of entering freshmen identified their political views as "liberal" or "far left," slightly up from the level of 1980, but well below the peak in 1971.

The "middle-of-the-road" freshman group increased during the 1970s, peaked at 60.3 percent in 1983, and has declined since then. In 1990 it stood at 54.7 percent, reflecting modest but steady gains from both the liberal and conservative sides.

However, the proportion of students who identified their political views as "conservative" or "far right" was 20.9 percent in 1990, up from 18.3 percent in 1980 and a low of 14.5 percent in 1973. Actually, as the figure shows, the proportion of students who call themselves conservative has been fairly stable over the past two decades. This seems surprising as the 1980s were supposed to be a period of "rising conservatism" among all Americans, including college students.

Political Orientation of College Freshmen, 1970–1990

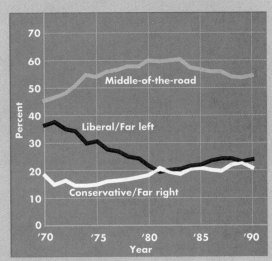

SOURCE: Higher Education Research Institute, UCLA

EXERCISE 13.4   Values in Conflict

Read the following situation and then answer the questions.

You have become good friends with your roommate since the beginning of the semester. You know he or she uses drugs once in a while, which usually results in some rowdy behavior you're not always comfortable with. He or she certainly doesn't use drugs every day, but you wonder if even occasional use is healthy. You've tried to discuss the topic with him or her and received very little response.

Last night, while under the influence of drugs, your roommate set fire to a number of flyers and posters on the hallway walls. Today your resident assistant (or house supervisor or landlord) wants an explanation and demands to know who is responsible. Your roommate doesn't seem willing to come forward.

Which of your values may come into play here? Will any of your values conflict with one another? How might your values conflict with those of your roommate? Your RA? How would you resolve the situation?

Share your answers in a small group. Discuss how changing one part of the scenario might change your response (for instance, what if your friend burned *your* posters on the door to your room?). Describe any similar situations you've experienced. How did you respond? Were you successful? How did you define success in the situation? (Note: If this exercise was particularly hard for you, you may find the section on assertiveness in Chapter 14 to be helpful.)

Are there better and worse ways to deal with these challenges to personal and moral values? The framework for an answer rests in an awareness of the nature of values themselves. As we saw earlier, true values must be freely chosen and cannot be accepted simply on the authority of another person. After all the purpose of values is to give active meaning to our lives. Trying to make sense out of the complex circumstances of our own lives by using someone else's values simply doesn't work.

At the same time, it is appropriate to talk about values with those with whom we seem to be in conflict. What are the other person's true values (consciously identified, freely chosen, and actively expressed)? Do his or her current behaviors correspond to those values? Much can be learned on both sides.

Many people make the mistake of fleeing from the challenge of diversity and failing to confront conflicting value systems. The problem with this strategy is that at some time in their lives, often within a year or two, these people find themselves unable to cope with the next set of challenges to which they are exposed. They do not grow as persons because they do not prize their own values and their behaviors are not consistent with what they say they value. Although it's only a first step, you must work through challenges to your own personal values by finding answers that truly make sense to you and help you to move ahead with your life.

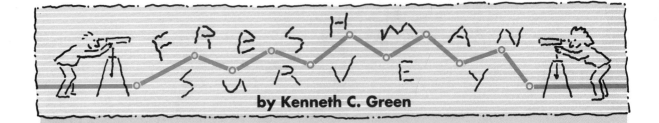

by Kenneth C. Green

Social and Political Issues

What were some of the personal values of first-year students in the late 1980s? Judge for yourself, based on the first figure.

What does the graph suggest about student attitudes on some key political and social issues between 1980 and 1990? Although it suggests a movement toward more liberal positions in recent years, entering freshmen have also become increasingly conservative on selected issues over the past decade, as the second figure shows.

Do any of these percentages surprise you? In what respect? Do you think these numbers would hold for your campus? What is the mood on political issues on your campus? Among your friends? How did you feel about the recent war with Iraq? Should we have waited longer for sanctions to affect Iraq instead of bombing Baghdad on January 17, 1991? (Were any of your friends or family members involved in the war?)

Freshman Attitudes on Political and Social Issues, 1980 and 1990 (percentage who "agree" or "strongly agree")

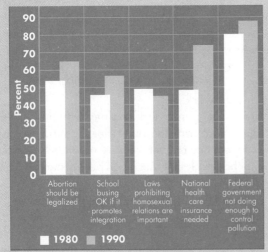

SOURCE: Higher Education Research Institute, UCLA

Freshman Attitudes on Crime-Related Issues, 1978 and 1990

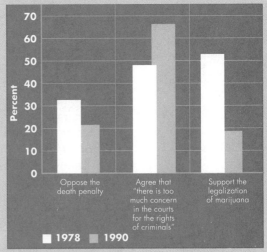

SOURCE: Higher Education Research Institute, UCLA

COLLEGE AND INTELLECTUAL VALUES

Intellectual values such as clarity, accuracy, rigor, and excellence cluster around the central value of truth. One of the most striking transitions that occurs during the college years has to do with the way in which a person's notion of truth changes.

Many students enter college assuming the process of education is one in which unquestioned authorities "pour" truth into the students' open ears. Some students believe that every problem has a single right answer and that the professor or the textbook will always be the source of truth. However, most college professors don't believe this, and their views on truth often initially shock these students (see Chapter 7).

Academics tend to see "truth" in a much more contextual, flexible, and variable way. It's not that the professor is cynical about the possibility of truth, but rather that the scholar's role is understood as involving an ongoing, open-ended search. The professor's interest is in seeking as many valid interpretations of the information as can be found. College instructors continually ask for reasons, for arguments, for the assumptions on which a given position is based, and for the evidence that confirms or discounts it.

Just as with personal and moral values, college-level education involves the assumption that as a student you will become a maker of your own meaning, on your own, with the ultimate responsibility for judgments of truth and falseness resting in your hands. The whole system of a university's intellectual values — openness, freedom of inquiry, tolerance, rigor, and excellence — is based on this approach, and there is no escaping it.

EXERCISE 13.5 Applying Your Values in College

While values are not always expressed directly and openly, they can be found in many places in your school's environment. Values surround you in the form of institutional mission statements, academic integrity policies, and behavior exhibited by you and the people around you. The variety of values expressed can often lead to conflict — within an individual, between individuals, or between an individual and the institution. From the following three topics, choose the one you're most interested in and work through the exercise.

A. *Institutional purpose.* Most institutions of higher education are based on a broad collection of values, beyond academic freedom and the search for truth (although these are vitally important). To learn more about your institution's guiding values, undertake a "document analysis." Obtain a copy of the institutional mission statement (it should be in your college catalog). As you read it, copy down phrases that seem to imply a value, identify the implied value, and then assess whether it concurs with a value you hold.

Phrase	Value(s) Implied	Fit with Your Values?
_____	_____	_____
_____	_____	_____
_____	_____	_____

Phrase	Value(s) Implied	Fit with Your Values?

If you disagree with one or more values, what will the consequences be for you? How will you respond?

B. *Academic integrity.* Recall the section in Chapter 6 dealing with academic integrity, which described the intellectual values held in higher education — honesty, freedom of inquiry, openness, and excellence. Academic dishonesty sometimes occurs when these values conflict with those of individual students. What values might lead students to commit academic dishonesty? How can this be avoided?

C. *Values and personal behavior.* Recall Chapter 2 on time management, which discussed prioritizing activities that are more important or less important to you. This is a way of expressing your values through actions. For the two values identified here, list a variety of actions that would express those values.

Achieving Excellence in College

1. *Reading one book each week not required for class but related to my major*

2. _____

3. _____

4. _____

5. _____

Maintaining a Great Social Life

1. *Spending weekends out of town with friends*

2. _____

3. _____

4. _____

5. _____

While achieving excellence and maintaining a social life may not seem like conflicting values, the actions that express the values may cause conflict. In other words acting on one value may prevent you from staying true to the other. Which of the actions you've listed in each column might conflict with one another? If you held these two values, how would you reconcile each of these conflicts?

RIGHT VALUES

We have stressed that the essential first step in developing a value system is for you to become your own maker of meaning whether in the sphere of personal, moral, or intellectual values. But it is only a first step; you must be aware not only of making meaning but also of making a meaning that can

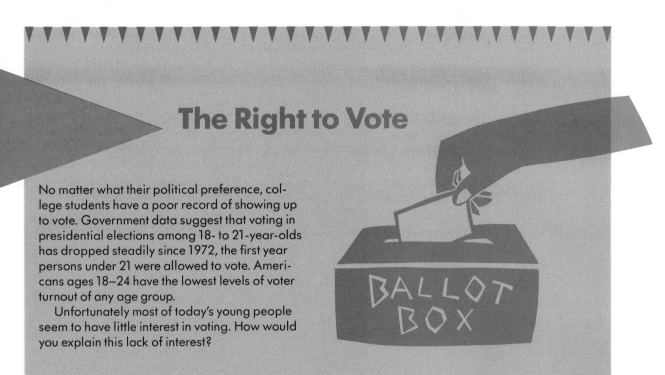

The Right to Vote

No matter what their political preference, college students have a poor record of showing up to vote. Government data suggest that voting in presidential elections among 18- to 21-year-olds has dropped steadily since 1972, the first year persons under 21 were allowed to vote. Americans ages 18–24 have the lowest levels of voter turnout of any age group.

Unfortunately most of today's young people seem to have little interest in voting. How would you explain this lack of interest?

lead to a coherent and fulfilling life. As crucial as it is to develop your own values, it is equally important that you find the *right* values. Little is accomplished if you develop a genuine system of values that leads to egocentric, dishonest, cruel, and/or irresponsible conduct.

The question of what the right values are cannot be answered simply. There are no automatic criteria (though perhaps the "Golden Rule" will serve as well as any). Yet clearly all of us who have accepted life in a democratic society and membership in an academic community such as a college or university are committed to many significant values. To participate in democratic institutions is to honor such values as respect for others, tolerance, equality, liberty, and fairness. Members of an academic community are usually passionate in their defense of academic freedom, the open search for truth, honesty, collegiality, civility, and tolerance for dissenting views.

Yet many issues relating to values are open for continuing and legitimate discussion and disagreement. For instance, to what extent should the university take it upon itself to ensure the success of each of its students? To what extent may it simply offer certain opportunities for learning and then let each student sink or swim?

Perhaps what college can do best with regard to values is teach a process for making value choices, for thinking seriously about values, just as a good education teaches us to think in other realms. That is, an education in values can teach us how to assess our values while leaving us to choose our own actual values. This might involve in part the posing of a series of overarching questions relating to values.

For example, are our values *consistent* with one another? Contradictions among values can be just as harmful and foolish as contradictions among ideas. Are our values sufficiently broad in *scope* — that is, do they provide us with a comprehensive outlook on life? We learn that our values may work very well within the small circle of our family but produce conflict with individuals from a different background. This presses us toward common ground, areas of agreement based on which we can overcome conflict. The pressure always to enlarge our circle of association, to move toward the universal sphere of the human family, beyond all divisions of race, sex, and the like — that is where we have to go to find our true and best selves.

Other tests can also measure the depth, the richness, and the adequacy of our values. We know that many of our choices fail to meet the test that *time* itself provides. Others fail to meet the test of *relative worth*. Life teaches us that transient satisfactions and pleasures leave us with little if they rob us of opportunities and accomplishments that may stay with us for a lifetime.

And so it goes. Life itself continually tests which of our values will create coherent, consistent, and enduring results, the greatest fulfillment of our potential. Just as we can be educated with regard to ways of thinking, so we can be educated with regard to our valuing and our choices. This too is what college is all about. The opportunity for growth is yours.

JOURNAL

This chapter suggests that any belief or behavior that is primarily a result of what someone else expects of us without our own active and free choice is not the expression of our own true values. It also suggests that for many students, college is a time and an experience in which everyone's true values are tested. Describe your current system of "true values" (chosen, affirmed, and acted upon). In what ways has college already tested or changed those values?

SUGGESTIONS FOR FURTHER READING

Bellah, R., R. Madsen, W. M. Sullivan, A. Swidler, and S. M. Tipton. *Habits of the Heart.* Berkeley: University of California Press, 1985.

Chickering, A. *Education and Identity.* San Francisco: Jossey-Bass, 1969.

Corey, G., and M. S. Corey. *I Never Knew I Had a Choice,* 4th ed. Pacific Grove, Calif.: Brooks/Cole, 1990.

Kolak, Daniel, and Raymond Martin. *Wisdom Without Answers: A Guide to the Experience of Philosophy,* 2nd ed. Belmont, Calif.: Wadsworth, 1991.

Lewis, Hunter. *A Question of Values.* New York: Harper & Row, 1990.

Morrill, R. L. *Teaching Values in College.* San Francisco: Jossey-Bass, 1980.

Niebuhr, H. R. *Faith on Earth.* New Haven, Conn.: Yale University Press, 1989.

———. *The Responsible Self.* New York: Harper & Row, 1963.

Pojman, Louis P. *Ethics: Discovering Right and Wrong.* Belmont, Calif.: Wadsworth, 1990.

Rokeach, M. *The Nature of Human Values.* New York: Free Press, 1973.

Simon, S., L. Howe, and H. Kirschenbaum. *Values Clarification.* New York: Hart, 1972.

CHAPTER

14

▼▼▼▼▼▼▼▼▼▼▼▼▼▼▼▼▼▼▼▼

Person to Person

Being Assertive – Not Passive or Aggressive
Ruthann Fox-Hines

Developing Relationships
Robert A. Friday

Getting Involved
Marie-Louise A. Ramsdale

Being Assertive – Not Passive or Aggressive

I can't bring myself to question my professor, even if I don't agree. I mean, who am I? Just a lowly student. I can't even manage to tell Fred off when he borrows my tapes. I don't want to ruin our friendship, but it sure bugs me. I just said, "Sure, take all the tapes you want this weekend. I'll just read the newspaper." Hope he got the message. I tried to tell him off once, but all he did was get upset. How do I say what's bothering me without getting everybody upset? Including me?

RUTHANN FOX-HINES *is a counseling psychologist at the University of South Carolina, Columbia.*

"There's a saying that you end up teaching what you need to learn. I think that fits me," she says. "In high school and in college I was shy and relatively passive. In graduate school I was a mix of passive and aggressive with increasing amounts of intuitively developed assertiveness. Then came Alberti and Emmons' 'Your Perfect Right' workshops, in which I studied the principles of assertiveness. Since then I have conducted hundreds of workshops, spoken, and published to expand the concepts. Assertive behavior has made such a difference in both my personal and professional lives. I hope this chapter motivates you to examine how you interact, to remember that the best behavior is based on mutual respect and personal responsibility, and to seek further training in assertiveness."

In college and beyond you will find it extremely important to stand up for yourself and communicate your wants, needs, feelings, and ideas in a positive manner. Concerned parents or teachers may not be around to look out for you, so it's up to you to look out for yourself.

Stop and think for a moment of the many occasions when you've wished you were more skilled in this respect. Perhaps you needed to talk to an advisor about getting a course changed or wanted to ask a professor to explain an obscure point in a lecture. Maybe you and your roommates hadn't agreed upon living arrangements and responsibilities. Resisting pressures from overly concerned parents, equitably sharing the work in a study group, speaking up in class, handling job interviews successfully, negotiating work issues such as salary and hours—all these challenges call for the skills of communicating positively and behaving assertively. Or perhaps you find it easy to stand up for yourself but often encounter negative reactions. If that happens, you may be standing up for yourself in a way that other people resent, that says you don't respect others' rights.

If standing up for your rights is very difficult for you, you may go through life hoping someone else will figure out what you want and do your standing up for you. The sad truth is that someone else rarely will. In this section you'll learn how to be assertive, rather than passive or aggressive, in defending your own rights and how to respect the rights of others.

ASSERTIVENESS VERSUS MISCOMMUNICATION

Most people pick up their communication skills in a rather disorganized manner. As children they begin by imitating parents, other family members, and peers. Such acquired communication behaviors tend to fall into one of three categories, or some combination of them:

- ► *Passive.* Failing to speak up, hinting, or whining
- ► *Aggressive.* Speaking up in a way that puts others down; demanding, pressuring, intimidating
- ► *Passive-aggressive.* Speaking up in a way that confuses others; saying one thing and doing another.

None of these styles of communicating is particularly well received by other people. The ineffective communicator is frequently disappointed, rejected, or even avoided.

Definitions of Assertiveness

The most effective and positive ways of standing up for yourself and communicating your needs and feelings properly are referred to as assertive behaviors. Unlike passive, aggressive, or passive-aggressive styles, assertiveness is clear, direct, respectful, responsible communication — verbal and nonverbal. With this style the chances of your being heard and understood are much greater, and the chances of the receiver of your communication drawing away, closing his or her ears to what you have to say, or lashing back at you are much less.

One popular definition of **assertive behavior** describes it as behavior that permits a person to stand up for his or her rights without denying others their rights. This definition is extremely important. If an individual stands up only for his or her rights, that person will probably come across as aggressive. If an individual focuses exclusively on the rights of the other person, he or she becomes passive. Attention to one's own rights *and* to others' rights is central to assertive behavior.

And what are those rights? They include personal rights, such as the right to your feelings and your opinions, and interpersonal rights, such as the right to ask others for what you want or need and to say no. To avoid denying others their rights, you need to be aware of and consciously acknowledge their rights. For example, you have the right to ask a favor; the other person has the right to refuse to grant it.

EXERCISE 14.1 Affirming Your Personal and Interpersonal Rights

For the following list of rights place a check mark next to those that are especially important to you. Then circle the ones you feel are important but that you have some difficulty acting on.

_____ 1. The right to lead my own life, make my own decisions, make choices, and take the consequences

_____ 2. The right to have my own values and to act on those values in a responsible way

_____ 3. The right to control my own time, body, money, and property

_____ 4. The right to have all my feelings, positive and negative, and to express these in a responsible manner

_____ 5. The right to have my own opinions, ideas, and perceptions and to express them in a responsible, nondogmatic way

_____ 6. The right to have needs and to act to meet them

_____ 7. The right to express my needs, make requests, ask for information, and ask for special consideration

_____ 0 8. The right to refuse requests and invitations

_____ 0 9. The right to *not* feel what others would like me to feel, to *not* share values and perceptions that others would like me to share

_____ 0 10. The right to be imperfect, make mistakes, and act to correct them

_____ 11. The right to change feelings, values, opinions, ideas, and behaviors

_____ 0 12. The right to stop and think when confronted, invited, asked to do a favor, or asked for an opinion

(Note that all these rights depend on your willingness to grant them to others; for example, you have the right to say no if you permit that right to others.)

Pick out one of the rights you marked as one you would most like to affirm or act on in the near future, and write it down in the following space. (You may be thinking, "I want *all* those rights," but for the purpose of the exercise, focus on just one. As that one becomes easier for you to act on, you may choose to go on to the others.)

_____

_____

Now practice making assertive verbal affirmations of your right in front of a mirror. Be sure to do the following:

1. Stand up straight and keep your head up.

2. Make eye contact with yourself in the mirror.

3. Keep your facial expression serious.

4. Make sure your voice is strong and goes down at the end of the affirmation of your right.

5. Go slowly enough to be meaningful; don't rush as you make the following statement:

I, _____, as a worthy human being who respects
          (your name)

the rights of others, have the perfect right to _____.
                                           (your right)

Practice several times until you accomplish an assertive affirmation. Verbalizing this affirmation every morning can strengthen your resolve to act on it during the day.

Three Essential Conditions of Assertiveness

To stand up for your rights assertively, three conditions completely or partially missing from the other ways of communicating must be present: (1) respect for self, (2) respect for others, and (3) the assumption of personal responsibility. When you behave assertively, in effect you are saying, "I respect myself and my right to my ideas, feelings, needs, wants, and values, and I respect you and your rights to the same. I take responsibility for myself. I do not require you to be responsible for me or to figure out what and who I am. I will figure that out myself." By contrast passive, aggressive, and passive-aggressive behaviors tend to show lack of respect for the self and/or lack of respect for the other person, and all three tend to be irresponsible.

An example may help you distinguish among the three nonassertive patterns. Suppose you are serving on a class committee, and one of the other students isn't doing her share of the work. You're becoming frustrated and worried about the grade you may receive on the project if this person doesn't get her part done. With **passive behavior** you might do her part as well as your own, clearly showing you don't respect your own rights. Or you might hint about the deadline and expect her to figure out that you're concerned. That approach shows that you are not respecting your own needs and feelings enough to make them known and that you are holding the other person responsible for figuring out what you need.

With **aggressive behavior** you might confront the individual in this manner: "You're messing this project up for the rest of us. How can you be so inconsiderate? If you don't have your part ready by Monday, I'm telling the professor." This attack is disrespectful in that it ignores the other person's feelings and possibly overlooks mitigating circumstances of which you may be unaware.

With **passive-aggressive behavior** you might complain to another committee member about the individual. This shows lack of respect for her. Haven't you said at times, "I wish he'd respect me enough to come to me instead of talking to others about me"? This behavior is also irresponsible because you probably hope that the person you complained to will take the responsibility of saying something to the individual at fault.

If these three approaches are incorrect and inappropriate, what is the assertive, or proper, approach? The assertive approach means respecting the other person and not attacking him or her, yet still dealing with the issues. It also means expressing feelings and wishes clearly, in specific words, not by implication or tone of voice.

In the case of the joint class project, assertive communication might sound like this: "Mary, I have a problem. Our project is due next week, and I'm worried we won't have it ready on time. I had my part done yesterday, the day we agreed on. Maybe you forgot we agreed on that date. Still, I'm sort of frustrated and worried that we won't have a good project. Would you please make this a priority? I'd like you to do your part so we can meet either tomorrow afternoon or noon the next day at the latest. That will give us the time we need to get it in shape and ready to turn in. I'd appreciate it a lot." The other person may feel embarrassed, but because you aren't attacking her, chances are she won't become defensive.

When people are attacked verbally, they defend themselves either by "flight" or by "fight." Flight can mean passively complying but harboring resentment that may surface later. Fight can mean openly throwing back accusations or acting subversively (passive-aggressively) by doing the work in a slipshod way. On the other hand, when you approach people in a respectful and open manner, chances are they will listen to you more carefully and respond in a positive manner.

A FORMULA FOR ASSERTIVENESS

Here is a formula that will help you act more assertively:

R →	(Respect for the other person)
R ←	(Respect for yourself)
+ S	(Specificity)
A	(Assertiveness)

What is considered a "respectful distance" in one culture may seem like "standoffishness" in another. People of different cultures and subcultures differ in how they interpret space and gesture.

R→: Respect for the Other Person

R→ reminds you to show respect for the other person. Respect as used here does not necessarily mean liking, admiring, or agreeing with that person. It simply means acknowledging that the other person *is* a person with the same basic rights as you. In other words you can dislike someone's behavior or disagree with him or her and still offer basic human respect.

Respect is communicated both in speech and in actions — in the spoken words and in the nonverbal expressions that accompany speech. Respectful verbal expression may be as simple as saying "Excuse me" as you move through a crowd to get off an elevator instead of silently pushing your way through. Your words may acknowledge that the other person also has a set of values and needs. For example, if you are about to discuss a possible grade change with a professor, you might begin by saying, "I realize you have established certain criteria for grades in this class." Respectful verbal expression may convey empathy: "I realize you have a heavy load." It may offer the benefit of the doubt: "It probably just slipped your mind." Respect for other people means giving them what you want to receive: courtesy, acknowledgment, and empathy.

Nonverbal expressions of respect for others may be communicated in gestures, facial expressions, and tone of voice, which often convey more meaning than the words themselves. For example, spoken in a certain tone of voice a phrase such as "I realize you're very busy" could sound hostile or sarcastic. Nonverbal expressions that communicate respect for others include a clear, relatively gentle, and unhurried manner of speaking; eye contact when another person is talking; uncrossed arms to signal openness; and appropriate physical space between people so they do not feel crowded or intimidated. As you learn effective and positive methods of standing up for yourself, also pay attention to your nonverbal communication.

Cultures often differ in the meaning and interpretation of nonverbal expressions. Thus you should be cautious about interpreting nonverbal behaviors as signs of disrespect when the individual is from a different cultural background. For example, Mediterranean, Latin American, and Middle Eastern people need much less space between themselves and others (as little as 12 inches) than do their northern European or North American counterparts (who require as much as 3 feet). If you are aware of these differences, you won't misinterpret such behavior as intimidating or disrespectful from one perspective or unfriendly and distant from the other.

R←: Respect for Yourself

R← reminds you to respect yourself and to accept personal responsibility for your feelings, wants, and actions. A major way to accomplish this verbally is to use the first-person singular pronoun: *I, me, my*. Say "I feel" instead of "You make me feel." Say "I need more time" instead of "Do you really want it done by . . . ?" which is indirect and suggestive, or "You've got to be kidding; it can't be done by . . . ," which is indirect but also a put-down. Instead of "Well, maybe" or "Heck, no! How could you ask me that?" say "I don't want to."

Nonverbal expressions of self-respect also include such things as eye contact and open body movements. Both imply you believe in what you are saying and have nothing to hide. Holding your head up instead of lowering it tends to communicate assurance rather than nervousness or lack of self-confidence. Softening and lowering your voice slightly at the end of sentences rather than tending toward a rising intonation communicates self-confidence.

S: Specificity

S reminds you to be specific. Through self-respect you accept responsibility for figuring yourself out as clearly as possible, and through respect for others you become willing to be as clear and specific as possible. Specificity implies a willingness to figure out your views, feelings, and wants and the ability to communicate those as clearly as possible. It means not applying labels to or making generalizations about other people and their behavior. Instead of saying "How can you be so inconsiderate?" when a smoker exhales in your direction, you might say, "I'm very bothered by smoke. Would you please blow it in the other direction?"

To attain specificity you need to avoid general labels such as *inconsiderate, lazy,* and *poor attitude,* which you would resent if applied to you. Instead talk about the specific behaviors that lead you to think about those labels. For example, you might think someone is aloof and unfriendly, but if you tell him that, he will probably become defensive. Ask yourself, "What does he do that leads me to believe he's unfriendly?" You may realize that he hardly ever smiles or speaks. Then you can mention to him how much you'd enjoy seeing him smile or hearing his ideas. His response will probably be much more positive.

You should also avoid ambiguous generalities such as *attention* and *respect,* for which people often have their own unique definitions. Instead determine the specific behaviors you include in your definition of these vague terms, and talk about those behaviors. For instance, if you want someone to look up from a magazine when you're talking to her, don't say, "You don't respect me." Instead say, "I'm uncomfortable when I talk to someone who doesn't look at me. When we talk, I'd appreciate it if you'd put your magazine down. It would help a lot."

Choosing the Proper Response: An Example

Now let's see how the formula might apply to a real-life situation.

Mark is a conscientious student while his roommate, John, seems to be majoring in partying. John cuts classes and regularly borrows Mark's notes from the two classes they have together. Although Mark has been rescuing John by giving him his notes whenever asked, he is beginning to feel resentful. In a sense "rescuers become victims." That is, "rescuers" do for others what others are capable of doing for themselves. When that happens, the other tends to victimize the rescuer, demanding more and more and valuing it less and less.

Mark's first mistake was to not make his position clear at the outset. The more a person takes responsibility for him- or herself (knowing his or her feelings, wants, and priorities and making them clearly known to others), the fewer problems he or she will have down the road. The first time John asked to borrow the notes, Mark could have responded: "I know you missed class and need the materials [acknowledging John's plight: R→], but I don't usually lend my notes. I'll let you use them this time, but in the future, don't ask me. Please, take your own notes, ask someone else, or talk with the professor ["I" statements of a clear policy and Mark's specific wishes: R← + S].

If John pressures him, Mark may need to protect himself by tightening his communication and using a technique known as the "broken record": No matter what John says, Mark responds by repeating the major message, "I don't like lending my notes" or "I do not lend my notes. Ask someone else."

Here is how the conversation might go if Mark has been lending his notes but wants to stop:

John: (breezing into their room) Hey, Mark, I couldn't make it to history class today; let me see your notes.

Mark: (finally deciding to stop being used; firmly but not sarcastically) I know I've been letting you use my notes, but I don't want to lend them out anymore. I'm beginning to feel as if I'm taking the course for you. Please get to class and take your own notes or ask someone else. I don't want to lend them to you any longer.

John: (laying a guilt trip) Ah, come on, I thought we'd take care of each other.

Mark: (resisting the guilt and focusing on the major issue) I do not want to lend my notes any longer.

John: (laying on more guilt and pressure) What kind of buddy are you? I thought I could count on you.

Mark: (saying John's name to get his attention) John, I do not want to lend my notes. Ask someone else.

John: (resorting to more guilt and pressure) I don't know anyone else in that class. You've always lent them to me before. Why stop now?

Mark: (speaking with increased firmness — more slowly and more deliberately) I know I lent them in the past, but I do *not* want to lend them out any longer. Talk to the professor, but don't keep pressuring me.

At this point John may storm out of the room in a huff.

Mark: Hey, John, I'm sorry you're taking it this way. I hope later you'll accept my position.

EXERCISE 14.2 Role Playing

A. Find a partner and read the parts of Mark and John in the previous script (or your instructor may ask for two volunteers to act out the script in class). What do you notice about the relationship between Mark and John as you read each part aloud or as you listen to the reading? Do you resemble either character? How?

B. With your partner (or observing others in class), act out the following situations. Take turns acting out the assertive role, and make sure to check with your partner and see if he or she feels defensive about any of your statements. This is a clue that your statement was probably aggressive or passive-aggressive instead of assertive.

1. One of your instructors speaks so fast in class you simply cannot take notes or make sense of his train of thought. Many students feel as you do, yet no one has talked to him about it. You decide to be the assertive student.

2. As you reach the parking garage, you see someone pulling into the reserved parking space you paid for. You approach the other student to be assertive in asking her to vacate your space; she tells you a hard luck story about why she needs to use it.

Mark's problem with John is compounded by the fact that he did not take care of this issue at the outset, and if he does not take assertive action, he faces several risks. He could slip into a passive approach, avoiding John as much as possible. He could lie and say he'd forgotten his notes and feel guilty about the deception later. This would be a combination of passive-aggressive and passive because the guilt would probably lead Mark to give in if asked again later. He could become passive-aggressive, complying with John's request but revealing frustration in his voice or giving John the wrong notes. Finally he could explode in an aggressive outburst: "Don't you ever take your own crummy notes? I'm sick and tired of doing all your work for you. Find someone else to mooch off. And, by the way, I'm also sick and tired of . . . " Here all Mark's other frustrations with John may come pouring out.

Any of these alternatives will result in added frustration, distancing between the two, or even flight or fight on John's part: loud arguments, sneak attacks, or stony silences. There's a good chance that if Mark does not assert himself, both he and John will be seeking new roommates at a time when reshuffling may be difficult.

While not guaranteeing that Mark will get what he wants from John, the assertive approach at least opens the door for such a possibility. The other approaches virtually guarantee that the door will be closed, even locked. First, Mark needs to specify the problems he has with John — notes, noise, privacy, whatever — and decide which issue to deal with first; handling individual issues is better than dumping a whole load of complaints on a person all at once. Mark should also find a time when he can talk with John alone. Complaints made in front of others tend to be disrespectful and cause the other person to be more defensive.

Here is another example of what Mark, applying the formula for assertiveness, could say to John: "John, I know I've been lending you my notes [by acknowledging his own part, Mark is showing John respect: R—→]. But I'm beginning to feel used. I don't mind lending my notes if someone is sick, but I really don't like doing it on a regular basis ["I" statement and clarity of feelings and wishes: R ←— + S]. I realize I should have said something earlier [again, R—→, acknowledging his part]. I want to break that pattern. From now on, I'm not lending my notes, and I'm asking you not to ask me for them. Find someone else or talk with the professor, or better still, take your own notes [more "I" statements and a clear statement of what he does and does not want from John: R ←— + S]." If John pushed, Mark could resort to the "broken record" tactic described earlier.

EXERCISE 14.3 What's Your Tendency?

Read the following scenario and the six potential responses. Place an M next to the way you would most likely handle the situation. (This can help you identify whether you tend to handle situations in a passive, aggressive, passive-aggressive, or assertive manner.) Place an X next to the option that best fits with the way assertiveness was described in this section. (The type of behavior each response reflects is listed in a footnote on p. 305.)

In a Friday class your professor announces a paper due on Monday. You have been working hard and had planned to reward yourself with a weekend at the beach with friends. The plans are all made and you're driving.

_____ 1. Forget about the paper, cut class Monday, turn the paper in late on Wednesday, and say you were sick.

_____ 2. When the professor announces the paper, accuse her of being unfair and demand that she give the class more time.

_____ 3. Go immediately to the dean's office and complain about the professor.

_____ 4. Explain to the professor that you have complicated plans that won't permit you time to do a proper job, and request an extension until Wednesday.

_____ 5. Go to the beach but work the whole time on the paper so your friends see how bad off you are. Don't get the rest and fun you need.

_____ 6. Cancel the plans, work on the paper, and complain about the professor to all your friends and classmates.

LEARNING ASSERTIVENESS SKILLS

Learning assertive communication skills is similar to learning to drive a car. First, you practice in a "safe" place such as the driveway or an empty parking lot. Later, you try your skills on uncrowded streets and, eventually, in rush-hour traffic. In the beginning, skills such as braking smoothly feel unnatural and awkward, but with practice they become second nature — you don't even have to think about how to do them.

The same is true with communication skills. In the beginning such behaviors may feel funny and unnatural, but with practice they feel less strange and can be tried in the "real world." Still later, after continued practice, they will become "natural."

A good way to learn assertive behavior skills is through special training seminars, groups, or workshops. Most college and university counseling centers and continuing education programs include assertiveness workshops. Community organizations such as the YMCA or YWCA may offer this training. You could also get together with friends or classmates and use the game "Assert with Love" if your instructor or college has acquired it.* The books listed at the end of this section may be helpful as well. Remember, though, that reading is not enough — practice is the essential thing.

EXERCISE 14.4   Seeing the Patterns

Read the following scenarios and then indicate the type of communication in the blanks: AS for assertive, P for passive, A for aggressive, and PA for passive-aggressive. (The type of behavior each scenario reflects is listed in the footnote on the next page.)

_____ 1. Naomi's parents tell her they want her to come home every weekend. She replies, "I know you love me and want what's best for me. Right now, with studies and the friendships I'm trying to establish, what's best for me is to spend most of my weekends at school. I don't want to come home except at breaks, but I will promise to write or call at least once a week. I'd appreciate your understanding."

_____ 2. Bill is asked to do a favor. He replies, "Are you kidding? Heck, no."

_____ 3. Brenda needs to borrow a party dress. She says to Helen, "I don't know what I'm going to do. I don't have anything to wear to Sara's party."

_____ 4. George pays Pete a compliment. Pete replies, "Thank you. I worked hard on getting that done."

_____ 5. Jan doesn't pay much attention to time. Her parents tell her they want her to call on Thursday evenings. She frequently forgets.

*High Consciousness Games, Inc., PO Box 3206, Kansas City, Kans. 66103.

JOURNAL

Reflect on your own basic behavior patterns in terms of your assertiveness or lack thereof. Write about a situation in which you were assertive and one in which you were not. Do you want to change your nonassertive behaviors? If so, what's your plan for doing so?

SUGGESTIONS FOR FURTHER READING

Emmons, M. L., and R. E. Alberti. *Your Perfect Right*. San Luis Obispo, Calif.: Impact, 1986.

Galassi, J., and M. Galassi. *Assert Yourself* (workbook). New York: Human Sciences Press, 1977.

Phelps, S., and N. Austin. *The Assertive Woman*. San Luis Obispo, Calif.: Impact, 1987.

ANSWERS (for Exercise 14.3 on p. 303): Type of behavior indicated by each response to scenario:
1. Passive-aggressive (lying)
2. Aggressive (accusing and demanding)
3. Passive-aggressive (getting her behind her back)
4. Assertive
5. Passive (acting the martyr)
6. Passive (acting the martyr) and passive-aggressive (getting her indirectly)

ANSWERS (for Exercise 14.4 on p. 304):
1. AS: Respect for others, "I" statements, and specificity are present.
2. AG: A put-down — respect for the other is missing.
3. P: Hinting, or forcing the other to figure out what is wanted, is irresponsible.
4. AS: Receiving a compliment graciously rather than brushing it off is the respectful thing to do.
5. PA: Forgetting is indirectly disrespectful.

Developing Relationships

I don't need to make friends with everybody; just give me one or two good friends . . . someone I can trust, pal around with . . . who knows when to leave me be. Lots of people I meet act like we're already pals, but I'm keeping my eyes open. I think I'd better go slow and watch my step. One good friend is worth all the rest put together.

ROBERT A. FRIDAY *is a corporate consultant in total quality management in the Pittsburgh, Pa., area. He is also the author of* Create Your College Success, *a book of activities and exercises in the Wadsworth Freshman Year Experience*_{SM} *Series.*

"In high school I stood back, afraid to try for a leadership role," he says. "When I went away to college, my goal was to be known as a friend by everyone on campus. I said 'Hi!' to everyone who made eye contact with me and talked with other students whenever I had a chance. I asked how they were feeling and what they were doing. I listened more than I talked. When I pledged a fraternity, my brothers encouraged me to run for student government because I was popular. Popular! I saw myself as a shy person who was trying hard to make a few friends. I ran and I won, and it changed my life. During the balance of my college career I held eighteen offices and worked with vice presidents and deans. I like to think that I majored in student government, minored in English literature, and learned to create success! I urge you to work on friendships based on cooperation, openness, and trust, and to be honest about mistakes because everyone makes them. That's the way to solve problems, create lasting friendships, and sleep well every night."

When I think about relationships, I hear my mentor, J. J. Johnston, Jr., saying, "Everything is based on relationships. You can have all of the business and professional training in the world, but if you can't develop relationships you won't get anywhere and you won't have anything worth living for." To that I would add that most people are generally unable to develop deep and lasting relationships with others until they have a good relationship with themselves. In these two statements is the essence of this section: First, get to feel good about yourself; then use those positive feelings to build meaningful relationships with others.

GETTING TO KNOW YOURSELF

It may seem strange to say that we have to work at getting to know ourselves, since we are with ourselves all of the time. Yet in our culture we tend to look outward and forward rather than inward and backward. To know yourself, you must look into your feelings and review your past. This *intrapersonal communication* — communication with yourself — requires spending time doing things that help you introspect, or look into yourself. As a first-year student, I spent a few hours several times a week jogging, exercising, or just taking a walk alone. Those moments always left me physically and mentally refreshed because I was giving myself time to sort through my feelings and problems and to make decisions for myself.

In the words of the Native American elder Rolling Thunder, "You have the power to think what you want to think, to say what you want to say, and to do what you want to do. And when you think what you want to think, say what you want to say, and do what you want to do, you are an adult." As you explore your origins and compare your family, background, and values with those of others, you will improve your understanding of why you think what you think, say what you say, and do what you do.

EXERCISE 14.5   Finding a Special Place to Think

Locate several places on or near your campus or home where you can relax and spend some time alone. Make at least two appointments a week with yourself to visit one of these places.

Take your journal. Do not involve yourself in conversations with others. As you observe people, nature, events, or things, record the first thoughts that come to you. Ask yourself where these thoughts originate.

Before you leave your special place, list problems or concerns that have come to mind during the visit. Ask yourself what you need to know to solve these problems. Write down where and when you plan to find the information you need. Write something that expresses why this problem is important to you at this time in your life.

HONESTY: THE KEY TO ANY RELATIONSHIP

Once you begin feeling comfortable with yourself, it's time to test the waters with others. You can do a number of things to establish successful interpersonal communication, but the glue that holds any relationship together is honesty. There may be some truth in what older people often say — that people used to be more honest. With each passing decade our society seemingly has wound the economic spring a little tighter. The pressure for material success seems ever greater, and the amount of cheating that goes on to gain success also seems to be increasing (see the section in Chapter 6 on academic integrity).

Rather than talk about right and wrong, we need to examine what effect dishonesty has on our relationships with ourselves and others. One peril is that when we are not honest with others, we force them to relate to a false image of ourselves. Until we can face up to ourselves truthfully, listen to the observations of others about ourselves, and honestly consider that some of what they say might be valid, we may be hiding in our own dream.

EXERCISE 14.6 **Comparing Yourself with Parents or Friends**

Write a few words to describe yourself in each of the following areas:

1. Sense of humor: _____

   _____

2. Important values: _____

   _____

3. Friendships: _____

   _____

4. Family relations: _____

   _____

5. Conflict resolution: _____

   _____

6. Strengths: _____

   _____

7. Weaknesses: _____

   _____

8. Interests: _____

   _____

Now do one or both of the following:

1. Consider how one or both of your parents might describe themselves in the same eight areas. How are you similar to each of them? How different? If you feel comfortable doing so, share this exercise with your parents the next time you visit with them, and see if they agree with your perceptions.

2. Compare your answers with how one or two of your best friends might respond about themselves. How are you similar or different? Next time you see them, share this exercise with them and see if they agree with your perceptions.

EIGHT KEYS TO SUCCESSFUL INTERPERSONAL COMMUNICATION

Successful interpersonal communication usually contains the following eight elements (Stinnett, 1977). Devise a plan for incorporating these elements or guidelines into your communication with friends, roommates, spouses, and dating partners. Once you do, you will find a new richness and growth in your relationships.

1. Practice Self-Disclosure

Because building any relationship starts with revealing yourself, you need to know who you are and express yourself honestly to others. If you begin by keeping secrets, you will always be on your guard, and your conversation will be stunted and uninteresting. Be open about what you feel and what you want. That's how to discover who agrees and disagrees with you and find others who like you for who you are.

When you explain to the other person what you like and don't like, you establish rules of behavior for your relationship. For example, if you sometimes like to drink when you are on a date, you can probably do so without offending someone who does not, as long as you do not get drunk. If you're looking for a sexual relationship, find a way to reveal this in discussion before you try it in action. Unannounced sexual advances are likely to be construed as a sign of disrespect. If you have difficulty talking about something, take your friend to a movie or play that explores the subject. Afterward find a nice place to have a snack and ask how he or she feels about the characters. This will give you an opportunity to express your own views as well.

2. Show Mutual Respect

The ideal person may exist in your mind, but he or she may be very hard to find on campus. Chances are the person sitting beside you in class or those you live with in the dorm, at home, or in an apartment do not fit all of your criteria for an ideal friend or intimate. Unfortunately you cannot change someone into your ideal. Trying to change someone is not only futile but disrespectful, because it reflects your nonacceptance of the person as he or she is.

3. Find a Common Frame of Reference

A shared background of experience and ideas makes it easier for two people to understand and appreciate each other. Having friends who appreciate the same cultural or social events increases feelings of belonging, whereas the lack of a common frame of reference can cause individuals to feel alienated or alone. Often people from different cultural, racial, or economic backgrounds have difficulty communicating and developing relationships. Remember, though, that while some experiences and traditions may be very different, there is always common ground. People who work at getting to know others from different backgrounds are usually richer for the experience.

4. Listen Actively

Paying attention to what someone says is only the first level of listening. Most communication between two people is nonverbal. If you don't believe that, try saying to someone, "Hey, glad to see you," while looking away. Ask what message you communicated. Chances are the person will wonder if you

"They Didn't Know Me"

I was never that popular in high school—in fact, I hardly dated. Suddenly in college all these guys were asking me out. They didn't know me. About all they knew was that I looked Asian.

In fact my father's Caucasian. He met my mother in Japan when he was in the merchant marine. He had one day of leave in Japan. They met for one afternoon, standing in line at a shrine in Kyoto when she was still in high school. They wrote to each other for four years before he went back and proposed. With that kind of courtship you might think they didn't know each other all that well, but I'm sure they did because I've seen the stacks of letters. They got married and came back to the States. My brother and I were born here.

I like to think that if I'm an unusual person it's not just because of things like my hair or the shape of my eyes. But you would be surprised how many guys in college would see me once and act like they already knew everything about me.

My freshman roommate had another kind of problem. She's black and in the first couple weeks she started dating someone who was also black. Then he kind of left her alone and started going out with whites. She might not have minded so much if there had been as many black men on campus as there were black women. But there weren't. She got pretty fed up with it—I guess lonely is the word.

My brother visited me one weekend in January, and we got to talking about this. He said his experience in college had been more like hers than like mine. Some women seemed to reject him simply because he looked Asian. At the same time, the Asian and Asian-American women were going out with whites. I was glad to hear him talk about this finally, but it also made me sad. My brother's a very sweet person, and I don't see why I should be accepted if he's not accepted also.

really are glad to see him or her. Facial expression, tone of voice, posture, and sense of physical, psychological, or emotional distance are all involved in active listening.

EXERCISE 14.7   Listening to Actions

We have all heard that actions speak louder than words. Try the following with small groups of classmates or friends: Have two teams each develop a list of ten everyday statements such as "Glad to see you," "I like your new jacket," and the like. One team should read one of its statements. Then members of the other team should spend a couple minutes saying the statement with as many conflicting nonverbal gestures as they can. (For example, say, "Glad to see you," sarcastically, while looking away, or say, "Want to have lunch?" while looking angry.)

Afterward review your feelings. Discuss the effects of the conflicting nonverbal "statements" on your reactions.

5. Check the Meaning of Communication

Most of us are rather sloppy with our language. Can you see any difference between the phrases "You make me angry when you . . ." and "I feel angry when you . . ."? The first statement implies that one person is causing a feeling to occur in another person. The second statement implies one person has a particular feeling in response to another person's actions. In truth nobody can *make* you feel anything; you are the one who must own your feelings. For instance, one person may feel upset or angry when a friend is late for a date while another person may think nothing of it.

Get in the habit of making sure you understand what the other person is saying. Use phrases like "I really want to understand what you're saying . . . ," "When you say that, do you mean . . . ?" and "If I'm understanding rightly, what you mean is . . ." When you check the meaning of a person's words, you express respect for what that person says and feels. You show that you are actively listening. It's not just in the beginning of a relationship that people need to check the meaning of communication. Human signals are so complicated that even between intimates it may be *years* before the need to do this is reduced.

EXERCISE 14.8 **Checking the Meaning of Communication**

Think of a time when you were angry with another person. Write a paragraph describing the event using the phrase "He or she made me angry when . . ." Write a second paragraph describing the event using the phrase "I felt angry when he or she . . ."

Volunteer to read your paragraph in class, and listen to others reading theirs. Discuss the difference between the meanings conveyed by the first and second paragraphs.

6. Empathize

When you put yourself in the place of other people and do your best to feel what they are feeling, you are in a position to understand their emotional state and meet their needs. However, you should not confuse empathy with sympathy. Whereas *sympathy* is an expression that you feel sorry for someone, *empathy* involves sharing the other's feelings. When you empathize you "walk a mile in a friend's shoes" — you place yourself in their situation and try to see the world as they do. When you empathize you take the time to sit with friends and explore who said or did what, why they said or did it, and what their words or actions mean. Empathy includes meaningful exploration and concludes with advice: "If I were in this situation I would . . ."

Who's More Romantic?

Research finds that men are much more vulnerable to falling romantically in love than are women, and they fall in love much more quickly than do women. For example, in one study in which men and women were asked how early in the affair they had become aware that they were in love, 20 percent of the men said they had fallen in love before the fourth date, as compared with 15 percent of the women. At the other extreme, 45 percent of the women were still not sure whether they were in love by the twentieth date, as compared with only 30 percent of the men.

Not only do men fall romantically in love more quickly than women, but they also cling more tenaciously to a dying love affair. And they are more depressed, more lonely, and function less effectively when the relationship ends. Men find it harder to accept the fact that they are no longer loved — that the affair is over and there is nothing they can do about it. Three times as many men as women commit suicide after a disastrous love affair. Women tend to be more philosophical and more practical in taking steps to meet new people and make new friends.

Although men fall romantically in love more quickly than do women, and cling more tenaciously to a dying affair, women are usually portrayed as being more romantic than men, dreaming more often about romantic fulfillment.

Do young women really spend more time immersed in fantasies about meeting a daring, dashing, handsome, and ardent admirer (the knight on the white charger) than young men spend daydreaming about their feminine ideal (the princess in the tower)?

In the absence of research one can only speculate. Women do buy and read the romantic novels of such writers as Barbara Cartland and such magazines as *True Romance*, whereas men tend to read *Field and Stream* and *Car and Driver*. Women are assumed to be more interested in discussing affairs of the heart, whereas men are traditionally expected to talk about sports, cars, and business.

In another reflection of popular culture — country-western songs — it is usually the woman who is portrayed as sacrificing everything for the man she loves. The man, on the other hand, is portrayed as having less urgent and more muted feelings. Moreover, the men in these songs are often drifters who brush aside passionate or tender emotions ("Baby, baby, don't get hooked on me").

Yet, nearly all love songs are written by men, as are virtually all ballets, operas, and ballads.

SOURCE: Adapted from Lloyd Saxton, *The Individual, Marriage, and the Family*, 7th ed. (Belmont, Calif.: Wadsworth, 1990).

7. Acknowledge the Legitimacy of Another's Feelings

As you probably know, feelings are not always logical. Each of us experiences physiological cycles, mood swings, varying reactions to similar situations, and so on. Though another person's mental and emotional states may sometimes seem inexplicable, you must acknowledge the legitimacy of those feelings.

Few friends or partners forthrightly state their feelings unless they have known each other a long time and have a history of good communication —

Find what you have in common. Recognize differences.

indeed, people who have been together a long time tend to become attuned to each other at this level. In the early stages of relationships most people send out little signals to see if the other will pick them up and respond, to test whether the person cares before they open up. As you seek to develop meaningful relationships, be sure to indicate that you sense the other wants to talk, and ask what he or she is thinking or feeling. This will help to deepen communication. For example, ask your partner or friend if he or she has ever discussed certain feelings or situations. If the person seems reluctant to respond, try explaining your thoughts on the subject and then ask for feedback. This approach will give each of you a better chance to understand where the other is coming from.

In our culture women tend to talk about feelings whereas men tend to keep feelings locked up inside. Very often in the early stages of dating, men do not treat feelings as a legitimate topic of conversation. However, true intimacy can develop only when each partner learns to talk about the things that are important to the other.

8. Accept Conflict

Even in relatively healthy relationships, fights are bound to occur (Bach and Wyden, 1969). Certainly most of us prefer to avoid conflict, not only because it can be unpleasant or painful but also because we have somehow developed the notion that conflict equals rejection. Nothing is further from the truth. Most often conflict between friends or partners indicates that one sees a problem in the relationship and wishes to correct it for the benefit of both. When conflict does occur, the important thing is to manage it according to certain standards of acceptable conduct — in short to fight fair.

"Fair fighting" is a form of revealing yourself. The fair fighter avoids blaming the other person and concentrates on expressing feelings and needs. When intimates assert themselves to each other in this fashion, they come to know each other's feelings and move toward accommodation. The best part of intimate communication lies in recognizing differences, arguing, resolving, and making up. If you can conclude an argument with greater appreciation for each other, you can be sure that you are building a positive intimate relationship.

When you want to raise an issue with a friend, partner, or roommate, be sure that you set the scene properly. Avoid the tension and defensiveness that result from abruptly springing a topic on someone. Don't try to deal with it while you are racing to class or when your roommate or friend is working on a term paper that is due the next morning. Try saying something like "I have been thinking about the way I have been consistently going past one of my limits when we . . ." or "I would like to discuss how I feel when you . . . Can we take a walk tomorrow after class and discuss our feelings on this?" The other person now knows the issue is going to be discussed and probably has a good idea of the role he or she has played in it. You have also allowed time for both of you to get ready. Remember, the objective is not to beat someone, but to arrive at a mutual agreement.

DECEPTION: THE BARRIER TO HONEST RELATIONSHIPS

Unfortunately some people fall into a pattern of exploiting other people for one-sided gain — they build relationships on deception. Many who communicate in this fashion are actually afraid of being rejected. Ironically, in their drive to be accepted, they violate most of the basic principles of good interpersonal communication. Such unsuccessful communication is usually characterized by these behaviors:

► Pretending to reveal yourself but actually exposing only those aspects of yourself that you think the other person will like

► Giving "lip service" respect to the other person that often is just empty flattery

► Attempting to share the perspective or take on the frame of reference of the other person, only to appear awkward and out of place

► Spending more energy on what you say than on listening to the other person

► Failing to check the meaning of what has been said because you do not really want any differences clarified — often out of fear of rejection

► Failing to empathize with the other person's feelings and holding back from expressing your own true feelings

► Denying or questioning the legitimacy of the other person's feelings with expressions like "You can't be serious" or "I've never heard of that before"

► Avoiding conflict because you are unwilling to lay your true feelings on the line and are incapable of sustaining an elaborate fiction over time

Many people feel unsure of themselves during a time of growth and change. Especially in the freshman year, when anxiety over the fear of rejection combines with other personal crises such as shifting identity and loss of contact with family and hometown friends, students worry whether they will make friends and be liked, loved, and accepted. Countless stories circulate of students who have lied or deceived others apparently in the hope that they will be accepted by the people around them.

If you find yourself deceiving people in order to fit in, it is time for some honest *intrapersonal* communication. Write a letter to yourself, your parents, or a close friend. Explore your development in your early years among your family and friends. Emphasize all of the times that people have loved and accepted you. Write about what you do well, why you like to do it, and how

"I Knew I Was Gay When I Was 13"

I knew I was gay when I was 13 years old. My friends were falling in love with members of the Fairview Little League team, and I was day-dreaming about Mary Sue Cook. Still, I didn't even know what a homosexual was until the AIDS virus hit. Kids in my middle school had cheerfully announced that some disease was killing all the fags, and I had said, "Good riddance!" No one had told me there was a word to describe me. Fags got AIDS, so I spent the rest of that year pretending to have crushes on the Little League boys.

By the time I was 15 I knew a whole lot about fags. I learned that faggots were actually pieces of kindling used to start a fire and that the term was transferred to homosexuals when they were burned at the stake for moral crimes. I learned about the National Gay Hotline and about the sodomy laws that still exist in most states. The Good Samaritan Church started a youth group for gay teens. Up until that point the word lesbian had been "the L word," because I had never heard it spoken in a positive way. Now it is a definitive term for everything I have been through.

We were a fairly insecure lot in those days. We fought against traditional values by coloring our half-shaved heads and dressing in black clothing. We spent our time crouching in mall emergency exits listening to Depeche Mode or Dead or Alive. We exchanged antique jewelry and jotted down poetry about an unjust world. We hid our faces behind heavy eyeliner and burgundy bangs. We were America's gay youth, and we had already learned that hiding was the easiest way to survive.

When I went away to college I was still a loathsome "closet case." My roommate and I seemed to hit it off, and I was afraid that my "news" might scare her away. God knows I didn't want her thinking I was interested in her. That may seem like a strange thing to say, but you would be surprised at the way the "straight" world views a friendship with a homosexual. I had known Wendy for almost three months, but I knew that everything would change when she found out. She would treat me like a different person, and yet I would be the same. I did finally confide in her after months of isolation and insecurity, and she stood by me despite her own fears. She even admitted that she would have blindly hated me if I had told her when we met. I guess I was supposed to be glad that I had lied.

After that, it was relatively easy to come out to my friends. One of the girls across the hall from me clipped out articles from the student newspaper about National Coming Out Day. She told me I should go to the Gay/Lesbian Student Association meetings to meet other people. There were hundreds of gay and lesbian students at the University of South Carolina, and perhaps thirty of them were comfortable enough to show their faces at the Gay/Lesbian Student Association.

I just knew that there would be a line of gay-bashers waiting to see just who went to those meetings. I finally worked up the nerve to walk over to Harper College one evening but quickly retreated when I realized that there were classes being held that I would have to walk in front of to get to the stairs. I skulked back to my room to tell my roommate of my misadventure. I really thought she'd pour out the sympathy over my pitiful condition. Instead, she got up, put her shoes on, and told me that the two of us were going to march right back over there and go to that meeting.

I have come a long way from my 13-year-old fears of getting AIDS. The "coming out" process is more than finding loopholes in society where you might feel safe. It's not just asking society to accept you, but learning to accept yourself.

SOURCE: Jen Bacon, Portfolio XI (no. 1), Fall 1990 (a University of South Carolina student publication). Used with permission.

good you feel doing it. Block out some time on your calendar that you can dedicate to doing what you like to do, and *do it*. Finally, look over all of the possible clubs, organizations, and activities that you can get involved in on or near your campus and join one. If you take part in an activity that you honestly enjoy, you will most likely find yourself making friends with those who share your interest.

The way you treat others is really a statement about yourself. For example, if you tell someone you are in love with him or her just so you can seduce that person sexually, you are treating him or her not as a human being but as a plaything. In such acts you also victimize yourself by denying the possibility of communicating your real feelings. Whether the goal is sexual pleasure, social status, information, or money, the result is still the same: What goes around comes around. Eventually the deceit becomes known because few people can live a lie for a lifetime or because subsequent events force the person to show his or her true colors.

ROOMMATE COMMUNICATION

Living with a roommate has a great impact on the lives of most resident freshmen. If you have not previously shared a room with a sibling or friend over a long period of time, your roommate will probably heighten your sense of private space and territory. You may never have thought that some "stranger" might open your closet and help him- or herself to your clothes. Yet your roommate may have always shared in this fashion and may assume that everybody acts this way.

In order to progress from being strangers to being friends, roommates must invest a great amount of time defining how they feel about a host of issues: the room temperature, policies about visitors, personal versus communal property, study and sleep habits, music and noise preferences, attitudes about drugs and sex, and above all, each other's needs for confidentiality. Treat communication between yourself and your roommate as confidential except in the rare instance when to keep a confidence would pose danger. And take time to get to know each other. Even if you never become close friends, you are living together and may learn much from the experience.

Sometimes roommates need to fight over issues like neatness or behavior. Suppose you prefer a clean, tidy living space but your roommate doesn't seem to care whether things are picked up or not. Pretending that everything is okay when you are furious that your roommate has left another mess will destroy your relationship in the long run. Your resentment will come out in other ways while the roommate assumes that everything is fine. So what should you do?

Look back at the discussion of assertiveness in the previous section for some good ideas about getting along with roommates. In such situations you need to explore beliefs and values together without making judgments. If you begin by trying to understand why your roommate tends to be sloppy, you might arrive at some mutual accommodation. (People who respect each other usually try to accommodate each other's needs.) Maybe you can agree that you will clean the room together every Saturday morning and try to keep it tidy during the week. By contrast, if you approach your roommate with disrespect, calling him or her a "pig" or a "slob," you will be provoking animosity instead of promoting harmony.

In any living situation you need to come to an agreement, sooner rather than later, on how the room or apartment should be managed. When either of you breaks the agreement, discuss it promptly. Put a "do not disturb" sign on the door, and proceed to explain, calmly and politely, how each of you feels about the situation. Give each other every opportunity to reflect, explore, and talk. Such conversations are rarely easy at first, but the experience will prepare you for a lifetime of positive communication with colleagues, friends, and intimates.

As roommates you must learn to identify and clarify the reason for the conflict and then discuss it together. Always remember to give each other the space to express individuality. If differences come up — as they should — be sure you are both talking about the same thing; that is, define the issue. If one person considers the issue to be serious, set aside time to discuss it. As in any relationship or communication situation, the moment you come home from work or school is not a good time to fight about an important issue. The quiet of the evening is a more productive time for most people to wrestle honestly with their differences. (For more on roommate negotiations, see Friday, 1988.)

EXERCISE 14.9   Living with Your Roommate

A. *Taking a look at your development.* Part of taking control of your social life involves learning to understand your automatic reactions to certain typical situations. This exercise will help you focus on how your early development is affecting the way you may relate to your roommate in daily living situations.

Following are several typical situations we find ourselves in from time to time. For each situation write an example that illustrates how your approach to it has been influenced by your family and your early developmental environment. Part of the influence will be the rules that your parents or guardians established for you, and part will be the social order established by your sibling(s) and/or friends.

1. Sharing personal items such as clothes, food, and favorite things

   _____

   _____

   _____

2. Sharing expensive items such as a typewriter, computer, or car

   _____

   _____

   _____

3. Being corrected by someone a few years older than you

   _____

   _____

   _____

4. Being corrected by someone a few years younger than you

   _____

   _____

   _____

5. Telling certain others what to do

_____

_____

_____

B. *Developing your contract.* Tell your roommate that you want to explore some issues that may help you avoid conflict in the future. See if you can arrive together at a written statement or contract in response to each of the following questions:

1. Should the room be kept messy or neat?
2. When should visitors be allowed in the room, and when should your space be quiet and private?
3. Should drugs or alcohol be allowed in the room?
4. Who should the telephone be billed to, and how should payments be made?
5. How should phone messages be taken and communicated?
6. Which items can be borrowed and which are personal?
7. Should smoking be allowed in the room?
8. What temperature is preferred for comfort in the room?
9. Should a television or stereo be on when either roommate is trying to study?

NETWORKING WITH FRIENDS AND COLLEAGUES

Whether in the context of love, academia, or business, sharing and giving relationships are the keys to advancement, to being loved, to new and refined ideas or increased profit. In the areas of academic advising, choosing a major, career development, and job hunting, your network is your biggest asset. Networking means building a web of relationships, beginning with those close to you and branching out to those close to others through referrals and interviews. You might be surprised to learn that about 70% of jobs are obtained through networking, not through sending out resumes or answering want ads.

The most successful networkers are kind, open, friendly, giving, and respectful of others' needs and wishes. All of the elements of successful communication between friends and intimates can be applied in a more formal way to successful communication between colleagues and others in your network.

Your relationships with roommates, neighbors, and good friends form the first level of your network. We have all heard the old saying "It's *who* you know, not *what* you know, that gets you . . ." Actually it might be more accurate to say, "It's *how* you know other people and *how* they know you that gets you . . ." If you are known to other people as an honest, caring, competent person, your reputation will precede you, and your road to success will be paved by your friends.

EXERCISE 14.10 Paired Listening

Pair up with a classmate to discuss a controversial topic (for example, abortion, legalization of marijuana, the drinking age, defense spending). Decide who will be "speaker" and who will be "listener." For the first 10 minutes the speaker should state his or her views on the topic. Each time the speaker makes a statement, the listener must (1) restate or rephrase what the speaker said to check for accuracy ("So you are saying . . .") and (2) request more information or clarification ("What led you to feel this way?" "Would you feel differently if . . .?" "How would you change the current situation?"). The listener should really concentrate on full understanding of the speaker and not be distracted by his or her own views on the topic. When the 10 minutes are up, switch roles and choose a new topic to talk about.

EXERCISE 14.11 Your Reputation Now and Later

Based on your actions, activities, and relationships thus far as a college student, list a few words or phrases describing the reputation you think you have among your friends at school.

_____   _____

_____   _____

_____   _____

Now list some words and phrases to describe the reputation you hope to have when you graduate from college.

_____   _____

_____   _____

_____   _____

Where do things stand right now? Apply the goal-setting strategy from Chapter 1 to something you would like to change.

All things in the universe, from the planets to the smallest virus, are defined by the nature of their relationships — their effects on other things. In the same way the meaning of your life to yourself and to others is defined by your relationships. If you are honest and trustworthy, that is how you will be known. But if you deceive others or yourself, that reputation will haunt you. College is a great place to redefine your relationships with others and yourself. You are going to meet many people in the next few years. Some of them will know you and work with you the rest of your life. Your roommates, new neighbors, dating partners, and classmates may become a part of your professional network. Be honest, respectful, and considerate of others, and they will help pave your road to success.

JOURNAL

Write about a relationship you have now that is important to you. Apply the eight elements of constructive interpersonal communication to this relationship. Which ones seem to fit best? How do you react to the comments about developing honest relationships?

REFERENCES AND SUGGESTIONS FOR FURTHER READING

Bach, George R., and Peter Wyden. *The Intimate Enemy*. New York: Morrow, 1969.

Boyd, Doug. *Rolling Thunder*. New York: Random House, 1977.

Crosby, John F. *Illusion and Disillusion: The Self in Love and Marriage*, 4th ed. Belmont, Calif.: Wadsworth, 1991.

Friday, Robert A. *Create Your College Success*. Belmont, Calif.: Wadsworth, 1988.

Fromm, Erich. *The Art of Loving*. New York: Harper & Row, 1956.

Hendrick, Clyde, and Susan Hendrick. *Liking, Loving, and Relating*, 2nd ed. Pacific Grove, Calif.: Brooks/Cole, 1992.

Lao Tsu. *Tao Te Ching*. Trans. Gia-Fu Feng and Jane English. New York: Vintage, 1972.

Laslett, Barbara. "The Family as a Public and Private Institution: An Historical Perspective." In *Intimacy, Family and Society*, ed. Arlene Skolnick and Jerome H. Skolnick. Boston: Little, Brown, 1974.

Patton, Bobby R., Kim Giffin, and Eleanor Nyquist Patton. *Decision-Making Group Interaction*, 3rd ed. New York, N.Y.: Harper & Row, 1989.

Scanzoni, John. *Sexual Bargaining: Power Politics in the American Marriage*. Englewood Cliffs, N.J.: Prentice-Hall, 1970.

Stinnett, Nick, and James Walters. *Relationships in Marriage and Family*. New York: Macmillan, 1977.

Getting Involved

Mom says I should stick to my studies. Dad says I should get a job. Sis tells me the best thing she ever did in her first year was join the geography club. Well, it was her major. 'Course, I'm a business major. I think there's a business club. My roommate went up to the campus radio station last week and she's already on the air! Maybe I can work one or two things into my schedule and still have time to study. . . .

MARIE-LOUISE A. RAMSDALE, *a student at Harvard University School of Law, is a 1990 graduate of the University of South Carolina, Columbia, where she was president of the student body, 1990 Omicron Delta Kappa National Leader of the Year, and a member of Alpha Delta Pi sorority. Involved in campus activities throughout her undergraduate years, she knows the benefits of participating in clubs and organizations.*

"While your freshman year of college can be exciting," she says, "it can also be a time of confusion and uncertainty. I hope some of the ideas I have included will help you get the most out of college by getting involved from the very beginning."

When I look back on my college experience, I think that I learned as much from activities *outside* the classroom as I did in it. In this section I'll share with you some of the benefits of taking part in **co-curricular** activities. I cannot imagine what my college years might have been like if I hadn't been involved, and I hope that by the end of this section you too will realize how much you can gain from becoming involved in campus life.

NINE REASONS TO JOIN A CAMPUS ORGANIZATION

You might be wondering whether it's that important to get involved in co-curricular activities. You might be thinking that between your schoolwork and your social life there won't be any time left for anything else. Or you may simply wonder what's in it for you. If so, consider the following:

► *You'll meet people.* Not only will you meet other students, but you will also have the opportunity to meet many other types of people, depending upon the groups you choose to join. Members of the NAACP at my school met actress Cicely Tyson. Members of the program union met former Secretary of State Henry Kissinger. Through interscholastic competition sports club members met students with the same interest from other schools. Members of honor societies, as well as sorority and fraternity members, traveled to their national conventions, meeting people from throughout the country. Being active in the campus community may also provide you with opportunities to meet college faculty and administrators. Within your organization you will meet a diverse group of people who share a common interest that brings them together, people who will offer not only valuable information about campus life but friendship.

► *You'll experiment and gain experience.* College is the perfect time to try something new, and joining a club or organization gives you the chance to do so. If you have always wanted to try sky-diving or ceramics, now's your chance. (And you can usually do so in college at a much lower cost through participation in a student organization.) Perhaps you've always wanted to act, but in high school you were afraid

I started out as an advertising major. I joined the Ad Club my first semester because I wanted to make sure I was on the right track. Some of the women in a sorority I was pledging and a dean of the college encouraged me to do this. The Ad Club helped me realize that advertising wasn't my thing but that I really did like public relations. The club gave me some experience right away in things I liked doing and put me in touch with some people in my major who've become my friends and given me a lot of good advice on courses.

Maryam

people would laugh at you if you tried out for a play. College life encourages you to experiment and explore, so audition for that play. Even if you realize you're no Dustin Hoffman or Meryl Streep, you might discover your hidden talent for stage managing. My sophomore-year roommate decided that she wanted to try mountain climbing, and before long she was hiking up mountains every weekend. The next year she even became secretary of the club—and this was a person who hated responsibility! You'll never know if something you've always wanted to do is fun until you take that first step.

EXERCISE 14.12 Taking a Risk

Off the top of your head, write down five activities you've always wanted to try. They may be sports, hobbies, recreational activities, or intellectual topics to explore. You will use these again in a later exercise.

1. _____

2. _____

3. _____

4. _____

5. _____

► *You'll improve your abilities.* There's nothing like giving an impromptu speech in the student senate on why smoking should (or should not) be banned on campus to improve your public speaking skills. Editing the literary magazine will give you insight into your own writing, and being responsible for planning the Riding Club's fund-raiser will do wonders for your organizational abilities.

► *You'll get the most out of college.* I've already mentioned briefly how being involved in co-curricular activities helps you get the full college experience. After college there will be more to life than working. Think of your college years the same way, and while remembering the importance of academics, don't spend all your time studying in the library. Look at college as your own community and be active in it.

EXERCISE 14.13 Leaving Your Mark

By this time in your college career (even if it's still only the first month!), you've most likely found things you like and things you don't like about your institution. You may even have a pet peeve. Your dissatisfactions can lead to involvement. If you could "leave your mark" by causing a change on your campus, what would it be? List two or three ideas here:

1. _____

2. _____

3. _____

Now take one of your ideas and do some research on how you might proceed to advocate for change. Why does the present situation exist? What alternative would you propose? Why would your alternative work? Who has the power to make the change? What group would you need to join that might provide the influence and help you will need?

Are you ready to take the plunge?

► *You'll feel at home faster.* There's nothing like serving barbeque at the homecoming cookout or planning the spring movie calendar to make you feel that you help make things "tick" at your school.

► *You'll manage stress better.* If you're worried about a test or if you had a fight with your boy- or girlfriend, call a friend from the Running Club and take a few laps around the track. If you're not athletically inclined, go and throw paint on a canvas with some friends from the Art Club. Several friends and I even started our own social group during our senior year to help us relax on Friday afternoons from the pressures of the week. We called it SOUL (for Stressed-out Overworked Underpaid Student Leaders), and some of the best times I had in college were during these Friday afternoon get-togethers.

► *You'll organize your time better.* Believe it or not, being busier helps you plan your day, your week, and your whole semester more efficiently. Knowing that you have responsibilities and must be somewhere at a specific time forces you to organize your life. If you know that you

My student activities complemented my classroom activities because I was a political science major and I did political activism. In my freshman year I got involved with our chapter of the statewide student public interest research group, which actually meant helping people with their actions in small claims court. From there I went on to working with the same group investigating and exposing problems with the city's taxi system that had resulted in some students being overcharged for fares. I really want to advance justice. I put a tremendous amount into what I did, and I got a tremendous amount out of it.

Andrew

are going to go into the city to visit museums this weekend with people you met at the Art Club meeting, then you also know you have to make the time to write that paper that's due on Monday morning before you leave for the weekend.

► *You'll improve your resume.* One of the best reasons to get involved now is your future after graduation. Competitive employers and graduate schools are looking for the well-rounded individual, not the person with straight A's who remained in the library all through college. The skills you learn in clubs and organizations today can make you far more marketable as a graduate. If you're an economics major, think about getting involved in the accounting societies, but also investigate such related possibilities as running for treasurer of some campus group. If you want to go to law school, look into volunteer work with the court system through your school's office of community service programs. But remember, you do not want to be exposed as a "resume stuffer." If you are going to list an organization on your resume, make sure you have done more than just pay your membership dues.

EXERCISE 14.14 Helping Out Your Career

What skills or experience are you likely to need for your work after college? Write down a job you might have after graduation and the skills you'll need for it. In addition to primary skills like accounting, singing, or research, be sure to include secondary skills like managing meetings, doing promotion, and writing grants. Now write down some ideas about how you can get the experience you need.

Potential job after graduation: _____

Skills or Experience Needed	Campus Activity or Organization Where I Can Get It
1. _____	_____
	_____
2. _____	_____
	_____
3. _____	_____
	_____
4. _____	_____
	_____

► *You'll meet organization advisors.* An unexpected bonus to members of many student groups (and one more reason to get involved) is the relationship they develop with the organization's advisor. The advisor, usually a faculty or staff member or interested person from the community, can lend support and advice not only to the organization and its officers but in many cases to the individual members as well. It's good to have someone at college to whom you can go for a different perspective from that of your peers. Club advisors are obviously interested in students or they wouldn't be involved with the organization, and if you need help or someone to turn to, the advisor of your club is a good person to start with. Even if the advisor doesn't have all the answers, he or she will at least be able to refer you to someone who does.

Let me tell you about the woman who advised the Greek system at my school. When I first held a position for which I needed her input, I found her hard to reach because every time I went to see her there was always someone in her office and more people waiting outside the door. As I worked with her over the next few years, I found out why there was always such a crowd waiting to see her: She was such a caring person. Whenever students visited her for help with organizational needs, she also took the time to find out how they were doing personally. This advisor seemed to care more about the students than about the organizations they represented. I and countless other students benefited from her concern and friendship. While all advisors may not be as outstanding as this one, my experiences in many different organizations have shown that developing a good relationship with a club advisor can be a very positive experience.

FINDING OUT ABOUT ORGANIZATIONS

Most colleges and universities have organizations for every type of interest imaginable, from racquetball to chess to foreign languages and literature. A brochure listing student organizations at my school included such types of groups as advocacy organizations; sports clubs; professional, service, and social fraternities and sororities; military reserve officer training corps (ROTC); numerous honor societies; special interest clubs; and religious

Rachel

Did you get one of those "student information packets" when you arrived on campus? I did. One of the slightly wackier things in it was an invitation to join the university band. Well, I walked in and they made me a saxophonist in the marching band! Even freshman year I got to go to New York for one game and a few other places, too. I also helped clean up the band room a few times and paid some pretty amusing dues by playing at the hockey games once football season was over. Actually by November of my freshman year I was a member of the band's junior staff. It took a lot of time — about as much time as a varsity sport! — but I got to know a lot of upperclassmen very quickly. They really took me under their wings and gave me some unusual perspectives on the university.

groups. To find out what clubs are established at your school, either ask your academic advisor or residence advisor or go to the student activities center, usually located in the student union, and ask for information about the co-curricular activities available at your school. Many schools also have organizational interest fairs in the early fall when members of different groups are available in a central location to recruit new members. The student newspaper and bulletin boards around campus are also good sources of information about club meetings.

Don't join any club because you are being pressured by one of the club members. If you are unsure about whether this club is really right for you after you have talked with some of the members, don't be afraid to say so. Of course you can always try one meeting to see if you like it; you don't have to sign up after you walk in the door if you find out that what you thought was the Astronomy Club is really the Astrology Club! Also, if more than one club seems interesting to you, go to several initial meetings. Attending a meeting doesn't bind you to membership for life in that organization, and going to several different meetings will provide a better perspective for choosing which clubs you actually want to join.

Here are some questions you might ask yourself as you think about what organizations to join:

1. *What am I already interested in?* If you have always been a "Francophile," then join the French Club. If you played football in high school and now want to play for fun and exercise, get involved with an intramural team.

2. *What abilities or skills do I want to improve or learn?* You went to England last summer and ever since then have had a burning desire to row crew. You sang in the chorus in high school and think that joining the concert choir would be a great way to continue this activity, if only you could get up the nerve to audition. Get up the nerve!

3. *How much time can I commit to this organization?* Does the organization meet once a week, every other week, or whenever the president decides to call a meeting? Does the meeting time fit into your schedule, or are you taking an eight-week course the second half of the semester

Go Greek or Geek. The possibly tongue-in-cheek Society of Nerds and Geeks has chapters on several East Coast campuses. Club members at Harvard say they'd rather spend their weekends sharing ideas than partying or watching football.

that conflicts with the club meeting time? What other club activities will you have to attend besides the regular meetings?

4. *Does this club have dues, and if so, can I afford them?* If the dues are high, is there a payment plan or do they have to be paid at one time? Do you pay dues every year or just when you join?

5. *What does this club require for membership?* Does it have an attendance policy that requires you to attend so many meetings in order to be able to participate in special club activities? Is there a certain pledge or initiation period before you can become an active or full member? Do you need to maintain a certain grade point average or take a special class in order to be a member?

MAKING IT HAPPEN

Admittedly it can be an overwhelming challenge during your first few weeks at college to think about entering a room full of strangers for a meeting that you have seen advertised on a bulletin board. First, remember that there will be other students in the room in exactly the same situation as you, as nervous if not more so. Don't be afraid to sit down next to someone and introduce yourself. It might also be a good idea to take your roommate or another friend with you to the meeting; in return you can attend a meeting that they are interested in. (Remember what we said about college being the time to try new things.) Also introduce yourself to the club officers after the meeting and let them know about your interest. Officers realize that new members are the future of their club, and more than likely they will be delighted to chat with you about their organization. If it hasn't already been mentioned, and you didn't want to ask during the meeting, this is an ideal time to ask about such things as membership dues, the club attendance policy, and other things you might want to know about before joining.

How to Be a Great Club Member

Get involved in those clubs and groups that you decide to join. You don't necessarily have to run for club vice president at your second meeting; just make a personal commitment to attend meetings and to be dependable. If

There didn't seem to be a lot of competition for Freshman Council. I thought, well, someone has to do it! So I ran and got elected. The Council was in its first year of existence, and the members set some pretty high goals. We also worked hard to achieve them. Fortunately it was a large group so the burden was spread out. I learned a lot about working with other people, particularly when things get stressful. I learned a lot about myself too. All that led to my going on in sophomore year to be elected to the student government cabinet. I guess the next step is the state assembly. . . .

Kim

you say that you will write that article on the new dean of students by Thursday, stick to your deadline. This will be easier if you know your limits and don't volunteer for something you won't have time to do or don't know how to do. Being a good club member doesn't mean that you have to volunteer for everything, but it also doesn't mean that you should tell everyone that you are a member of the Rugby Club if you've never even attended a practice.

Let me tell you about two types of club members I worked with during my four years of involvement with different campus organizations. Although Ann didn't hold a tremendously important position, the organization could not have operated as smoothly without her. If she told you that she would take care of something, you never had to worry about whether it would be done. If there was a job that no one else wanted to do, she would volunteer for it and then find some way to make it fun. Many of us will never forget the night of the Christmas party when Ann transported food for sixty people by herself to the room where the party was to be held. Meanwhile her efforts did not go unnoticed; she won an award at the end of the year and was one of the first people asked to attend any special events that were held.

Another student I worked with had become overinvolved in her freshman and sophomore years and as a result was burned out by her junior year. Although Julie had volunteered for an important position in student government at the end of her sophomore year, she just didn't have the time or the energy to be active in the club when she returned to school the following fall. This attitude was also apparent to people in several other clubs in which she had previously been an active member. While people tried to be supportive of Julie and realized that she was going through a difficult time, she eventually dropped out of all the clubs in which she was involved to spend time improving her grades.

If you budget your time wisely and pick a few groups you really want to get involved with, like Ann did, you will get a lot out of your participation in college activities, as well as give a great deal back to your organization. On the other hand, if you overextend yourself like Julie, you may find your grades falling and yourself resenting the time you spend with club activities you had previously enjoyed.

EXERCISE 14.15 Taking the Plunge

Get a list of campus clubs and organizations from the appropriate office on your campus. Now, using information from the first three exercises in this section, identify five clubs you might be interested in joining. Choose one club, attend a meeting, and try to speak with an officer of the club. Obtain the following information:

Name of club: _____

Purpose: _____

Meeting schedule: _____

_____

Dues: _____

Activities: _____

_____

_____

Membership requirements: _____

_____

Are you interested in joining? Write down your thoughts about it below. Your instructor may ask you to make a brief presentation in class about your experience at the meeting.

_____

_____

_____

_____

_____

How to Start Your Own Organization

What do you do if the type of club you want to join doesn't exist on your campus? Start it yourself! While I was in school, new clubs were started all the time, just as other clubs in which students had lost interest were deactivated. Begin with the facts. Since schools have various regulations for starting a new club or organization, go to your campus activities center, or the equivalent on your campus, and request the guidelines. Read them carefully. It might also help to talk with the student affairs professional in charge of new student organizations before getting started. Then consult with this person regularly as you develop your group.

Get out the word about your group. Use bulletin boards in the student union classroom buildings, and residence halls. Find out about getting your group's meetings publicized in the campus events calendar. The student media, particularly the newspaper, may even run an article on your group.

Be organized and set goals for the group, even if they are small ones at first. Having goals lends structure to your group and gives members something to strive toward accomplishing. A good way to set goals is to organize a retreat at which all members participate in planning what the group hopes to accomplish over the next month, semester, and year. Once goals have been set, be sure to refer to them regularly to see if you are on target or if the goals need adjusting.

You'll need to have a good idea of the purpose of your club and plan activities accordingly. For example, if your club was established to promote environmental awareness, fall semester activities could include sponsoring lunchtime forums with environmental activists as speakers. In the spring you could hold monthly recycling days during which students could bring materials to be recycled to a central location staffed by club members. If you get club members excited and involved in club activities, they will keep coming back to meetings and might even bring their friends!

Plan how your group is going to be funded. You may not need much money, particularly at first, but virtually every group needs funds for advertising and mailing costs. Look into your school's funding procedure for student organizations. At many colleges organizations have to be established for a certain period of time before they can receive funding from student activity fees. Also consider fund-raisers that members can assist with. Your campus activities center should be able to provide ideas for student organization fund-raisers. Fund-raisers at my school ranged from bedtime story readings to raft-a-thons on the duck pond in front of the library to the standard bake sales and car washes.

Keep in mind that while starting a new club can be very rewarding, it can also be challenging and, at times, frustrating. Before you decide to start an organization, take a good look at yourself to see if you have the necessary energy and time to get the club off the ground. If you feel that you do, then go for it, and good luck to you!

JOURNAL

What's your reaction to the author's advice that "college is the perfect time to try something new"? To what extent have you already become involved in campus life? What organizations have you visited or joined? What's been your experience so far? Is there anything you'd like to try but are somehow reluctant to? How might you overcome your reluctance?

SUGGESTIONS FOR FURTHER READING

Chickering, A. S. *Education and Identity.* San Francisco: Jossey-Bass, 1969.

DeCoster, D. A., and P. Mable, eds. *Student Development and Education in College Residence Halls.* Washington, D.C.: American Personnel and Guidance Association, 1974.

Feldman, K., and T. M. Newcomb. *The Impact of College on Students.* San Francisco: Jossey-Bass, 1970.

Sanford, N. *The American College.* New York: Wiley, 1962.

CHAPTER 15

▼▼▼▼▼▼▼▼▼▼▼▼▼▼▼▼▼▼

Wellness — More Than Just "Okay"

Nutrition, Fitness, and Sexuality
Lisa Ann Mohn

Alcohol, Other Drugs, and You
N. Peter Johnson with
Preston E. Johnson

Stress Management
Kevin W. King

Nutrition, Fitness, and Sexuality

I'm sick of hearing about sex and AIDS and birth control. Don't tell me what I should eat! Or how much sleep I need. Or how much exercise. Listen, I'm grown up; that's how I got into college. I know all about these things, and it's embarrassing to hear them all over again, especially in mixed company if you know what I mean. So I'm roly-poly. And maybe I am a little affectionate and not overcareful. So what? I'm happy!

LISA ANN MOHN *is director of health and wellness programs at the University of South Carolina, Columbia.*

"My first two years of college life were not spent, shall I say, living the healthiest of lifestyles," she recalls. "During my junior year I joined a campus health organization and the world of wellness opened before me. In fact I became so excited at the physical and emotional results of my new lifestyle that I decided to change from a career in advertising to one in health education. I particularly enjoy my work with college students because most of them are in a stage of transition, and the time is ripe to begin new behaviors and discover new selves. I sometimes wonder how I might have been different had I learned these lessons as a freshman. That's why I hope you can benefit from the joys of wellness, starting now."

Wellness, as we shall use the term, goes beyond the usual notion of health, beyond just feeling "okay" and not suffering from disease; it also goes beyond general physical conditioning. Wellness means striving toward your maximal potential for physical and emotional well-being. There is always a higher level of wellness you can aspire to and achieve.

You may be surprised at how many of the students at your school accept a fairly low level of wellness as the norm. You may know someone who gets up feeling sluggish, drags through classes, and has to take a nap in the afternoon in order to be able to study. You may then witness that same person staying up late to complete assignments, only to get up the next morning and start the process all over again. Yet a young person who is not sick has little reason to feel this way on a regular basis. Wellness offers something better.

Wellness requires two things. The first is self-responsibility. Feeling good takes conscious effort; sometimes you have to go a little out of your way to find the low-fat, high-energy meal that will give your body what it needs. It certainly takes effort to maintain an exercise program or to consciously reduce stress. Responsible sexual decisions — also crucial to wellness — likewise do not come about by accident.

The second thing is moderation. While it's difficult to stay well if you're constantly "burning the candle at both ends," you also don't have to lead a "perfect" existence. It's a balancing act. Wellness, like life, involves some trade-offs.

Picture your well-being as a bucket: You can fill it with positive things, such as a good night's sleep, physical exercise, a healthy spiritual life, preventive medical care, and good nutrition. But you can also fill it with negative things, such as the stress of academics, tension in certain relationships, junk food, lack of exercise, too little sleep, tobacco, alcohol, and drugs. If you fill your bucket with more negative than positive things, your health and well-being are likely to suffer. Especially during midterm and final exam periods, unhealthy behaviors tend to mount up. Not surprisingly, this is when the student health center is probably at its busiest.

Perhaps this is the first time you've been on your own to make decisions about what to eat, when to sleep, and so on — decisions that can either enhance or hinder your college experience. Most likely your current priorities are to get good grades, have fun, meet new people, and perhaps form or maintain a romantic relationship. Staying well and fit helps you do all of these things. If you take care of yourself, you'll look better, feel better, have more energy and self-confidence, and approach each day with a zest for life.

This section discusses some common wellness issues such as nutrition, fitness, weight control, and sexuality. Stress management and alcohol/drug use are discussed in subsequent sections in this chapter.

EXERCISE 15.1　Your Personal Wellness

A. Now that you've learned about the general concept of wellness, you can do your own "wellness assessment." Take a few minutes to write down some healthy and some unhealthy behaviors that are part of your lifestyle. Then give an overall assessment of your level of wellness. This will be helpful as you continue to read about how to improve your health.

1. What "fills your bucket"?

_____

_____

_____

_____

2. What empties it?

_____

_____

_____

_____

3. What's your current level of wellness?

_____

_____

_____

_____

B. Your wellness is influenced by your biological inheritance and by the diet and other practices of the family you grew up in. Ask your parents or other family members about their health histories and those of previous generations. What does their experience suggest about problems you are having now or may encounter in the future?

NUTRITION

More than a few students have complained about the food choices in their campus dining halls. It is often more difficult to eat a healthy diet when you don't prepare your own meals, because you can't estimate portion sizes and calories, you can't be sure of the ingredients used, and you may not like a particular food when it is prepared in an unfamiliar manner. However, it is possible to eat healthfully if you are willing to make certain choices. Before you read the discussion of these choices, complete the following exercise to determine your nutritional ranking. The "quiz" will show areas in which you can use some improvement.

EXERCISE 15.2   Testing Your Nutrition

To help you assess your nutritional habits, try the following self-test.* It is important to recognize what your current habits are before beginning to make changes. Score 1 point for each statement that is applicable to your diet.

Part I

_____ 1. I have 1–2 cups of milk or milk products (yogurt, cottage cheese) per day.

_____ 2. I use low-fat or skim (2 percent or less butterfat) milk and/or milk products.

_____ 3. I eat ice cream or ice milk no more than twice per week.

_____ 4. I use margarine instead of butter.

Part II

_____ 5. I do not eat meat, fish, poultry, or eggs more than once per day.

_____ 6. I do not eat red meats (beef or pork) more than three times per week.

_____ 7. I remove or ask that fat be trimmed from meat before cooking (also mark 1 point if you do not eat meat).

_____ 8. I have no more than one to three fresh eggs per week, either in other foods or separately.

_____ 9. I have meatless days and have such meat substitutes as legumes (beans, peas, and so on) and nuts.

_____ 10. I usually broil, boil, bake, or roast meat, fish, or poultry.

Part III

_____ 11. I have one serving of citrus fruit (for example, oranges) each day.

_____ 12. I have at least two servings of dark green or deep yellow vegetables each day.

_____ 13. I eat fresh fruits and vegetables when I can get them.

_____ 14. I cook vegetables without fat (if I use margarine, it is added after cooking).

_____ 15. I usually eat fresh fruit rather than pastries.

*Prepared by Dr. Roger Sargent, Professor, School of Public Health, University of South Carolina. Used with permission.

Part IV

_____ 16. I eat whole-grain breads and cereals.

_____ 17. I prefer high-bran or high-fiber cereals.

_____ 18. I buy cereals that are low in added sugar.

_____ 19. I prefer brown rice to common white enriched rice.

_____ 20. I usually have four servings of whole-grain products (cereals, breads, brown rice, and so on) per day.

Part V

_____ 21. I am within 5–10 pounds of my ideal weight.

_____ 22. I drink no more than 1½ ounces of alcohol per day.

_____ 23. I do not add salt to food after preparation and prefer foods salted lightly or not at all.

_____ 24. I usually avoid foods high in refined sugar and do not use sugar in coffee or tea.

_____ 25. I normally eat breakfast, and it usually consists of at least bread or cereal and fruit or fruit juice.

SCORING

Now total your points for each part and place your score on the appropriate line:

	Excellent	Good	Fair	Poor	Your Score
Part I	4	3	2	1	_____
Part II	5–6	4	3	2	_____
Part III	5	4	3	2	_____
Part IV	5	4	3	2	_____
Part V	5	4	3	2	_____

Total Score   23–25: Excellent
19–22: Good
14–18: Fair
9–14: Poor

Whether you eat in a campus dining hall or not, you can do a number of things to improve your eating habits.

Reducing Fat and Cholesterol

Probably the most important things to be concerned about in developing a healthy diet are fat and cholesterol. Elevated cholesterol levels are one of the three major preventable risk factors for heart disease, the leading cause of death in our country. (The other two are high blood pressure and cigarette smoking.) Diet is an important component in lowering cholesterol levels because excess fat and cholesterol in the diet typically raise cholesterol in the body.

The issue of fat and cholesterol is particularly important for college students. Although we think of heart disease as something that happens to middle-aged and older adults, younger people have often been found to have elevated cholesterol levels. Experts believe that heart disease is a process that begins at an early age. Thus, if you establish healthy eating behaviors now, you reduce the chances of having problems later in life.

Some definitions may be helpful. Cholesterol is a waxy, fatlike substance that all animals produce. Therefore, not only does your body produce it, you also consume it when you eat anything that comes from an animal: pork, beef, poultry, eggs, dairy products. Fat is a nutrient that supplies us with energy and fat-soluble vitamins. Fat is either saturated or unsaturated depending on its chemical structure. Unsaturated fats tend to lower cholesterol levels in the body while saturated fats tend to increase cholesterol levels. One way to determine if a fat is saturated or not is by its consistency: Unsaturated fats are usually liquid at room temperature while saturated fats are solid. The main exceptions to this rule are coconut and palm oils, which are used commonly in processed foods and which are liquid but highly saturated.

In order to reduce the amount of fat and cholesterol you consume, you must eat less fried food. Choose low-fat or skim-milk dairy products such as the low-fat varieties of cottage cheese and yogurt; limit the amount of cheese you eat; and choose ice milk or frozen yogurt over ice cream for a sweet snack. Beef and pork are high in saturated fat and cholesterol, so you should eat these no more than three times a week. Instead eat chicken, turkey, and fish (preferably broiled or baked) and meatless meals on occasion. Quantity is also important. When you eat beef, choose a small (3–4 ounce) serving rather than a large (8–10 ounce) serving. Load up instead on vegetables, potatoes, and rice.

Other foods you should eat only in limited quantities, if at all, are fatty luncheon foods like bologna and hot dogs, "junk foods" like potato chips and french fries, and prepared baked goods or foods from vending machines. They are not all bad, but you should get into the habit of reading labels. Look for coconut and palm oil and try to avoid these. Be aware that you can still eat all the foods that you love, but you should eat the high-fat ones in smaller quantities. Moderation is the key!

Increasing Fiber

Also known as roughage, fiber is a nutrient that can make a difference in your current and your long-term health. Fiber helps you feel full because it expands in the stomach and is more complex than processed and refined foods. It also helps with digestion and with keeping your bowels regular. Evidence suggests that a high-fiber diet may help prevent colon cancer and reduce cholesterol in the body. Fiber is found in plant foods such as fruits, vegetables, whole grains, and cereals. When whole grains are processed into white flour and white rice, all of the fiber and many of the vitamins and minerals are removed. Foods can be fortified with vitamins and minerals, but fiber cannot be added back in. To increase your fiber intake, choose a whole-grain cereal for breakfast — that is, a cereal whose first ingredient is "whole" wheat, corn, oats, rice, or bran. Eat fresh fruits and vegetables every day, and whenever you have the opportunity, eat whole-wheat bread and brown rice instead of the white (bleached and processed) variety. Nuts and beans

are also good sources of fiber, so choose foods made with these items to add fiber to your snacks or meals. You may really see a difference in how you feel.

Limiting Sugar

You should limit the amount of sugar in your diet. The main health problem caused by refined sugar is cavities. Sugar is also a contributing factor in obesity, though it's not sugar in itself that causes people to gain weight, but the fact that it adds calories beyond what a person may need. Sugar provides "empty calories" because it is void of any nutrients. All it adds to the diet is calories.

Sugar can sometimes create problems for college students. Consider Mary, who gets up at 8:30 for her 9:00 A.M. class, leaving herself barely enough time to get dressed and no time for a healthy breakfast. She breezes through the cafeteria grabbing two donuts and a Coke, which she gobbles down on her way to class. Unfortunately there's more sugar than anything else in the donut, and there's an average of 9 teaspoons of sugar in a 12-ounce sweetened soft drink! All the sugar, in addition to the caffeine, gives her a temporary lift. She's pretty alert for the first part of class, but about 45 minutes into it she begins to feel sluggish and drowsy. She has a hard time keeping her eyes open for the rest of the session, feels lethargic and irritable, and has difficulty concentrating during her other morning classes. What happened to Mary? The refined sugar gave her blood sugar levels a temporary boost. But refined sugar is absorbed quickly in the body, so her energetic feeling was short-lived. To compound the problem, the large dose of sugar caused her metabolism to release a large dose of insulin, bringing her blood sugar abruptly down.

You can probably see how too much sugar can interfere with your daily peformance and well-being. Don't be distressed, however, by the presence of naturally occurring sugars in some foods, particularly in milk products

Caffeine Content

Have you ever wondered how much caffeine you consume in an average day? The following chart should give you a good idea.

Item	Caffeine (milligrams)
1 cup brewed coffee	85
1 cup instant coffee	60
1 cup tea	30–50
12-ounce cola drinks	35–65
Many aspirin compounds	30–60
Various cold preparations	30
1 cup cocoa	6–142
1 cup decaffeinated coffee	3

and fruits. These sugars are not as refined as "table sugar," and in combination with the other nutrients in these foods, they do not cause the dramatic fluctuations in blood sugar discussed here. In fact they have the advantage of promoting a rise in blood sugar without the accompanying fall. In Mary's case a good whole-grain cereal, toast, fruit, and other high-fiber foods would have been absorbed more slowly and would have stayed with her longer to give her a good nutritional start for the rest of the day.

Controlling Caffeine

Tea and coffee, many soft drinks, and foods made with cocoa all contain caffeine, unless the product has been specifically developed to eliminate it. Some drugs (both prescription and over-the-counter) also contain caffeine. In moderate amounts (50–200 milligrams per day) caffeine increases alertness and reduces feelings of fatigue. However, when this range is exceeded, many negative physical effects may occur: nervousness, headaches, irritability, stomach irritation, and insomnia. If you do consume caffeine, keep it to a level that will give you the positive effects without the negative.

Reducing Salt

People who have high blood pressure need to be particularly concerned about their salt intake. Salt causes fluid retention, which in turn increases the pressure on the walls of the blood vessels. People who have a high-salt diet may be more predisposed to high blood pressure. For most college students, though, salt is not the primary concern in developing a healthy diet. However, if you have just begun to be more independent in your food choices, this is a great time to begin modifying your intake of salt. Experts believe that salt is an acquired taste; if you slowly cut down on the amount of salt in your diet, you will probably desire it less and less. College is an ideal time to begin choosing less salty foods and to stop adding salt at the table if you were brought up to do so.

Some Suggestions for Eating on Campus

To ensure that you are eating well, try doing the following:

1. If you feel there aren't enough healthy choices in the dining halls on your campus, speak with the food service managers in those facilities. If there's enough demand, they are usually willing to modify their menus.

2. Plan ahead, so you are not stuck with unhealthy choices as your only options. If you know you get hungry between meals, carry fruit or healthy snacks with you to class. Dried fruit and small bags of nuts make easy snack food that won't spoil.

3. If you have the choice, prepare some meals in your room. Low-fat lunch meat and cheese on whole-wheat bread offers a healthy, low-calorie alternative for lunch, as does soup (though high in salt, usually), a peanut butter and jelly sandwich, or tuna fish.

4. For late-night snacking, keep fruit in your room. Choose popcorn (preferably not the microwave varieties, which are usually high in fat) instead of convenience foods like potato chips or candy bars. If you order out for pizza, try plain cheese. And share it with a few friends so you are not tempted to eat the whole thing.

EXERCISE 15.3 Food Diary

Keep a record of everything you eat and drink for a week on photocopies of the chart on p. 343. Also keep notes on how you feel on a daily basis. At the end of the week, review your record and see if you are able to identify any patterns in what you eat and how you feel. How does your diary record compare with your responses in Exercise 15.2?

FITNESS

People approach exercise with differing attitudes. Some students were very active in high school but feel the increased responsibilities of college keep them too busy for a regular exercise program. Other students who were active before college continue their personal fitness program and/or partake in some sort of intramural activity for fun and fitness. Still other students have little prior athletic experience but see college as the perfect place to begin a personal fitness program, given the availability of quality workout facilities and opportunities for interaction with fellow students.

We hope you will remain or become more active in college. Many students complain about not having enough time for a physical fitness program, but

Day: _____

Time	Quantity and Type of Food	Special Circumstances (Were you very hungry? Anxious? With friends?)
A.M.		
P.M.		

Notes about how you feel this day: _____

_____

_____

_____

_____

_____

_____

_____

_____

_____

perhaps you can look at it this way: You probably have *more* time and flexibility now than you ever will again! It certainly won't get easier as family and career obligations mount after college. Also many colleges offer exercise facilities to students at little or no extra charge, including many opportunities for competitive sports at the amateur level. If you establish a program now, you will be more likely to continue throughout your college years and later in life. If you wait until you're a junior, you may never do it.

Choosing an Exercise Program

Consider the benefits of various types of exercise. Competitive sports, such as intramurals, are excellent ways to meet people and have a good time, and they often involve only a once- or twice-a-week commitment. On the other hand, such activities don't always offer a strenuous enough workout to qualify as good exercise. Also games such as softball, flag football, or volleyball have fairly high rates of injury. Other activities, geared more toward conditioning and building strength, do more for fitness than do most intramural sports but are still of somewhat limited benefit. The most common exercise in this category is weight training, which has become a popular activity for women as well as men. Lifting free weights and training on a circuit with weight machines are excellent activities for building muscle, reducing body fat, and providing tone and shape to your body. The main drawback is that weight training is not an aerobic activity, which is the type of exercise most beneficial to your health.

Aerobic activities — swimming, jogging, brisk walking, cycling, vigorous one-on-one racquet sports, to name a few — strengthen your cardiovascular system, which improves overall health and has many feel-good benefits. Students report more energy, less stress, better sleep, weight loss, and an improved self-image. Aerobic exercise also tends to increase endurance, lower blood pressure and cholesterol levels, and result in other healthy physical changes.

Especially on a large campus you may feel that you get plenty of exercise just walking to and from classes, your car, or the dining hall. In order to get all the benefits of an aerobic exercise program, however, you need to follow certain guidelines. If you don't, it doesn't mean that your exercise is wasted. Any time you are moving instead of being a couch potato, there is some benefit. But to truly experience all the great things exercise can offer, you need to meet some minimum criteria:

► *Mode.* Pick an exercise that you enjoy and will continue. You can cross-train doing different exercises, as long as they cumulatively meet the other criteria listed here.

► *Frequency.* Exercise at least three times per week. You will see greater improvements, however, if you gradually build to four to six times per week and maintain this frequency. Give yourself *at least* one day a week free of exercise so your body can recover.

► *Duration.* Exercise for at least 20–30 minutes at a time. Even when you begin, it's important to maintain exercise for 20 minutes, although this may mean you need to slow down quite a bit periodically.

► *Intensity.* Monitor the intensity of your workout. Intensity refers to how vigorously you work out. In order to get aerobic benefits, your heart must be beating at a target heart rate. Use the formula in Exercise 15.4 to calculate the heartbeat range you should achieve to make your exercise work the best for you.

EXERCISE 15.4   How Hard Should You Exercise?

Determine your target (exercise) heart rate by completing the blanks in the formula below.

$220 - \underline{\hspace{1.5cm}}_{\text{(your age)}} = \underline{\hspace{1.5cm}} \times .60 = \underline{\hspace{1.5cm}}_{\text{(beats/minute)}}$ (lower end of target)

$220 - \underline{\hspace{1.5cm}}_{\text{(your age)}} = \underline{\hspace{1.5cm}} \times .75 = \underline{\hspace{1.5cm}}_{\text{(beats/minute)}}$ (upper end of target)

For example, if Jan is 20 years old, her maximum heart rate is about 200 beats per minute. (She never wants to exercise at *that* intensity.) Her target heart rate would be 60–75 percent of 200, or 120–150 beats per minute. If she measures her heart rate a few minutes into her workout and finds it lower than 120, she knows that she has to work a little harder. If she finds that it's much more than 150, then she knows she needs to slow down. This is just a guideline to ensure that the exercise is truly aerobic.

EXERCISE 15.5   Campus Fitness Resources

With a classmate or friend find out about opportunities and resources for physical fitness on your campus. These may include classes, equipment and courts, and clubs/organizations. List some of the opportunities below, along with operating hours and phone numbers for several you are interested in pursuing.

1. _____

   _____

   _____

2. _____

   _____

   _____

3. _____

   _____

   _____

Suggestions for Success in Exercise Programs

To get the most out of your exercise program, try doing the following:

1. If you are trying to begin a program or are having trouble continuing one, find an exercise partner. A friend's support and motivation can be invaluable.

2. Begin slowly. There's probably nothing more discouraging at first than being muscle-bound for a week, but keep in mind that your body needs time to become fit.

3. Think of exercise as a life-long commitment, and choose an exercise you can continue for a long time. Fitness is not stored; you need to exercise regularly. Keeping it up is a lot easier than starting over, too!

4. Make sure you have the appropriate equipment and clothing for your sport. Dress for the weather conditions, and don't take undue risks at night or in hazardous weather. Good shoes are generally the most important thing (except for cycling and swimming, of course!).

5. If you are a young, healthy college student, you probably do not need a physical exam before beginning an exercise program unless a preexisting medical condition or past injury poses some limit or risk.

6. Don't use the excuse "I don't have time." Schedule exercise into your day as you would classes or studying, and don't let anything interfere with it. Finding time is often a matter of setting your priorities.

WEIGHT CONTROL

Many freshmen are afraid of the "Freshman 15"—the 15 pounds (more or less) many resident students (men and women) gain during their first year away at college. First-semester weight gain often results from having many tempting (or at least high-fat) foods to choose from, late-night snacks in addition to three meals a day, the stress of academics, and access to an unlimited quantity of food at mealtime or foods not previously eaten at every meal, such as dessert.

Whatever the reason for the Freshman 15 (and it varies from student to student), it is certainly not inevitable. Choose the low-fat and lower-calorie foods for the sake of your weight as well as your health. Try to eat only when you're hungry, not because you're studying or because your mealcard says you still have $3.00 left for the day. And exercise—lots. Any extra calories you may be taking in from the change in your diet can probably be burned up in an aerobic exercise program. If you find you are gaining weight anyway, try to deal with it as soon as possible. Generally the longer you wait, the tougher it becomes to shed those extra pounds.

You may find help on your campus at the student health center, the physical fitness center, the counseling center, or even in your residence hall. There may be some good community resources in your area such as Weight Watchers or hospital-based weight loss programs. Whatever you do, seek a slow, sensible approach to losing weight and keeping it off. Many people want a quick fix, such as protein shakes, diet pills, laxatives, or starvation. Not only can these be dangerous to your health (and often cause you to feel lousy), but they generally don't work in the long run. In fact they often don't work in the short run. There's no magic potion or foolproof formula for weight loss, other than burning more calories than you are taking in.

Anorexia and bulimia affect many college students. These eating disorders are very different from each other, but in both cases food is abused in some way as a focal point in the illness. The vast majority of those affected are women. Anorexia often starts in adolescence and is characterized by an irrational fear of getting fat. This fear leads anorexics to participate in self-imposed starvation or excessive compulsive exercise, or both, to lose weight. As a result they are usually very thin. Bulimics, on the other hand, may be slightly plump or of normal weight, because their illness is characterized by a syndrome known as "bingeing and purging." The bulimic goes through periods of consuming vast quantities of food, and then getting rid of it, usually by vomiting or taking laxatives.

You don't have to be sick to use your college's student health service. It's a great place to get information about contraception, STDs, and other health-related issues.

Eating disorders are very complex, having physical, psychological, and social dimensions. Therefore they usually don't go away by themselves and often require intensive treatment. If you suspect that you or someone you know is developing anorexia or bulimia, there are a variety of resources you can consult: a physician at your student health center, the counseling center on your campus, local hospitals that may have specific programs dealing with eating disorders, and private physicians or mental health practitioners in your community. Often the hardest part is admitting that there is a problem and deciding to seek help.

SEXUALITY

Not all freshmen are sexually active. However, college seems to be a time when recent high school graduates begin to at least think more seriously about sex. Perhaps this has to do with peer pressure or a sense of one's newfound independence, or maybe it's just hormones. Regardless of the reasons, it can be quite helpful to explore your sexual values and to consider whether sex is right for you at this time. It is important to keep in mind that love and sexuality can be expressed through many sexual behaviors other than intercourse. For the purposes of this discussion, however, "sex" will mean intercourse, because sexual behaviors that aren't intercourse do not generally lead to consequences as serious as pregnancy or sexually transmitted diseases.

While the "sexual revolution" of the 1960s and 1970s may have made premarital sex more socially acceptable, people have not necessarily become better equipped to deal with this sexual freedom. There is an alarmingly high rate of sexually transmitted diseases (STDs) among college students, and unwanted pregnancies are, unfortunately, not uncommon.

Why is it that otherwise intelligent people choose to take sexual risks? Well, sex isn't the only thing that college students take risks with. If you are

18 or so, you may feel you are invincible or immune from danger. Although you know certain risks exist, you may never have been sufficiently exposed to them personally to believe your own life could be touched. Or perhaps it's simply that sex and relationships are a confusing business. While there are many pressures to become sexually active, certainly many factors may discourage sexual activity as well. The following list compares these factors:

Encouragers	Discouragers
Hormones	Family values/expectations
Peer pressure	Religious values
Alcohol/drugs	Sexually transmitted diseases
Curiosity	Fear of pregnancy
The media	Concern for reputation
An intimate relationship	Feeling of unreadiness
Sexual pleasure	Fear of being hurt or "used"

As you can see, there are some powerful pressures on each side. Consequently some people get confused and frustrated and fail to make any decision. Or they may allow the encouragers to persuade them but not feel comfortable enough with that decision to take responsibility for their actions — the "If I don't think or talk about it, then I can pretend I'm not really doing it" syndrome. This irresponsibility or indecisiveness carries a risk: that sex will occur without the means to prevent pregnancy or STDs.

For your protection try to clarify your own values and then act in accordance with them. Those who do this usually wind up happier with their decisions. Take a moment now to reflect on whether you plan to be sexually active. Whatever you decide, think about how you will reinforce your resolve to abstain from sex or only practice safer sex and how you plan on communicating that decision to your partner. The following exercise will help you consider these points.

EXERCISE 15.6 **Personal Reflection on Sexuality**

Have you taken time to sort out your own values about sexual activity? What is it that might prevent you from taking time to think about these issues, and what can you do to ensure that you act in accordance with values, taking into account the health of both you and your partner? On a separate sheet of paper write some of your thoughts and intentions about this. No one else will read this, but the activity of writing will help you organize your thoughts. Committing your values to paper will help ensure that you live by them when making tough decisions (see Chapter 13, "A Personal System of Values").

Contraception

What is the best method of contraception? Any method that you use correctly and consistently, each time you have intercourse. While one method may be more effective than another, if a couple does not prefer it, they will be less likely to use it consistently and correctly, and therefore it's not better for them. When choosing a method of birth control, consider all aspects of the method before you decide. Table 15.1 (pp. 350–351) compares the major features of some common methods of birth control.

As the table indicates, all methods have their advantages and disadvantages. You need to make sure that whatever method you choose, you feel comfortable using it. You should consult your physician for the methods requiring a prescription and make sure to read all package inserts thoroughly, particularly for any over-the-counter methods you purchase. And always discuss birth control with your partner so that you both feel comfortable with the option you have selected. For more information about a particular method, consult a pharmacist, a medical practitioner at your student health center, a local family planning clinic or Planned Parenthood affiliate, the local health department, or your private physician. The main thing is to get information somewhere and to resolve to protect yourself and your partner each and every time you choose to have sexual intercourse.

About Condoms

In the 1990s the condom needs to be a "given" for those who are sexually active. Other than providing very good pregnancy protection, it can help to prevent the spread of STDs, including AIDS. The most current research indicates that the rate of protection provided by condoms against STDs is similar to its rate of protection against pregnancy (90–99%). Other methods of birth control, particularly spermicides containing Nonoxynol-9 in a 4 percent concentration, may provide some extra protection against STDs, but no other method rivals the protection offered by condoms. Because STDs are epidemic on most college campuses, and because AIDS is a deadly disease, it becomes more and more important to use condoms.

To some degree, however, this is easier said than done. The condom has long had a reputation of being a less spontaneous method of birth control and of diminishing pleasurable sensations. It may take some discussion to convince your partner that using condoms is the right thing to do. Perhaps he or she will respond negatively to the suggestion. If this happens, here are some comments that may help you in your discussion:

Your partner: Condoms aren't spontaneous. They ruin the moment.

You: If you think they're not spontaneous, maybe we're not being creative enough. If you let me put it on you, I bet you won't notice that it's not spontaneous!

Your partner: Condoms aren't natural.

You: What's not natural is to be uptight during sex. If we know we're protected against unwanted pregnancy and disease, we'll both be more relaxed.

Your partner: It just doesn't feel as good with a condom. It's like taking a shower with a raincoat on.

You: I know it may not feel exactly the same, but I'm sure we can both work toward making it feel really good. Besides we can't have sex without one. Using a condom is going to feel a lot better than not having sex at all.

Your partner: I can't believe you carry condoms with you. Does this mean you'll "do it" with anyone?

You: Of course not! In fact I carry condoms because I think sex *is* special. I want to be responsible about it. Also I care about you, and if we decide to have sex, I want to make sure we're both protected.

Table 15.1 Methods of Contraception

ABSTINENCE (100%)*

What It Is
Celibacy.

Advantages
Only method that provides total protection against pregnancy and STDs.

Disadvantages
Not everyone willing to abstain from sex at all times.

Comments
Not an acceptable practice for many people.

STERILIZATION (99.5%)

What It Is
Tubal ligation in women; vasectomy in men.

Advantages
Provides nearly permanent protection from future pregnancies.

Disadvantages
Not considered reversible and therefore not a good option for anyone wanting children at a later date.

Comments
While this is a common method for people over 30, most college students would not choose it.

ORAL CONTRACEPTIVES (97–99%)

What They Are
Birth control pills.

Advantages
High rate of effectiveness; allows spontaneity by not interfering with the sexual act. Most women have lighter and shorter periods.

Disadvantages
Many minor side effects (nausea, weight gain), which cause a significant percentage of users to discontinue. Potential for major side effects exists, but usually in women over 35 and smokers.

Comments
Pill must be taken daily. Available by prescription only.

INTRAUTERINE DEVICE (IUD) (94–98%)

What It Is
Device inserted into the uterus by a physician.

Advantages
Once inserted, may be left in for one year, affording sexual spontaneity.

Disadvantages
High rate of serious complications associated with IUD — pelvic inflammatory disease and infertility.

Comments
Only one type widely available in the United States. Women who have not had a child may have a difficult time finding a doctor willing to prescribe it.

CONDOM (90%)

What It Is
Rubber sheath that fits over the penis.

Advantages
Only birth control method that also provides good protection against STDs, including AIDS. Actively includes male partner.

Disadvantages
Less spontaneous than some other methods because it must be put on right before intercourse. Belief of many men that it cuts down on pleasurable sensations.

Comments
Experts believe that most condom failure is due to *nonuse* of condoms rather than breakage. Has been shown to be up to 98% effective, especially when a spermicide is also used.

DIAPHRAGM (80–95%)

What It Is
Dome-shaped rubber cap, inserted into the vagina, that covers the cervix — a "barrier" method

Advantages
Safe method of birth control with virtually no side effects. May be inserted up to 2 hours prior to intercourse, making it somewhat spontaneous. May provide some protection against STDs.

*Percentages in parentheses refer to effectiveness rates.

Your partner: I won't have sex with a condom on.

You: Well, we can't have sex without one. There are other things we can do without having intercourse. Why don't we stick to "outercourse" until we can resolve our differences?

Sexually Transmitted Diseases

The problem of STDs on college campuses has been receiving growing attention in recent years, as the number of infected students has reached epidemic proportions. The consequences of the most common STDs reach far beyond the embarrassment most students feel when diagnosed with a sexually related illness. The idea that "nice" young men and women don't catch these sorts of diseases is more dangerous and ridiculous than ever before. If you choose to be sexually active, particularly with more than one partner, exposure to an STD is a very real possibility.

Disadvantages
Wide variance of effectiveness based on consistent use, the fit of the diaphragm, and frequency of intercourse. Multiple acts of intercourse during the same wearing require additional spermicide.

Comments
Must be prescribed by a physician. Must always be used with a spermicide (usually jelly) and left in for 6–8 hours after intercourse.

CONTRACEPTIVE SPONGE (80–90%)

What It Is
Small polyurethane sponge containing the spermicide Nonoxynol-9.

Advantages
Easy to obtain (over-the-counter) and use. No need for additional spermicide because it already contains it. Once inserted, effective for 24 hours, providing greater spontaneity.

Disadvantages
Frequent difficulty with removal. For women who have had a child, effectiveness is less than indicated here.

Comments
Must be left in for 6–8 hours after intercourse.

CERVICAL CAP (80–90%)

What It Is
A cup-shaped device that fits over the cervix.

Advantages
Similar to diaphragm.

Disadvantages
At the present time few medical practitioners have received the training necessary to prescribe this method.

Comments
The cap was only recently approved by the FDA to be marketed in the United States, and the long-term effects, if any, are not known.

SPERMICIDAL FOAMS, CREAMS, AND JELLIES (75–80%)

What They Are
Sperm-killing chemicals inserted into the vagina.

Advantages
Easy to purchase and use. Seem to provide protection against STDs, including AIDS.

Disadvantages
Somewhat ineffective as birth control. May increase likelihood of birth defects should pregnancy occur.

Comments
As with condoms, it is suspected that failure is due to nonuse. However, spermicides seem to work better in combination with other methods (such as condoms).

NATURAL FAMILY PLANNING (80%)

What It Is
Periodic abstinence based on when ovulation is predicted.

Advantages
Requires no devices or chemicals.

Disadvantages
Requires a period of abstinence during the month, when ovulation is expected. Also requires diligent record-keeping.

Comments
For maximum effectiveness, consult a trained practitioner for guidance in using this method.

COITUS INTERRUPTUS (80%)

What It Is
Withdrawal.

Advantages
Requires no devices or chemicals and can be used at any time, at no cost.

Disadvantages
Relies heavily on the man having enough control and knowing when ejaculation will occur to remove himself from the vagina in time. Also may diminish pleasure for the couple.

Comments
Ejaculation must be far enough away from partner's genitals so that no semen can enter the vagina. Provides no protection against STDs and, if not practiced carefully, can result in unwanted pregnancy.

You are probably wondering what "risk factors" make a person most likely to become infected with an STD. In general there are three: (1) being 15–24 years old, (2) having multiple sexual partners, and (3) not using a condom. For those who are sexually active, monogamy is certainly safer than having sex with many partners. If two people enter into a sexual relationship free of any diseases, then the risk of contracting an STD is nil. Unfortunately you can rarely be positive of someone's disease status, unless they have never had sex before. (And even then you can't be 100 percent sure. AIDS, for example, is transmitted in several ways, not only through sexual contact.) Condoms were discussed earlier, but remember that they do provide excellent protection against STDs and that failure to use one puts you at greater risk of infection.

The STDs that students need to be most concerned about are chlamydia and gonorrhea, herpes, venereal warts, and AIDS. The rates of all the diseases besides AIDS are very high on college campuses. In fact the rate of STDs continues to increase faster than that of any other illness on campuses

Condoms

When selecting a condom, always consider the following:*

1. Use condoms made of latex rubber. Latex serves as a barrier to the virus. "Lambskin" or "natural membrane" condoms are not good because of the pores in the material. Look for the "latex" on the package.

2. A condom with a spermicide may provide additional protection. Spermicides have been shown in laboratory tests to kill the virus. Use the spermicide in the tip and outside the condom.

3. Condom use is safer with a lubricant. Check the list of ingredients on the back of the lubricant package to make sure the lubricant is water-based. Do not use petroleum-based jelly, cold cream, baby oil, or cooking shortening. These can weaken the condom and cause it to break.

*From *Understanding AIDS: A Message from the Surgeon General*. HHA Publication No. (CDC) HHS-88-8404 (Washington, D.C.: Government Printing Office).

today. Approximately 5–10 percent of visits to college health services nationally are for the diagnosis and treatment of STDs. While AIDS does not pose the same kind of threat in terms of likelihood of exposure, students surely need to be concerned about it because of the potentially life-threatening consequences. The following is a brief synopsis of these illnesses. For more information about any of them, contact your student health service or local health department.

Chlamydia. The most common STD in the United States is chlamydia, with over 4 million new cases diagnosed each year. Chlamydia is particularly threatening to women because a large proportion of women who are infected do not show symptoms, allowing the disease to progress to pelvic inflammatory disease (PID), now thought to be the leading cause of infertility in women. When present, symptoms of chlamydia in women may include mild abdominal pain, change in vaginal discharge and in frequency of urination, and pain with urination.

In men symptoms may include pain and burning with urination and discharge from the penis, though occasionally the symptoms will be too mild to notice. Men who go without treatment may also become infertile, although this happens much more rarely than it does in women. In both sexes symptoms usually manifest themselves one to three weeks after exposure. Even if symptoms are not apparent, an individual infected with chlamydia is still contagious and runs the risk of transmitting the disease to subsequent sexual partners. If detected, chlamydia is completely treatable with antibiotics.

Gonorrhea. Gonorrhea is a bacterial infection that produces symptoms similar to chlamydia. While not quite as common as chlamydia, with approximately 2 million new cases a year, it still has a significant impact on the health of Americans. As with chlamydia, men will usually show symptoms, but women often do not. Gonorrhea is treatable with antibiotics, but in recent years new, more resistant strains of gonorrhea have made this process more difficult. Untreated gonorrhea, like chlamydia, can lead to more severe infections in men and women.

Herpes. Before AIDS came along, herpes was considered the worst sexually transmitted disease one could get, because there is no known cure. While it is not quite as common as the other diseases mentioned here, it still affects a significant percentage of sexually active people in our society — about 1.5–1.8 percent. Genital herpes is very similar to the cold sores and fever blisters people get on their mouths, and in fact they are both caused by varieties of the herpes virus. Symptoms appear on the genitals two to twenty days after exposure in the form of small blisters or lesions that erupt into painful sores. The first outbreak is usually the most severe, and about 50 percent of those infected will never have another outbreak. The other 50 percent are likely to have outbreaks several times a year, particularly when they are under stress or their immune system is being taxed.

Although there is no cure, the prescription drug Zovirax seems to reduce the length and severity of herpes outbreaks. When there are open lesions, or any suspicion of them, it is important to abstain from any genital-to-genital contact. For those who engage in oral sex, abstinence would also be recommended when a partner is having an outbreak of herpes, as it is possible to transmit the infection from one region of the body to another. Potentially serious complications also exist for babies born through vaginal deliveries to mothers suffering from a herpes outbreak. (Fortunately, cesarean section is an effective way to deal with the latter.)

Venereal Warts (Condyloma). These warts are caused by the human papilloma virus (HPV). While chlamydia may still be the most common STD diagnosed nationally, venereal warts have become the leading STD affecting the health of college students. There has been a 600 percent increase in this disease among college students in the last twenty years, and it's estimated that as many as 10–15 percent of sexually active college students are infected with HPV, with rates increasing yearly. A typical incubation period for venereal warts is one to three months, though symptoms may not appear for several years after exposure. Genital warts may be small, flat, pink growths, or they may be larger, with a cauliflowerlike appearance. In either case they are usually not painful though they may cause itching, bleeding, or burning. They are usually found on the shaft of the penis, on the vaginal lips, and in the rectum, but in women they may extend up through the vagina to the cervix, and in men they may grow in the urethra causing eventual blockage requiring surgery.

Because venereal warts are caused by a virus, there is no cure, but treatments such as freezing, burning, or chemical applications have been effective. It is suspected that the virus recedes into the cells, which may account for future outbreaks of warts and which makes it difficult to determine whether a person remains contagious and for how long. The reason for recent concern over this STD is that it is being identified in college students at an alarming rate, and it seems to be connected with an increasing incidence of cervical cancer in college women.

AIDS. This STD is very difficult to discuss briefly. The main thing you need to know is that AIDS is still a problem. In 1990 the number of AIDS cases had grown to over 150,000 in just a few short years, and the Centers for Disease Control was predicting that the number would be over 250,000 in 1992. As of 1990 it was suspected that about 1–1½ million people were infected with HIV, the virus that causes AIDS.

Living with AIDS

Most people only die once. I've already died twice. The first time was in the fall of 1981 when I surrendered to the fact that I was an alcoholic and pillhead. The second time was on a warm, sunny day in late April 1987, when my doctor said, "With these symptoms, I have to conclude that it's the AIDS virus."

Being dead can have its advantages. Sometimes I say to myself, "You're dead, you can do whatever you want. What are they going to do, shoot you?" You get to eat what you like. In fact, like the scene from Sleeper, the doctors encourage you to eat steaks and ice cream. People don't castigate you when you sleep in. Planning for the future means drawing up a will. You don't save for retirement, you should live that long. I have a friend who went $27,000 into debt and then kicked the bucket. Now, he got the joke.

Generally, though, being dead isn't much fun. Old friends often treat you like the proverbial hot potato, or like a time bomb. They pass you around, hoping you don't go off around them. Not that I blame them: We've all gone to too many funerals.

So you find yourself gravitating to the other HIVs. Then the game becomes more like musical chairs. Who's the next one out? When your friends start the fast slide, they are instantly old men, the shadow-dead. Hair turns into fragile wisps, bodies gaunt down, eyes disappear into the recesses of emaciated faces. Then everyone knows, not much longer for this one.

Some are deserted by their families. More often, families kill with a kind of kindness. Well-intentioned, misguided, they nurse you through the last months, but they really want you to go out on their terms. I have a friend who was an invalid for his last six months while his . . . family screened out all gay callers and "converted" him to Christ and prayer and away from the gay life.

Another unpleasant thing about being dead is that people objectify you, treat you like a thing rather than a person. This is, of course, what we do to dead things. Bad enough that the doctors and hospital medical staff treat you like a faulty piece of equipment to keep running and keep clean (although I've had indigent friends who were denied even that slim dignity in the final countdown). You begin to wonder how to justify all this expense and bother. Soon you hear subtle messages like, "Do you realize how much your decision to stay alive is costing us?"

Then there is all the shame that goes with being too sick to meet obligations, with losing your looks, with becoming helpless. Shame is an awesome thing. My mother, who has otherwise been remarkable, cannot tell her friends that her son has this virus and is probably dying. She simply cannot do it.

Then there are all the lies. I lost a job because they found out why I was sick. I lost a job because I couldn't risk telling them I was sick. Better to leave with a question mark than with that trailing after you. Outside of the gay community I tell only a select few. I'll be [damned] if I'll surrender my personal power. . . .

Gradually the gritty process of closing out a life begins. Can't make it into the office at nine? Go on disability. Can't keep your apartment up? Move in with Mom and Dad. Learn to like daytime television. Let's not even talk about a sex life. You end up disempowered, nudged to the edge of things by the busy, ignoring untouched, living in limbo. . . .

Memorize this equation: silence = death. The mountains of medicine labor to bring forth a mouse. When you get an undeserved death sentence, you have the right to be angry. It is only the most belligerent and unpleasant among the sick who can hope to hope.

SOURCE: Adapted and reproduced, with permission, from the Student Union (a publication by students at Carnegie-Mellon University), 6, no. 3 (1990).

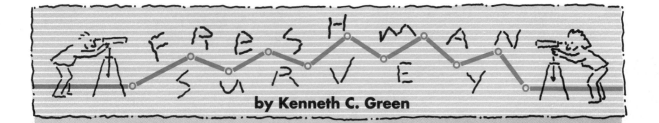

FRESHMAN SURVEY

by Kenneth C. Green

AIDS Testing?

College freshmen support liberal positions on many social issues, but not regarding testing for AIDS. In 1988 the UCLA Freshman Survey conducted what was probably the first large national survey of attitudes toward AIDS testing among the traditional college-age population. Slightly over two-thirds (67.7 percent) of the Fall 1988 freshmen agreed with the statement "the best way to control AIDS is through widespread, mandatory testing." Freshman support for mandatory AIDS testing has remained fairly stable since then. In 1989 and again in 1990, about two-thirds (roughly 67 percent) of the entering freshmen agreed that "the best way to control AIDS is through widespread, mandatory testing."

This response raises an interesting question. College-age individuals would obviously be a prime target of any widespread testing for AIDS. Groups that favor testing might cite these data as proof that young people are willing to submit to testing. Groups opposed to testing might see it as evidence that college students do not fully understand their constitutional rights to privacy and the potential political consequences of testing.

How would you feel if you had to take a mandatory AIDS test to enroll in college? What if your institution required a mandatory AIDS test for everyone on your campus? What arguments would you make for or against it?

The most common routes of transmission continue to be through semen and blood, though vaginal fluids also may transmit the virus. While AIDS has not yet spread in the heterosexual community to the degree that was predicted earlier, this may change. Heterosexuals who engage in risky behaviors (sharing needles and having unprotected sexual intercourse) are still at risk for contracting the disease. While the rate of infection in the heterosexual population has not risen significantly, the actual number of heterosexuals infected with HIV and who have AIDS certainly continues to grow.

AIDS has not been a major problem on most college campuses, as of the early 1990s. However, as more and more people come down with HIV-related illnesses, more college students likely will contract AIDS as well. Because of the long incubation period suspected for AIDS, students may become infected with the virus while they are in college but not become sick until several years afterward. The main concern is that since other STDs are occurring at such a high rate, many students obviously are engaging in the behaviors that put them at risk for STDs, including AIDS. Each person must try to evaluate his or her own risk of becoming infected and take precautions against these risks. As with other STDs, abstinence, monogamy, and condoms (in that order) are the best ways to prevent the sexual spread of AIDS. Get as much information as you can through your student health service, your local health department, or the National AIDS Hotline (1-800-342-AIDS).

Sex – Yes = Rape

I can remember a friend of mine talking about a party that she went to this summer. She was telling me about how she liked this guy and was flirting with him a little bit. She ended up having too much to drink and passed out in a friend's room. In the morning she woke up next to the guy she had been flirting with the night before. She thought that she was OK because she had all her clothes on, but when she was walking home she noticed that her underwear was in her pocket.

Every day I walk to school and in the past couple of weeks I have noticed stencils on the sidewalk—one saying "stop raping" and the other saying "sex – yes = rape." The sight of these are kind of eerie to me. Where are the rape victims on our campus? Do they have no one to turn to and therefore resort to marking their concerns and hurts on the sidewalk?

This graffiti makes me think of the statistics that I hear floating around about 1 out of every 3 women getting sexually assaulted by the time they graduate from college. Sometimes I feel lucky because I got my one time over with already and the person did not get very far except for scaring me. But then I tell myself I am not that lucky—this could happen again at any time.

I was standing against a fraternity wall and someone that I knew pretty well came up to me and pushed his body against mine and started putting his hand up my shirt while trying to kiss me. I kept turning my head against the wall so he couldn't kiss me on the lips and I was trying to push him away by pushing on his shoulders. It was scary because he was bigger and stronger than I was. Even though I was pushing as hard as I could, he was stronger. After about a minute, which felt like an eternity, he got really embarrassed and backed off and said, "I'm sorry, I'm sorry, I know I shouldn't do that to you," and then he ran away.

That incident made me feel very uncomfortable and very scared. Uncomfortable because I felt a little guilty—like maybe it was my fault. I asked myself, "Why didn't I scream? What if someone else saw?" I was scared because something like that could happen to me and I was not strong enough to stop it. Also it scared me that this was someone that I knew. I had spent time alone with him in his room in the past and he had never touched me. I was confused about why all of a sudden, in the middle of this party, he would attack me. I became distrusting of him, but also of other men that I am not very close to.

It's very frightening to think about, but too often there comes a time when a woman's resistance to sexual advances is simply chalked up to her need for further seduction, for further convincing. Suddenly the female in question is no longer a feeling individual, she's just a woman, one of the ones who would eventually say "yes" anyway. At this point an act of what might have been sexual desire turns into a desire to control the situation and the woman. It is in these cases, when the someone is denied the right to say NO, that sexual assault occurs.

To understand even faintly what the experience of sexual assault is like, you must consider what it would be like to be robbed of something very personal. There are very few things that we can personally exert control over in this life, and when someone takes the control of your own body away from you, it is devastating. When something that you own is stolen, you will be justifiably upset and insecure. When your body is violated and control over your own person is taken from you, you can never regain the security of knowing that your self (physical, emotional, mental) is your own.

SOURCE: Reproduced, with permission, from Ingrid Bromberg, "Rape Does Happen at CMU," the Student Union (a publication by students at Carnegie-Mellon University), 6, no. 3 (1990).

Rape

Until now the discussion of sexuality has focused on sexual activity involving the consent of both partners. However, date and acquaintance rape — forced sexual intercourse involving two people who know each other — is an all-too-common occurrence on college campuses. Major studies done at colleges and universities suggest that as many as 15–35 percent of women will be the victims of rape or attempted rape before they graduate from college. A discussion of rape can become very involved, and there is not enough space here to cover it adequately. The most important things that you need to know are that (1) rape is a common occurrence, (2) it is *never* okay for a man to force a woman to have sex against her will, and (3) while there is no absolute prevention for rape, there are many things a woman can do to reduce her risk of being raped. For more information about this topic, contact a rape crisis center in your community, your student health service, or local organizations that address women's issues.

As you consider the issue of wellness, keep these ideas in mind. First, you have the ability to greatly influence your health and well-being on a day-to-day basis. Second, you will have to determine for yourself what risks you may face in neglecting a healthy lifestyle, just as you will have to take action to prevent those risks. Third, how you decide to live does make a difference in how you feel and whether you will succeed in other areas of your life. Finally, most college campuses provide resources to help you learn the information and skills that will lead you to be a healthier person.

Are you prepared to take responsibility for your own wellness?

EXERCISE 15.7   Contracting for Change

Now that you've learned about aspects of wellness, you may feel the desire to make changes to improve your own health. This behavior change contract should help by giving you some structure and providing a reward at the end!

Behavior Change Contract

1. Specific behavior I want to change:

   a. Current behavior: _____

   b. Ideal behavior: _____

2. How will I go about making the change?

   _____

   _____

   _____

3. What are some negative thoughts I have that keep me from changing the desired behavior?

   _____

   _____

   _____

4. What can I say to myself that might be more helpful?

_____

_____

_____

5. (Optional) Who will be my support person(s)? What will their responsibilities be?

_____

_____

_____

6. What rewards will I give myself when I meet my goal?

_____

_____

_____

Signed:

My name: _____ Date: _____

Support person: _____ Date: _____

JOURNAL

Evaluate your own behaviors in support of your wellness (diet, exercise, and so on). Comment on any of the author's suggestions that seem particularly applicable to you. What about her discussion of sexuality as it pertains to wellness? What advice might she have offered college freshmen that perhaps she didn't?

SUGGESTIONS FOR FURTHER READING

Body, Jane. *Good Food Book: Living the High Carbohydrate Way*. New York: Norton, 1985.

Boston Women's Health Collective. *The New Our Bodies, Our Selves*. New York: Simon & Schuster, 1984.

Cooper, Kenneth H. *The Aerobic Program for Total Well-Being*. New York: Evans, 1982.

Otis, Carol, and R. Goldingay. *Campus Health Guide*. New York: College Entrance Examination Board, 1989.

Parrot, Andrea. *Coping with Date Rape and Acquaintance Rape*. New York: Rosen, 1988.

Smith, Sandra, and Chris Smith. *The College Student's Health Guide*. Los Altos, Calif.: Westchester, 1988.

Travis, John W., and Regina Sara Ryan. *Wellness Workbook*. Berkeley, Calif.: Ten Speed Press, 1988.

Alcohol, Other Drugs, and You

Pretty soon they're going to tell you nothing's good for you, and you're going to starve to death. I mean, you get uptight from studying and doing papers and reading assignments; you have to loosen up sometimes. So I have a couple of beers every night and go to sleep. You gotta get your rest, too, don't you? The way I see it, we're old enough to make those decisions on our own. So what if I drink a few beers? What's the big deal?

N. PETER JOHNSON and PRESTON E. JOHNSON *collaborated to write this section. Peter is coordinator of alcohol and drug studies in the department of neuropsychiatry and behavioral science, School of Medicine, University of South Carolina, Columbia. He has been a medical educator since 1972 and an alcohol and drug educator since 1978. In 1988 he was a distinguished lecturer for the American Medical Association. In his spare time he assists students and others who are in distress as a result of alcohol and other drugs.*

"I struggled with this section," he recalls, "until I hit on the idea of asking my son to react to what I had written. The words you are about to read began as a series of letters to my son, Preston, and his responses helped me find a focus for this complex and highly charged subject." Preston is an undergraduate at Emory University, Atlanta.

Writing a piece on alcohol and other drugs for students entering college is hardly an easy task. It's very tempting to come down on anyone who uses any form of drugs. For example, I could share with you my belief that you should never drink alcoholic beverages, that there is no such thing as "recreational use of drugs," and that even the caffeine in coffee can produce effects that will inhibit your chances for success in college and beyond.

If that's all I wrote, however, no matter how strongly I might believe it, you probably would think, "There's another guy preaching to me like he's my parent." I could hardly blame you. I gave considerable thought to this issue when my own son, Preston, began his college career at Emory University. I decided to write to Preston about my feelings on this subject. As an alcohol and drug educator I felt the professional part of me wanting to let him know all I knew about alcohol and other drugs, yet the parent in me warned me not to overdo it.

When I was in high school, I was a jock and actually followed my coaches' advice when they said, "Stay away from women, cigarettes, and booze." However, when I started college at the age of 16, the school I attended had few sports, and none in which I was any good. With no athletic niche for me, I immediately developed a profound interest in girls, cigarettes, and drinking. As a result of this change my freshman grades were so bad that I left college to join the Army. I don't recommend this course of action to anyone. I hope you will be more mature than I was.

So after much thought, and reams of drafts that ended up in the trash, I think I finally began to make sense to myself as well as to my son. I began by telling him that, in spite of what we read in the newspapers, college students use drugs far less frequently than young people who do not attend college. Over the past ten years the number of college students using drugs other than alcohol has actually fallen. For instance, in spite of the image projected by "beach 'n' beer" movies, virtually no one takes sedatives such as Quaaludes. The only people you hear saying things like "Duh, like wow man, this is really heavy" either are truly dumb or are smoking marijuana, a topic we shall get to in due time. Two drugs whose use has not decreased on campus, unfortunately, are cocaine and LSD.

However, college students are more prone to heavy alcohol usage than are their noncollege peers. Heavy drinking has been increasing on campus even as it declines among young people not in college. So college students use fewer drugs, but drink more alcohol. Male college students use more drugs and alcohol than female college students, with one exception: More college women than men are smokers.

EXERCISE 15.8   Alcohol and Drug Use on Your Campus

In a small group review the following list of questions, and add three or four of your own.

1. What percentage of students on this campus do you think are problem drinkers?
2. What percentage of students do you think use illegal drugs?
3. What drugs, excluding alcohol, are most popular on your campus?
4. What are the rules pertaining to alcohol and other drugs on your campus?
5. How many students have discipline problems due to alcohol and drug use?
6. What are the consequences of these discipline problems?
7. Why do students use alcohol and other drugs?

8. _____
9. _____
10. _____
11. _____

Now, using these questions, interview people from at least three of the following seven categories and note their answers. Each group member should report at least one interview.

First-year student   Dean of students or person in that office
Upperclass student   Health center staff person
Alcohol/drug educator   Discipline officer
Counseling center staff person

Discuss your findings. How are their answers similar? What would account for any differences in their answers? What did you learn that surprised you about alcohol and drug use on your campus?

I went on to tell Preston about several basic principles that have been important in my life. First, I believe in a "no use" drug policy because of the effects of drugs on the thought process, on academic performance, and on life in general. Second, I recommend a "no use" alcohol policy because not only does alcohol affect mental and physical performance for several days, it blocks long-term memory. I believe in this principle even though I know that about 80 percent of college students drink alcoholic beverages at some time.

I refuse to minimize the consequences of using drugs and alcohol, and I detest the term *responsible drinking*. This phrase sounds suspiciously like something the beer industry coined in order to sell more beer. What it means is, "We know you're going to drink; therefore, we want you to drink responsibly." Perhaps the industry would like you to believe that drinking is inevitable for everyone, yet the truth is that 38 percent of U.S. adults don't drink.

I don't support the term *recreational drug use* either, because there is no such thing. No one actually uses drugs recreationally. The word *recreation* derives from the Latin *recreatio*, meaning to restore to health. Its use here implies that health is somehow related to drug use, when the exact opposite is true. In general, drug users are less healthy, physically and mentally, than the rest of us.

So now that you know where *I* stand, let me pass on some further information about specific drugs to help you decide where *you* stand.

ALCOHOL

Alcohol consumption is the number-one cause of problems for college students. In fact drinking alcohol has become such an expected part of life on many campuses that some consider it to be "normal." Most of us forget or ignore its consequences until forcefully reminded by friends who suffer broken bones, head injuries, automobile accidents, sexual assaults including date rape, academic failure, near deaths, and death itself. Then we ignore or forget again until still another tragedy strikes.

Many people can paraphrase the 1985 report (widely publicized by the alcohol industry) indicating that moderate drinking could improve health. Fewer people know about other research since then showing that even moderate drinking can negatively affect the heart (enlarging and weakening the ventricles) and skeletal muscles.

Let's talk about alcoholism. Alcoholism is a disease in which a person consistently and continually causes harm to him- or herself or others as a result of drinking. Alcoholics are people who cannot resist drinking frequently or who cannot limit themselves when they do drink. In general terms the alcoholic drinks four or more days per week or has five or more drinks in a row. Six percent of adults in the United States are alcoholics—10 percent of all drinkers in this country.

You or a friend might say, "That definition doesn't apply to me. Everybody I know drinks that way." Well, as you also know, "Birds of a feather flock together." Drinkers tend to hang around with drinkers, while nondrinkers tend to prefer the company of others like themselves.

But what if you drink? Even then, a little knowledge may lessen the damage you can inflict. For example, you should know that the alcohol in beer, wine, and distilled liquors is all the same alcohol. You can become intoxicated, or alcoholic, just as easily from drinking one as from drinking another.

You should also know that there are ways to reduce the quantity of alcohol you consume per hour. If you tend to gulp drinks, try alternating noncarbonated, nonalcoholic drinks with mixed drinks to keep the alcohol quantity down. Stay away from college drinking games, such as "quarters," "thumper," and "Indian," in which participants must consume large quantities of alcohol in short periods of time. Heavy drinkers frequently initiate these games so that their drinking will appear normal. The games require that others become involved; try to be the student who is not enticed. And never drink on an empty stomach; the stomach rapidly absorbs alcohol, especially from carbonated beverages, when empty.

Male Drinking Is on the Skids

According to national surveys the percentage of men who use alcohol dropped from 75 percent in 1981 to 64 percent in 1989. Per capita consumption has fallen to its lowest level in twenty years.

What has convinced males to cut down on their alcohol? The symbolic meaning of drinking has changed. Men who imbibe are no longer regarded as macho. Boozing is not a requirement for manhood anymore.

Up until ten years ago Americans exalted alcohol as liquid masculinity. In our movies, our stories, our advertisements, drinkers were very male. They were aggressive and fearless, ready for anything. Drinking was the first rite of passage for teenage boys. Later it greased the way for friendship and acceptance. Almost every male gathering included alcohol. No wonder, then, that alcohol abuse became such a staggering problem, affecting 18 percent of all men.

The impetus for change came from two movements that took hold in the 1970s: the rejection of traditional sex roles and heightened consciousness about health and safety.

The opening challenge to "manly" drinking occurred in 1980 when women, disgusted by carnage on the highways, formed Mothers Against Drunk Driving (MADD). Before MADD, male-dominated legislatures had been reluctant to impede men's prerogative to live dangerously. MADD forced the public to realize that intoxicated men, who made up 90 percent of drunken drivers, weren't just "being men." They also were murderers. Statehouses began to stiffly punish impaired offenders, raise the minimum age for drinking, and lower the legal blood alcohol level for drivers.

The movement filtered down to the student level, and Students Against Drunk Driving (SADD) was organized. The former epitome of wimpiness — asking your parents to drive you home if you were drinking — became respectable. In 1987 the concept of "designated drivers" went mainstream. For the first time it could actually be manly to stay sober in order to look after one's buddies.

Canned macho? Today, masculinity and alcohol no longer go hand in hand, and in fact, the number of men who use alcohol has declined since 1981.

Hollywood joined the trend to take manliness out of drinking, following a 1983 report by the entertainment industry that described how movies and television had glorified alcohol.

The close affiliation of drinking with sports also began to erode in the mid-1980s. Stadiums implemented a variety of drinking restrictions. Athletes have been discouraged from drinking heavily. The National Football League routinely tests for alcohol abuse, and in a number of clubhouses, drinking is forbidden.

Even in the military, the ultimate bastion of macho, change is afoot. The biggest blow came in 1988, when officers got orders from the top to take the glamour out of alcohol use. As a result heavy alcohol use in the armed forces has decreased by 25 percent.

Although drinking will always have a place in our culture, we may yet see the day when it ceases to be a means by which men prove themselves.

SOURCE: Adapted, with permission, from a syndicated 1990 article by Russell Lemle, chief of the alcoholism clinic at the San Francisco Veterans Administration Medical Center, and Marc E. Mishkind, Yale University.

EXERCISE 15.9 Responses to Peer Pressure

Sometimes it's difficult to be the only one in the group not drinking. You may not receive *direct* pressure from others, but there may be a subtle message that you should drink to "be like everyone else." Using the assertiveness techniques you learned in Chapter 14, write potential responses to these remarks, made in situations in which you choose not to drink.

1. C'mon, you're not gonna be any fun if you don't loosen up and down a

   couple! _____

   _____

2. Just have one before you hit the road. _____

   _____

3. Hey — alcohol is *healthy* for you, y'know! _____

   _____

4. Man, you don't want to be sober all by yourself, do you? _____

   _____

5. No, don't give _____ any — *he's/she's* not drink-
   (your name)

   ing tonight! _____

   _____

You should also know that time is the only thing that will sober you up after drinking. The enzymes in your liver process absolute alcohol at a rate of about half an ounce per hour. Cold showers, coffee, and exercise will not help at all. The joke is that coffee only makes for a more wide-awake drunk, but it really isn't funny.

Just as important is that rate of intoxication depends on age, body weight, gender, and acquired tolerance levels. For example, women and older persons produce higher blood alcohol levels for the same amount of alcohol consumption, even if body weights are the same as those of younger men. Also, because of differences in body fat distribution, a stomach enzyme, and hormones, a woman weighing the same as a man may need only drink 45% of what the man drinks to reach the same level of intoxication.

If you play sports, be aware that moderate drinking results in loss of muscle coordination for at least 12–18 hours after consumption. The decreased muscle tone and other effects last for days, long after the alcohol is undetectable in the bloodstream. And since processing alcohol disrupts the liver from its normal process of making fuel for the body, muscles tend to tire faster. For 48 hours or longer you can also expect impaired reaction time, balance, and eye–hand coordination; distorted perception; reduced ability to make smooth, easy movements; decreased strength; increased fatigue;

Beer, Wine, or Liquor — Alcohol Is Alcohol

If you drink, know how much alcohol you are consuming. The absolute alcohol content varies according to the type of alcoholic beverage.

- ► Can of beer (2.3 percent alcohol) $12\ oz \times .023 = .28\ oz$ absolute alcohol
- ► Can of beer (5 percent alcohol) $12\ oz \times .05 = .60\ oz$ absolute alcohol
- ► Wine cooler (5 percent alcohol) $6\ oz \times .05 = .30\ oz$ absolute alcohol
- ► Glass of wine (12 percent alcohol) $5\ oz \times .12 = .60\ oz$ absolute alcohol
- ► Glass of wine (15 percent alcohol) $5\ oz \times .15 = .75\ oz$ absolute alcohol
- ► MD 20/20 (20 percent alcohol) $6\ oz \times .20 = 1.20\ oz$ absolute alcohol
- ► Liquor (80 proof/40 percent alcohol) $1\ oz \times .40 = .40\ oz$ absolute alcohol
- ► Liquor (100 proof/50 percent alcohol) $1\ oz \times .50 = .50\ oz$ absolute alcohol
- ► 151 rum (75.5 percent alcohol) $1\ oz \times .75 = .75\ oz$ absolute alcohol

and a host of other problems. Alcohol impairs memory, too; isn't college tough enough as it is?

Drinking and driving is a special problem for college students. Were you aware that the highest automobile accident rates are for persons ages 18–24? These same people also rank highest in binge drinking and per capita alcohol consumption. Almost 250,000 college students are arrested for driving under the influence (DUI) each year, and 75 percent of first-time DUI offenders will later be diagnosed as alcoholic. The likelihood of alcoholism for second-time DUI offenders is 90 percent. Driving a motor vehicle under the influence of alcohol also costs in many ways: jail time, legal fees (at least $500), and increased insurance costs (up to $1,000). The estimated lifetime cost in 1991 for DUI offenses is $10,000, even if no repeat occurrences take place.

Alcoholism should be a special concern for you if alcohol problems have occurred in your immediate family. Anytime a parent, sibling, aunt, uncle, or grandparent has a problem, your susceptibility increases. At the end of the section is a test that may help you determine whether you have a family problem with alcoholism. People who score high on the test should be particularly careful about drinking or avoid it entirely.

It Isn't Over Till It's Over

How long do the behavioral effects of marijuana last?

A group of scientists wanted to determine how long after smoking marijuana a person's judgment and performance might still be impaired. To do this, they trained ten experienced, licensed private pilots for 8 hours to perform a simple takeoff and landing procedure on a flight simulator. After this training each pilot smoked a cigarette containing THC, the principal active ingredient in marijuana. Each cigarette contained 19 milligrams of the drug, roughly the same amount a person is likely to smoke in a social setting. Some hours after smoking this drug, the pilots tried the landing task again.

The pilots' mean performance on the landing task showed impairment on all variables, including significant impairment in vertical and lateral deviation on approach to landing and distance off center from the runway.*

The pilots reported no awareness of impaired performance.

How long after they had smoked the drug would you guess that the pilots were tested?

a. 3 hours   **b.** 6 hours
c. 12 hours   **d.** 24 hours

(The answer may be found in the footnote on p. 368.)

*Jerome A. Yasavage et al., "Carry-Over Effects of Marijuana Intoxication on Aircraft Pilot Performance: A Preliminary Report," *American Journal of Psychiatry* 142, no. 11: 1325–29.

MARIJUANA

I read recently that a custodian at a college campus was busted for possession of marijuana. Seems marijuana is everywhere and everyone is using it, doesn't it? Actually that's not so. Less than 20 percent of college students use marijuana, but about 5 percent of all college students develop pretty serious habits. That's disturbing, because marijuana is a strange drug. When I was in college, the authorities warned us about "killer weed," and since most of us knew it wasn't deadly — at least in the short term — we disregarded everything anyone told us. Actually marijuana has some pretty bad attributes. The ingredient most responsible for the "high" is delta-9-tetrahydrocannabinol, or THC, which is absorbed through the lungs and into the bloodstream immediately. If you detest tobacco smoking for what it does to the body, you should know that smoking marijuana has the same effect on the lungs. In fact it is even more cancer-causing than tobacco, though people generally smoke less of it. In addition strains of marijuana available today contain higher levels of THC than ever before. For example, sinsemilla reportedly is as much as 600 times stronger than the marijuana of the 1960s and 1970s.

Once in the bloodstream, THC is absorbed by, stored in, and gradually released by fat cells. A single puff of marijuana has a half-life in the body of between three and seven days, depending on the potency and the smoker. After a period of chronic, heavy use, it can take as long as a month for THC

Effects of Marijuana

If you think marijuana isn't really that bad for you, perhaps you should consider the following list of potential adverse effects from chronic use.

- ► Chronically slowed reaction times
- ► Decreased tracking capability by the eyes
- ► Impaired eye–hand coordination
- ► Altered perception of time (for example, "slow motion" sensations)
- ► Impairment of depth perception
- ► Impairment of recent memory
- ► Increased suggestibility, suspiciousness, and fearfulness
- ► Apathy, loss of drive, unwillingness or inability to complete tasks, low frustration tolerance, unrealistic thinking, increased shyness, total involvement in the present at the expense of future goals
- ► Increased likelihood of lung infections

- ► Increased likelihood of cancer (marijuana contains *ten times* more cancer-causing agents than found in cigarettes)
- ► Breast enlargement in males

to clear your system. One acquaintance of mine lost a job because marijuana showed up on a drug test even though he was not a user. Rather, for the previous year he had been exposed to the second-hand smoke of a roommate and family members. He had stored up so much THC it was as if he were smoking marijuana himself.

Recently one of my students asked me to help him stop smoking marijuana. He was about to graduate and was afraid he might be tested for drugs during his preemployment physical. I suggested that he stop at least long enough to clear his system. He said he wasn't sure he could stop smoking that long, since it had been several years since he had gone without marijuana. We worked together, and after a month of abstinence, he commented that he could now think and remember much more clearly. The decrease in his thinking abilities had occurred so gradually that he was unaware of it. This can be a major problem for students who need to memorize quantities of information. Recent research shows that the measurable pharmacologic effects of marijuana can last for one full day, and the behavioral effects may last much longer.

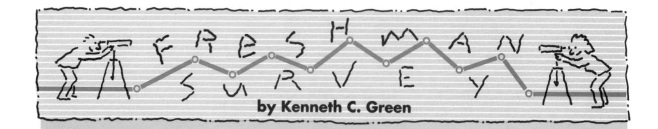

Drug Testing?

In the 1990 UCLA Freshman Survey, 80.4 percent of first-year students agreed with the statement "employers should be allowed to require drug testing of employees or job applicants." (Presumably that would include alcohol, which is certainly a drug.) Do you think their agreement reflects students' willingness to submit *themselves* to drug testing?

What's your opinion about drug testing? Have you ever had to take a drug test for a job? How do you feel about drug testing for college and professional athletes? How do you think students on your campus would respond to the statement "colleges should be allowed to require drug testing of students and faculty"?

COCAINE

Cocaine is a powerful chemical extracted from the leaves of the coca plant. People in the Andes Mountains use coca mixed with a little lime to avoid hunger pangs and to make work at high altitudes go easier. In concentrated form cocaine is a powerful stimulant; it overstimulates the pleasure centers of the brain. The user literally loses touch with even basic biological needs during a cocaine "high." Laboratory animals have been observed to self-administer cocaine until they die of thirst or starvation, ignoring their needs for food, water, and sex. Cocaine is one of the most addictive drugs known.

The street drug cocaine hydrochloride (what most people call cocaine) is sniffed into the nose. "Crack" is smokable cocaine from which the hydrochloride has been removed. Once the drug is in the bloodstream, both forms produce the same symptoms although the way the drug is delivered (smoked or snorted) causes differences in the immediate severity. Snorting cocaine causes runny noses, and in the long term it can "burn" a hole through the septum of the nose. Smoking crack causes respiratory problems and has destructive effects on the lungs and breathing tubes. Incidentally these same problems occur with methamphetamine, or "ice," in smokable form.

ANSWER (to question in box on p. 366): **d.** The pilots were tested one full day after smoking. At this time they were still clearly impaired in their ability to perform the flight simulation. Yet they were unaware of their impairment or of any continuing effect of the THC on performance, mood, or alertness.

Effects of Cocaine

Cocaine use can lead to a staggering number of physical, mental, and emotional problems, both short- and long-term. Consider the following:

Adverse Effects from the Cocaine "High"

- Accelerated but unfocused thinking, disrupted concentration
- Misjudgment of timing and accuracy
- Misjudgment of physical and mental power
- Jumpiness
- Covered-up pain, increasing the possibility of injury
- Increased aggressiveness and sense of hostility toward others
- Extreme rises in body temperature (heat prostration)
- Heavy sweating, dehydration, and muscle cramping
- Rapid heart rate
- Heart irregularities and heart attack
- Stroke and seizures due to increased blood pressure
- Increased rate and depth of breathing (hyperventilation)
- Visual hallucinations ("coke lights")
- Restlessness and insomnia
- Shakes
- Convulsions
- Mental problems similar to schizophrenia (including hallucinations)
- Loss of appetite
- Cross-problems with alcohol including heavy drinking

Adverse Effects from the Postcocaine "Crash"

- Auto and other accidents from too much alcohol consumption while using cocaine
- Extreme hunger
- Decrease in energy
- Loss of motivation
- Inability to concentrate on specific tasks
- Depression ("coke blues")
- Suicidal thoughts and attempts

Adverse Effects from Chronic Cocaine Use

- Restlessness and inability to consistently study
- Continued insomnia and loss of sleep, leading to an increased use of cocaine and/or alcohol for sleep and other reasons
- Isolation from other people
- Irritability and fear
- Profound depression
- Seizures and convulsions
- Suicidal thoughts and actions
- Feeling that something is crawling under the skin ("coke bugs")
- Extreme hunger and self-induced vomiting in response to overeating

Causes of Death Related to Stimulants Including Cocaine

- Convulsions (seizures)
- Coma (loss of consciousness)
- Heart attack
- Stroke

Cocaine produces an intense experience by enhancing certain chemical processes in the brain. For the cocaine user thoughts seem to come more quickly, each of the five senses seems heightened, physical energy seems unlimited, attitude becomes one of unwavering self-assurance, and fatigue and hunger disappear. It is easy to see why some students are attracted to this potent drug.

Naturally, however, what goes up must come down — and in this case, rather quickly. A cocaine high starts in a few minutes, peaks in 15–20 minutes, and goes away in less than an hour. A crack high peaks within seconds and lasts about a minute. During the crash the user may feel tired and unmotivated. Mood may swing rapidly to depression and agitation, and the user may feel paranoid and restless and be unable to sleep.

CAFFEINE AND TOBACCO

Many students use lots of caffeine to stay awake while cramming for tests. A much better way to prepare, of course, is to study on a regular basis (see the chapters on developing sound study habits). But if you're in the habit of cramming, you should know that caffeine is often abused by students who would never consider using "real" drugs. Because it is legal and readily available, many people assume caffeine poses no genuine health risks, but caffeine toxicity can produce serious ill effects. If introduced today, many caffeine products would be restricted by the Food and Drug Administration as too potent for unregulated distribution and consumption. (See the previous section on nutrition for data on the caffeine content of various substances and beverages.)

I haven't said much about tobacco, the number-one killer drug, because very few college students smoke. Because more women than men now smoke, the rate of cancer in women has surpassed that in men. The easiest time to break an addiction is before it starts. After that it takes courage and willpower, but in the long run it's worth it. I smoked for sixteen years and now regret every minute of it. Now that I've not smoked for another sixteen years, I resent people who make me breathe their smoke. The number of reported cancers from passive inhalation continues to go up, and I don't want to be one of the victims.

The best defense against alcohol and drug abuse is information, and there's plenty of it available. You can start by contacting the alcohol and drug program on your campus. Hospitals are another excellent source of this sort of information. You can also call the National Clearinghouse on Alcohol and Drug Information at 1-800-728-2600. For cocaine information call 1-800-COCAINE.

College is a valuable time in the lives of each of us fortunate enough to reap its rewards. The more one remembers the value of education, the less one is likely to take risks that could devalue that experience. This is why I hope you will think long and hard about what I have said in these few pages. I've tried not to preach to you, and I hope I have succeeded in presenting the facts as objectively as possible. As an alcohol and drug educator, I obviously have strong feelings about alcohol and drug use. As a human being so may you. All I ask is that you consider what I have written, discuss it with people you admire, and make a decision for yourself based on *your own* values, not on the prevailing attitudes of others.

EXERCISE 15.10 Campus Resources

Visit the places on your campus where resources and assistance related to alcohol and other drugs is available. You may find help in these places:

Health center
Student activities office
Residence life office
Minister or chaplain's office

Counseling center
Drug/alcohol education office
Discipline office

Note below the offices you visited, their phone number and hours, and the types of resources they offer to students.

Office: _____

Phone: _____ Hours: _____

Resources: _____

Office: _____

Phone: _____ Hours: _____

Resources: _____

Office: _____

Phone: _____ Hours: _____

Resources: _____

EXERCISE 15.11 Screening Test for Alcoholism

For each of the following items answer Y for yes or N for no.

_____ 1. Do you feel you are a normal drinker? ("Normal" means you drink less than or as much as most other people and you have not developed recurring trouble while drinking.)

_____ 2. Have you ever awakened the morning after some drinking the night before and found that you could not remember part of the evening?

_____ 3. Do either you, your parents, any other close relatives, your spouse, or any girlfriend or boyfriend ever worry or complain about your drinking?

_____ 4. Can you stop drinking without a struggle after one or two drinks?

_____ 5. Do you feel guilty about your drinking?

_____ 6. Do friends or relatives think you are a normal drinker?

_____ 7. Are you able to stop drinking when you want to?

_____ 8. Have you ever attended a meeting of Alcoholics Anonymous (AA)?

_____ 9. Have you been in physical fights when you have been drinking?

_____ 10. Has your drinking ever created problems between you and either your parents, another relative, your spouse, or any girlfriend or boyfriend?

_____ 11. Has any family member of yours ever gone to anyone for help about your drinking?

_____ 12. Have you ever lost friends because of your drinking?

_____ 13. Have you ever been in trouble at work or at school because of drinking?

_____ 14. Have you ever lost a job because of drinking?

_____ 15. Have you ever neglected your obligations, your schoolwork, your family, or your job for two or more days in a row because you were drinking?

_____ 16. Do you drink before noon fairly often?

_____ 17. Have you ever been told you have liver trouble or cirrhosis?

_____ 18. After heavy drinking, have you ever had severe shaking or heard voices or seen things that really weren't there?

_____ 19. Have you ever gone to anyone for help about your drinking?

_____ 20. Have you ever been in a hospital because of drinking?

_____ 21. Have you ever been a patient in a psychiatric hospital or in a psychiatric ward of a general hospital where drinking was part of the problem that resulted in hospitalization?

_____ 22. Have you ever gone to a psychiatric or mental health clinic or to any doctor, social worker, or clergy for help with any emotional problem where drinking was a part of the problem?

_____ 23. Have you ever been arrested for drunk driving, driving while intoxicated, or driving under the influence of alcoholic beverages or any other drug? (If yes, how many times? _____)

_____ 24. Have you ever been arrested or taken into custody, even for a few hours, because of other drunk behavior, whether due to alcohol or another drug? (If yes, how many times? _____)

Now compute your total score based on the point values listed here for each Y or N answer.

1. 2N	5. 1Y	9. 1Y	13. 2Y	17. 2Y	21. 2Y
2. 2Y	6. 2N	10. 2Y	14. 2Y	18. 2Y*	22. 2Y
3. 1Y	7. 2N	11. 2Y	15. 2Y	19. 5Y	23. 2Y**
4. 2N	8. 5Y	12. 2Y	16. 1Y	20. 5Y	24. 2Y**

* Score 5 points for hallucinations or delirium tremens.
**Score 2 points for each occasion.

Compare your total score with the numbers listed below.

0–3 points = probable normal drinker

4 points = borderline score

5–9 points = 80 percent associated with alcoholism/chemical dependence

10 or more = 100 percent associated with alcoholism

Regardless of your score, if you have some concerns about your drinking, assistance is available. Make an appointment to talk with someone on your campus who can help. This may be a counselor, alcohol/drug educator, minister, or someone else with whom you feel comfortable. Take advantage of the assistance they can provide.

EXERCISE 15.12 Children of Alcoholics Screening Test

Place a Y for yes next to each question that you answer affirmatively.

_____ 1. Have you ever thought that one of your parents had a drinking problem?

_____ 2. Have you ever lost sleep because of a parent's drinking?

_____ 3. Did you ever encourage one of your parents to quit drinking?

_____ 4. Did you ever feel alone, scared, nervous, angry, or frustrated because a parent was not able to stop drinking?

_____ 5. Did you ever argue or fight with a parent when he or she was drinking?

_____ 6. Did you ever threaten to or actually run away from home because of a parent's drinking?

_____ 7. Has a parent ever yelled at or hit you or other family members when drinking?

_____ 8. Have you ever heard your parents fight when one of them was drunk?

_____ 9. Did you ever protect another family member from a parent who was drinking?

_____ 10. Did you ever feel like hiding or emptying a parent's bottle of liquor?

_____ 11. Do any of your thoughts revolve around a problem-drinking parent or do difficulties arise because of his or her drinking?

_____ 12. Did you ever wish that a parent would stop drinking?

_____ 13. Did you ever feel responsible for and guilty about a parent's drinking?

_____ 14. Did you ever fear that your parents would get divorced due to alcohol abuse?

_____ 15. Have you ever withdrawn from and avoided outside activities and friends because of embarrassment and shame over a parent's drinking problem?

_____ 16. Did you ever feel caught in the middle of an argument or fight between a problem-drinking parent and your other parent?

_____ 17. Did you ever feel that you made a parent drink alcohol?

_____ 18. Have you ever felt that a problem-drinking parent did not really love you?

_____ 19. Did you ever resent a parent's drinking?

_____ 20. Have you ever worried about a parent's health because of his or her alcohol use?

_____ 21. Have you ever been blamed for a parent's drinking?

_____ 22. Did you ever think your father was an alcoholic?

_____ 23. Did you ever think your mother was an alcoholic?

_____ 24. Did you ever wish your home could be more like the homes of your friends who did not have a parent with a drinking problem?

_____ 25. Did a parent ever make promises to you that he or she did not keep because of drinking?

_____ 26. Did you ever wish that you could talk to someone who could understand and help with the alcohol-related problems in your family?

_____ 27. Did you ever fight with your brothers and sisters about a parent's drinking?

_____ 28. Did you ever stay away from home to avoid the drinking parent or your other parent's reaction to the drinking?

_____ 29. Have you ever felt sick, cried, or had a "knot" in your stomach after worrying about a parent's drinking?

_____ 30. Did you ever take over any chores or duties at home that were usually done by a parent before he or she developed a drinking problem?

Now compute your score by assigning 1 point for each Y answer, and compare the total with the numbers listed below. (Note: This test is *not* nationally standardized.)

   0–3 points = probably normal family

   4 or more points = indication that someone in your family *does* have a drinking problem

   10 or more points = severe dysfunction

Again, if you are concerned about family alcohol use and/or the effect it has had on you, visit with someone on your campus who is qualified to help.

JOURNAL

You probably found the author of this section very straightforward in saying what he believes. Be equally direct in discussing your views on alcohol and other drugs. In what respects do you agree? In what ways do you disagree? Try writing in response to specific new information you may have gathered from the reading. For instance, what do you make of the study of marijuana use by airplane pilots?

REFERENCES AND SUGGESTIONS FOR FURTHER READING

Cohen, S. "The Effects of Combined Alcohol/Drug Abuse on Human Behavior." Chapter 1 in *Treatment Research Monograph Series: Drug and Alcohol Abuse — Implications for Treatment*. Washington, D.C.: Department of Health and Human Services, Alcohol, Drug Abuse, and Mental Health Administration, 1981.

Gilbert, R. M. "Caffeine as a Drug of Abuse." In R. J. Gibbins et al., *Research Advances in Alcohol and Drug Problems*, Vol. 3. New York: Wiley, 1976.

Gold, M. S. *800-COCAINE*. New York: Bantam Books, 1984.

———. *Facts About Drugs and Alcohol*. New York: Bantam Books, 1986.

Griffin, T. M. *Paying the Price*. Center City, Minn.: Hazelden Foundation Press, 1985.

Johnson, N. P., ed. *Dictionary of Street Alcohol and Drug Terms*. Columbia: University of South Carolina Press, 1988, p. 163.

Johnston, L. D., P. M. O'Malley, and J. G. Bachman. *National Trends in Drug Use and Related Factors Among American High School Students and Young Adults, 1975–86*. Publication No. 87-1535. Washington, D.C.: Department of Health and Human Services, 1987.

Kaufman, D. W., L. Rosenberg, S. P. Helmrich, and S. Shapiro. "Alcoholic Beverages and Myocardial Infarction in Young Men." *American Journal of Epidemiology* 121 (1985): 548–54.

Kinney, J., and G. Leaton, eds. *Understanding Alcohol: A Handbook of Alcohol Information*, 3rd ed. St. Louis: Mosby, 1987.

Schwartz, R. H. "Marijuana: An Overview." *Pediatric Clinics of North America*, 34, no. 2: 305–17.

Strauss, R. H., ed. *Drugs and Performance in Sports*. Philadelphia: Saunders, 1987.

Whitfield, C. L., J. E. Davis, and L. R. Barker. "Alcoholism." Chapter 21 in *Principles of Ambulatory Medicine*, 2nd ed. L. R. Barker, J. R. Burton, and P. D. Zieve, eds. Baltimore: Williams and Wilkins, 1987.

Stress
Management

*H*ey you! Yeah I said you! Watch where you're going. I mean, move and let me get by. I've gotta get to class, and I don't have time to hassle with you. What's the big rush? . . . What? Who are you tellin' to slow down, mister? I am not stressed out. Hey, I was up till four gettin' ready for class . . . so maybe I'm a little edgy today. So butt out, will ya?

KEVIN W. KING *is director of assessment and faculty relations in the University Career Center, University of South Carolina, Columbia. He also regularly conducts workshops on stress management for students, faculty, and staff at USC.*

"My freshman year was a catastrophe!" he recalls. "I earned a 0.5 grade point average during my first semester and found that my university cared very little whether I or any of my classmates were able to dig our way out of that hole. Obviously I did, and my research in public speaking anxiety and performance anxiety were partially motivated by my own experiences and my desire to find a way to help others succeed more easily than I did."

Stress is natural. So, to the extent that stress is a sign of vitality, stress is good. Yet most of us, as we grow and develop, don't really learn how to cope effectively with stress-producing situations, and the result is that stress can overwhelm us, interfering seriously with our ability to perform. The primary way to manage stress is to modify it with something that enhances our feeling of control in the situation. For me relaxation is also very important in counteracting stress. It's impossible to be tense and relaxed at the same time, and relaxation is a skill that we can learn just like any other skill.

Did you realize you have actually *learned* to be tense in most stress-producing situations? Now you can learn how to identify the warning signs or symptoms of stress. And once you are aware of the warning signs, you can *choose* how you will react. That's what this section is all about.

WHAT HAPPENS WHEN YOU ARE TENSE

The signs or symptoms of stress are easy to recognize and differ little from person to person. Basically your rate of breathing becomes more rapid and shallower, your heart rate begins to speed up, and the muscles in your shoulders and forehead, the back of your neck, and perhaps even across your chest begin to tighten. Probably your hands and perhaps even your feet become cold and sweaty. There are likely to be disturbances in your gastrointestinal system, such as a "butterfly" stomach or diarrhea, vomiting, and frequent urination. Your mouth may become parched, your lips may dry out, and your hands and knees may begin to shake or tremble. And your voice may quiver or even go up an octave.

A number of psychological changes also occur when you are under stress. These changes are the result of your body and mind trying to "defend" you from some real or imagined threat. The threat could be from an actual situation, such as someone approaching you with a gun in hand. Or it could come from something that hasn't actually happened but that you are worried about, because the part of the brain that controls your defensive reactions doesn't do any thinking — it simply reacts. The stress you typically feel is just part of that defensive reaction. As a result you're more easily confused, your memory becomes blocked, and your thinking becomes less flexible and much more critical. Along with these reactions your body's adrenal glands produce adrenalin and a group of hormones called corticoids. If the situation persists over a long time, you may also find it difficult to concentrate, and you may experience a general sense of fear or anxiety, insomnia, early waking, changes in eating habits, excessive worrying, fatigue, and an urge to run away.

EXERCISE 15.13 Your Signs of Stress

Recall your last troublesome experience. What signals from your mind or body (for example, worry, frightening thoughts, tense muscles, headache, stomach distress) let you know this was a distressing situation? How did you respond to those signals? What might you do next time to handle the situation more effectively?

The urges to stand and fight or to run away are two of the human body's basic responses to stress. But many times both urges must be suppressed because they would be inappropriate. For instance, a person taking an exam may want to get up and run out of the exam room, but it probably would not help the grade to do so, and it's pointless to fight with a piece of paper. So we often find we must cope with a situation in a way that allows us to stay and face it and to do so using our potential and skills to the maximum. This is where learning to manage stress effectively can make a difference!

IDENTIFYING YOUR STRESS

Stress has many sources, but there are two prevailing theories as to its origin. The first is the life events theory, which attributes health risks and life span reduction to an accumulation of stress from events that have occurred in the previous twelve months of a person's life.

EXERCISE 15.14 The College Readjustment Rating Scale

The College Readjustment Rating Scale* is an adaptation of Holmes and Rahe's Life Events Scale. It has been modified for college-age adults and should be considered as a rough indication of stress levels and possible health consequences.

*Adapted with permission from T. H. Holmes and R. H. Rahe, "The Social Readjustment Scale," in Carol L. Otis and Roger Goldingay, *Campus Health Guide* (New York: CEEB, 1989).

In the College Readjustment Rating Scale each event, such as the first quarter/semester in college, is assigned a value that represents the amount of readjustment a person has to make in life as a result of change. In some studies people with serious illnesses have been found to have high scores on similar scales. Persons with scores of 300 and higher have a high health risk. Persons scoring between 150 and 300 points have about a 50–50 chance of serious health change within two years. Subjects scoring 150 and below have a 1 in 3 chance of serious health change.

To determine your stress score, circle the number of points corresponding to the events you have experienced in the past six months or are likely to experience in the next six months. Then add the circled numbers up.

Event	Points	Event	Points
Death of spouse	100	Sexual difficulties	45
Female unwed pregnancy	92	Serious argument with significant other person	40
Death of parent	80	Academic probation	39
Male partner in unwed pregnancy	77	Change in major	37
Divorce	73	New love interest	36
Death of a close family member	70	Increased workload in college	31
Death of a close friend	65	Outstanding personal achievement	29
Divorce between parents	63	First quarter/semester in college	28
Jail term	61	Serious conflict with instructor	27
Major personal injury or illness	60	Lower grades than expected	25
Flunk out of college	58	Change in colleges (transfer)	24
Marriage	55	Change in social activities	22
Fired from job	50	Change in sleeping habits	21
Loss of financial support for college (scholarship)	48	Change in eating habits	19
Failed important course or required course	47	Minor violations of the law (for example, traffic ticket)	15

If your score indicates potential health problems, it would be to your benefit to seriously review the "stress relief smorgasbord" that appears later in this section and select and implement some strategies to reduce your stress.

If you find that your score on the preceding exercise is 150 or higher, it would be good preventive health care to think about why you experienced each of the scored events. In addition, you might consider what skills you need to learn to either repair the damage that these events caused or prevent their recurrence. It would also be interesting to find out how the rest of the class scored on the scale. If there seems to be a need, the class might draw upon a resource person to help everyone develop better coping or learning skills. You might also find out that you already have experts within the class who might share with you how they have handled these or similar events.

The other major theory about the sources of stress attributes our general level of stress to an overload of personal hassles and a deficit of uplifts or reliefs. This theory encourages us to evaluate our immediate problems but, while doing so, to focus on what's good about our lives and to strive to notice positive events instead of taking them for granted. We are all going to experience reversals, whether it's because we don't get along with our roommate, can't register for the course or time slot we want, can't find a parking space, can't find the classroom, can't seem to handle the freedom of college, can't find the time to do all that we might, can't get into the "right" Greek or social organization, can't get our parents to "understand," can't find the money to do it all, and so on. What we can control is our *reaction* to these hassles. If we can adopt the attitude that we will do what we can do, seek help when appropriate, and not sweat the small stuff, we won't be as negatively affected by disappointments and hassles. It also helps to keep a mental tally of the positive things in our lives. The following exercise will help you to take positive stock of your life and to become more aware of the barriers to letting go of useless worries.

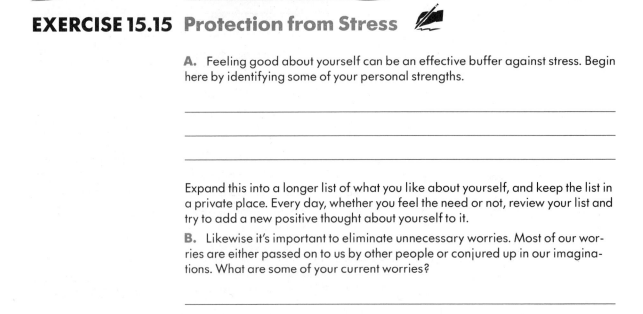

EXERCISE 15.15 Protection from Stress

A. Feeling good about yourself can be an effective buffer against stress. Begin here by identifying some of your personal strengths.

_____

_____

_____

Expand this into a longer list of what you like about yourself, and keep the list in a private place. Every day, whether you feel the need or not, review your list and try to add a new positive thought about yourself to it.

B. Likewise it's important to eliminate unnecessary worries. Most of our worries are either passed on to us by other people or conjured up in our imaginations. What are some of your current worries?

_____

_____

_____

What can you do to eliminate one or more of them?

_____

_____

_____

A STRESS RELIEF SMORGASBORD

Everyone finds different activities relaxing. To provide yourself with a sense of relief, you need to do those things that help you to let go of stress or invigorate your mind and body. However, many of the traditional things that

Take a break and have some fun! Physical activity is a great stress reliever.

people do with the intention of relieving stress — things like drinking alcohol, taking drugs, sleeping, or eating — don't relieve stress and may actually increase it! There are many other ways of handling stress that actually work, and I offer the following as more effective methods of coping with stress.

Get Physical

1. *Relax your neck and shoulders.* Slowly drop your head forward, roll it gently to the center of your right shoulder, and pause; gently roll it backward to the center of your shoulders and pause; gently roll it to the center of your left shoulder and pause; roll it gently forward to the center of your chest and pause. Then reverse direction and go back around your shoulders from left to right. Remember that your goal is to slowly stretch muscles into relaxation.

2. *Take a stretch.* In any situation, if you pause to stretch your body you will feel it loosen up and become more relaxed, so stand up and reach for the sky!

3. *Get a massage.* Physical touch can feel wonderful when you are tense, and having someone else help you to relax can feel very supportive.

4. *Exercise.* Physical exercise strengthens both mind and body. Aerobic exercise is the most effective type for stress relief.

Get Mental

1. *Count to ten.* Many people discount this method because they think that it is too simple. Your purpose is to master self-control and to gain a more realistic perspective or outlook. To give yourself time to gain that new outlook or to come up with a "better" way to handle the situation, count slowly while asking yourself, "How can I best handle this situation?"

2. *Control your thoughts.* The imagination can be *very* creative — it can veer off in frightening directions if allowed to do so. To gain control of negative thoughts or worries, imagine yelling "STOP!" as loudly as you can in your mind. You may have to repeat this process quite a few times until you master it, but gradually it will help you to shut out angry or frightening thoughts.

Road Warrior

A student who commuted twenty-three miles to school was tailgated just before arriving on campus one day. The accident was minor, but unfortunately she had been sipping coffee at the time of the collision, and it splashed all over her dress. She was so embarrassed that she didn't go to class. Unfortunately that was a particularly important class, and her absence eventually cost her a full letter grade.

If you commute a long distance, carry a store of supplies. Leave your "survival" kit in your car if you drive, or in a locker at school if possible. Here are some things you should have in your kit. Talk with other students about other items that might be useful and add them to the list.

1. Spare key to your house/apartment
2. Emergency medical supplies
3. Flashlight
4. One dollar in change
5. Some pencils and paper
6. A spare checkbook
7. Jumper cables
8. Local bus schedule
9. Rag or towel
10. A spare set of clothes
11. A spare car key hidden underneath your car
12. _____
13. _____
14. _____
15. _____

3. *Fantasize.* Give yourself a few moments. Let yourself take a minivacation, or remember the pleasure of an experience you enjoy. Hear a child laugh, or just let your mind be creative. Make a list of some places or activities that make you feel relaxed and good about yourself. Next time you need to "get away," refer to the list, close your eyes, and take a minibreak.

4. *Congratulate yourself.* Give yourself pats on the back. No one knows how difficult a situation may have been for you to handle, or even how well you may have handled it, so tell yourself, "Good going."

5. *Ignore the problem.* This may sound strange at first, but many problems just don't need to be dealt with or can't be solved right now. Forget about the problem at hand and do something more important or something nice for yourself.

6. *Perform self-maintenance.* Stress is a daily issue, so the more you plan for its reduction, the more likely it will be reduced.

Get Spiritual

1. *Meditate.* All that meditation requires is slow breathing and concentration! Look at something in front of you or make a mental picture while you gradually breathe slower and slower, and feel the relief spread through your body and mind.

Sharing a laugh with a good friend can help to keep things in perspective.

2. *Pray.* It is not necessary to go through life feeling alone. Prayer can be a great source of comfort and strength.

3. *Remember your purpose.* Sometimes it is very valuable to remind ourselves why we are in a particular situation. Even though it may be a difficult situation, you may need to remind yourself that you have to be there and to realize that the situation's importance outweighs its difficulty.

Use Mind and Body Together

1. *Take a break.* If possible, get up from what you are doing and walk away for a while. Don't let yourself think about the source of the problem until after a short walk.

2. *Get hug therapy.* We need at least four hugs a day to survive, eight hugs to feel okay, and twelve hugs to tackle the world. "Hugs" can come from many different sources and they can take many different forms. They can be bear hugs, smiles, compliments, or kind words or thoughts. If you have forgotten how to hug, ask a small child you know to teach you. Young children know that every time you give a hug, you get one back as a fringe benefit!

3. *Try progressive relaxation.* Perform a mental massage of each muscle in your body from your feet up to your head. Take the time to allow each muscle to relax and unwind. Imagine that the muscles that were all knotted and tense are now long, smooth, and relaxed.

4. *Laugh.* Nothing is so important that we must suffer self-damage. The ability to laugh at your own mistakes lightens your load and gives you the energy to go back to a difficult task.

A Relaxation Process

Settle back and get comfortable. Take a few moments to allow yourself to listen to your thoughts and to your body. If your thoughts get in the way of relaxing, imagine a blackboard in your mind and visualize yourself writing down all of your thoughts on the blackboard. By doing this you can put those thoughts aside for a while and know that you will be able to retrieve them later.

Now that you are more ready to relax, begin by closing your eyes. Allow your breathing to become a little slower and a little deeper. As you continue breathing slowly and deeply, let your mind drift back into a tranquil, safe place that you have been in before. Try to recall everything that you could see, hear, and feel back there. Let those pleasant memories wash away any tension or discomfort.

To help yourself relax even further, take a brief journey through your body, allowing all of your muscles to become as comfortable and as relaxed as possible.

Let's begin that journey down at your feet. Begin by focusing on your feet up to your ankles, wiggling your feet or toes to help them to relax, then allowing that growing wave of relaxation to continue up into the muscles of the calves. As muscles relax, they stretch out and allow more blood to flow into them; therefore they gradu- ally feel warmer and heavier. Continue the process on up into the muscles of the thighs; gradually your legs should feel more and more comfortable, more and more relaxed.

Then concentrate on all of the muscles up and down your spine, and feel the relaxation moving into your abdomen; as you do so you might also feel a pleasant sense of warmth moving out to every part of your body. Next focus on the muscles of the chest. Each time that you exhale, your chest muscles will relax just a little more. Let the feeling flow up into the muscles of the shoulders, washing away any tightness or tension, allowing the shoulder muscles to become loose and limp. And now the relaxation can seep out into the muscles of the arms and hands; gradually your arms and hands become heavy, limp, and warm.

Now move on to the muscles of the neck — front, sides, and back — imagining perhaps that your neck muscles are as floppy as a handful of rubber bands. And now relax the muscles of the face, letting the jaw, cheeks, and sides of the face hang loose and limp. Now relax the eyes and the nose, and now the forehead and the scalp. Let any wrinkles just melt away. And now, by taking a long, slow, deep breath, cleanse yourself of any remaining tension.

5. *Find a pet.* Countless studies have demonstrated that caring for, talking to, holding, and stroking pets can help to reduce stress.

Develop New Skills

1. *Learn something.* Sometimes your problem is that you lack information or skills in a certain area. The sooner you remedy your deficiency, the sooner your distress will end.

2. *Practice a hobby.* If you have one, use it; if you don't currently have one, then it's time that you did. The purpose of a hobby is to immerse yourself in an activity of your choice that provides you with a sense of accomplishment and pleasure.

EXERCISE 15.16 **Adding to and Using the Stress Reduction List**

A. Over your lifetime you've discovered some additional things that work to relieve stress for you. List them here:

_____

_____

_____

Expand your list still further by comparing notes with other students in the class.

B. Try at least one stress relief technique suggested in this section for two weeks. Give it a *good* try. To assist yourself in changing from a stress habit to a control habit, resolve in your mind that you deserve to be a more relaxed, confident person. Share your experience with someone.

The stress management habits that you are currently acquiring and practicing are likely to be the same ones that you will use for the rest of your life! Learning to handle stress in a healthy fashion is important not only to survive your freshman year and do well but to cope with the demands and opportunities of adulthood. A healthy adult is one who treats his or her body and mind in a respectful manner. When you do that, you communicate to all other adults that you are handling yourself well and don't need them to "baby" you or to tell you how to live your life.

Sometimes our lives or problems are either too overwhelming or too complex to resolve by ourselves. If you find that to be the case for you, you might benefit from checking out the services provided by your college counseling center. Counseling centers often offer individual or group sessions on handling difficult times or situations in our lives, and the support and skills of a trained professional can help make the most difficult issues a lot more manageable.

EXERCISE 15.17 **Your Social Support Network**

Your social support network can be extremely helpful to you in difficult times, but many people aren't sure whom to count on for support or how to ask for it.

You first learned about getting support from your family. Think back to a time when you felt you really needed support. Was it when you were trying to accomplish something or when you felt discouraged or defeated? Whom did you ask for support? How did you ask? Did they respond in the way that you needed them to? Did you get the caring or comfort that you wanted?

Life's early lessons usually get reinforced over the years. Probably by now either you feel good about the level of support in your life or you don't.

Imagine you have a problem with a roommate that you want to discuss with someone else. Whom would you choose? Would you expect that discussion to leave you feeling the way you want to feel, or are you just used to feeling that you never get the support you need to feel good about yourself?

In different situations you may need different people for support. Are you still relying primarily on your family, or have you expanded your resources to get support from friends, professors, co-workers, and so on? Who is in your support network? Make a list of people you would support. Make a list of situations in which you sometimes need support. List the people who support you in them. Do you need to add someone to your network? Write yourself a note about how to get that person's support.

You may also want to consider the values that your current physical, emotional, and spiritual circumstances reflect. Are those values similar to or different from those of your family and friends? Are you acting in accordance with your values? Is this a source of stress? (See Chapter 13 for more about values.) Remember, whatever you do to cope with stress, you will be coping either productively or counterproductively — it's your choice. Go forth and manage stress!

EXERCISE 15.18 A One-Week Checkup

To control stress, we need to heed its warning signs. Photocopy the chart on the next page and use it for one week to keep track of troublesome experiences and your *reactions* and *responses* to them. If at first you don't notice any reactions, pay attention to your general state during the day. Times when you feel suddenly fatigued, tense, angry, upset, frightened, and so on are stress points in your day.

After the week is over, analyze the chart. Look for both positive and negative patterns. Based on this information, write down a plan for stress management:

I will _Relax, stop and think rationally_

I will _get enough sleep, do homework in advance before day before deadline_

I will not _Stay up late_

I will not _plan Alot of things on the weekend that I cannot handle_

Event	Signals		Your Response	What (If Anything) Would You Do Differently Next Time?
	Physical	Emotional		
Catched A cold	✓	✓	Upset Tense	Relax Sleep + drink Fluids
Arguement with Girlfriend		✓	Angry Tense	Calm down Talk it out
Worrying About Homework		✓	Frightened Tense	Calm down Relax and get the work done
Not enough sleep	✓	✓	Fatigued Upset	Make sure I get enough sleep Next time
Planning my weekend		✓	Tense Fatigued	Calm down, think what I really need to do
Finding a Job		✓	Upset Angry tense	Notice that many people Are out of work

JOURNAL

Which stress theory described in this section makes the most sense to you? Explore your reaction by recording some personal examples or experiences. Comment on some of your stress relief strategies. How effective are they for you?

SUGGESTIONS FOR FURTHER READING

Benson, H. *The Mind/Body Effect*. New York: Simon & Schuster, 1979.

Benson, H., and M. Z. Klipper. *The Relaxation Response*. New York: Morrow, 1976.

Brown, B. *Supermind*. New York: Harper & Row, 1980.

Butler, P. *Talking to Yourself*. New York: Stein and Day, 1981.

Clum, George A. *Coping with Panic: A Drug Free Approach to Dealing with Anxiety Attacks*. Pacific Grove, Calif.: Brooks/Cole, 1990.

Emmons, M. *The Inner Source*. San Luis Obispo, Calif.: Impact, 1978.

Glasser, W. *Positive Addiction*. New York: Harper & Row, 1979.

Green, E., and A. Green. *Beyond Biofeedback*. New York: Delta, 1977.

Hyatt, C., and L. Gottlieb. *When Smart People Fail*. New York: Simon & Schuster, 1987.

Kinser, N. S. *Stress and the American Woman*. New York: Ballantine Books, 1980.

Martin, R. A., and E. Y. Pollard, *Learning to Change*. New York: McGraw-Hill, 1980.

Otis, C. L., and R. Goldingay. *Campus Health Guide*. New York: College Entrance Examination Board, 1989.

Pelletier, K. *Mind as Healer/Mind as Slayer*. New York: Delta, 1977.

Pennebaker, James W. *Opening Up: The Healing Power of Confiding in Others*. New York: William Morrow, 1990.

Powell, Trevor J. *Anxiety and Stress Management*. New York: Routledge, 1990.

Rice, Phillip L. *Stress and Health: Principles and Practice for Coping and Wellness*, 2nd ed. Pacific Grove, Calif.: Brooks/Cole, 1992.

Smith, Jonathan C. *Stress Scripting: A Guide to Stress Management*. New York: Praeger, 1991.

Sutherland, Valerie J., and Cary L. Cooper. *Understanding Stress*. New York: Chapman & Hall, 1990.

Vorst, J. *Necessary Losses*. New York: Fawcett, 1986.

AFTERWORD ▼▼▼▼▼▼▼▼▼▼▼▼▼▼▼▼▼

Although This Is the End, It Isn't Over

If you're excited about how far you've moved up the ladder toward self-sufficiency during this first term or first year, we believe you're going to like what happens to you during the next few years even more.

Just think. If you're not already taking classes in your major field of study, you soon will be, along with enrichment courses in the liberal arts and sciences. At some point, you will begin to recognize how all learning is related, and from that understanding will blossom the critical thinking, creative, and communication skills that can prepare you for the "real world," as some would call it.

But think about this also: Isn't your college experience part of your "real world," too? Keep that in mind and make every class, every activity, and every opportunity for a meaningful relationship count during these years. As a result, you will acquire the skills and knowledge that form the basis for making meaningful changes in your future as well as in the future of others.

We hope this book has helped you understand the value of college. If we've done a good job, we'd like to hear from you. If we've missed something important, we need to know that as well, so that the next edition will be better. Drop us a line (or use the tearsheet at the back of the book) % Wadsworth Publishing Company, 10 Davis Drive, Belmont, California 94002. We'll answer your letter and let you know we're listening.

Finally, we hope you will put this book in a safe place once the course is over. Like any good reference tool, it may come to the rescue more than once as you make your way through college. We know we speak for all our contributors in wishing you the best during this exciting and meaningful period of your life.

John N. Gardner
A. Jerome Jewler

How to Read Your College Catalog

MARY STUART HUNTER *is a co-director of the University 101 freshman program at the University of South Carolina, Columbia.*

"In the fifteen years I have worked with college students," she says, "I have learned to appreciate just how empowering information can be. I find that the more students know about their institution, the more comfortable they are as students and the more successful they are throughout their college careers. This has caused me to encourage all students to learn as much as they can about the colleges they have chosen — by asking for information and not being satisfied until they get it."

College catalogs and bulletins were probably an excellent resource for you when you were choosing which college to attend. Now that the decision has been made, you may be inclined to leave your institution's catalog on a shelf to gather dust or even toss it in the trash, thinking it's no longer needed. Don't.

Suppose, like many of your fellow students, you decided to invest in a personal computer to help you through college. Once you've purchased that complex and expensive machine, you certainly wouldn't throw away the user's manual that came with it. College is also complex and expensive, and the college catalog is really a sort of user's manual for your institution. Learn what's in your catalog — it should be a valuable resource throughout your college years.

WHAT'S IN THE CATALOG?

First and foremost, the catalog is the official publication of your institution and contains valuable information about it: regulations, requirements, procedures, and opportunities for your development as a student. While the catalog doesn't contain *everything* students need to know, it does provide an excellent summary of critical information available in greater detail elsewhere on your campus. The style of catalogs varies, but most provide you with the following information.

Publication Date

Most college catalogs are published yearly; some are published twice a year. The publication date is generally shown on the cover. It is important for you to know which catalog was on record when you **matriculated** (that is, enrolled for the first time) rather than when you applied for admission, because you are subject to the rules and regulations that were in effect when you matriculated.

Colleges and universities are constantly changing admissions standards, degree requirements, academic calendars, and so on. But the catalog in use at the time of your matriculation will generally stand as your individual "contract" with the institution. This constancy is to your benefit. Imagine the chaos if you had to adjust to a new set of degree requirements with each new yearly catalog! The catalog in effect at your matriculation is the one that defines the requirements for your degree, unless it states a time limit to complete the degree under those requirements.

General Information

The introductory information in the catalog usually stresses an institution's unique characteristics, mission, and educational philosophy. While philosophies and mission statements are sometimes discounted as unimportant, in reality they may determine whether or not you will find a good "fit" at the institution. For example, if you are interested in a broad liberal arts education, you might think twice about enrolling in a school that stresses business and engineering. Likewise, if engineering or computer technology are your areas, you may want to think again about the fit of a small liberal arts college.

Opening sections of the catalog frequently also list the governing officers and officials, describe the physical plant and facilities, recount a brief history of the school, and state its current **accreditations** (accredited institutions and programs are those that have met specific national standards). Accreditation is important because it assures you that a program is of an acceptable quality. Future employers and graduate school admissions officers pay special attention to the accreditation status of undergraduate schools.

Admissions Information

College catalogs serve many purposes, including student recruitment. So there is almost always admissions information in the catalog. This section will list the various categories of admissions and specify admissions procedures, application deadlines, and criteria for admissions decisions.

General Academic Regulations

General academic regulations include requirements, procedures, and policies that are applicable to all students regardless of individual majors or student classifications. Fully understanding and complying with these rules will help you progress through your academic years without running into roadblocks.

Academic regulations are often distorted or misinterpreted by undergraduates. To be fully and accurately informed, don't rely on second-hand, "grapevine" knowledge. Become familiar with these rules directly from the catalog.

The regulations section outlines the institution's **core courses** (courses that all undergraduates must take) and enrollment and registration procedures. It also explains the grading system, course credit options, grade point average calculation, and academic suspension system and describes academic honors and graduation requirements as they apply to students throughout the school. It may also detail students' rights, including the confidentiality of student records and the right to appeal or petition for relief from certain academic regulations.

General Nonacademic Information

College catalogs nearly always include a useful section on student life at the institution. Out-of-classroom activities should certainly be an integral part of your development and education. This section may list student clubs, campus interest groups, organizations, programs, and facilities.

Financial Information

Your catalog may also discuss the current costs of attending your institution: academic fee schedules, costs of various housing options, prices of meal plans, and outlines of fines, refund policies, and payment options. Government-assisted schools also include rules for resident and nonresident status and resulting fee differentials.

The high cost of a college education concerns most students, as it does most college administrators. Not only may cost have affected your choice of a school, but costs will probably continue to rise throughout your years in college. But the financial section may have good news for you: detailed information on financial aid, scholarships, loans, and work opportunities. Study this section for sources of financial help.

Academic Calendar

Every college catalog includes a current academic calendar, which states the beginning and ending dates of the academic terms as well as dates of holidays and other events within each term. Being familiar with the calendar in advance will help you make sound decisions. For example, if you are not doing well in a particular class, you may want to drop the course rather than receive a failing grade, but you must do so before the deadline for withdrawal. To facilitate general planning, some catalogs give the academic calendars for several years in advance.

Academic Program

By far the lengthiest part of most catalogs is the section on academic programs. This summarizes the various degrees offered, the majors within each department, and the requirements for studying in each discipline. The departmental outlines include most of the information that is unique to each department, supplementing any institution-wide rules and regulations. They also list any special admissions criteria for special programs, as well as the progression, curriculum, and degree requirements.

The academic program section also describes the individual courses offered at your institution. Basic information usually includes course number, course title, units of credit, prerequisites for taking the course, and a very brief overview of the course content.

Remember, the catalog is only a *summary* of information. Individual department offices frequently offer more detailed information in the form of course descriptions, curriculum checklists, departmental advisement guidelines, and so on. Your academic advisor may also have such supplemental information.

The Faculty

Catalogs usually list the faculty, along with their academic degrees and other credentials. This information may appear in the academic program section. You can often measure the strength of a department by the strength of its faculty credentials. You can also learn about the backgrounds of teachers whose courses you are considering taking.

FINDING, KEEPING, AND USING YOUR CATALOG

Where should you go to find your matriculation catalog, or the subsequent catalog you may need to plan your yearly program? If you have not already received it, check first with your advisor. If your advisor does not have a copy for you, contact the admissions office, the registration office, or the department office of your academic major.

Your catalog should be the key item in a file that you keep throughout your college years. Other items to include in the file are your grade reports, advisement forms, fee payment receipts, schedule change forms, and other proof of financial and academic dealings with your institution. Retain all these things until your diploma is framed and hanging on the wall.

Why is it so important to keep all these forms and receipts? When you apply for graduation, your department will conduct what is frequently called a *senior check, degree audit, senior audit,* or *graduation check.* This process involves comparing your transcript with the academic requirements for the degree you are seeking. Any discrepancy between what you present as your academic record and the requirements in the catalog must be reconciled. Should university records be incomplete or inaccurate, your own file might make a difference in your favor.

Your catalog is but one of many resources that will be valuable to you throughout college. Along with other handbooks and guidelines, it can answer many questions. Use it alongside your telephone directory, your dictionary, and your thesaurus as an indispensable college resource.

APPENDIX B ▼▼▼▼▼▼▼▼▼▼▼▼▼▼▼▼▼▼

How to Manage Your Money and Obtain Financial Aid

RAY EDWARDS *is director of student financial aid at East Carolina University, Greenville, North Carolina.*

"Because I teach freshmen, I know that many of them are not prepared to deal with the financial aspects of paying for college," he says. "Instead they leave it to mom and dad. That's neither helpful nor necessary. Finding sources of financial aid and managing your money both require effort. I hope the techniques I discuss here will make it easier for you to take charge of your finances, so you don't find your semester lasting longer than your money!"

If you are like most college freshmen, an overabundance of money is not your problem. However much of it you have, when you are in control of your money, you can eliminate financial worries and focus your energies on getting the best education possible. Most likely you'll also be able to afford a bit of enjoyment, too.

SOME BASIC MISCONCEPTIONS

Perhaps you suffer from one or more of the following misconceptions about the management of money.

► *Misconception 1.* Financial management is a magical process known only by a few wizards. (The truth is, there's nothing mysterious about it. Financial management is a skill that you can certainly learn if you have been able to get into college.)

► *Misconception 2.* In order to *manage* money, you need a lot more of it. Otherwise what is there to manage? (Actually it is probably more important to manage your money well when you don't have much than it is when you have money to burn.)

► *Misconception 3.* If you have enough money, you don't need to worry about how you spend it. (As a first-year student you may be handling your own finances for the first time now — paying for your room and board, buying expensive books, and so on — and you may feel that you have more money than you need. Nevertheless you need to keep track of where that money is going.)

► *Misconception 4.* You can keep track of your personal finances just by balancing your checkbook. (Balancing your checkbook is certainly important, but it has little value in relation to planning for your financial needs.)

Fortunately money management represents nothing more than the application of common sense, planning, and self-discipline — applying some simple techniques in an organized, logical way. If you learn these techniques and apply them, you will stay on top of your finances.

THE MONEY-MANAGING PROCESS

Money management boils down to three primary activities: analysis, planning, and budgeting.

Analysis

Analyze your finances by identifying and comparing your expenses with your resources. Unless you know what your costs are and how much you have available, you are not going to be in control of anything. Think in terms of the academic year (August or September through May or June).

Expenses. Start by making a list of all the expenses you can think of, under two main categories of costs: educational and noneducational. *Educational expenses* are those you incur because you are a student, including tuition, fees, books, supplies, lab equipment, and so on. *Noneducational expenses* include all your other costs: housing, food, transportation, and miscellaneous and personal needs.

Be especially careful as you identify noneducational expenses because these costs are often hard to estimate. For example, it is easy to determine how much your tuition and fees are going to be (you need only consult your institution's published schedule of costs), but it is not so easy to estimate utility bills or food and transportation costs. Be as methodical as you can. If you are careless, you may end up being "nickeled and dimed to debt."

Table B.1 shows most of the types of costs you will face. If you have other expenses, add them to the list.

Resources. Next, identify your resources. Again list your sources of financial support by category (savings, part-time work, financial aid, parents, and so on). Be realistic — neither overly optimistic nor too pessimistic — about your resources. Table B.2 lists some common types of student monetary support. List any additional sources.

Comparing Expenses to Resources. Once you have identified your expenses and resources, compare the totals. Remember that this is a tentative tally, not a final evaluation. This is especially important to note if your costs exceed your resources.

To bring your finances in focus, you must now complete the third step of your analysis: setting priorities and revising. To do this, classify your expenses as fixed or flexible. *Fixed expenses* are those over which you have no control; *flexible expenses* are those you can modify (flexible does not usually mean completely avoidable). Tuition, fees, and freshman dormitory costs are generally fixed, since the institution requires you to pay specific amounts. Food may be fixed or flexible, depending on whether you are paying for a residential board plan or cooking on your own.

Table B.3 shows some typical freshman costs divided into fixed and flexible expenses. The flexible expenses are listed in order of importance.

If the total of your expenses exceeds the total of your costs, you can start revising your flexible costs, such as telephone, clothing, and entertainment. Although cutting wardrobe and entertainment costs may be less than enjoyable, good money management means maintaining control and being realistic.

Table B.1 Identifying Expenses (academic year)

Educational Costs

Tuition	$ 800
Fees	$1,200
Books	$ 325
Supplies	$ 75
Subtotal educational costs	$2,400

Noneducational Costs

Housing	$1,250
Food	$1,500
Personal	$ 100
Phone	$ 120
Transportation	$ 750
Clothing	$ 450
Social/entertainment	$ 360
Savings	$ 250
Subtotal noneducational costs	$4,780
Total educational and noneducational costs	$7,180

Table B.2 Identifying Resources (academic year)

A. Parents	
Cash	$1,000
Credit union loan	$1,500
B. Work	
Summer (savings after expenses)	$1,000
Part-time during year	$1,500
C. Savings	
Parents	$ 0
Your own	$ 150
D. Financial Aid	
Grants	$ 400
Loans	$ 700
Scholarships	$ 0
E. Benefits	
Veterans	$ 0
Other	$ 0
F. Other	
ROTC	$ 900
Relatives	$ 0
Trusts	$ 0
Total	$7,150

Planning

Having analyzed your costs and resources, you now have a good overall perspective on your financial situation. Next you need to plan how you will manage your money. Focus on timing, identifying *when* you will have to pay for various things.

For planning you will need an academic schedule for your school (which probably appears in your college catalog or bulletin) and a calendar, preferably organized on an academic schedule such as August through July. First, review your institution's academic schedule for its overall time frame and specific dates. Determine your school's registration and payment schedules. When is the latest you can pay your housing deposit for living on campus? What is the deadline for tuition and fees? What is the school's refund policy and schedule? Enter these critical dates on your own planning calendar for the entire academic year.

Then turn your attention to other important dates that are not institutionally related. For example, if you pay auto insurance semi-annually, when is your next big premium due?

After you have recorded the important dates of your major expenditures, do the same thing for your revenue. This knowledge is essential for planning, since you can't very well plan *how* you're going to pay for things if you don't know *when* you'll have the money. For example, financial aid is typically disbursed in one lump sum at the beginning of each academic term, whereas paychecks come in smaller, more frequent installments.

Do you have any timing problems? Are there going to be points at which your costs exceed your cash? If there are, you must adjust either when you must pay or when your income will arrive. If you will be a bit strapped paying all of your tuition and fees at the start of the semester, see if your school has an installment plan that will let you stretch out the payments or if you can reschedule semi-annual car insurance premiums as monthly payments.

Table B.3 Expense Priorities (academic year)

Fixed Expenses

Tuition	$ 800
Fees	$1,200
Books	$ 325
Supplies	$ 75
Housing	$1,250
Subtotal fixed expenses	$3,650

Flexible Expenses

Food	$1,500
Transportation	$ 700
Clothing	$ 450
Personal	$ 100
Phone	$ 120
Social/entertainment	$ 360
Savings	$ 250
Subtotal flexible expenses	$3,530
Total fixed and flexible expenses	$7,180

Table B.4 Sample Monthly Budget (September)

Resources

Summer savings	$1,000
Parents	$ 750
Financial aid	$ 500
ROTC	$ 100
Part-time job	$ 166
Total	$2,516

Fixed Expenses

Tuition and fees	$1,000
Books	$ 175
Dorm room	$ 625
Total	$1,800

Flexible Expenses

Food (meal cash card)	$150
Supplies	$35
Personal	$35
Phone	$15
Transportation	$10
Social	$40
Total	$285

Summary

Total resources	$2,516
Less total expenses	$2,085
Less savings	$ 50
Balance	$ 381*

*Carried forward to October.

Once you have determined the critical dates of income and expenses, planning becomes very simple. But keep in mind that most significant of all planning destroyers, the dreaded Murphy's law: If something can go wrong, it will — and at the worst moment. For example, you might leave the cap off your car's radiator and accidentally crack the engine block. Or a roommate might suddenly split for Bali, leaving you to pay extra rent.

How can you prepare for and minimize the damage caused by unscheduled calamities? Frankly you can't do everything, but you can prepare to some extent by being emotionally ready to deal with such things when they happen, by building up an emergency fund (even a small one), and by not departing from your money management plan. These principles are not only important for you now, they are also good habits to follow throughout your life.

Having completed the process of planning your expenditures, you should feel much more in control of your finances. Being totally aware of where you are will alleviate much potential stress.

Budgeting

The last step in developing a sound money management plan is budgeting. Budgeting takes self-discipline. Develop both a monthly budget and an academic year budget.

The budgeting process overlaps with the financial planning you did when you identified the timing of your "big ticket" items and income. The academic year budget transforms what you have on your academic calendar into a scheme that also includes your smaller, less dramatic, ongoing expenses.

The monthly budget is a specific plan for each month's income and outgo — the final details necessary to make your management system work. It eliminates any confusion about what you must do in the near future, within a manageable block of time. It is also your method for continual control over your finances. Since it coincides with the cycle of your checking account, it also facilitates monthly balancing and scheduling.

To develop your monthly budget, put your expenses and income together onto one sheet, as shown in Table B.4 on p. A9. After listing your fixed expenses, your flexible expenses, and your resources, subtract expenses from resources to create a summary for the month. Settle your fixed outlays, and revise the flexible ones as necessary to achieve a reasonable balance. The September budget shown in the chart happens to include the major "start-up" costs for tuition, fees, and so on. Make sure your budget is comprehensive and keeps track of how you spend what you spend.

Financial worries can be stress-inducing, but you can minimize this stress by analyzing, planning, and budgeting well. Good money management supports your total health and well-being.

The way you handle your money in college says a lot about how you approach life in general. When you manage your personal finances well, you are facing up to realities that will confront you for the rest of your life. Developing the required seriousness and skill will continue to pay off long after you have finished college.

COLLEGE COSTS IN PERSPECTIVE

Once you're doing everything to manage your current finances well, you may still need more money. How you acquire additional financial aid has both immediate and long-term implications. Even if you're fortunate enough to have parents helping you through college, don't leave the problem up to them. Paying for college is a major undertaking that should be shared. Most parents will make whatever sacrifices are necessary, within their means, to help their children go to college. Not all students should work while they are in college, but most students find ways to pay at least part of their college expenses, and a large majority work at least part-time.

Over the past fifteen years inflation has eroded the savings of many families. In fact the United States currently has one of the lowest percentages of per capita savings among industrialized countries. Most American families today are not paying for their children's college education out of savings. Because of this, and because the price of a college education has risen sharply over the same period, most students must now rely mainly on their family's current income and loans to finance college.

Such overreliance on current income and loans has been harmful to parents and their student/dependents in two ways. First, families are forced to make difficult sacrifices. Second, the repayment "legacy" of educational loans often extends long after the student has finished college.

For their part colleges and universities have been caught by the same economic forces as families, and college expenses over the past fifteen years have risen faster than the overall inflation rate. It simply costs more each year for schools to provide the same level of service. Both public and private colleges have had little choice but to increase fees, and you will likely have to pay more each year you are in college.

The annual cost of an education at a public four-year institution averages between $5,000 and $11,000, depending on whether the student officially resides in-state or out-of-state. Most students graduate in about four-and-a-half to five years (not in the formerly "traditional" four years). Thus a typical college degree at a public four-year school costs from $23,000 to $52,000. At private institutions, where the average annual expenses range from $10,000 to $15,000, the total is even more dramatic — from $47,000 to $72,000 — and at the most prestigious schools it is even higher. For most American families today, financing a college education is an investment challenge second only to purchasing a home.

If you are going to be able to deal with your college expenses, it is essential that you see them realistically. Only by knowing how much your education is going to cost can you go about planning how to pay for it. If it is clear that you and/or your family cannot handle all of the costs, you should certainly apply for financial aid.

TYPES OF FINANCIAL AID

Financial aid refers to any type of funding you receive to assist yourself in paying for college. Most financial aid money is given on the basis of need, often according to "demonstrated financial need." **Demonstrated financial**

need is eligibility determined by some specific financial scale, most commonly the federal needs analysis system called the congressional methodology. Other types of financial aid awards may not depend on this type of eligibility.

Financial aid is categorized as either gift or self-help assistance. **Gift assistance** is that which does not have to be repaid. **Self-help assistance** requires you to do something in return, such as work or repay the money. An academic scholarship is gift assistance; a student loan is self-help assistance.

The basis upon which financial aid is awarded varies, but typical criteria are academic merit, financial need, or some combination of the two. The large federal aid programs and most state programs are based on financial need and acceptable progress toward a degree.

Financial aid can be further categorized into two types of gift assistance — grants and scholarships — and two types of self-help assistance — loans and work opportunities.

Grants

Grants are gift assistance and so do not have to be repaid. Most institutions offer numerous grants programs, the largest funded by the federal and state governments. Generally grants are aimed at students with the greatest demonstrated financial need. Students can often receive more than one type of grant simultaneously, but institutions do place limits on the total amount of grant assistance they will award to any one individual, since such funds are limited. Most schools want to spread grants out among as many students as possible.

Scholarships

Scholarships are awarded on the basis of superior academic achievement or merit, although financial need may also be a criterion. Most colleges and universities have scholarships for incoming freshmen as well as for students in the upper years. Thousands of scholarships are also available from hundreds of national foundations, organizations, state and federal agencies, businesses, corporations, churches, and civic clubs.

The best way to find scholarship opportunities is to start with your institution and work your way out. Check the availability of scholarships from groups and organizations in your home region. Review information from the primary education-related agency or organization in your state. Go to the library or financial aid office at your school to ask for assistance and to review publications listing scholarships. Our best advice is, *ask, ask, ask.*

Loans

In the past decade long-term, low-interest educational **loans** have become the major means for financing college. There are a number of public and private student loan programs, most of which allow extended repayment periods (up to ten years, depending on the amount borrowed) and very reasonable rates (5–10 percent). Though the practice is not recommended unless absolutely necessary, it is possible to receive assistance from more than one loan program at a time.

The large federal student loan programs are based primarily on need. In addition to student loans there is also a federally sponsored loan program for parents that does not require demonstrated need. The interest rate for

A Caution About Loans

Student loans are an extremely valuable component of the total financial aid picture, but it is important to remember that they are exactly what they are called: loans. They must be repaid. Failure to repay a student loan can have very negative consequences, including damaged credit, garnishment of wages, confiscation of income tax refunds, and litigation. Be very careful in assuming loan indebtedness during college, since a sizable monthly loan repayment can become a heavy burden. Take out student loans only to the extent that they are absolutely necessary for you to stay in school. Keep track of exactly how much you have borrowed as you go. Otherwise the student loan that seems like such a boon now may be a tremendous bane later.

this program can be as high as 12 percent, and repayment generally begins shortly after the loan is made. This program has become popular among parents whose dependents do not qualify for need-based aid.

Work Opportunities

Part-time work is a valuable type of self-help aid. The College Work–Study Program is a federal student aid program based on need that lets you earn some of the aid for which you may be eligible through employment, generally on campus. In addition many schools have their own programs through which students earn money or in-kind support such as board. This type of assistance has two advantages. First, you are not indebted after graduation. Second, you may be able to work in areas related to your major, thereby gaining an edge in later job hunting.

Contrary to some opinion, a reasonable amount of part-time work does not interfere with the academic performance of most working students. Indeed some national studies have indicated just the opposite effect, because students who work must be more self-disciplined and must manage their time and energies more wisely.

Cooperative education programs are another great opportunity for students at many institutions. These programs provide employment off campus in public and private agencies, business, and industry. Work may parallel education (part-time course load, part-time work) or alternate with it (full-time study one term, full-time work the next). This type of experience can also be invaluable when you look for that first job after graduation. Many graduates are offered permanent, full-time positions as a result of co-op experience.

THE FINANCIAL AID PROCESS

Unfortunately, where there is money, there is bureaucracy. Consequently you are going to have to deal with red tape — sometimes a great deal of it. This may be frustrating, but remember that the potential payoff can be well worth the aggravation. Be prepared to fill out forms.

The largest financial aid programs are those based upon need and regulated by state and/or federal agencies. For these, most institutions require at least two basic documents: a needs analysis document and an institutional application/information form. Another routine financial aid form is the scholarship application. Such forms vary widely depending on the scholarship sought and the organization awarding it, but they usually gather information about past performance, honors, leadership, and so on.

The Needs Analysis Document

The term **needs analysis** is sometimes used to refer to the general process of analyzing a student's financial resources in order to determine whether the student needs any further assistance to attend college. Frequently, however, it refers specifically to the federal system called the congressional methodology. This system, established by the U.S. Congress, provides a consistent national standard for deciding who will get federal financial aid. Because it is an extremely complex and sophisticated method for allocating limited financial aid resources, it really doesn't determine an individual's "need" in the pure sense, but merely one's eligibility. Of course need is relative. How much help a student or family may feel they need in order to send someone to college depends on many subjective opinions and feelings. At best needs analysis is simply a relative measure comparing a given family's ability to pay for a college education with that of other families.

In order to operate this system, the federal government requires certain basic information for determining a student's eligibility, and all students must provide this information on a needs analysis document. A variety of such forms are in use nationally, each provided and processed by a different processing agency. You must submit some form of the needs analysis document in order to apply for federal student aid. Before you fill one out, however, check with the financial aid office at your school to determine which version of the form it accepts or prefers.

The Institutional Application/Information Form

Many institutions have their own financial aid forms in addition to the needs analysis document. These forms typically ask for different information than is requested in the needs analysis.

Applying for Financial Aid

When you apply for financial aid, remember to do the following:

1. *Plan ahead.* Planning is critical. Find out what is available at your institution, how to go about applying, and when you must apply. You also need to determine what information will be required and allow for the time it may take you to gather that information.

2. *Allow sufficient time for the process to work.* The financial aid application process is often slow, taking several weeks to several months, depending on the type of aid you are applying for, your school's application volume, processing mechanisms, and the time of year. (Summer is the peak season, so allow extra time in the summer.) After you have submitted your initial application, you may be asked to provide addi-

tional information to support or clarify it. Be prepared to do this promptly and to experience further delay.

3. *Keep copies of everything.* Maintain a file with copies of everything you complete or send regarding your application for aid, including the date it was completed or sent. This will help you avoid confusion and/or costly delays due to miscommunication or things getting lost in the mail.

You are responsible for helping to finance your college education. Aside from working, whether from necessity or desire, to help earn some of what you need, you can contribute in two other ways.

First, you can stretch your dollars. Be as frugal as possible in areas where you can be flexible, such as personal expenses. Think twice before you spend your money. Is what you're spending it on necessary, or can you live without it? Budget and manage your money wisely.

Second, you can be serious about your college education. By applying yourself to the best of your abilities, managing your time wisely, keeping up in your classes, and, above all else, not having to repeat courses because of poor grades, you will get the most value possible for your investment. By going about your college education with dedication and focus, you will save both time and money.

SUGGESTIONS FOR FURTHER READING

Adams, Janelle P., ed. *College Check Mate: Innovative Tuition Plans That Make You a Winner.* Alexandria, Va.: Octameron Associates. Published yearly.

———. *The A's and B's of Academic Scholarships.* Alexandria, Va.: Octameron Associates. Published yearly.

The College Cost Book. Princeton, N.J.: College Scholarship Service of the College Board. Published yearly.

College Planning/Search Book. Iowa City, Iowa: American College Testing Program. Published yearly.

Directory of Special Programs for Minority Group Members, 4th ed. Garrett Park, Md.: Garrett Park Press, 1986.

Earn and Learn: Cooperative Education Opportunities with the Federal Government. Alexandria, Va.: Octameron Associates. Published yearly.

Feingold, S., and M. Feingold. *Scholarships, Fellowships, and Loans,* Vol. 8. Arlington, Mass.: Bellman, 1987.

Financial Aid Fin-Ancer: Expert Answers to College Financing Questions. Alexandria, Va.: Octameron Associates. Published yearly.

Guide for Students and Parents. Iowa City, Iowa: American College Testing Program Need Analysis Service. Published yearly.

Keesler, Oreon. *Financial Aids for Higher Education,* 4th ed. Dubuque, Iowa: Brown, 1991.

Kennedy, Joyce, and Herm Davis. *The College Financial Aid Emergency Kit.* Cardiff, Calif.: Sun Features. Published yearly.

Lovejoy's College Guide. Red Bank, N.J.: Lovejoy's College Guide. Published yearly.

Mohr, Lillian H. *Fiscal Fitness for Students: How to Have Paying Power.* Tallahassee, Fla.: Florida State University Press, 1986.

Need a Lift? Indianapolis, Ind.: American Legion, National Emblem Sales. Published yearly.

Schlacter, Gail A. *Directory of Financial Aids for Women.* Santa Barbara, Calif.: Reference Service Press, 1991.

Schlacter, Gail A., and Sandra E. Goldstein. *Directory of Financial Aids for Minorities.* Santa Barbara, Calif.: Reference Service Press, 1989.

Student Consumer Guide. Washington, D.C.: Government Printing Office. Published yearly.

G L O S S A R Y ▼▼▼▼▼▼▼▼▼▼▼▼▼▼▼▼▼

Mary Stuart Hunter
Co-Director, University 101
University of South Carolina, Columbia

In addition to the terms boldfaced in the text, this glossary defines a number of terms that you may encounter in the college environment.

Academic advisor Colleges have many people who carry the title of advisor or counselor. Your academic advisor may be a faculty member in the academic field you've chosen or a full-time administrative employee who works in a counseling office of the school. You'll be assigned an advisor once you begin college. While academic advisors will help you plan your college schedule or choose a major, they can also offer much more. Ask about anything that concerns you, and you may save both time and money.

Academic freedom The ability of faculty and students to pursue whatever inquiry they wish without undue external influence and to speak about it in classrooms without fear of censorship. It can also be described as the open search for truth, honesty, collegiality, and civility, as well as a tolerance for dissenting views.

Academic program See **Degree program**.

Accreditation Colleges and universities are judged, or accredited, either by an organization of other colleges and universities or by professional organizations. Accrediting teams visit on a regular basis and judge schools on faculty, degrees offered, library facilities, laboratories, other facilities, and finances. Southern schools are accredited by the Southern Association of Colleges and Schools. A law school may be accredited by the American Bar Association. A college of business may be accredited by the American Association of Collegiate Schools of Business, and colleges of communications or

journalism may be accredited by the Association for Education in Journalism and Mass Communications. Accredited schools and programs are usually the best of their kind and are recognized as such by many future employers.

Active listening A process whereby the recipient of spoken communication becomes actively involved in the transfer of information through note-taking, questions, and appropriate responses of affirmation. Active listeners hear with their minds in addition to their ears.

Aggressive behavior Behaving in a manner that puts others down; demanding, pressuring, intimidating.

AIDS Acquired immune deficiency syndrome; a sexually transmitted disease for which there is currently no known cure. As the disease progresses, it gradually breaks down the body's immune system and thus lowers its defense mechanisms, making it impossible for the body to function normally or properly.

Alumnus A graduate of a college or university. Schools have alumni offices, which may ask you for money or other support after you graduate.

Arts The academic disciplines that explore and represent human thought and behavior in creative works. Creating works of art is a way of both coming to understand and expressing ideas and feelings.

Assertive behavior Behavior that is clear, direct, respectful, and responsible; behavior that permits a person to stand up for his or her rights without denying others their rights.

Assistant professor See **Professor**.

Associate degree A two-year degree, in the arts or in science (A.A. or A.S.). Many associate degree programs are offered at community and junior colleges and at technical schools, but many large universities also offer such programs. Just because you earn an associate degree does not mean you're halfway toward a bachelor's degree. Some states have agreements (called "articulation agreements") that require state colleges and universities to accept all or most classes satisfactorily completed toward an associate degree and to count those credits toward a bachelor's degree.

Associate professor See **Professor**.

Bachelor's degree The formal name for a four-year college degree. Two major types are the Bachelor of Arts (B.A.) and Bachelor of Science (B.S.). Requirements for these degrees vary depending on the standards of the school or college.

Board plan A meal plan that you may have an opportunity to purchase while enrolled as a student. It tends to be less expensive than buying meals individually as it offers a "package deal" on a certain number of meals at a discounted price.

Bookstore More than a place that sells textbooks, a college bookstore may also sell running shorts, pens and pencils, greeting cards, and a host of other items. Be certain you purchase the proper edition of required texts, and see if used copies are available at a reduced price. Always keep your book receipt, and do not mark in the book until you're sure you'll keep it, or you may have trouble obtaining a refund. Bookstores are usually located in student centers or college/university unions.

Bribery A form of academic misconduct that involves trading something of value for any kind of academic advantage.

Bulletin See **Catalog**.

Cafeteria or **dining hall** These terms mean the same thing on some campuses but different things on others. The dining hall may be a part of a dormitory, and your food may be already paid for if you purchased a meal card or board plan. In a cafeteria you pay for each item you select; it may be located in the student center.

Career counseling/planning Most campuses began offering this service in the 1970s because students saw a direct relationship between what they were studying in college and the job market. Students wanted to know where the jobs were and what they needed to achieve to be eligible for them. Career planning services include, but are not limited to, self-assessment and interest tests, job search workshops, decision-making workshops, and resume workshops. These services are usually located in counseling centers, student affairs offices, or placement offices.

Carrel A study room or numbered desk and chair in the college library that can be assigned to students. You must request a carrel from the college librarian; however, not everyone is eligible for one.

Catalog The official publication of the institution containing information about its regulations, requirements, and procedures, as well as opportunities for growth as a college student. It focuses on general information, admissions information, general academic regulations, general nonacademic information, financial information, and academic programs and includes an academic calendar. In Canada the catalog is called a calendar.

Chancellor Title given to a high academic officer at some colleges and universities. The chancellor is usually the chief executive officer of a campus or a collection of campuses.

Cheating A form of academic misconduct that involves using unauthorized assistance of any kind during an academic exercise.

Class standing Most colleges link your standing to the number of hours you've earned, not the number of years you've attended school. A freshman is working to complete the first one-fourth of college work. A sophomore is in the second fourth. A junior has passed the halfway point, and a senior has three-fourths of his or her requirements completed. This practice applies to students on the quarter and semester systems in four-year undergraduate programs. See also **Quarter system** and **Semester system**.

CLEP Stands for College Level Examination Program, a series of tests you may take to demonstrate proficiency in various college subjects. If you pass the test, you will earn credit for certain college courses. CLEP subject exams cover individual courses, such as Introductory Psychology; CLEP general exams incorporate several courses, such as the one for social studies. Be aware that some colleges will accept CLEP subject exams, but not general exams. CLEP tests are usually administered through the college testing office. You can also obtain information about CLEP tests from your admissions office and/or your advisor.

Co-curricular A word describing activities, clubs, or organizations you may join and participate in, above and beyond your academic courses. Such activities provide fun and friends and also look good on your resume, but keep in mind that some are more valuable than others. Ask a counselor for advice, since certain activities may lead you into career choices. Activities include student government, student media, clubs, volunteer work, and faculty/student committees.

Coeducational A school that admits men and women. Most colleges are coeducational. Some schools have coeducational residence halls where men and women live in the same building, but not in the same room.

Cognate A group of courses related to a student's major and approved by his or her advisor. Such courses are required for graduation at many colleges. Cognates are junior- and senior-level courses. Colleges that don't require a cognate may require a minor. See also **Minor**.

Commencement A ceremony in which colleges award degrees to graduating students. Some schools hold two or three commencements annually, but the largest ones are held in May or early June.

Communication skills Oral and writing skills that are extremely important for effective communication in any work or social setting; the ability to write and speak clearly and effectively.

Community college A two-year college; may also be known as a junior college or technical school. These colleges award associate degrees, and technical colleges may offer other types of degrees or certificates as well.

Be certain that the community college you select is accredited, and remember that there's no guarantee that all courses you take at a two-year college will transfer to a four-year college or university.

Commuting students Represent about four out of five college students on American college and university campuses today. They live off campus and have to commute, or travel, to campus each day.

Comprehensive examination Some schools use this term to describe final exams, which are given during the last days of the term. The word *comprehensive* means that all material covered during the term may be included on the exam. Graduate students may also take comprehensive exams to earn the master's or doctoral degree.

Computation skills Quantitative, or mathematical, skills.

Continuing education Over the years the meaning of this term has changed. Some schools may still refer to such programs as "adult education." Continuing education programs enable the nontraditional college student to take classes without having to be admitted as a degree candidate. While continuing education students may take college courses for credit, some colleges have established noncredit learning programs under this name.

Cooperative education program Provides students with an opportunity to work off campus in public and private agencies, as well as in business and industry, either by parallel scheduling (going to school part-time and working part-time) or alternate scheduling (staying out of school for an academic term and working full-time).

Core courses/distribution requirements/basic requirements/general education These terms all mean the same thing. Colleges require that all students complete specific groups of courses. These courses are usually offered at the freshman and sophomore levels and include English, math, science, history, and other requirements. Since many of these lower-numbered courses must be completed before other courses can be taken, it's wise to complete your core courses as early as possible. See also **Prerequisite**.

Counseling center Counseling is provided by trained professionals at your college. Counselors can help you with various adjustment problems and may refer you to other services. There are many types of counselors; you'll find them in the following offices: admissions, financial aid, residence halls, career planning, placement, veterans' affairs, study skills, academic advising, and counseling. Counselors treat in confidence whatever you tell them. Once you determine that you need some type of counseling, seek it out — your tuition is paying for it.

Course number Different colleges number their courses in different ways. Most undergraduates take courses at the 100 level through at least the 400 level, but this will vary on different campuses. Graduate-level courses carry higher numbers. The 100-level courses are usually survey courses introducing that subject, while upper-level courses may spend an entire term covering a narrower topic in more detail. Some 100-level courses must be completed before you can take upper-level work in that subject. Check your catalog and ask your advisor for help.

Credit hour See **Quarter hour**.

Critical thinking Careful observation of a problem or phenomenon followed by thoughtful, organized analysis resulting in a logical, reasoned response that improves our understanding of our world.

Curriculum All courses required for your degree. Some colleges refer to all courses in the catalog as the curriculum, and many schools provide students with curriculum outlines or curriculum sheets in addition to the catalog. These sheets show what courses you must take and may indicate the order in which you must take them. That order is called "course sequencing."

Dean A college administrator who may have been a professor. Some deans are academic deans, which means they head colleges. Some colleges and universities have a dean of student affairs, a dean of business affairs, and a few still have deans of men and of women. The academic dean is a person who oversees your degree program. He or she can grant exceptions to academic policy. The other types of deans are executives who may or may not work directly with students, although most work in student services. Some deans may have associate or assistant deans to help them.

Dean's list If you make high grades, you'll make the dean's list at the end of the term. This academic honor looks good on your resume and on applications for graduate study or employment. See what your school requires for you to make the list, and make it as many times as you can.

Deficiency This word can mean more than one thing. You may be told you have a one-course deficiency that you must make up before graduation or entrance to a particular program. Your grades may be fine, but the deficiency exists as a prerequisite for what you want to do. Deficiency can also mean that your grades are so low that you may not be permitted to return to school.

Degree program All the courses you must take to earn a degree in a specific field. Programs vary greatly. Your academic advisor is a source of information for program requirements.

Demonstrated financial need The eligibility for financial aid you are determined to have by whatever means is used to determine such eligibility; it is most commonly determined through the federal needs analysis system (the congressional methodology).

Department A college is often organized into academic departments. For example, a group of history faculty will develop a curriculum for students studying history. The history department will offer all history courses for every student at the school, including history majors.

Dismissal At most schools dismissal means the same thing as suspension, and you will be told to leave the school for academic or disciplinary reasons. College catalogs explain the circumstances for dismissal, and you should learn these rules and obey them. Dismissal or suspension usually is noted on your official record or transcript, and the requirements to reenter college will vary. See also **Leave of absence** and **Probation**.

Dissertation One of the final requirements for the highest academic degree a student can earn in most fields, the doctorate, or Ph.D. In some fields the dissertation is book length. The graduate student is expected to break new ground in research and must defend her or his dissertation before a faculty committee. See also **Graduate student**.

Diversity A reference to the growing variety of today's college student bodies, which include men, women, minorities, foreign students, and other groups that have never been so well represented on college campuses.

Doctoral degree Requires additional years of study beyond the bachelor's and/or master's degrees; is rewarded upon successful completion of course work, the dissertation, and orals. Most of your professors probably have a Ph.D. (doctor of philosophy); other types, including the M.D. (medical doctor) and J.D. (doctor of jurisprudence) also require extensive study.

Dormitories See **Residence hall**.

Drop Most colleges allow students to drop courses without penalty during specified periods of time. Dropping a course can be dangerous if you don't know the proper procedures, since you'll need to complete certain forms and obtain official signatures. If you're receiving financial aid, your status may change if you drop a course. Finally, dropping courses certainly will affect your graduation date.

Electives Students who say, "I think I'll take an elective course," may think that electives differ from other course requirements. This is only partially true because electives are required for most college degrees. An elective is a course you may select from an academic area of interest to you. The course will not count in your core, major, or minor/cognate. Each college decides the number of electives you may take, and you may take them at any time. Ask your advisor if he or she recommends that you complete core courses before choosing electives.

Evaluation of courses See **Validation of credits**.

Exchange program One of several options that may be available at your college or university that will enable you to broaden your academic experience by attending another college or university for a specific time period at the same cost and for the same credits as spent and earned, respectively, at your own institution.

Extracurricular See **Co-curricular**.

Fabrication A form of academic misconduct that involves intentionally inventing information or results in the course of academic work.

Faculty All the teachers at your college. The names of faculty positions and the ranks held by individuals will vary. See also **Professor**.

Fees At most colleges fees are required costs in addition to tuition. Fees may be charged for housing, health care, labs, parking, and many other things. Most college catalogs give a good idea of what fees you'll have to pay and when you must pay them. See also **Tuition**.

Final exams Some schools call them comprehensive exams and hold them during an examination week, a period when your instructors may find out how much you've learned from them. Most finals are written rather than oral. Professors usually tell students about finals near the beginning of the term; however, not all professors require them. A final may count as much as one-half of your grade, or it could count much less. Some schools may also schedule midterm exams.

Financial aid A complicated subject in recent years. Most colleges have a financial aid office to provide information to students on scholarships, grants, and loans. Some forms of financial aid are gifts, but others are loans that must be repaid with interest. Some aid is offered only to new freshmen while other sources of financial aid are available to all students. Many grants and loans are provided through federal government assistance; government regulations control this money. To determine your eligibility for any aid, see your financial aid counselor as early as you can. The application process for financial aid for a fall semester usually begins during the preceding January.

Fraternity See **Greeks**.

Full-time student Students enrolled for a specified number of hours, such as 12 semester hours or more. At most schools part-time students receive the same benefits as full-time students. At others part-time students may receive limited health care and no athletic tickets. Ask your advisor about the advantages of going full-time, but remember, if you must work, raise a family, or handle other obligations, a part-time program may be the more sensible one to pursue.

Gender-balanced curriculum A curriculum that includes information about women equivalent to the quality and quantity of information traditionally included about white men.

Gender referencing Attributing occupational, personality, or other characteristics to individuals of a specific gender, for example, "the nurse gives *her* client."

Gift-assistance Any type of financial aid that does not have to be repaid.

Grade point average (GPA) Sometimes called the cumulative average, grade point ratio (GPR), or quality point average (QPA). Most colleges base grades on a four-point scale, with points assigned to each grade (A = 4, B = 3, C = 2, D = 1, F = 0). To compute your GPA for one term, you need only complete three simple mathematical steps: multiply, add, divide. *Multiply* the number of points representing the grade you receive for each course times the number of credit hours for the course. *Add* the points for all courses to determine the total number of points you've earned for the term. *Divide* the total points by the number of credit hours you attempted that term. The result will be your GPA. Some colleges complicate this with a three-point system or by using grades in addition to A through F. College catalogs explain the system at individual schools.

Grades or **grading system** Most schools use the A–F system. A is the highest grade and F means failure. A–D are passing grades for which you will earn points and credits. If you transfer colleges, however, the D grades may not transfer. Most colleges require a minimum 2.0 GPA, or C average, for graduation; in addition, you might lose financial aid, housing, and other benefits when your GPA falls below a certain level. Bad grades and low GPAs also lead to dismissal or suspension. Some schools have pass/fail grades (P/F or S/U) and an incomplete grade (I), the latter representing work not completed during the term it was taken. Learning the grading system of your college should be one of your first priorities.

Graduate student A person who has earned at least a bachelor's degree (B.A. or B.S.) and is presently enrolled in a program granting a master's degree (M.A. or M.S.) and/or a doctorate (Ph.D.). Students in law school, medical school, and other specialized programs beyond the bachelor's level are also classified as graduate students.

Grants A type of financial assistance that does not have to be repaid and is available at most institutions, with the largest being funded by the state and federal governments. They are usually given to the students with the greatest amount of demonstrated need.

Greeks Used to describe students who join fraternities or sororities. Discuss the possibility of becoming a Greek with someone whose opinions you value.

Higher education Any college courses you take or any degree you earn after completing high school (secondary education). Also called postsecondary education.

Honors Most colleges recognize good grades in the form of academic honors. Dean's list is the most common award. Honors are also awarded at graduation to superior students, and the following Latin words are used: *cum laude* (with praise), *magna cum laude* (with great praise), and *summa cum laude* (with highest praise).

Hours Another word for credits. If you enroll for 15 hours this term and pass all five of your 3-hour courses, you'll earn fifteen credits. There is usually a relationship between the number of hours you spend in the classroom each week and the number of credits you can earn from the course. After you accumulate the proper number of credits/hours, you will graduate with an associate or bachelor's degree.

Humanities The academic disciplines that study human thought and experience through the written record of what people have thought, felt, or experienced in a variety of cultures. Subject areas include languages and literatures, philosophy, history, and religion.

Hypothesis An unproved theory, supposition, or assumption used as a basis from which one can tentatively draw a conclusion.

Incomplete See **Grades** or **Grading system**.

Independent study Can mean at least two things. An independent study course is one in which you complete course requirements on your own time, under the direction of a professor, and outside a classroom setting. This term may also describe some work you've done, either by yourself or with others, that is creative and that shows your ability to work with minimal direction.

Information Age The age in which the transfer of information became as important as the production of goods and services. This was made possible partly by the development of more sophisticated computers.

Instructor See **Professor**.

Internship An arrangement that permits students to work and receive college credit in their major. Internships are required for graduation in some fields, such as psychology, nursing, and medicine. Prerequisites must be completed before you take an internship, and you must complete an application and obtain the proper signatures before you will be allowed to intern.

Interpersonal skills Those skills that enable you to communicate with and relate to people effectively using tact, persuasion, listening, and understanding.

Junior See **Class standing**.

Junior college See **Community college**.

Labeling Naming in such a way to indicate relative position of power, usually a superior–inferior relationship, for example, using *girl* to refer to an adult woman.

Laboratories Science courses often include laboratories that provide opportunities to apply principles learned in lectures. Many large universities call other learning experiences "laboratories." For example, courses in foreign languages, computer science, education, psychology, and journalism may have labs where new skills are practiced (languages) or experiments conducted (psychology). Many courses require labs whether you want to take the lab or not, but in other cases labs may be optional. Check your catalog to see what labs are in store for you.

Leave of absence Another way to say you've withdrawn completely from college. Most students take a leave of absence while still in good academic standing, with the intention of seeking readmittance at a later date. Remember to read the rules and regulations in your catalog because colleges have different ideas about the meaning of a leave of absence.

Lecturer See **Professor**.

Liberal arts A broad course of study including courses taken in the humanities (such as philosophy, history, English and other languages, art, music, and religion) as well as the social sciences (political science, psychology, sociology, and anthropology).

Liberal education Education in which the major goal is to free you from the biases and prejudices you held before you came to college. Most educators view a liberal education as consisting of studies in the humanities, the social sciences, and the physical sciences.

Loans Form of financial aid that requires repayment. In the case of educational loans the repayment "legacy" extends long after the student has left college.

Lower division Many colleges and universities have divided their academic programs into lower and upper divisions (also called preprofessional and professional). Your standing depends on the number of hours you've accumulated, prerequisites completed, forms completed and signed, and grade point average. Students in the upper division usually enjoy greater privileges and certainly are closer to graduation.

Lying A form of academic misconduct that involves any type of misrepresentation in academic endeavors.

Major Your field of specialization in college. As much as 30 percent of the courses you need for graduation may fall into this category. Major courses usually carry higher course numbers. Your advisor will explain the requirements of your major to you.

Master schedule See **Schedule of classes**.

Master's degree students Students who have chosen to continue their education in either a master of arts (M.A.) or master of science (M.S.) program. Master's students may have entered a different program from the one in which they earned their bachelor's degree. Comprehensive exams, a thesis, and/or practicums and internships may be required. See also **Thesis**.

Matriculate A term used by the admissions office. It means you've applied for a degree program, have been accepted in that program, and have enrolled for classes. At that point you're considered to have matriculated.

Mentor In a college environment a faculty or staff member who cares enough about an individual student to take time to teach, guide, show, challenge, and support the student's educational and personal growth and development.

Minor A group of courses that may or may not be required for your degree. Not all colleges require a minor. Your advisor may tell you that your minor must be "academically related" to your major, as government is to history. Minors may also consist of courses taken in a professional school, such as business administration.

Multiple submission A form of academic misconduct that involves earning credit more than once for the same piece of academic work without permission.

Needs analysis The system or process of applying a specific set of computational criteria to your and/or your family's financial resources in order to determine your eligibility for financial aid.

Noneducational expenses The costs you would incur regardless of whether you were enrolled in college (housing, food, transportation, and so on).

Nonparallel terminology Unequal terms used within the same context of reference, for example, *men* and *girls*.

Oral An examination during which your professor will ask you questions about your class and you will answer aloud. Undergraduate students usually don't have to undergo orals.

Orientation Most colleges now set aside a single day, several days, or an even longer period of time for orientation. During this period new students and their parents are introduced to academic programs, facilities, and services provided by the college. Orientation may also include academic advisement and preregistration for classes.

Part-time student See **Full-time student**.

Pass/fail or **pass/no pass** or **satisfactory/unsatisfactory** Many colleges allow you to take certain courses on a pass/fail system. By passing the course, you will earn credits toward graduation, but the grade will not count in your GPA. Pass/fail grades do not have grade points assigned to them. Most schools will not allow you to take core courses, major courses, or minor/cognate courses on this system, but may allow free electives as pass/fail options. To take courses pass/fail, you must fill out the proper forms before the established deadline in the term.

Passive-aggressive behavior Behaving in a manner that confuses others; saying one thing and doing another.

Passive behavior "Poor-me" behavior; failing to speak up, hinting, whining, and/or showing a general lack of assertiveness and initiative.

Patronization Overindulging or overcomplimenting in a way that actually puts someone down; treating others in an offensively condescending manner.

Peers Those with whom you share equal experiences and interests, such as your fellow students.

Physical and biological sciences The academic disciplines that study the physical world, its inhabitants, and the symbolic relationships within it.

Placement Several definitions are appropriate here. Placement tests tell academic departments what level of knowledge you've achieved in their subject. A college placement office can help you with resume writing and interviewing. This office may, with your permission, keep a job file on you and release information to prospective

employers upon request. Recruiters from business and industry often recruit graduating seniors through college placement offices.

Plagiarism A form of academic misconduct that involves presenting another's ideas, words, or opinions as one's own.

Portfolio building Building a portfolio or "package" of skills, contacts, experiences, and credentials to present to potential employers.

Practicum Generally a practicum experience covers a limited amount of material in depth, rather than trying, as an internship does, to provide an overview of an area. The terms may be used interchangeably, however, and refer to practical types of learning experiences, usually for college credit.

Preregistration Many colleges employ preregistration systems (often computer-assisted) to simplify the process of signing up for courses. Preregistration usually occurs in the middle of the term prior to the one you're registering for. This early registration also tells colleges what courses students want, when they'll want them, and what professors they request. Preregistration gives students a greater chance of getting into the courses and sections asked for.

Prerequisite A prerequisite is a course or courses that must be completed as a condition for taking another course. Catalogs state prerequisites. Often a GPA or class standing may constitute a prerequisite for certain classes.

President The chief executive officer of the university or college. Presidents report directly to governing boards (trustees). Unless you attend a small school, you probably won't see this person often, except at official functions such as commencement.

Probation A warning that you are not making satisfactory academic progress toward your degree. Probation is followed by suspension/dismissal unless the situation is corrected. Probation may also exist for disciplinary reasons.

Procedural knowledge A knowledge or understanding of the procedures or structures that different disciplines apply to their subject matter. Literary critics do close analytical readings of texts and historians trace causes.

Professional degree Refers to a study in business, journalism, pharmacy, nursing, or one of the sciences where what you learn is directly linked to what you will be seeking professionally.

Professor College teachers are ranked as teaching assistant, lecturer, instructor, or professor. Professor is the highest rank and includes three levels: assistant professor, associate professor, and (full) professor. To avoid confusion, note how your teacher introduces him- or herself the first day of class. When in doubt, use "professor." While many professors have earned a doctoral degree, this is not a rigid requirement for holding professorial rank.

Proficiency exam A test used to measure whether you've reached a certain level of knowledge. Such exams may allow you to exempt, with or without credit, certain lower-level courses. Math and foreign language departments often use proficiency exams.

Quantitative studies The academic subjects that create systems for describing the physical world or human behavior in abstract or mathematical terms. They include mathematics, statistics, and computer science.

Quarter hour A unit of credit given at colleges whose terms are called quarters, which last approximately ten weeks. See also **Semester hour**.

Quarter system Colleges operating on this system have four terms, or quarters: fall, winter, spring, and summer. If you attend full-time and plan to finish in four years without attending summer school, you'll take courses for twelve quarters. See also **Semester system**.

Racism Discriminatory or differential treatment of individuals based on race.

Registrar The college administrator who maintains your transcript, directs the registration process, and performs other academic duties as assigned by the faculty. When faculty submit final grades, the registrar posts them to your transcript and mails you a copy.

Registration The act of scheduling your classes for each term. Whether you preregister or sign up just prior to the term, you should seek academic advising first to be certain you're taking the proper courses. When in doubt, ask your advisor first! See also **Preregistration**.

Reinstatement or **readmission** A return to college following suspension or a leave of absence; you must apply for reinstatement or readmission. In some cases you'll be readmitted with no restrictions. If your GPA is low, you may be readmitted on probation. Check the academic regulations at your school.

Residence hall A contemporary term for dormitory. A residence hall is operated by the college as student housing. Ask your residence hall or dorm counselor to explain the rules that apply to your place of residence on campus.

Residency State-supported colleges and universities charge a higher tuition to students who do not reside (maintain residency) year round in the same state and who are not considered legal residents of that state. If you live in the same state in which you attend college, you have residency in that state and are eligible for in-state tuition, provided you meet other specific requirements of your school.

Resident advisor or **resident assistant** An undergraduate student who lives in a residence hall and works with students to provide personal help and assistance; manage and facilitate small groups; facilitate social, recreational, and educational programs; provide information or act as a referral source to appropriate university or community offices and agencies; interpret and enforce university rules and regulations; and maintain a safe, secure environment that is conducive to the academic pursuits of students.

Respect Treating others as fellow human beings, even if not necessarily liking them, admiring them, or agreeing with them.

Retention The condition of remaining enrolled in a college or university.

Sabbatical A period of paid or semi-paid release time awarded every six or seven years to professors, who are expected, during this period (either one-half or one full year), to make a contribution to their continuing professional development.

Schedule of classes Also called a master schedule, this is a listing of all classes that will be offered during the coming term, including days and times of class meetings, name of instructor, building and room, and other registration information.

Scholarship A financial award made for academic achievement. Many scholarships are reserved for new freshmen and may be renewed annually, provided grades are satisfactory. The money is applied to tuition.

Section The different classes offered for a single subject. For example, a large college might offer fifty sections of freshman English. Depending on the section you register for, you may have a different teacher, different textbook, and different meeting time than your friends who are taking other sections of the same course.

Self-help assistance Any type of financial aid for which you must do something in return — usually work or repayment.

Semester hour The unit of credit you earn for course work that takes a semester to complete. Many college courses carry three credits, or semester hours.

Semester system As opposed to the quarter system, a semester system consists of a fall semester, a spring semester, and summer school.

Seminar A class containing fewer students than a lecture class (usually a small number), in which the teacher leads discussions and all students participate. The majority of classes in graduate school are operated this way, although you'll find seminars in undergraduate programs as well.

Senior See **Class standing**.

Sexism Discriminatory or differential treatment of individuals based on sex.

Sexual harassment Behaviors such as unwelcome sexual advances, requests for sexual favors, or demeaning sexist remarks that affect or become a condition of an individual's employment or educational status or that create an atmosphere interfering with an individual's academic or work performance.

Sexuality An awareness of the sum characteristics, perceptions, attitudes, values, and issues surrounding being male or female in society.

Social sciences The academic disciplines that focus on human beings and their behavior from a variety of perspectives: as individuals (psychology), as groups (sociology), within cultures (anthropology), or even as economic or political entities (economics and political science).

Social scientists Those who study and teach the social sciences, such as psychologists, sociologists, anthropologists, economists, and political scientists.

Sophomore See **Class standing**.

Sorority See **Greeks**.

Special student In most colleges this is a student who has not matriculated (has not been accepted into a degree program). A special student may have one degree, but may wish to continue his or her education by selecting courses without regard to a degree program. Military personnel are often admitted as special students. Special students may be exempted from certain prerequisites, but they can't receive financial aid or free athletic tickets.

Spending audit An analysis exercise to determine where you spend your money by listing for a specific time period each and every expenditure.

Stereotyping Using expected categorical distinctions within our society. Such distinctions may be far from accurate when applied to individuals.

Student teaching An internship that undergraduate education majors must complete before graduation. During the internship the student spends a period of time in a school situation (elementary or high school) under the supervision of a teacher. The student progresses from observation to successfully assuming complete responsibility for the teacher's workload.

Student union A building where you can eat, see a movie, meet friends, and take part in co-curricular activities. On many campuses student support services such as counseling and career planning may be located in the union buildings. Also called the student center.

Study abroad One of several options that may be available at your college or university that will enable you to broaden your academic experience by attending a college or university in another country for a specific time, earning credit that will apply toward graduation requirements at your institution.

Summer session or **summer school** For students who wish to make up deficiencies, get ahead, or just can't seem to get enough of school. Classes meet every day for longer periods than during the regular sessions. Since things move quickly, good academic advisement is essential before you consider summer school. You may also take summer school as a transient student at another school, provided your advisor has given you prior approval. Since many schools will not let you take courses you failed at another school, be careful.

Suspension See **Dismissal**.

Syllabus One or more pages of class requirements a professor will give you on the first day. The syllabus acts as a course outline, telling when you must complete assignments, readings, and so on. A professor may also include on the syllabus her or his grading system, attendance policy, and a brief description of the course. Be sure you get one and use it.

Technical (tech) schools Technical education systems established by many states offer specialized two-year degrees and certificates. While these schools may be accredited, course work may be so technically oriented that it won't transfer to a bachelor's degree program. If you plan to attend a tech school, be certain to ask about the "college parallel curriculum." See also **Associate degree**.

Tendering of information This represents a form of academic misconduct that involves giving work or exam answers to another student to copy.

Tenure In higher education it is the securement of a lifetime faculty position after a specified period of time and the meeting of specified requirements. Tenure is tantamount to a lifetime guarantee of employment that can be terminated in only a few select conditions. At most colleges and universities a high percentage of the faculty will be tenured.

Term paper Not all professors require one, but when you're assigned a term paper, you should treat it as a very important portion of the course. The instructor may give you the entire term to research and write a term pa-

per—hence, its name. Be certain to know which style manual (for example, the Modern Language Association or American Psychological Association manuals) your teacher prefers, and follow it.

Thesis A longer research paper, usually written as partial fulfillment of the requirements for a master's degree. Some schools require a senior thesis from graduating students.

Theory Like a hypothesis, an assumption or supposition used to explain something.

Transcript The official record of your college work, which is maintained and updated each term by the registrar. Your courses, grades, GPA, and graduation information will be included in your transcript.

Transfer credit If you should transfer from one college or university to another, the number of courses the new college accepts and counts toward your degree are your transfer credits.

Transient student A student who receives permission from his or her regular college to take courses (usually in the summer) from another college.

Tuition The money you pay for your college courses. See also **Fees**.

Upper division The opposite of lower division and much closer to graduation. See also **Lower division**.

Validation of credits Procedure in which a school determines which credits from another school may be transferred. Despite good grades not all of your courses may be accepted. A grade of D normally will not transfer. If you ever consider transferring from one college to another, it is your responsibility to learn which courses and grades will transfer.

Values clarification A structured approach designed to assist students to understand, choose, and act on a personal value system (behaviors as exhibited by attitudes, beliefs, feelings, and concepts).

Withdraw Although you may withdraw from one course, this term usually denotes the dropping of all courses for one term and leaving school for whatever reasons you may have. Withdrawal requires a form and signatures, and if you don't follow the prescribed procedure, you may receive failing grades on all courses, which could place you on academic suspension. Withdrawal in good academic standing, following established procedures, will allow you to request readmission later. See also **Reinstatement** and **Leave of absence**.

Women's movement Began in the 1960s during turmoil over American governmental policies, the Vietnam War, and the fight for equality and civil rights. An attempt to begin recognizing the equality of women with men in terms of work performance, status, independence, compensation, hiring, promotion, and so on.

Women's studies Area of study where women become the center of research and teaching, acknowledging the experiences and contributions of women to history. On many campuses you can receive a major or a minor in this area of study.

Work/study A federal student aid program based on need, which provides the opportunity for students to earn some of the aid for which they are eligible through employment, generally on campus.

Index

Page entries in *italics* refer to figures in the text.

Organization, and writing, 169–170
Organizations, student considerations, in joining, 328–329
finding out about, 327–329
how to start, 331–332
involvement in, 329–330
meeting advisors of, 327
reasons for joining, 323–327
Organize, defined, 144
Orientation programs, for older students, 271
Otis, C., 358
Otis, C. L., 388
Outlining, 169, 170–171
defined, 105
Owens, H. F., 15, 24

Paluda, M. A., 243
Paraphrasing, 117
Parker, C. A., 24
Parks, S., 24
Parrot, A., 358
Part-time enrollment, for older students, 267
Pascarella, E. T., 24
Passive-aggressive behavior, 295, 297, 298, 302
Passive behavior, 295, 297, 298, 302
Patton, Bobby R., 321
Pauk, W., 64, 77
Paulsen, M. B., 276
Pease-Windy Boy, J., 246
Peer groups, 270
Pelletier, K., 388
Pennebacker, J. W., 388
Perry, W., 64
Persistence factors, 6
Personal development, during college, 19–20
Personality characteristics and career choice, 216, 219
and lifestyle, 52
Personal space, 300
Phelps, S., 305
Phillips, A. D., 93
Physical studies, 180
Pirsig, R., 127, 137, 174
Plagiarism
defined, 116
versus referencing, 116–117
Planning
financial, A8–A9
time management, 27–46, 109, 186–187
Pojman, L. P., 292
Political views, 286, 288
Pollard, E. Y., 388
Powell, T. J., 388
Prayer, 383
Précis, writing, 90
Premises, examining, 193
Preparation, lack of, and cheating, 121
Priorities
identifying, 28
setting, 27–30
Problems
academic advisor and, 200
common, 9
Procrastination, 29, 81, 82
Professional programs, and liberal arts, 181

Professors, 127–137. See also Instructors
college reading of, 129
expectations of, 129
good, finding, 134–136
versus high school teachers, 127–128
interests of, 127–128
means of address, 133
motivations of, 129
qualities of, 134–135
rank of, 133
relating to, 131–132
responsibilities of, 130
teaching styles of, 135
tenured, 132–133
on "truth," 289
understanding, 128–132
Prophecies, self-fulfilling, 9
Proving, defined, 105
Psychological types, and instructor's learning style, 52–53
Puerto Rican students, 251

Quality Education for Minorities Project, 163, 245, 246, 257–251
Quantitative studies, 180
Quotas, 253

Race, relevancy/irrelevancy of, 249
Racism, 255, 256
Oprah Winfrey on, 262
Ramsdale, Marie-Louise A., 323
Rape, 356–357
Reading, for general information, 168
Reading, of textbooks, 82–84, 89, 91. See also Textbooks
active, 84, 89, 91
flexibility in, 91
procrastination in, 81, 82
taking notes on, 163–164
Reasoning
incorrect, 190–191
patterns of, 186–187
Recall column, 71, 72–74
super recall column, 99, 101
Recitation, 72
Referencing, versus plagiarism, 116–117
Relationships
defined, 105
developing, 307–332
honesty in, 308–309, 315, 317, 320
interpersonal communication in, 310–315
Relaxation, 381
progressive, 383, 384
Rendón, L. I., 245
"Rescuing" behavior, 301–302
Research
bibliographic, steps in, 144–152
primary, versus secondary, 128
Respect
communication of, 299–300

mutual, 310
for others, 297, 299
for self, 297, 300
Responsibility, personal, 300, 335
assumption of, 297
sexual, 335
Resume
planning, 228
student activities and, 326
Review, defined, 105
Review courses, 268
Revising, 173–174
Rice, P. L., 388
Rice, R. L., 3
Riechmann, S., 51–52
Rights, personal and interpersonal, affirming, 296
Risktaking, 185
Ritter, D. A., 112
Rokeach, M., 292
Rolling Thunder, 307
Romantic love, 313
Roommates, communication with, 317–318
Rosenberg, L., 375
Rosser, S. V., 233, 243
Roth, A. J., 158
Ryan, R. S., 358

Sagan, C., 196
Salane, L. B., 211
Salt in diet, reducing, 341–342
Salzman, M., 228
Sandler, B. R., 240, 243
Sanford, N., 24
SAT, mathematics test scores, 194
Satisfaction, perception of, 216
Sauer, K., 276
Scanzoni, J., 321
Scheduling. See Block scheduling; Time management
Schlacter, Gail A., A15
Scholarships, A12
Schwartz, R. H., 375
Science courses, 261–262
changes in freshman interest in, 226
Sciences, 180
empirical versus nonempirical, 188
Self-assessment, and grades, 235
Self-control, 381–382
Self-discipline, maintaining, 109
Self-disclosure, 310
Self-esteem, growth in, 19, 20
Self-fulfillment, 273, 274
Self-knowledge, 307
Self-management, and academic integrity, 121
Sensing/Intuition scale, 52–53
Sexism
in classroom, 237, 240–242
in course content, 238–242
in language, 234–236
Sexual harassment, 241

Sexually transmitted diseases, 347, 350–355. See also specific diseases
Sexual relationships, 347–355
responsibility in, 335
Shapiro, A. H., 243
Shapiro, S., 375
Sheehy, G., 276
Sign stimuli, 44–45
Simon, S., 292
Skills
career decision and, 214
development of, 227, 324–325, 384
identifying and evaluating, 213, 214, 227
and stress management, 384
Smith, C., 358
Smith, J. C., 388
Smith, R. M., 93
Smith, S., 358
Social issues, views on, 288
Social sciences, 180
Sotiriou, P. E., 46, 77, 93
Space, personal, 300
Specificity, in communication, 298, 300, 301, 303
Spivack, J. D., 228
Spouses, 272
Stairt, L. B., 228
Stereotyping, 235–236
Stinnett, N., 321
Stiver, J. L., 196
Strauss, R. H., 375
Stress
identifying sources of, 378–380
management of, 325, 380–388
signs of, 377–378
Stretching, 381
Streufert, D., 228
Student Consumer Guide, A15
Student-professor relationship, 131–132
Students Against Drunk Driving (SADD), 363
Study abroad, 225
Study groups, 258, 260, 270–271
Study location, 45
Study time, planning for, 30, 31, 32, 33, 34, 36, 37, 38
Subject departments, 180
Success, 215, 216
academic advising and, 6, 199
in college, suggestions for, 6–9
Sugar in diet, limiting, 340–341
Sullivan, W. M., 292
Summary, defined, 105
Support systems, 258, 261, 270–272, 385–386
Sutherland, V. J., 388
Suzuki, B. H., 246, 263
Swidler, A., 292
Synthesis, 189

Tait, F. E., 179
Takaki, R., 246–247
Teaching careers, changes in freshman interest in, 227

PLEASE TELL US HOW YOU LIKE THIS BOOK

Thank you for using *Your College Experience*. We hope you've enjoyed reading it as much as we enjoyed writing it and that you've found it useful, stimulating, and well worth keeping.

For the sake of future editions and of future students at your school, please tell us how you liked this first edition. Only through your comments can we learn how to make this the best possible resource for first-year students. Write your comments below or on a separate sheet of paper.

1. What did you like most about this first edition of *Your College Experience*?

   _____
   _____
   _____
   _____

2. Which chapter did you enjoy most? Why?

   _____
   _____
   _____

3. What additional topics would you like to see included?

   _____
   _____
   _____

4. How else might we improve this book in its next edition?

   _____
   _____
   _____
   _____
   _____
   _____

May we have permission to quote your above remarks?

Yes _____   No _____

We hope you found the personal experiences recounted in this book interesting. Have you yourself had some experience in your first year of college that you'd like to write about and possibly see published in the second edition of this book? Send us a brief statement of your experience (one or two typed, double-spaced pages), ℅ Wadsworth Publishing Company. We'll be delighted to hear from you!

John Gardner   Jerry Jewler

Name _____   School _____

Instructor's Name _____

Address _____

City/State _____   Zip _____

FOLD HERE

CUT PAGE OUT

FOLD HERE

NO POSTAGE
NECESSARY
IF MAILED
IN THE
UNITED STATES

BUSINESS REPLY MAIL
FIRST CLASS   PERMIT NO. 34   BELMONT, CA

POSTAGE WILL BE PAID BY ADDRESSEE

John N. Gardner/A. Jerome Jewler
Wadsworth Publishing Company
10 Davis Drive
Belmont, CA 94002